STONEWALL JACKSON,
BERESFORD HOPE,
AND THE MEANING OF THE
AMERICAN CIVIL WAR
IN BRITAIN

STONEWALL JACKSON, BERESFORD HOPE,

and the Meaning of the

AMERICAN CIVIL WAR

in BRITAIN

MICHAEL J. TURNER

Louisiana State University Press

Baton Rouge

Published by Louisiana State University Press
www.lsupress.org

Designer: Michelle A. Neustrom
Typeface: Goudy Old Style BT

Cover illustration: Postcard image of Stonewall Jackson's statue,
Capitol Square, Richmond, Virginia, ca. 1917.

Library of Congress Cataloging-in-Publication Data

Names: Turner, Michael J., author.
Title: Stonewall Jackson, Beresford Hope, and the meaning of the American Civil
    War in Britain / Michael J. Turner.
Description: Baton Rouge : Louisiana State University Press, [2020] | Includes index.
Identifiers: LCCN 2020009004 (print) | LCCN 2020009005 (ebook) | ISBN 978-0-
    8071-7108-0 (cloth) | ISBN 978-0-8071-7449-4 (pdf) | ISBN 978-0-8071-7450-0 (epub)
Subjects: LCSH: United States—History—Civil War, 1861–1865—Foreign public
    opinion, British. | Beresford Hope, A. J. B. (Alexander James Beresford), 1820–1887.
    | Jackson, Stonewall, 1824–1863—Public opinion. | Public opinion—Great Britain.
    | United States—Relations—Great Britain. | Great Britain—Relations—United
    States.
Classification: LCC E469.8 .T87 2020 (print) | LCC E469.8 (ebook) | DDC
    973.7/210941—dc23
LC record available at https://lccn.loc.gov/2020009004
LC ebook record available at https://lccn.loc.gov/2020009005

For my favorite southerner
(who also happens to be my favorite historian)

CONTENTS

ACKNOWLEDGMENTS

I am grateful to Rand Dotson and everyone at Louisiana State University Press who played a part in the publication of this book and to the anonymous referee who commented on the original book manuscript. I would also like to thank colleagues and students at Appalachian State University for their interest in my work and, above all, family and friends on both sides of the Atlantic for their love and encouragement. Special mention must be made of the Regular Joes and others at ABF in Boone, who did more than they probably know to keep me focused when the going got tough! My wife, Catherine, continues to astonish me with her capacity to help and advise in so many ways, and this book is dedicated to her. Our children, Grace, Jill, and Ethan (though they are not really children anymore), have been supportive, too, in their different ways, and they also deserve my thanks.

Any errors or shortcomings in this book are entirely my own responsibility.

STONEWALL JACKSON,
BERESFORD HOPE,
AND THE MEANING OF THE
AMERICAN CIVIL WAR
IN BRITAIN

INTRODUCTION

This book is situated within and combines two historiographical trends, one organized around international perspectives on the American Civil War and the other organized around British-American interactions of the nineteenth century and British responses to the American crisis of secession, war, and Reconstruction. The goal is to expand knowledge and understanding in these fields, not least by offering fresh insights gleaned from research into previously neglected sources and historical agents. At the book's core is the question of why so many people in Britain sympathized with the South during the American Civil War.

New avenues of inquiry into British opinion are opened up by an analysis of the ideas and activities of Alexander James Beresford Hope (1820–87), one of the leaders of the pro-southern lobby. Hope was a wealthy Conservative politician, High Churchman, author, collector, ecclesiologist, patron of the arts, and champion of the Gothic Revival. His lectures and speeches, pamphlets, articles, letters to the press, and private correspondence, along with British and American press coverage of his pro-southern endeavors, point both to his own importance as an activist and to the reasons why the Confederacy gained support in Britain.

Much is already known about the role of economic interest, political ideas, and concern about Britain's global reach and geostrategic position. People in Britain might have been drawn toward the southern cause because they knew that Britain needed cotton and they envisaged a close economic partnership with the independent Confederacy; or because their view of American history and the U.S. Constitution made them think a certain way about states' rights, slavery, American public life, and the balance of representative weight between North and South; or because they expected that Britain's trade, influence, and imperial possessions (especially those in the Americas) would be more secure if the Union was broken up. Hope spoke

and wrote about these matters at length, but he also brought in other considerations. He believed that there were social, cultural, and religious reasons
why British people should favor the South. In modern scholarship, insufficient attention has been paid to these motives.

During the war, Hope noticed a tendency—which he forcefully expressed
and encouraged—to prefer the South over the North on the basis that southerners were engaged in a "heroic" struggle. The South seemed to be a place
of heroes, its warriors, statesmen, and civilians evincing a fortitude and a decency not seen in the North. By the 1880s, Hope was suggesting that respect
for southern heroism was the main reason why British people had wished
the Confederacy well.

The lasting popularity in Britain of a great southerner, Thomas Jonathan "Stonewall" Jackson, indicates that Hope was on to something. Using
Hope's activism to cast light on pro-southern sentiment, this book also uses
the British reputation of Jackson from the 1860s into the early twentieth century to facilitate a deeper grasp of contemporary ideas and affiliations. No
such study has previously been published.

Jackson became a British hero because of what was known about his merits as a soldier and a man and because he was taken to represent values and
goals that had wide approval. He emerged as a legendary figure in a very
short space of time. For all the verifiable facts that the British collected about
him, there were also errors and falsehoods. While he was condemned in
some quarters (usually because he could be accused of fighting to preserve
slavery), Jackson's reputation in Britain during and after the war was remarkably positive. Such was his stature, indeed, that a group of pro-southerners
led by Hope arranged to set up a memorial in his honor. A public fund was
opened. More money was collected than was needed, which is a telling signifier of British preferences. Some of the donors were wealthy, but much of
the money was raised through multiple small donations.

This book includes a detailed discussion of the Jackson statue, the controversy surrounding it, and what it reveals about the meaning of the American Civil War in Britain. It was not completed until 1875, ten years after the
end of the war and more than ten years after Jackson's death. It was unveiled
in Richmond, Virginia, in circumstances quite unlike those that had prevailed in 1863, when it was commissioned. Its British promoters and subscribers were expressing their support for the South and admiration for Jackson when they commenced the project. That it was still important to them

in 1875, that they had persisted despite all that happened in the intervening years, shows that their former commitment had not diminished.

The American war was not just America's war. It fascinated people across the world. They felt themselves involved in its causes, course, and outcome. They had no doubt that the world would be changed (some thought for better, some for worse) and that the pressing issues of the day would be settled or at least clarified. This internationalization of the war has been much discussed in recent years. For Don Doyle, the war was a pivotal struggle that boosted democratic idealism. "America's Civil War lies at the heart of the story Americans tell about themselves," he suggests, but another story can be told, one about "a conflict that mattered greatly to the wider world. At stake were nothing less than the fate of slavery and the survival of . . . the embattled experiment in government by the people."[1] Ian Tyrrell has called for more synthesis in the writing and learning of American history, for a fuller appreciation of "experiences of connectedness" and the "porous" boundary between American and external developments. He thinks that secession, war, and Reconstruction should be studied less for their uniqueness than for their place in wider political, economic, and social patterns.[2] David Gleeson and Simon Lewis argue that the war must be studied "not just as a local conflict but as a global one, whose causes, conditions, and consequences were all affected by transnational concerns and whose outcome in turn has had profound effects on world history." This is to abandon the "intense localism" of the historiography, and Gleeson and Lewis believe that by doing so, by pursuing a broader investigation, the differences between pre- and postwar circumstances become clearer.[3] In a similar manner, Jörg Nagler, Don Doyle, and Marcus Gräser have pointed to the global impact of the war and to its shaping of economic interdependencies, governmental changes, and theories of nationalism. They highlight the interconnectedness of events and the need to "avoid a U.S.-centric view." They emphasize that people *at the time* realized that the war would have effects around the world. There was an "electric chain" of "action and retroaction."[4] Questions about the secession of the South and the nature of southern identity have also been addressed in this wider perspective. One approach has been to trace relationships within an "Atlantic world."[5]

By such means, historical interpretation has been enriched and extended. The pros and cons of "Atlantic" and other methodologies will continue to be debated, but few scholars would dismiss them entirely.[6] The American

Civil War is now examined more thoroughly as, among other things, a momentous stage in an ongoing ideological contest centering on liberty and order. The reputation of democracy and republicanism, and the power of their vocabularies and principles, were bound to be affected. At the same time, the viability of nation-states could be queried and the conservative reaction to the 1848 revolutions in Europe vindicated, adding strength to traditional authority. Austria and Russia faced their own problems, with imperial cohesion endangered by secessionist movements, and Prussia had ambitions for territorial adjustments leading to a German union. America was not cut off from the rest of the world, and that world influenced and was influenced by what happened in America. "Transnational meanings" were given expression. The local and global could frequently be seen to merge. That they had a relevance to each other—and that "exceptionalism," American and southern, has become more complicated than previously assumed—is undeniable. Before, during, and after the war, Americans and non-Americans shared some of the same interests, and both had a heavy practical, intellectual, and emotional investment in the war's causes and consequences.

How Britain and America regarded each other remains a major concern. Nimrod Tal treats the war as a "transatlantic encounter" and advises against framing British responses as purely "autonomous" and "domestic" since many in Britain based their view of the war on American sources and on prevalent assumptions about American society. In addition, some of these British commentators exported their representations of the war to America. No other foreign war was so frequently and passionately discussed by the British, and the fascination lasted. The American Civil War occupied a "central place in British culture," and over time, people in Britain adapted it to their own purposes.[7]

During the war and afterward, most British commentators did not actually go to America. They needed American information and took up American narratives, and then they disseminated their own version of events. Each generation looked at the war again, to aid an understanding of the United States and with the feeling that the war was part of Britain's own history.[8] Tal also notes the rise of a neutral, conciliatory, unifying perspective on the war and its consequences, in both America and Britain. But to claim, as Tal does, that "extreme Civil War ideologies have had little place in Britain" is to underestimate the influence and extent of pro-southern sentiment during the war and in the postwar decades.[9]

The war came at a time of constant transatlantic interaction. By the 1850s, many people in Britain were eager to find out more about America. The British were themselves having to manage problems at home—not least, pressure for reform and class animosities—and abroad, with Britain's prestige and status affected by the Crimean War (1854–56) and Indian Mutiny (1857–58). America was often brought into discussion of these matters. Notions about class, for example, were not separated from attitudes toward slavery. Reminders of how connected Britain was to the United States arose in other forms: U.S. business failures and financial panic in 1857 harmed British trade and banking, and U.S. interventions in Central America raised suspicions in Britain, which had its own plans for the region. The outbreak of the American Civil War was of great importance to the British, many of whom expected the conflict to contribute to the resolution of broader difficulties. Could slavery survive? Would the credibility of democratic government be ruined or upheld? Citing a contemporary, Brent Kinser agrees that the war was indeed "the trial of the century."[10]

According to Duncan Campbell, the majority British response to the war might have been indifference. Many in Britain saw no reason to get behind either side, disliking both northerners and southerners; and if they were interested in the issues at stake, their attention was increasingly drawn to other matters at home or in Europe or the empire. By 1864, both Union and Confederacy had been "dismissed" from their minds.[11] This is an exaggeration, but Campbell does demonstrate that along with the indifference, or the waning of interest, there was strong pro-northern and pro-southern partisanship in Britain. British observers realized that the war was not just an American war but one that was likely to have wider importance.

The war's effect on political philosophies in Britain is elucidated by Kinser, but he employs an outmoded framework: the liberal minded backed the Union because they favored democracy and the conservative minded were led by their hatred of democracy to wish for the Union's collapse. This is to oversimplify British opinion, for there were nuances and divisions within each camp, liberal and conservative. There was no consensus on whether secession and war in America revealed democracy's flaws, and the North's victory over the South did not necessarily mean that democracy had proven itself. The war did affect British reform, but it had been moving forward anyway, and the 1867 Reform Act was less a response to what happened in America than a British event with mainly British causes.

An economic explanation for British preferences has been advanced by Mary Ellison, who argues that textile workers in Lancashire sided with the Confederacy because of the wartime cotton shortage. Ellison notes strong pro-southern feeling in those districts most affected by economic hardship, contending that this correlation is the key to understanding British opinion and that political party, social class, and religious denomination were less important in motivating people to support North or South. Ellison wants, in particular, to undermine the old claim that Lancashire operatives patiently endured suffering because they preferred the North and believed that the war would free the slaves. This "lingering misconception" was largely a postwar creation, part of the campaign for parliamentary reform. The inferred wisdom and restraint of the war years would be used by reformers to make a case for limited working-class enfranchisement.[12] There is a difficulty with Ellison's thesis in that the need for cotton might have led some to support the North rather than the South. If the main point was to end the U.S. blockade of southern ports, restoration of the Union could do this just as well as Confederate victory in the war.

Campbell's analysis demonstrates that British opinion is not easy to pin down, for it was subject to many forces, political and social, local and regional, and it was highly sensitive to the course of events in America. Opposition to slavery did not inevitably result in support for the North. Criticism of U.S. policy did not necessarily indicate attachment to the southern cause. British people in general, even if they took sides, were not ready for direct intervention in the war or formal recognition of the Confederacy as an independent country. The British government and Parliament were reluctant to be drawn in, and the prospect of involvement in hostilities so soon after the conflicts in the Crimea and India was unwelcome. As for political ideas, it is likely, based on Campbell's findings, that those who had committed themselves for or against reform would have remained so whatever the outcome of the war in America. Campbell relies on a limited sample of publications, mostly London based, to describe and explain British opinion, but he effectively brings out the dominant trends in that opinion, and he establishes that class identities did not determine pro-northern or pro-southern preferences. Alfred Grant has also explored the key points of interest for the British through their newspapers and periodicals, but his account, though informative, is more useful in terms of breadth rather than depth, for he discusses a range of topics without providing the detail and explanation given by Campbell.[13]

Many of the same topics are covered in Thomas Sebrell's study of northern and southern efforts to win British approval through propaganda organs the *London American*, which ran from May 1860 to March 1863 and became an advocate of the Union cause, and the *Index*, which appeared from May 1862 to August 1865 and served the Confederacy. Sebrell shows that American events and British opinion were linked, and he also conveys some impression of the busy campaigning of the main partisans of North and South in Britain.[14] Sebrell nevertheless has to admit that the *London American* and the *Index* probably made little difference. Neither could induce the British to do anything they did not want to do. Pro-southerners would have been pro-southerners whether or not the *Index* existed. Parliament would have debated northern offenses against Britain's rights and interests without the fuss made by the *Index*. The *London American* was of scant importance to the U.S. government, which refused to finance it, and the appeal of both publications was limited by their editorial policies (the *Index* was proslavery, and the *London American* insulted British institutions). Despite all this, Sebrell's research confirms a crucial point: the *London American* and *Index* might not have been very influential, but they did not have to be. Plenty of British organs attached themselves to either the Union or the Confederacy, and throughout the war, they did all they could to present and comment upon American news in a way that served their purposes. More material arrived in Britain from the North than from the South, largely because of the fortunes of war, and those British papers that favored the South therefore had to work even harder to make a case.

This need for ceaseless exertion was not lost on the leaders of the pro-southern lobby, and they played their part too. None did more than Beresford Hope. Through his speaking and writing, he constructed a full and sophisticated basis for British sympathy for the South. At the time and afterward, he was known on both sides of the Atlantic for his consistency and determination and for the strength of his convictions. There were many who disagreed with him, many who ridiculed him, but he carried on regardless.

Though one did not have to be a wealthy upper-class Conservative to side with the South, Hope was of this social standing and party allegiance.[15] He was born into privilege. His father, Thomas Hope, was of Dutch and

Scottish descent, the eldest son in a family of Amsterdam merchants and financiers who became a respected writer, scholar, and art collector after settling with a large fortune in England. His mother, Louisa Beresford, hailed from the landed and clerical elites of Ireland. Alexander James Beresford Hope, born in 1820, was their third and youngest son. Thomas Hope died in 1831, and in the following year, Louisa married her kinsman William Carr Beresford, Viscount Beresford, a decorated veteran of the French Wars and holder of several lucrative offices. Alexander James lived with his mother and stepfather (his older brothers having by this time embarked on their own careers). He did well at Harrow, one of the most prestigious English public schools, and in 1837 went up to Trinity College, Cambridge, where he won prizes for his academic accomplishments. He was subsequently a notable benefactor of his college. While at Cambridge, he was founder-member of the Camden Society, later renamed the Ecclesiological Society. In time, he became an acknowledged expert on architecture and church doctrine and history. He was an enthusiast for Gothic style and a devout High Churchman, respecting traditional teachings, the sacraments, the authority of the episcopate, ritual, and continuity in the Church of England. He put his money into the projects, organizations, buildings, objects, publications, and institutions that accorded with his personal tastes. He would be president of the Royal Institute of British Architects in 1865–67 and a principal promoter of and participant at the annual Church Congresses, which began meeting in 1861. In 1842, he married Lady Mildred Cecil, eldest daughter of the second Marquess of Salisbury (and sister of the third marquess, the future Conservative prime minister). They had ten children.

Hope was first elected to Parliament in 1841. He served as MP for Maidstone from 1841 to 1852 and 1857 to 1859, for Stoke-upon-Trent from 1865 to 1868, and for Cambridge University from 1868 to 1887. He had a connection with each of these constituencies: he inherited large properties in Kent and Staffordshire, and he was a Cambridge man who kept up with university affairs. In the House of Commons, he was a frequent speaker, especially on religious and educational matters, and he was skeptical about political reform. He was a prolific writer—of articles for newspapers, essays for learned and professional journals, books, poetry, and in later life society novels. In 1855, he established the *Saturday Review*, which became one of the most highly regarded metropolitan weeklies. As its owner and a regular contributor, he helped to set a direction and tone for the *Saturday Review,* but talent was the main criterion for its writers, not agreement with Hope's opinions.

Having inherited some of his father's property and items from a rich uncle, Hope was the chief beneficiary of his stepfather, who died in 1854. (The legal form of his surname now became Beresford-Hope.) His mother had died in 1851. Hope and his wife, Lady Mildred, cared for Lord Beresford in his declining years, and when he died, they took over the estates at Bedgebury Park (Kent) and Beresford Hall (Staffordshire). They also had a London mansion in Connaught Place, close to Hyde Park. They often attended court functions, political dinners, and charitable and other events and hosted many lavish occasions of their own.

Hope was avidly pro-southern during the era of secession, war, and Reconstruction in America. Given his wealth, influence, family and friends, political associations, and newspaper contacts, he was not wrong to think he could be useful. His ideas and activities during and after the war add much to what is already known about British support for the South, and they are investigated in the first part of this book.

Chapter 1 is contextual. It discusses the changing relationship between Britain and the United States during the nineteenth century, especially in the decades before the war. Elements of both friendship and enmity are explored. There is some consideration of transatlantic links such as trade and emigration, and in particular, on the British side, there are preliminary remarks about government policies and popular attitudes.

Part 1 of the book uses Hope's thoughts, words, and deeds to mount a sustained analysis of British sympathy for the South during the war. In chapter 2, the focus is on the economic and political justifications for secession and on British understanding of the compatible economic interests of the Confederacy and Britain (free trade, and British manufactures to be exchanged for southern products) and the political implications of the war (what it suggested about the Union, republicanism, democracy, national self-determination, and individual liberties). Hope advocated free trade, opposed democratization, and endorsed states' rights. He was certain that the division of America into two—and in time maybe more—sovereign nations would be to the general benefit.

Chapter 3 lays open a sense of social and cultural similarity, expressed by many British people toward the South. Hope's rhetoric of "our brethren"—

deserving of British approval and assistance—is tied in with evidence of southern exceptionalism, which was partly based on beliefs about ethnic identity. Hope expressed the views of those in Britain who favored the South because they saw it as essentially different, and superior, to the North. There was agreement with southerners' own self-definition.

In chapter 4, attention centers on the vexed questions of slavery and emancipation. Pro-southerners in Britain argued that slavery was not the cause of the war, that the independent Confederacy would move toward emancipation and was already improving conditions for the slaves, that northern society was more racist than the South, that northern abolitionists were dangerous extremists, that the U.S. government was not genuine about emancipation, and that to free the slaves without proper planning would be disastrous. Hope repeatedly professed himself an enemy of slavery but just as often added qualifications with respect to the South in order to make slavery seem less important.

Chapter 5 explores the religious grounds on which Hope based his pro-southern appeals. Being a staunch Anglican, he was interested above all in the fate of the Episcopal Church in America. He saw the schism in the American church as a boon to Anglicanism globally and a gain for religious truth because each branch of the church could advance more quickly by it-self. Hope envisaged a righteous competition between northern and southern Episcopalians, with each pushing the other toward improvement. But Hope also declared that the church and indeed Christianity were stronger in the South than in the North, as evidenced by southern moral standards, social order, and religious observance. The southern church had the right policy on slavery, moreover, teaching that slaves must be treated well and that reform leading eventually to freedom was better than immediate emancipation without the necessary preparations. Hope thought that the southern church would grow stronger owing to the South's cultural and social advantages over the North, talented bishops to lead, and increasing interaction with Britain. He argued that the northern and southern churches, like the peoples they served, were irreconcilable. The northern church was too political. The southern church was an expression of national distinctiveness.

Chapter 6 is about the course of the war and the responses of British commentators to major battles and political events in America. Britain's dealings with the two belligerents and the war's effects on Britain were controversial. British interest in American affairs continued after the war because of the difficulties of Reconstruction. Hope went on writing and speaking about the U.S. system of government, economic and racial issues, and British-American relations. He did not give up his pro-southern preferences. In 1881, Hope wrote that the primary reason why so many people in Britain had supported the Confederate cause during the war was their appreciation of southern heroism.

Part 2 of the book describes and explains the British reputation of the greatest southern hero, Stonewall Jackson. Chapter 7 covers the period between Jackson's rise to fame in the Valley Campaign of spring 1862 and his death in May 1863. Chapter 8 covers the period between Jackson's death and the end of the American Civil War in 1865. Jackson and his legend gained a remarkable purchase over the British imagination. Though not uncontested, his reputation in Britain was overwhelmingly positive, and no other foreign-born celebrity was discussed in the same way or to the same extent. He was a brave, talented, successful soldier. He was a pious Christian. He was a kindly gentleman, a fond husband and father, a victor over adversities, a self-made exemplar, a patriot, a moral paragon. He withstood comparison with any of Britain's native heroes. He had a relevance to contemporary political, social, and religious discourses in Britain, and as a key player in the captivating drama that was unfolding across the Atlantic, he attracted enormous attention.

As established in chapter 9, this attention did not fade after the war. Into the twentieth century, Jackson was still being written and talked about. His name and fame were serviceable instruments. During the First World War, for instance, Jackson was used to encourage British youth to patriotic sacrifice, even though there was no shortage of figures from Britain's own history who fit the bill. After 1865, in Britain, there was continuing discussion of Jackson's British ties. His religious fervor, military talents, and successes in battle were still admired. Information about his character, appearance, and habits was much sought after; he was the subject of songs, lectures, and readings; and he was often mentioned in material about America and British-U.S. relations. The Jackson legend not only survived, it flourished. In Britain, the values, behavior, and bearing associated with Jackson ensured that there would be no loss of heroic status. Rising to fame only during the last two years of his life, and foreign-born, Jackson nevertheless retained his hold over the interest and affection of a large section of the British people. In part, the unique historical connection between Britain and America made him seem more familiar. But his appeal had more to it than this because he personified moral standards and had an importance socially, religiously, and politically that other legendary figures did not, and the qualities that British commentators attributed to him—whether or not they had much basis in fact—gave him lasting influence.

British regard for Jackson was strikingly expressed, thanks mainly to Beresford Hope, in the statue unveiled in 1875 in Capitol Square, Richmond. It was a British memorial. Organized by "English gentlemen," promoted in the press, and funded through public subscription, this memorial was a tangible sign of the high esteem in which Jackson was held. Chapter 10 brings together the Jackson statue and the efforts behind it, pro-southern sentiment in Britain, Hope's activism and the ideological and practical contributions he made to wartime and postwar controversy, heroic and other representations of the war, and Jackson's British reputation.

The conclusion offers some reflections on icons and their role, then and now. It also assesses the impact of Hope's agitation on behalf of the South and relates the nature of British opinion to the creation and maintenance of Jackson the hero.

FRIENDLY RELATIONS?

By the end of the nineteenth century, Britain and the United States were moving toward what many call "the special relationship." The two governments and peoples regarded each other in a special way and assumed a unique connection. British dealings with America and America's with Britain were quite unlike their dealings with anyone else.[1] Closeness and cordiality were evident, though there were reservations on both sides, a reminder that the relationship in earlier times had not been so friendly. For much of the nineteenth century, indeed, there was open rivalry. Britain was uneasy about the growing influence of the United States and the challenges it foreboded, and there were periods—above all, during the American Civil War—when animosity, not amity, was the order of the day.

After the American war, too, several problems affected British opinion about the United States. The Irish question was among them. Ireland played an important role in British-American relations. Trade was another concern, linked as it was with the impact of U.S. tariff increases and a resurgent struggle between protectionists and free traders. For many in Britain, consideration of these issues was shaped by the premise that the U.S. political system would remain exemplary to British reform movements, although, as in the decades before secession and war, admiration for the United States in some pro-reform circles was matched by disappointment in others. The prospects for rapprochement at the governmental level improved after wartime disputes, but this did not mean the end of suspicion and stereotyping. Americans still described the British as enemies to democracy, and British visitors to the United States still presented a picture of the vulgar, pushy, uncultured American.[2]

Some British observers were struck by the fact that even in America, the great republic and beacon of liberty, national cohesion was no easier to maintain than it was in Britain and Europe. The shock of civil war and instability of the Reconstruction period indicated, as Eugenio Biagini puts it, "contrasting forms of national identity," something that pro-southerners in Britain had highlighted during the war years. Britain had its Irish question and the potential dismemberment of the United Kingdom, and historic, ethnic, religious, social, regional, and other centrifugal forces across Europe meant that the unity of the French, Italian, Spanish, and German states was far from assured. How to reconcile nationalism, constitutionalism, central authority, popular sovereignty, and community was one of the preoccupations of the late nineteenth century.[3] There were no easy solutions in Britain or Europe or in America. If the ideal was a harmony of different groups and interests within the nation, all enjoying equal status, it was not clear that such a nation existed. British writers on America referred to its egalitarianism, but equality did not guarantee unity. Reconstruction did not remove sectionalism. There remained in America an "essential bipolarity," as Robert Kelley terms it. To Kelley, economic conditions, religious beliefs, social and ethnic identities, and reform debates were just as likely to divide people in the United States as in Britain. On both sides of the Atlantic, "there was a struggle going on between majority and minority cultures," between those who wanted pluralism and those who wanted homogeneity.[4]

For all this, Britain and the United States were drawing together. Previous conflict between the governments had been mitigated. When the Americans sought overseas territories, they targeted Spain, not Britain, and there was a shared anxiety about the rise of Germany. U.S. naval power allowed the British to withdraw vessels from waters that could be policed by the Americans. Transatlantic commerce was important to both countries. Cooperation might also have been facilitated by social changes, for the arrival in the United States of people from southern and eastern Europe aroused American nativism and clarified the notion of natural kinship between Britain and America.[5] This kinship had been under consideration for a long time. Jonathan Parry has argued that in the formation of a British liberal-progressive tendency, much was made of perceived contrasts and affinities with other cultures, races, and polities. Britain's political and economic maturity compared to other nations reinforced the idea, stronger after the 1848 revolutions, that a large part of Europe was underdeveloped. In this context, a sense of Anglo-Saxon superiority had evidence behind it. By the 1870s, it was usual to group the United States and Britain's white settler colonies with Britain in the front rank. The rest of the world lagged behind.

Various schemes were proposed to bind Anglo-Saxon people together and inculcate their values as widely as possible.[6] In Britain, these attitudes promoted a continuing interest in American events, but it was also thought that superiority might be jeopardized by the costs of the common British and U.S. quest for ascendancy.

At the end of the century, troublesome consequences of urbanization and industrial expansion elicited much comment. Social surveys influenced the outlook of politicians and philanthropists, and there were new ideas about taxation, planning, and the role of trade unions and churches. Reformers in Britain and America, rethinking the division of responsibilities between public and private, decided that government should be doing more as an agent of reform. Daniel Rodgers has shown that several initiatives were rooted in a rejection of free markets and that reformers on either side of the Atlantic were eager to learn from each other, an alliance also stressed by Duncan Campbell. British reformers were disappointed by the slow advance of corrective policies in America. Constitutional deadlock in Washington was blamed. But gradually, reform proceeded. There was more press backing. Legislation in one place became a template for legislation in another. Conferences, studies, correspondence, and visits brought different groups together, and in Britain and America, there was a strong spiritual dimension to all this, seen in the "social gospel" and in Christian socialism.[7]

America's image as the land of liberty and opportunity was not as strong as it had been in Britain, and old assumptions about the link between democracy and material progress were questioned, which had implications for democratization in Britain. Conservative spokesmen who had derided the U.S. Constitution were more likely now to point out that it placed limits on democracy (through the division of powers, authority of the Supreme Court, and indirectly elected Senate). Though some progressive commentators went on as before, praising American government and society, others had lost confidence in America. Among younger British radicals, who had not been active during the American Civil War or the struggle for the 1867 Reform Act, the experience of urbanization and industrialization focused their efforts against the exploitation of labor, social distress, inequality, monopolies, the power of capital, and class legislation.[8] Strikes and other disturbances in the United States suggested that political democracy did not necessarily deliver social and economic justice.

Interaction between Britain and America at the end of the nineteenth century, therefore, promoted a mix of positive and negative assessments. Variability of opinion was also characteristic of the first half of the century. Many British people arrived at firm conclusions about America, whether or not they went there to see for themselves.

In a discussion of "America through foreign eyes," Stephen Brooks brings out both the fascination that the United States stimulated in observers from afar and the eagerness of Americans to be admired by others. Through the generations, people saw what they wanted to see in America, to which they attached "expectations of greatness."[9] Historians have often remarked upon this. In the late 1940s, Allan Nevins declared that America had remained a "favorite observation-ground of Britons" for well over a hundred years. He used such categorizations as "practical investigation," "condescension," "mixed criticism and praise," and "unbiased portraiture" to demonstrate some common findings by British observers of America during the nineteenth century.[10] Nevins also recognized the desire of Americans to know what others thought of them and, in particular, a sensitivity to British comment. Despite America's autonomy, there remained a "cultural dependence" on Britain. The wish for British favor meant that British disapproval stoked resentment. Some Americans were conscious only of disdain from the British, but it was less prevalent than they supposed. Opinion about the U.S. system of government, for instance, was divided, reflecting political disagreements that already existed in Britain.[11] George Lillibridge's *Beacon of Freedom*, published in 1955, elucidated British reformers' pro-American leanings, and it was followed by works by others in the same vein. *Beacon of Freedom* was a book of its time, and the statements of Nevins also reflect the time in which they were published. One reviewer of Max Berger's *British Traveler in America, 1836–1860* (originally published in 1943) remarked in 1945 that the book was "particularly pertinent in days like these, when Anglo-American analyses are assets for common understanding."[12] An intellectual accord arose during the twentieth century, resting on British historians' emphasis on past evidence of friendship between Britain and the United States and on American historians' privileging of their own national paradigm, America as the home of liberty and destined to spread its benefits to the rest of the world. British-U.S. cooperation in the two world wars and the Cold War encouraged scholars to play down previous tensions. The agreed framework was that a common heritage and shared goals made for inevitable harmony.[13]

Nevertheless, relations since the American Revolution have been unde-niably complex. In the era of America's war for independence, argues Kevin Phillips, pro-American sentiment in Britain was strongest among groups and in places that had a "history of economic innovation, religious dissent, and political assertiveness." This pattern endured. America was created mainly by refugees from Britain, who took with them their traditions and ideas and contributed to a wider discussion on both sides of the Atlantic about political and religious rights. George Lillibridge argues that when re-formers in nineteenth-century Britain used the model of American democ-racy to condemn "the old order," they upheld "the American destiny," the belief that America's one purpose was to exhibit the blessings of liberty. To Fred Leventhal and Roland Quinault, "evolving democratic aspirations in both countries can be ascribed to mutual parentage."[14] This helps to explain why British visitors to the new republic during the late eighteenth and early nineteenth centuries—people who were curious about America but had no plans to remain there—made favorable comments.[15] Some were impressed by the contrast with the Britain of this period, a country blighted by war and debt, repressive legislation, and the dislocating effects of industrialization, in comparison with which America looked peaceful and prosperous. Most of all, perhaps, these visitors could take pride in a young and thriving nation that was a British offspring. They joined in the debate about "English liberty overseas."[16] The transfer of "liberty" from one place to another was not easy, and there were doubts about the viability of republicanism and democracy as alternatives to monarchical and aristocratic structures and about the place of slavery in the Union. But still, America could be thought of as "British," and Americans could feel that they shared something meaningful with Britain.[17]

Economic links were no less important than cultural or institutional ones. The formation and progress of an "Anglo-world" ("sub-global but intercon-tinental") has been traced by James Belich through production and con-sumption, booms and speculation, migration and settlement. People were attracted by the promise of a new life as the frontier was opened up—that is, Britain's imperial frontier and the American frontier—and development was sustained by money and commodities sent out from Britain to the em-pire and the United States. Sections of this Anglo-world traded primarily with each other, with metropolitan generators of growth in London and New York, which dispersed what was needed in the ever-widening area of settlement. Belich contends that Britain and the United States only separated after 1900, by which time America provided its own markets and capital.[18] Other scholars have argued that British and U.S. economic growth went together for much (if not all) of the nineteenth century and that the symbiosis remained important into the twentieth century, when more than a few British firms adopted American methods.[19]

While objections might be raised to some of Belich's claims, he does make plain the numerous ways in which patterns of settlement and economic activity made for a lasting connection between Britain and America. He also attends to the differences between the two countries—particularly the wider franchise and greater political decentralization in America—and he suggests that the spread of ideas and structures owed more to the conditions created by expansion than to a wish to "clone" from British originals. Separateness was clearer in the United States by the late nineteenth century because America's further development did not need supplementing by Britain, but before the "decoupling," Britain and the United States were "in some respects a single economy." Commentators before and after the American Civil War were conscious of this and other types of unity (cultural, intellectual, ethnic, legal).[20]

Ties have also been stressed by historians who focus on religion, including Jonathan Clark, who presents the American Revolution as a "war of religion" and declares that opinion in both countries was shaped by sectarianism rather than politics. Clark argues that religious affiliations were basically the same in the new country as they had been in the old. The rebellion against British rule was carried forward by people whose religious traditions included former acts of defiance against the "unified sovereignty" of church and state. Religious heterodoxy played a "central role in activating principled opposition to the established order," and rebellion was really a clash between "militant imperial Anglicanism" and "sectarianism and ethnic diversity."[21] More Anglicans in America were rebels than were loyalists, however, and some Dissenters opposed the rebellion. Denominational attachment alone cannot explain rebellion or loyalism or neutrality. Nevertheless, Clark does illuminate some of the things that mattered to contemporaries. William Van Vugt is another who highlights a "shared Anglo-American religious tradition" (based on his reading of letters written by people who had left Britain to live in America).[22] Clark also adds to the work of other scholars in raising the possibility that there was a single intellectual setting.[23] Religious connections continued throughout the nineteenth century and were evident in charitable efforts, the temperance and antislavery movements, and Protestant revivalism. Richard Carwardine has explored transatlantic contact, with personnel, publications, information, and ideas passing back and forth. Revivalists in Britain took up American techniques, and British criticism of slavery "reinforced the element of social morality within American revivalism." If there were religious differences between Britain and the United States, there were also similarities. Religious fervor was augmented in both countries by the insecurity associated with industrialization; in both, it was thought that true and vital Christianity would end division and promote social peace, and evangelicals in Britain and America "saw themselves as branches of the same closely-knit family."[24]

At the diplomatic level, taking a long-term view, it might be thought that cooperation and goodwill were more typical of relations between the British and U.S. governments than hostility. Phillip Myers insists that the relationship was pragmatic and cordial before the American Civil War. Thereafter, despite wartime quarrels between London and Washington, both needed friendship to be preserved. They desired the advantages that would accrue. According to this line of argument, the approach to diplomatic problems did not change much over time. Both governments favored negotiation and compromise.[25] It is true that disputes before and during the war did not bring an irreversible breach. The British and U.S. governments did have to be pragmatic, as Myers emphasizes, but this does not mean that conflict was entirely eliminated.

Frequently, government policies and popular attitudes indicated more discord than concord. David Crook's *American Democracy in English Politics* was published in 1965, ten years after the appearance of George Lillibridge's *Beacon of Freedom*. Crook thought that Lillibridge had exaggerated British reformers' affection for America. He warned against the distortion of history with "hind-knowledge about the triumph of liberalism and American-type democracy in the West."[26] A related trend in the historiography has been to highlight what was most distinctive about nineteenth-century Britain. If British people believed in and valued their uniqueness, it must have mattered more to them than any sense of affinity with America. This raises questions about the thesis of Kevin Phillips, who wrote of "the triumph of Anglo-America" in the late 1990s, when multiculturalism had fallen into disfavor in some circles. To Phillips, the seventeenth-century civil wars in Britain, the American Revolution, and the American Civil War were all part of a single process that led to the global primacy of "Anglo-America," based on values associated with Calvinism, military strength, territorial expansion, and commercial success. The holders of these values saw themselves as a chosen people.[27] This concept of Anglo-America does not take account of a large body of research into religious beliefs, economic theory and behavior, and political languages and principles. To assume that ethnic and cultural identities were automatically expressed in political choices and that people in America who had come from Britain retained the habits and opinions of their homeland, unaltered by American conditions and experiences, is inappropriate. Changing ideas about nation and empire in the nineteenth century also need to be considered.

The extent to which Britain was distinctive, and proudly so, was also the extent to which assertions of harmony with America could be eschewed. Studies of the political culture of Victorian Britain have established that there was indeed an impression of its excellence and exceptionality. British political culture rested on interlinking concepts of freedom, rights, and opportunity that were mostly positive, generous, and uplifting in motivation.[28] Reform was pursued, though there was also resistance to change. Opinions about democracy were various and fluctuating. There was the prospect of class-based politics as industrialization and urbanization proceeded apace, but there was no linear transition to democracy in Britain, notwithstanding the enlargements of the electorate in 1832, 1867, and 1884. In some ways, politics might have become less participatory, for political reform had uneven effects.[29] Lauren Goodlad sees Victorian Britain as "idiosyncratic, self-consciously liberal, decentralized, and self-governing," its liberalism shaped and reshaped by diverse pressures and demands, including individual free will, political expediency, social needs, and trust in progress.[30] The British were creating a society that allowed for both individual rights and collective responsibilities and different ideas about how to balance them, though political contention was mostly carried on within constitutional channels. Historians disagree about the results of reform and about how and when organized national parties and class-based politics arose. Opinions differ, too, on the merits of libertarian and conservative views of the constitution, on the role of radicalism and popular protest, and on levels of agency and inclusion in the system of government.[31]

Pride in the constitution was integral to a sense of Britishness, yet the constitution could be viewed in contradictory ways, and if constitutionalism was flexible and contingent, nationalism was no less so. There was no single British identity. England's legislative unions with Scotland (1707) and Ireland (1801) did not ensure integration in other spheres. The United Kingdom of the nineteenth century remained united but with plural histories and cultures.[32] Imperial expansion and Britain's interaction with its colonies stimulated debate about whether one could be British having been born and raised outside Britain, and there was disagreement about who should be granted political and other rights in the empire. A pluralist, egalitarian approach to these matters was not typical.[33]

A number of historians have asserted that there was understanding and acceptance of what it meant to be British. Linda Colley argues that a pervasive sense of Britishness had arisen by the 1830s, rooted in Protestantism, imperialism, and warfare against a foreign "other," France.[34] But this has to be weighed against the importance of multiple identities, rifts within Protestantism, cases of Francophilia, the contrast between forms of patriotism discernible in peacetime and those evident in times of war, and controversies over race and ethnicity that came to the fore after the 1830s. In Peter Mandler's study of "national character," an older focus on the sovereign, law, and Parliament gave way to a modern consciousness associated with "the people." The supposition that virtue resided in the people boosted libertarian movements. Conservatives, meanwhile, saw virtue in leaders, traditions, and institutions. A general notion that there *was* a "national character" gained influence during the nineteenth century and peaked in the first half of the twentieth. Racial theories were present, though not dominant, and language, attitudes, and definitions varied over time, which suited a diverse society.[35]

Victory in the wars against France, which ended in 1815, ushered in an era of security, prosperity, and confidence. Britain's success was hailed as a success for liberty. Parliament exulted in its role as the guarantor of rights, and the 1848 revolutions in Europe added to the mood of British superiority and uniqueness. That Britain had no revolution and remained stable and wealthy when much of Europe succumbed to disorder was taken as proof that Britain's institutions were sound. A distinction was made between constitutional, inclusive, humanitarian Britain and the autocracy and republicanism seen on the Continent. Britain's political objective, argues Jonathan Parry, was effective and fair government under the rule of law, which was in line with the dominant liberal version of national identity— self-improvement, social reform, moral probity, political inclusivity, economic opportunity, civic responsibility, and the overcoming of intolerance and dogmatism.[36] This identity could incorporate many, and it held out the prospect of advancement and happiness for the whole world, assuming the spread of British values.

For most interested observers, there was no great desire or expectation that America and Britain should resemble each other more closely. While British people who visited the United States in the mid-nineteenth century might have been impressed by what they found, there was no overriding inclination to transplant American institutions to Britain and no serious suggestion that America ought to conform to a British model.[37] In his study of the comparisons that were made with different polities, Robert Saunders indicates that the democracy seen elsewhere was not wanted in Britain. After all, America, "of interest for its Anglo-Saxon culture and as an example of democracy in a large and opulent state," descended into sectionalism and civil war.[38] Britain was different and had to remain so.

This may have been a majority viewpoint, but quarrels continued in Britain about rights, liberty, and national identity and about class, race, and gender.[39] Religious belief remained an important component of identity, and yet while he posits a lasting Anglo-American coherence, Jonathan Clark also accepts that the gap between Britain and America grew larger because the two had "partly-incompatible theories of their own exceptionalism."[40] These ideas were unsettled. America often featured in British debates, but for many contemporaries, it was the contrasts between the two countries, not the similarities, that were most significant, and they were grateful for these differences. They did not complain about them. Even within nineteenth-century British radicalism, there could be condemnation of America as well as praise.[41] When some radicals compared Britain with America, it was Britain that disappointed. The United States enjoyed esteem for its written constitution and guarantee of personal rights, its republican system and wide suffrage, its religious toleration and the absence of an established church, its freedom from the weight of tradition and rank, its well-developed local government and active civic participation. But plenty of radicals faulted America for its expansionist foreign policy, protective tariffs, and slavery; for its inability to stop the slide into civil war; for its massive inequalities in wealth and influence; and for its failure to live up to the lofty principles upon which it was supposed to be founded.[42]

Despite their links, America and Britain in the nineteenth century evinced discrete political cultures. In America, as Jon Roper has explained, liberty was associated with the struggle for self-government, the republic, and the egalitarian philosophy expressed in the Declaration of Independence and Constitution. Liberty would increasingly be thought about in circumstances created by industrialization, the westward spread of settlement, institutional maturity, and economic growth. In Britain, meanwhile, liberty was associated more with political continuity, inherited wisdoms, social hierarchy, and parliamentary representation. Equality, it seemed, might bring instability, break up the consensual respect for the past, and endanger liberty. This disparity between America and Britain affected the way that many issues were considered. Democratic elements did come into the British polity but gradually.[43] American examples were cited, and it was not only conservatives who denied their relevance to Britain. Prominent reformers also criticized American democracy. They doubted that it was truly liberal and representative and suited to complex societies. Robert Saunders suggests that what they really wanted was to popularize the constitution without democratizing it along American lines.[44]

Differences between British and American practice can also be discerned in electioneering rhetoric and the relationship between politicians and publics. Andrew Robertson argues that a shift from "government by gentlemen" to "government for, if not by, the people" did not have the same results in the two countries. The growth of electorates obliged politicians to rethink their methods. It was no longer sufficient for polite and decorous leaders to present themselves as worthy of support by speaking of their character and conduct. Now they had to rouse voters and speak about issues. Elections became more deliberative in nature and political language more disruptive, emotional, and confrontational. These developments came earlier, and had more impact, in the United States. They emerged more slowly in Britain, where the electorate remained comparatively smaller, taxes on the press higher, and the power of elites easier to defend.[45]

Disputes between the British and U.S. governments affected popular opinion on both sides of the Atlantic. Notwithstanding the revisionist account of Phillip Myers—that relations between the two governments were consistently good—it is clear that for most of the nineteenth century, they were not. British and American people also had reservations about each other. The distance between them was not merely geographical, and it was remarked upon before America's war for independence.[46] In the early nineteenth century, writers in Britain and the United States engaged each other in a war of words, defending what they took to be national honor. This political and cultural squabble was a journey toward self-awareness, for both British and American contestants.[47] In her account of "the American idea of England," Jennifer Clark highlights the uncomfortable mix of wishing for a break from the old country while also being conscious of necessary links with it.[48] Connectedness was expressed in countless images and objects.[49] According to Sam Haynes, though, Anglophobia was one of the striking features of U.S. politics and society between the 1820s and 1850s. Still a self-consciously "developing" nation, Americans were determined to create a separate identity and sought to undermine lingering assumptions in America about British superiority. For many Americans, the routine was to see British hostility behind all their problems.[50] In time, these problems were attributed to other causes, and Anglophobia faded, but some Americans still disliked Britain, and the sentiment was reciprocated. Duncan Campbell argues that the number of British people who committed themselves to the Union or Confederacy during the American Civil War was smaller than the number who decided that neither was worthy of support.[51] Many of the visitors who crossed the Atlantic to America before and after the war encountered more that was strange than familiar, and there were Americans who could not get used to particular British manners and customs. There was bias and misconception on both sides.[52] Some of the British who settled permanently in America went there precisely because it was different (although they probably integrated more quickly and easily than non-British groups).[53] By the late nineteenth century, most people in Britain and the United States were aware of the contrasts between the two countries, not just in politics but also in other spheres, including their differing rates of economic growth, differing cityscapes and residential patterns, and differing attachments to class and ethnicity.[54]

A "contradictory dynamic" in British discourse has been explored by Hugh Dubrulle using the concept of "postcolonial" mentality. As Americans pushed toward full independence in the nineteenth century, the British— still mindful of the old imperial link—could see them both as Anglo-Saxon and equal *and* as former subjects and inferior. They could be proud of America but also patronizing.[55]

Britain and America had representative forms of government, but these had evolved in different ways. The British were mostly unwilling to accept instruction from Americans on the meaning of liberty.[56] Separateness was acknowledged. By the 1830s, argues Linda Colley, the presumption that Americans were basically British was passing away. Americans had "rejected both the authority of the British parliament and in the end their own residual British identity." This led people in Britain, conservatives as well as reformers, to think again about their nation in comparison with others. Colley shows that one result was a new focus on slavery. The British slave trade was abolished in 1807 and slavery in the empire in 1833, helping to restore the reputation of British liberty after the American Revolution. America retained slavery, allowing British commentators to counter its claims to superior freedoms.[57] By such means, the propensity to regard Britain's institutions, whatever their flaws, as better than those existing elsewhere was reinforced. Before and after the American Civil War, the extent to which America might be an exemplar and the interdependency of ideas and events between the two countries were fiercely disputed.

Secession and war in America had considerable impact in Britain. Government and people, Parliament and press, could not agree on the line that Britain should take in response to the American crisis. The vulnerability of Canada, instability in Europe, lack of confidence in France, ambivalence toward both the Union and the Confederacy, and concern about public opinion at home all affected policy makers to some degree. The initial expectation that the war would soon be over had to be discarded, and it was sometimes difficult for the British government to stick to its declaration of neutrality. For many observers, the American crisis was a conflict about slavery, but this was not the only way of looking at it. British attitudes were confused and shifting. There was no simple division of opinion based on social class, political allegiance, or economic interest. The assumption that British workers and reformers favored the North and aristocrats and conservatives the South has long been discredited. Nevertheless, discussion about the war was certainly influenced by contention over the suffrage, free trade, social policy, slavery, and colonial affairs. Quarreling about the "Americanization" of British politics, which had been present for some time, became more intense. Some anti-reform groups in Britain did sympathize with the Confederacy because they saw in the Union the institutions and aspirations they opposed. This also explains why some reformers wished for a Union victory in America.

After the war, British-U.S. relations were affected as before by America's domestic problems. Now it was the course of Reconstruction that commanded attention. There was also wrangling between the two governments left over from the war. Washington's claims for compensation relating to the *Alabama* and other vessels built in Britain, which had been taken into the Confederate navy, were especially controversial. The assertive and prosperous United States competed with Britain for international influence, but transatlantic trade was expanding too, much to the benefit of both countries. Soon there was a struggle between protectionists and free traders as British economic growth slowed down and U.S. industries flourished behind a tariff wall.

In addition, the American Civil War made the Irish question more complicated. Union and Confederacy had both recruited well among the Irish in America, and the gaining of military experience had direct consequences for the Irish struggle against British rule. More important, the ideological aspects of the American crisis, especially the rhetoric of liberty, and concepts of nationhood shaped by European as well as American events meant that the British Parliament and people had to take more seriously the Irish bid for self-government. Attitudes after the American war were influenced by interpretations of that war. Advocates of a federal system in Britain, with Ireland still part of the United Kingdom but in charge of its own affairs, could point to the survival of the American Union as salutary, while opponents of devolution used the war to warn against secessionist tendencies. As Irish nationalists took more extreme paths, some took up arms for full independence—that is, disunion—and rejected those readings of the American war that accentuated the blessings and necessity of unity. These campaigners and their adversaries both sought American approval. The rise of the United States as a global power made American opinion more important, and the Irish question was discussed in ways that Americans could understand, while the lessons of the American war became flexible tools for employment by British authorities, Irish separatists, and others on each side of the debate about Ireland's future.[58]

Cooperation between the British and U.S. governments increased after 1865. Though they were competing for influence, there was also a realization in London and Washington that they should work together on shared concerns and in those parts of the world where their interests coincided. A substantial body of opinion in Britain had by now come to accept that the

United States would be a great power and that its institutions, having survived secession and war, were worthy of respect (though not replication). American regard for Britain at the popular level was also rising in the late nineteenth century, in part because it was channeled into agreeable avenues, including, as Walter Arnstein has shown, a fondness for Queen Victoria.[59]

British viewpoints altered as more information became available about the United States (particularly through travel writing, lectures, and newspapers). It is possible that both affection *and* animosity between the Americans and British have been exaggerated by scholars. Perhaps there was majority indifference alongside the minority Anglophobia and anti-Americanism. As for the political likes and dislikes between the two, they each had different versions of "liberty," and whether it was appropriate and sensible or not, there was bound to be discussion about which version was best. In Britain, abstract political theory was usually depreciated or ignored (going back to the excesses of the French Revolution). Numerous British politicians and writers argued that liberty required order and that, without order, it descended into licentiousness. Here was yet another interpretive paradigm that could be used with reference to America, for there were times when the United States was thought by some to be heading toward licentiousness. Yet it was not illogical to claim that representative institutions, by breaking the control of unearned privilege, would guarantee stability. If people were able to participate in the system of government, so this argument ran, they would be less likely to rise up against it. As ever, America was a testing ground. Howard Temperley highlights the mutual respect between sections of British and U.S. society and the level of involvement in each other's affairs. He also admits, however, that misrepresentation occurred as people focused on the things they found most admirable or most offensive. There were inaccuracies in the images presented.[60] Disagreement about America persisted in Britain. It was understood by British reformers, for instance, that the success of United States could raise the reputation and appeal of liberty around the world, but by the end of the nineteenth century, a growing number of them thought that something had gone wrong. They saw America's rich exploiting its poor and unresolved problems relating to urban living, capitalism, industrialization, race, and immigration.[61]

"Foreigners often have ambivalent feelings about America," notes Stephen Brooks. "The United States has the ability to excite in outsiders contradictory feelings of admiration and repugnance."[62] This was true of the nineteenth century. Among British commentators were both ardent admirers of the United States and persistent denigrators.

It is unsurprising, in view of the wide range of opinions about America, that when the nation faced national emergency, many in Britain were willing and able to attach themselves either to the Union or the Confederacy. They had kept up with American news. They were interested and informed. They had strong views on what was happening across the Atlantic and on the likely ramifications for Britain and for British-American relations.

I

Beresford Hope's Civil War

2

ECONOMIC MEASURES AND POLITICAL IDEAS

B eresford Hope emerged as one of the leading pro-southern activists in Britain during the American Civil War. Wealthy and well-
connected, he could arrange events, make introductions, provide
hospitality, pay for printing, organize loans or make direct gifts of money,
write letters, and give speeches. He explained the American crisis by exploring its economic aspects and, more commonly, through a discussion of
political ideas, especially interpretations of U.S. history and the American
Constitution. He often pointed to the evils of the "democracy" that could be
associated with the North. He argued that southern society was distinctive—
demonstrably not the same as the North—meaning that the separation of
the two was natural and inevitable. Hope also offered his thoughts on national character. Northerners were corrupt and dangerous, while southerners had strong affinities with England.

Hope made his views clear, and tried to convince others to adopt or act
upon their own pro-southern sentiments in a series of lectures, speeches,
and articles, some of which were revised (usually enlarged) and published in
pamphlet form. The pamphlets went into several editions to satisfy demand
as the first print runs were sold out. Two pieces in the High Church quarterly
Christian Remembrancer for January 1862 and January 1863 became the shilling
pamphlets *Two Years of Church Progress* (1862) and *The American Church in
the Disruption* (1863). Lectures delivered at various locations in Kent (Kiln-
down, twice, in November 1861; Hawkhurst in January 1862; and Maidstone
in March 1862 and January 1863) became the sixpenny pamphlets *A Popular
View of the American Civil War* (1861), *England, the North, and the South* (1862),
The Results of the American Disruption (1862), and *The Social and Political Bearings of the American Disruption* (1863).[1] There were other speeches—notably
in Maidstone in November 1861, Stoke-upon-Trent in September 1862, and

Liverpool in October 1863—and much can also be gleaned from Hope's letters to the press and from newspaper coverage of his lectures and advertising of his publications. As founding owner of the *Saturday Review*, moreover, Hope was in a position both to write his own pieces about America for that influential weekly and to invite contributions from others.

In all the things Hope said and wrote about the American crisis, he gave the least attention to its economic aspects. This was not because he considered them unimportant. On the contrary, he ranked them among the principal factors, along with political and constitutional disagreement, that had shaped recent American history. He dealt with economic issues only briefly because he assumed that the people he was addressing already appreciated their role. Rather than go into detail, he preferred to move on to other matters that to him (and possibly to his audiences and readers) were more interesting. Economic arguments carried most weight in districts that were directly affected by the disruption of trade between Britain and America, especially the cotton towns of Lancashire. Elsewhere there might have been less concern.

Hope condemned U.S. tariff policy. The Morrill Tariff was passed at the beginning of March 1861, just before Abraham Lincoln took office as president. Named after its sponsor, Justin Smith Morrill of Vermont, in its first year of operation it increased the rate of duty on selected imports by about 70 percent. Hope emphasized that the tariff was approved by a rump Congress, after the departure of southerners. Protection had been a key part of the Republican platform in the 1860 elections, and in Hope's view, the purpose was to strike at the South—which favored free trade—while rewarding northern businessmen and workers for their political backing. The North's economic program was furthered thereafter by the wartime blockade of southern ports.[2] During a lecture of January 1862, Hope was applauded when he remarked that "the North was all for protection—the South for free trade," and he went on to complain about New York's growing control over commerce and shipping. He denounced northern policy as "nothing less than a selfish conspiracy against the free trade and legitimate privileges of the world."[3] Hope declared on another occasion that secession and war could not be understood without reference to the North's "selfish commercial and manufacturing system." He suggested that necessity, the fact that the North had obstructed the economic progress of the South, was the primary reason for the establishment of the Confederacy.[4]

At a large gathering in Stoke-upon-Trent in September 1862, Hope said that sectional animosity had been growing long before secession because of a northern plot to subjugate the South. Tariffs were one of the tools to this end.[5] Hope subsequently spoke of the collapse of the Union as the result of a conflict between free traders and protectionists.[6]

The problem for the South within the former Union was that it had been reduced to minority influence in the national government by the United States' territorial growth and economic and demographic changes. Protective tariffs and navigation laws helped northern interests at the South's expense and led to the overweening dominance of New York and its "reckless trading and bubble banks." Britain preferred economic liberalization, as the South did, but the North wanted to impose a self-serving regulatory order. U.S. policies "have prevented the South from finding the market for its agricultural produce, to its own greatest disadvantage, in the free harbors of the world, where it would be able to purchase foreign goods at a fair rate in return." To release itself from the power of the North—augmented by tariffs and the unbalanced system of representation—the South had been forced to leave the Union.[7]

Hope's opinions about the economic aspects of the American crisis had already been endorsed in the *Saturday Review*. In July 1861, for example, one article insisted that the U.S. Congress was using the war to enrich a few northerners, in keeping with the pattern seen in preceding years. Economic discrimination against Britain was openly discussed, and northern businessmen were determined that the secession of the South should allow them to make profits.[8] Hope was right to suppose that there were economic motives behind secession, but his arguments were based mainly on the idea that the South was pushed into it. In his view, the South had been on the wrong end of an economic hegemony within the United States.

Perhaps there was more optimism than anxiety in southern calculations. Matthew Karp has suggested that the producers and traders of cotton had faith in their ability to win for the independent Confederacy an assured place among the giants of global commerce.[9] Britain's dependence on southern cotton was a given. So were secessionist expectations about the leverage it would provide, although, as Brian Schoen demonstrates, northerners were determined to frustrate the pro-cotton and proslavery agenda.[10] Many southerners did believe that they were economically disadvantaged within the Union. Yet Schoen points not to a sense of economic backwardness but to a forward-looking and dynamic project: establishing the Confederacy squarely on the basis of interaction with the rest of the world. Brian Ward and John McCardell have also noted this economic ambition.[11] Quarrels about tariffs and slavery reflected divergent economic visions in America. Schoen argues that the southern vision was not defensive and reactionary but rational and modernizing.[12]

Much of this was wishful thinking, or propaganda, but southern self-confidence must be taken into account when assessing secession. If there was anxiety and resentment about the South's economic position within the Union, there was also enthusiasm surrounding the consequences of separation from the North. Hope's writings and speeches made much of the South's economic subjection and emphasized that the South would be better off as an independent country. A number of scholars have denied that the South was stuck in the past and that slavery was a barrier to economic change.[13]

While laying out the economic considerations that he thought justified the South's bid for independence, Hope went more deeply into political ideas, interpretations of U.S. history and the American Constitution, and what he regarded as the shortcomings of "democracy." He had already publicized his low opinion of U.S. politics and of schemes for political reform in Britain that might introduce American traits into the British system of government.[14]

In November 1861, Hope explored the historical roots of secession and war and the political principles at stake. He wanted to show—from "my reading, my acquaintance with many Americans, and the interest that I feel in the matter"—why the American crisis had importance for Britain. He discussed the original colonies and suggested that their revolt against British rule was morally and politically valid because George III and his ministers had tried to govern without the consent of the governed. The Americans had framed their own federal system, and under the U.S. Constitution, each state retained sovereign rights within its own territory. It was a loose union, unlike anything known in British history, and the secession of states from that union was legitimate because of their sovereign rights. This scenario would not be possible in Britain because the same local sovereignties did not exist.[15]

States' rights might be considered one of the strengths of the American system, Hope thought, but in other respects, it was flawed. Checks and balances had not worked. Electoral Colleges, for instance, did not place the best candidates in high office and, "instead of having a deliberative voice of their own, are merely the mouthpieces of those by whom they themselves are appointed." As for an independent judiciary headed by the Supreme Court, which was meant to prevent the government from breaking the law, Hope pointed to the recent conflict between Chief Justice Roger B. Taney and President Lincoln on habeas corpus: "The American Constitution resembles, in outside form, that of England—having its two Houses of Legislature, its old Saxon privileges, its common and statute law, and its trial by jury." But "all these glorious bulwarks of freedom, all these well poised safeguards of order, are alike overruled and trampled down by that miserable, levelling democracy and universal suffrage which is so rapidly landing the Northern States in a perfectly Assyrian despotism."[16]

Hope discussed these matters with friends, including the bishop of Labuan, Francis McDougall, and Sir John Kirkland, of Queen's Wood, Kent, a former army agent and banker.[17] He invited both of them to hear him speak in Maidstone in November 1861, and it was the bishop who followed Hope by proposing a vote of thanks for his "instructive and interesting" comments. The bishop agreed with what Hope had said about "the turbulent sea of democracy": "Whenever agitators, as was their wont, lauded Republican institutions, we might retort upon them, 'Look at your dear friends in America.'"[18] Hope also discussed the American crisis with E. A. Freeman, the prolific writer and prominent man of letters, fellow of Trinity College, Oxford, and future Regius Professor of History at Oxford. Hope and Freeman shared enthusiasms in history, literature, religion, and architecture. In the spring and summer of 1861, as Freeman was finishing a book on federal government, the two corresponded about America, and Hope formed the impression that Freeman would dedicate his work to Confederate president Jefferson Davis.[19] As Freeman told Hope, and as he wrote in the book, he had long been planning to write a history of federalism, but the "late events in America" prompted him to quicken the process. His purpose was to promote a better understanding of "federal ideas."[20]

Freeman offered firm opinions about what was going on in America, several of which Hope had expressed privately and in public. To Freeman, federal government meant "any union of component members, where the degree of union between the members surpasses that of mere alliance, however intimate, and where the degree of independence possessed by each member surpasses anything which can fairly come under the head of merely municipal freedom." To work well, it needed a high level of "refinement" and "political education," continuing over "many generations," and practically and institutionally, it required the unified government to be sovereign over all external matters with each member of the union having independent control over its own internal concerns. Freeman argued that federalism, like other forms of government, was not perfect. They all had strengths and weaknesses, and secession and war in America did not prove anything against federal government in the abstract.[21]

Nevertheless, "mismanagement in the conduct of the American Republic" was clear enough, and it was probable "that circumstances have rendered it undesirable that the whole Union should remain united by a single Federal bond." Freeman was not convinced that the South had a constitutional right to secede: "On the ground of expediency," however, "a plausible case can be made." The states in the Union lacked "that degree of mutual sympathy . . . without which a Federal Government cannot be successfully carried on." In addition, "the Union, as it stood, was too large to be properly governed as one Federal commonwealth."[22]

On states' rights, Freeman stressed that no union could last unless its members respected each other's authority over their internal affairs (and slavery was not an exception, since the U.S. Constitution had not prohibited it). On democracy, Freeman was equivocal. The growth of political participation and understanding could be advantageous, but it might also pose problems because "it is possible that where everybody is a statesman, nobody will be a great statesman."[23]

Hope was more scathing in his assessment of democracy both in the abstract and in its American form. Early in 1862, he wrote that Britain and Europe should learn from America's experience and count themselves fortunate that they had not fallen into the same errors. He ridiculed the northern definition of secession as "rebellion." Had the United States not originally been established through rebellion? This led to another question. Was rebellion always wrong, no matter what the circumstances? The U.S. Constitution upheld state sovereignty, and it was no more fitting to call Jefferson Davis "a rebel" than it was to call Abraham Lincoln the same. "They respectively and legitimately represent different readings of a document not meant to be straightforward by those who framed it, and who carried it with long delays, only in consequence of its ambiguity, through the legislatures of thirteen jealous sovereignties."[24]

The conduct of the North up to early 1862 struck Hope as a useful corrective to the claims of those in Britain who extolled the U.S. system of government as a model and used it to recommend reforms at home. Hope pointed to the North's debt, its "barbarous" military tactics, the blockade of southern ports, the Lincoln administration's violation of individual liberties, and the *Trent* affair.[25]

He complained that too many British people lacked a sure grasp of American political history. Deeper understanding, he believed, would prompt support for the South. No reasonable person would think of the Glorious Revolution of 1688 as rebellion and probably not the Declaration of Independence of 1776 either. The establishment of the Confederacy should not be classed differently, Hope went on, since it was rooted in the same right to self-government. It was unfortunate that the good intentions behind the U.S. Constitution had been ruined by democratic suffrage, party machinations, and anomalies in the system of representation. Government in the Union had fallen into disrepair, and secession became necessary to preserve the proper pattern of sovereignty because northerners wanted to put the Union above states' rights. A careful reading of the Declaration of Independence, the Articles of Confederation of 1781, and the U.S. Constitution of 1787 revealed that the southern states had never resigned their separate sovereignty to the federal government. All powers not explicitly given to that government were retained by the individual states.[26]

Therefore, the North had no constitutional grounds for engaging in a war against the South, and it was not easy for Hope to take this line, he explained, because most of his American friends were northerners and he received more publications from the North than from the South. Despite all this, he was certain that the South had been faced with no alternative but to secede. Had there been some mention in 1781 and 1787 of freedom to leave the Union as well as join it, a clause to be invoked, a process to be followed, the present crisis might have been easier to resolve. "We must own that secession was irregular, but we cannot pronounce it unjustifiable," and here Hope brought up 1688, government by consent, and the duty to resist tyranny.[27]

Hope showed why the system of representation in America had hurt the South. Clearly, the weight of numbers was bound to shift with the addition of new states to the Union (there were thirty-three by 1860) and the growth of towns and industries in the North. Apportioning representation according to population, while reasonable in theory, made the South a minority influence in practice. Only the North could benefit "in a country where representation is based on numbers, and where the electoral districts are carved out according to the whole population (including women) and not according to the number of voters." Counting a slave as three-fifths of a person did not help. "No doubt it was a less disadvantage than their total omission would have been; but on any theory which admits that representation should take account of property as well as of mere numbers it was a disadvantage." Southerners had wanted some of the new states admitted to the Union to be slave states for political reasons that had nothing to do with the moral or economic viability of slavery, and the South could not be other than alarmed as the North used its representative power for "oppression and fraud." For years, northern leaders had attacked southern rights, and finally an anti-southern faction had taken control of the national government.[28]

While Hope realized that in Britain there were varying opinions about secession, he thought it difficult to quibble with the results in constitutional terms, for the Confederate constitution had some admirable features. He welcomed its express prohibition of the slave trade. Beyond this, he thought it would generate political practices and relationships that were better than those of the North. There would be less of the scrambling for offices, the machine politics, the scandals, patronage, and bribery seen in the United States. These flaws had constantly lowered the standard of statecraft and administration, partly because the best men refused to demean themselves by engaging in politics. Hope commended such provisions in the Confederate system as term limits, offices tenable during good behavior, dismissals subject to review, and clear rules about public spending. He did not expect officeholders in the South to profit from their posts, and he did not expect the legislature to rush bills through or to mix too much together in one measure or to tack unnecessary items to necessary ones.[29]

It had long been assumed that the American Constitution was "much like ours," and some in Britain had even embraced it as superior, thinking it made for cheaper and more efficient government. Hope set out to dispel such notions. Recent events, he asserted, had demonstrated that there was more disparity than similarity between the two systems. Whatever the affiliations of those who heard his speeches or read his pamphlets, he trusted that all would wish to maintain "our dear, good, old, and tried English Constitution." In *fundamentals,* the American version could not be regarded as better or even similar. The British system "pre-eminently allows freedom of thought, freedom of action to every citizen," but in the United States, freedom went "beyond those limits which providence, nature, and common sense have laid down," and in effect, the individual was reduced "to the condition of a mere fragment of a great machine—a something whose personal freedom is entirely in abeyance, if not rather forfeited in the interest of the political section or party to which he belongs." Under Lincoln and the Republicans, the Union was becoming notorious for "arrests by telegraph, military occupation, military search, suppression of newspapers, imprisonment without trial, and all the other devices by which free thought and action can be checked." Nothing like this was possible under the British system. Britain, moreover, abided by true principles of representation, with "full swing to local interests." Each constituency had its own MP. Electors and MPs interacted with each other, and political communication was unfettered. The United States had wire-pullers and party machines, "the despotism of irresponsible committees," and political violence instead of rational debate, and the constant reapportionment of representatives made for unstable, irregular electoral districts.[30]

The saving grace was states' rights, which the South was trying to defend against the "federal imperialism" of Lincoln and his accomplice, U.S. secretary of state William H. Seward. Hope approved of states' rights because they ensured an orderly balance of interests. Slavery was only a "secondary" concern, according to Hope, and the British should not be led by their hatred of slavery into forgetting that the war was really about "constitutional right and wrong."[31]

"The Union is gone forever," Hope declared in March 1862, claiming that this was the opinion even of many northerners. However sound it had been conceptually, the U.S. system of government had not functioned well.[32] Hope was willing to recognize, among leaders of the American Revolution, the contributions of George Washington, Alexander Hamilton, and James Madison but singled out Thomas Jefferson as "mischievous" and "bad" because Jefferson had corrupted states' rights by adding "an ultra-democratic bias, with which that doctrine had no natural affinity." Early in 1863, Hope ridiculed "universal suffrage" as a "philosophic absurdity, bred of Jefferson and the French Revolution."[33] He went on to reiterate that the factors behind the breakup of the American Union were mainly political and that a state that had exercised its freedom to join the Union also had the freedom to leave it. Nobody who understood sovereignty and liberty could think otherwise, and here Hope pointed to aspects of the Glorious Revolution and the wars leading to the independence of Greece (1832) and Italy (1861). After the secession of the South, he continued, the Lincoln administration brazenly usurped some of the rights of individual states and interfered in their internal affairs. This had prompted some in the North to become more vocal in their commitment to states' rights. Northern Democrats were not entirely trustworthy, but at least they were trying to restrain Lincoln, and by arguing for "the Union as it was," they were helping people in the North to understand what had caused the war.[34]

These comments reflected Hope's view of American political parties and recent electoral cycles. He recalled the first parties—the Federalists, who were for strong government and "English values," and the Democrats, led by Jefferson, who favored weak government. Gradually, the Federalists became Whigs, who were strongest in the North and no longer advocated English-type government. The Democrats were strong in the South and represented conservative and rural interests. In the election of 1852, the Democrats won a resounding victory, leading to the disintegration of the Whig Party. The new president was Franklin Pierce, who appointed Jefferson Davis, former senator for Mississippi, as secretary of war. Disputes over slavery intensified during the 1850s, and various compromises were tried. "Slavery, you perceive, is not a matter of sentiment, of philanthropy, of religion, but a card which either side plays to suit its own purposes," Hope argued. Southerners feared that slavery would not be allowed in new states admitted to the Union, which would upset the balance of electoral influence. This was why they wanted to annex Cuba: a plan, Hope emphasized, that was a consequence of membership of the Union. As an independent nation, the Confederacy posed no threat to Cuba.[35]

With the defeat of the Whigs in 1852, a "cunning" faction led by New Yorkers—notably Seward, "who amongst the unprincipled politicians of the day holds an exalted place"—began to combine former Whigs and discontented Democrats into a new party, the Republicans. They picked up support by irritating the South, "playing with the slave question," and laying claim to Canada. The Republican candidate in 1856 was the former soldier, explorer, and senator for California John C. Frémont, a celebrity rather than a statesman, in Hope's view, who stood against the former U.S. minister in London, James Buchanan, "a man of great plausibility and personally popular, but wanting in deep or stable views." Buchanan won, but his Democratic administration was weak, as Pierce's had been, and sectional tension continued to grow. The Democrats splintered. In the North, they nominated Illinois senator Stephen A. Douglas for president in 1860, while in the South, they nominated John C. Breckinridge of Kentucky, Buchanan's vice president. Most Republicans expected Seward to be their candidate, but the party leaders wanted someone who could beat Douglas, seen by them as the main threat. They knew that his state was electorally crucial, so they chose an Illinois man, Lincoln, who had served in the state legislature and U.S. House of Representatives. Lincoln won in 1860. He had reportedly been a boatman, a clerk, and a rail-splitter, before training himself to be an attorney. Raised on the frontier, his manners were "rough" and his education limited. Hope considered him unfit for the presidency. That such a man, at such a critical moment for America, should rise to rule "thirty million of the Anglo-Saxon race" proved that there was a serious deficiency in U.S. politics.[36]

While the U.S. Constitution did not explicitly provide for secession, Hope thought that a fair assessment of underlying principles and comparable historical events, in 1688 and 1776, would favor the South. Respected political philosophers seemed to agree that the responsibilities assumed in 1688 and 1776 were appropriate. Therefore, it could not be argued that the secession of the South was inappropriate. The southern states had established themselves as an independent federal republic with its own constitution, which was an improvement on the U.S. Constitution. In terms of political leadership, the Confederacy also had the better of the Union. Lincoln was a ridiculous nonentity. The South had Davis, a true statesman, and Hope also admired Confederate vice president Alexander Stephens of Georgia.[37]

If the South's secession was correct, what about the North's response? Lincoln had won the election in November 1860 but did not become president until March 1861. In these last months of the Buchanan administration, the Republicans baited the South, making an accommodation impossible. They had won votes in the North by making promises, notably on economic policy, and the departure of southerners from Congress allowed them to pass a protective tariff designed to boost northern industry and damage southern agriculture. This, and antislavery rhetoric, did not suggest to southerners that the North was interested in reconciliation. The Confederate attack on Fort Sumter on 12 April 1861 was provoked by the North, for the fort was being reinforced despite assurances to the contrary. Now there was a "fever" that could arise only in democracies. The northern mob wanted revenge for the attack, Republicans were intent on punishing "rebels," and northern

Democrats were angry about losing their party's southern wing. Lincoln and Seward "veered with the wind" and opted for war.[38]

In September 1862, Hope stood in a parliamentary by-election at Stoke-upon-Trent (he was defeated by the Liberal candidate, banker Henry Grenfell). Speaking before polling, Hope reproached pro-North apologist John Bright, MP for Birmingham, for writing a letter against him and having it circulated in the constituency. Annoyed because Hope had insulted the president and people of the United States, Bright claimed that Hope was the enemy of liberty. Hope dismissed the allegation as nonsense, insisting that Bright was trying to interfere with the free choice of Stoke voters and that, as an ally of Lincoln, *he* was the friend of despotism, not Hope. Sectional animosity had grown in America only because the North subordinated the South economically and politically.[39]

In his speech at Stoke, Hope also noted that American events were influencing the course of British politics, in particular the discussion of proposals for parliamentary reform. Radicals like Bright, who wanted to reshape the British system along American lines, were pressing for suffrage extension and vote by ballot. Hope agreed that the electorate ought to be enlarged and that there were many deserving men of the working classes who should be able to vote. The excitement caused by the American war, however, could not be allowed to determine the question. Time must be given for reflection, and if there was to be reform, Hope was adamant that it should not include the ballot. The consequence of voting by ballot in America had been a lowering of the quality of public men and manners. The secrecy that ballot campaigners wanted was "unmanly and un-English."[40] On 22 September 1862, in his speech at the nomination of candidates in Stoke, Hope said that the ballot turned electors into a "flock of sheep" and made them more vulnerable to pressure. Rather than embrace "Americanized institutions," he argued, the British people should rely on their own traditions.[41]

Hope continued to treat the American crisis as a clash of political ideas. The Central Association for the Recognition of the Confederate States was set up in April 1863, and its leaders' view of the American war was summed up in its "general constitution," dated 10 August 1863: "a struggle involving the highest interests of liberty and self-government." Hope was one of the vice presidents of the Central Association. In October 1863, he addressed a meeting of the Liverpool Southern Club, an affiliate of the Central Association. In reporting his speech and that of a "Colonel Lamar" in the same week at an "agricultural meeting" in Chertsey, *John Bull* reasserted their main point: the South was fighting for the sake of civil liberty and constitutional government.[42] Colonel Lamar was Lucius Lamar of Mississippi, sent by President Davis to Britain and France following a spell as Confederate envoy to Russia.

Pieces in the *Saturday Review* reflected Hope's idea about breaches of constitutional principle. Rights were suspended in Maryland, and Baltimore was placed under "military rule." Recognition of "a revolutionary State Government in Western Virginia" amounted to an "audacious violation of that Federal compact which the North has armed itself to vindicate and maintain." British observers were aware that while the relationship between individual states and the Union might be open to debate, "the unity of each State within itself has hitherto never been disputed." By encouraging its dismemberment, the United States became to Virginia "a wrong-doer" and "foreign enemy." The same thing was likely to happen in Missouri, with rival governments operating in separate parts of the state.[43]

Northern commentators accused British publications—especially the *Times* and Hope's *Saturday Review*—of bias against the United States. The *Saturday Review* expressed surprise that Americans did not understand the purpose of the British press. The *Saturday Review* was not written for Americans and had no responsibility to them. Its conductors did not seek an extensive American circulation (and knew that if they gained one, their work would be pirated by unscrupulous American publishers). The *Saturday Review* was designed for British readers and only discussed those American events that were significant to British readers. Since "there are influential politicians in England whose whole repertory of political wisdom consists of assertions of the excellence of American institutions," it would be wrong for the *Saturday Review* to leave their "noisy Radical prejudices" unchallenged, and when the *Saturday Review* commented on the conduct of the United States, these remarks were honest reactions to what was taking place. If Americans disliked the truth, they should stop reading the *Saturday Review*.[44]

In August 1862, the *Saturday Review* issued one of its many attacks on pro-northerners Richard Cobden and John Bright, the leaders of provincial middle-class radicalism. According to this contribution, their appeal was "waning" because of their association with the United States. American democracy, "which they used to hold up to their countrymen," had afforded "no security against . . . moral and political evils." So much for the bestowal

of power upon "a half-educated multitude." Britain could not trust the judgment of the Cobden and Bright school.[45]

In January 1863, the *Times* suggested that as more of the American continent became settled and organized, several republics would be formed. Individual states would coalesce with each other according to their own interests, and the existing federal government would cease to exist.[46] Hope had
already made similar remarks. He did not believe that four or five confed-
erations was out of the question. Perhaps the Confederacy formed in 1861
would end up being the largest union in America because it had already
commenced the necessary work of adjusting the relationship between central and state governments. Some pro-northerners in Britain, particularly
Bright, expected the old Union to be restored and to increase in size. Hope
thought this unlikely—and undesirable. Several smaller political units would
be much better for America than the "Yankee empire" envisaged by Bright.[47]

What would be best for Britain? "We still hope and believe that the
Anglo-Saxon race will eventually lead the world. But there must be a head
somewhere to that race." The primacy was Britain's, "with its ancient civilization and ordered freedom." Britain had a natural ally in the Confederacy, and the two were not to be "overmastered by a system compounded of
the greed of New York and the fanaticism of New England." Hope wished
for the success of the Anglo-Saxon race and especially "our own section
of it." The future of that race could not be dictated by the North, and the
independence of the South would help to prevent such a calamity, all the
more if it led to the division of the whole continent into several unions, established on sound principles and able to coexist and prosper.[48] Hope connected this vision with the status of Canada. Perhaps there was a "design of
Providence" for North America to consist of independent nations—South,
Central, Pacific, Northwest, as well as the present post-secession Union—a
configuration that would benefit all concerned. When Canada was ready
for self-government, Britain would have to behave in the way that the North
should have treated the Confederacy. Hope expected that, together, Canada and the South, with agricultural economies, could maintain an equilib-
rium with the more industrial (and "turbulent, blustering, and aggressive")
United States.[49] He maintained that "we have not seen the end of secession."
He called on the government and people of the North to accept this future
and to begin by letting the South go.[50]

His outspokenness provoked the ire of northern newspapers, especially the *New York Times*, which began complaining about him at the end of 1861. It described him (not quite correctly) as "MP, and the leading editor of the *Saturday Review*, famous for its attacks on America," and declared that "Mr. Beresford Hope is wholly in favor of the South. He has no misgivings . . . There is nothing good in the North; there is nothing bad in the South."[51] Early in 1863, the *New York Times* argued that Hope was an enemy of the United States because he was an enemy of democracy. Like other foreign friends of the South, he wanted the rebellion to succeed "because they hope to see, in our confusion, humiliation, and defeat, the overthrow of those political doctrines which we have now, for eighty years, represented in the eyes of the world." The "aristocratic party in England" hated what Americans loved: education, a free press, the rights of labor, religious equality, peace, manhood suffrage. Hope and his colleagues longed for the Union to fail, for this would justify "in their eyes, class privileges, the restriction of knowledge and of a share in the Government to the few, the maintenance of standing armies, the maintenance of Church establishments, the cost of regal Courts, and the injustice of primogeniture and the absurdity of entails." Still, the *New York Times* was less concerned about what Hope was doing in Britain than about the use made of his arguments in the North by opponents of the Republican Party and abolition.[52]

Newspapers of Boston and Philadelphia also argued that it was his commitment to "aristocratic" rule that made Hope side with the South. His detestation of U.S. democracy was stronger than his opposition to slavery, but there were Liberals and reformers who were writing and speaking in a different vein. Hope might relish the applause of "a stupid assembly," but the course of the war and the tide of British opinion were against him.[53] Several northern commentators noted Hope's defeat in the Stoke-upon-Trent by-election of September 1862. One saw in it "the working of the principles of democracy." Another remarked that Hope based his electoral appeal "chiefly on his public advocacy of the recognition of the Southern Confederacy." He was "the first man in England to introduce that question into the politics of the country," but the voters had rejected him.[54]

Whenever Hope was condemned by pro-reform and pro-northern lecturers in Britain, his enemies in the American press were quick to celebrate. In April 1862, they gave space to Henry Vincent, the radical temperance and antislavery campaigner, who had criticized Hope during a speech in Bedford. In March 1864, it was the turn of "eloquent and popular Irish orator" Mason Jones, who, having toured the United States, was appearing in Manchester.[55]

As the war was drawing to its close in April 1865, the *Saturday Review* expressed regret that the North would win because such an important victory might blind the world to democracy's flaws.[56] Certain that the North was a defective and nefarious polity, Hope saw trouble arising from restoration of the Union. Many in Britain shared his pessimistic outlook. One did not have to be a pro-southerner to be suspicious of American democracy.[57]

The war did reshape ideas about the nature of political power and the meaning of liberty. Some of the combatants believed that they were fighting for personal freedom, to be extended to cover slaves, while for a slave owner, interference with property rights meant the destruction of liberty. Lincoln thought that the war would decide the future of democracy in the wider world, which made him more determined to uphold the Union, for the freedom and opportunity offered by a republican form of government had to be safeguarded.[58] Related discussion of political participation and education was in keeping with Lincoln's belief that the authority of government rested upon an informed public.[59] Seward acted on the same idea when he arranged for the publication of diplomatic communications between the United States and Britain (though Charles F. Adams, the U.S. minister in London, advised against the publication of details that might complicate his dealings with the British).[60]

The main correspondent for the *Times* in the early part of the war, William Howard Russell, became increasingly favorable toward Lincoln (but hostile to Seward). Though northerners denigrated Russell's journalism, his diary and correspondence show that he wished to see the North win the war.[61] Hope was unmoved, but in some British circles, assessments of Lincoln and the U.S. system of government became more positive. Nevertheless, disagreements about American democracy continued.[62]

Hope would remain an active protagonist in these quarrels, as would the *Saturday Review*. All the quality periodicals sought to spread the word for or against democracy. Reformers and conservatives alike realized that the American crisis had lessons to teach. The *Saturday Review* was adamant that Americanization would be catastrophic for Britain. A more balanced perspective was that democracy was admirable in principle but difficult to operate in practice. This was the point made in 1862 by the editor of the moderately liberal *Edinburgh Review*, Henry Reeve, who published a new edition of Alexis de Tocqueville's much-respected *Democracy in America* (originally published in two volumes in 1835 and 1840) because of its obvious relevance to present-day deliberations. Reeve's introduction was quite despondent— he was concerned that reform might go too far.[63]

The American Civil War was a promoter of change in the wider world. In part because it marked the rise of U.S. power, it extended the discourse of democracy. There was acute awareness in Britain that even after the Reform Act of 1867, the franchise was still more restricted at home than it was in America.[64] Different outcomes would have emerged had the South won the war. Northerners believed that republican government and "free soil" went together, while southerners believed that liberty meant the protection of property, including slaves. The southerners' version of liberty was *regulated* liberty, to which they attached conservative religion and social stability, and binding all together was respect for authority (including racial hierarchy— some were fit for rights, and some were not).[65]

In cahoots with some Conservative politicians in Britain, Confederate agents and propagandists sought international approval for the creation of a "conservative world order" in which American and European problems would be addressed together. In short, Britain, France, and the Confederacy would cooperate to steady a world in transition. Balance and continuity, peace, trade, and the ascendancy of property owners were among the ends in view—as was southern independence. For a time, this project had the enthusiastic support of Hope's brother-in-law Lord Robert Cecil, the future Conservative foreign secretary and prime minister (as Marquess of Salisbury) and a regular contributor to the *Saturday Review*, among other periodicals. Discussion of the conservative world order increased in 1864 because there was a prospect of the Conservatives returning to office in Britain, the Confederates were inflicting heavy casualties on the Federals in America, and Napoleon III of France was pressing ahead with his intervention in Mexico. Southerners urged their Conservative friends in Britain to connect the balance of power in America (to contain U.S. democracy and aggression) with the balance in Europe (to restore calm after the Polish and Schleswig-Holstein crises). Alliance between Britain and France seemed to offer a means of control over events on both continents. But British Conservatives decided on an alternative plan, employing different tactics in different parts of the world. If Britain became embroiled in Europe, the United

States would take advantage in the Americas, and if Britain got more involved in the Americas, France would make advances in Europe. Therefore,
it seemed wisest to step back, relying more on the empire and the Royal
Navy as props for British influence.[66]

In Britain, even campaigners for substantial reform did not want democracy. The goal, rather, was to extend participation—to "popularize the constitution," in the phrase of Robert Saunders—without creating a democratic
system that would ruin the character of British parliamentary government,
the envy of the world. The Reform Act of 1867 was designed to bring change
without veering toward U.S.-style democracy.[67] Yet there is evidence that
some of the British who had settled in America warmly embraced the democracy they found there. Those from a rural background tended to take little interest in American politics and thought of American liberty as freedom
from taxes and tithes, while those with urban and industrial experience were
more mobile, less prejudiced against American ways, and more political.[68]

Just as Hope and other pro-southerners feared, the victory of the North
was a victory for democracy. This outcome directly affected British-American
interaction, and there were other ramifications. For instance, U.S.-Russian
relations looked set to improve, in the eyes of at least some northerners,
because of common interests beyond trade: the United States and Russia
were both rivals of Britain, both embarking on fundamental reform (the end
of slavery and serfdom, respectively) and both challenged by rebels (in the
South and in Poland, respectively). Pursuing "liberty" was not a national but
an international concern.[69]

At the end of the war, many in America and beyond thought that liberty
would be seen above all in rights and opportunities for former slaves. Yet
the emancipation process in America was no unproblematic leap forward
for democracy, which is a caution against uncritical acceptance of a "progress" narrative.[70] Those in Britain who were skeptical about U.S. emancipation and worried about the political, social, and economic adjustments
that might have to be made to accommodate the freedmen must have been
relieved when the democratic bogey turned out not to be as dangerous as
they had formerly imagined.

Hope's unequivocal comments about the nature of the Union point to
related considerations that absorbed the attention of his contemporaries.
Pro-southerners in Britain easily assimilated a Confederate interpretation of
American history. As Brian Schoen explains, southerners came to have an

idea of what America should be that was not the North's idea. Paul Quigley stresses the "unfinished" form of American national identity. Southerners believed that the original Union was based not on equality but on liberty, and liberty was meaningless if it did not protect the people from intrusive government. States' rights were a guarantee. The federal power could not interfere with property—that is, slavery. Southerners accused antislavery northerners of breaking with the values of the American Revolution. These northerners were the ones who were destroying the Union, unlike the southern architects of a secession that was but a principled response to what happened in the North.[71] It is odd that constitutional principles feature so rarely in John McCardell's account of "the idea of a southern nation," for states' rights were essential to that idea.[72] Peter Onuf recognizes the importance of the separatist inclination but argues that it did not gather strength until the very eve of war. Most southerners, influenced by popular patriotism and a democratic culture, were proud to be American. The shift came with the prospect of war, which gave to patriotic feeling in the South a more separatist character.[73]

This delay might cast doubt on historic and self-conscious southern exceptionalism. At the time, however, Hope and other pro-southerners in Britain had no qualms about approving of secession on the grounds of the South's separate identity and interests. Hope insisted that the South had irrefutable reasons for detaching itself from the North. For its own economic prosperity, political strength, and constitutional soundness, the South had to be independent, and its people were standing up for values that were also cherished in Britain.

3

SOCIAL AND CULTURAL
AFFINITIES

A longside his discussion of economics and his political and constitutional arguments, Hope made a case for the distinctiveness of southern society. The South was not the same as the North, he claimed, not in identity, manners, culture, ideas, or experiences. Separation was natural and unstoppable because North and South were like strangers to each other. Hope also argued that the South had stronger connections with England.

In lectures of November 1861 that were published as *A Popular View of the American Civil War*, Hope outlined some contrasts between North and South. While admitting that the growth of towns and industries in the North had been impressive, he looked behind the aura of prosperity and progress and saw greed, materialism, and "a feeble national character, no political faith, no corporate virtues." Hope had friends in the North, and he knew of excellent people there, but he discerned an alarming tendency, largely the result of the democratic suffrage, for everyone to be dragged down to the same level. In the North, there was infidelity and superstition, "habitual divorce," tawdry newspapers, a lack of principle—in short, "the lowest depths of meanness." Despite "great wealth, great science," the North had "no heart, no steady feeling, no abiding union," and it was sinking further into this mess as discontented and destitute hordes poured in from Germany and Ireland. The South did not present so disappointing a spectacle. Though most white men could vote, there was no "mob power." Landowners played their part in public affairs, and government pursued the general rather than selfish interests. It was no accident that before secession, southern politicians had enjoyed great influence in the Union: they had the understanding and skills to rise to the fore. But an equally striking fact about North and South was their political divergence, so entrenched by the 1850s that the Whig Party dominated in one section and the Democrats in the other.[1]

Writing early in 1862, Hope again emphasized the moral and social failings of the North and argued that southerners were different and superior. In the former Union, New York had risen to dominance. Yet it was a sinkhole, a disgusting mix of vice, luxury, rowdyism, and mendacity. Secession was a blessing because it would prevent the further ascent of New York to control the whole of the New World (and possibly the Old World too). In Boston, there was intellectual and religious skepticism. New England poets, authors, and artists had long been highly regarded, but Hope wondered why. He found much of their work neither Christian nor respectable. He condemned the *Atlantic Monthly*, published in Boston, so often praised as the product of the "cream" of American intellect. To Hope, its content was not edifying but morally destructive. How could it be otherwise in the declining North, governed by criminals in Washington whose schemes were contrary to law and freedom? The South was quite unlike the North. Hope thought it similar to England, having the same spirit of "conservative moderation," seen in both its government and its people. Hope believed that Confederate leaders would not allow themselves to be corrupted. He pointed to the absence of "mob" mentality in the South and to the greater social cohesion, lower divorce rate, and more widespread civility and kindness in the South compared to the North. Unsurprisingly, northerners did not like to be reminded of such things. Hope had learned that Edward Stearns, an Episcopalian clergyman in the diocese of Maryland, was likely to be prosecuted for remarks he had made in a sermon. He had done no more than compare standards of morality in the North and South, but his critics accused him of justifying secession.[2]

In exploring the differences between North and South, Hope sought to show that they had moved away from each other socially and economically and that party politics both contributed to and reflected this cleavage (though party distinctions tended to be weaker in the South than in the North). The Republican Party represented northern business and consolidated its position by fomenting hostility toward the South. The Democrats had divided into northern and southern camps and could not be a majority party unless the two wings combined.[3]

North and South had discordant attitudes toward Britain. The North was jealous, assertive, and hostile and the South respectful, friendly, and generous. An independent Confederacy would be open to British influence, much more than the old Union had been. It was in Britain's interests that the two sections should separate, but even more, it was for their own good. North and South were too dissimilar. Each had its own destiny to seek, and it was better that separation should happen now instead of later, when it would be more disruptive and difficult.[4]

This was also the line taken by the *Saturday Review*. A contribution published in July 1861 pointed to the "howl of unprovoked hostility" toward Britain from northern politicians and newspapers, the "bad temper and bad taste" and "disgraceful folly of American writers and speakers," which only partially subsided as the British government made clear its intention to remain neutral. Pro-northerners in Britain claimed that the North wanted British friendship, yet the North was not behaving like it did. All the bluster and criticism of northerners—aggrieved, apparently, because Britain had not rushed to support them—alienated rather than attracted. At the beginning of the war, most British people, because they opposed slavery, were ready to side with the North—even "the vulgar insolence of the Republican faction" could not make them accept slavery. But now the words and deeds of northerners meant that the British were unlikely to wish them well.[5]

This piece in the *Saturday Review* also complained that the House of Commons had shown undue "deference" to the United States by refusing to discuss British recognition of the Confederacy. Hope was not in Parliament at the time—he was without a seat between May 1859 and July 1865—but he could encourage and assist those pro-southerners who were, and several of them were happy to act as proxies. Hope's friend William Henry Gregory, Conservative MP for Galway, had given notice of a motion to recognize the Confederacy. (Gregory had visited America in the 1850s and befriended a number of southern personalities, including James M. Mason of Virginia, the future Confederate envoy to Britain, and during the war, Gregory would be involved in many of the same pro-southern initiatives as Hope.) In the Commons on 7 June 1861, Gregory was urged to withdraw his motion. The MP for North Lancashire, John Wilson Patten, another Conservative, said that it would be unwise to proceed. He spoke for "a great number of persons" who wished to maintain friendly relations with the United States. Gregory agreed to postpone his motion, indefinitely, but not until he had explained the motives behind it. Parliament and people needed a "perfectly impartial statement" of the reasons for the schism in America. Most information reaching Britain came from the North, and "he thought it only fair" that the southern states "should have an opportunity of justifying the course which they had taken." Another motion had been announced, by William Edward Forster, the pro-northern Liberal MP for Bradford, which opposed as inexpedient any interference on behalf of "Citizens of the United States who are now in insurrection against their Government." Since Gregory had relented, Forster withdrew his motion. This exchange was also notable for the interjection of Hope's brother-in-law Lord Robert Cecil, then MP for Stamford, who made plain his preference for the Gregory over the Forster motion.[6]

In March 1862, Hope lectured by invitation at the Maidstone Literary and Mechanics' Institution. He questioned the widespread impression that the North represented a "higher" civilization than the South. Pro-northern journals such as the *Daily News* in London were trying to sustain the claim, but it was a myth. Though the North *seemed* advanced, because it was populous and prosperous and distinguished in literature and science, there was more to civilization than this. The American crisis was instructive: "All over the North gigantic jobbing, the grossest political turpitude, ostentatious disregard of principle, cynical self-seeking," while "in the poorer, less cultivated, more thinly populated South we have discovered a unity of feeling and of action perfectly astonishing." In the South, liberty was respected. There was no suspension of habeas corpus or restrictions on the press. Defeats in battle were acknowledged calmly and in a way that reinvigorated the national will to carry on the fight. Southern industries were growing. Political life was not marred by instability and demagoguery, as in the North. Men of position, talent, and wealth came to the fore as "natural leaders," and the people were ready to make sacrifices for their independence. Hope gathered from all this that the South surpassed the North in "moral spirit." Whatever strengths the North possessed, whatever its claims to civilization, it "has not shown the still higher civilization of corporate action, or corporate feeling, or of organized patriotism." Anybody in Britain who doubted this characterization, Hope said, should read a piece in *Blackwood's Magazine* of December 1861, "A Month with 'The Rebels.'"[7]

Its author had journeyed through the North and found it disappointing. The people were scruffy and vulgar; anti-British sentiment was freely expressed; greedy war contractors were making huge profits; reports from the front were patently deceitful (Confederate troops either ran away or were hungry, ragged, and ready to surrender); and northerners blithely assumed that they could not possibly lose the war since they had more men and money than the South. The author, wishing to see the South for himself, was obliged to go via Kentucky and noted that U.S. authorities had resorted to arbitrary rule along the border, prompting more sympathy for the Confederacy. Across the North generally, "a raging democracy now supports a Ministry which bears no reproof and will endure no criticism." When he was in the South, the author witnessed unity and spirit. The troops were remarkable for their "determination and reckless daring." They respected private property and paid for the supplies they took from the surrounding country as they made camp or marched to meet the enemy. The author spoke with many of them. They came from every social class. All showed the same devotion. They were backed by the whole southern people, who willingly gave what money and material they could to the war effort, who were manufacturing for themselves what they used to obtain from the North, who had formed hundreds of voluntary societies to make clothes for the soldiers, and who in the author's experience—his travels took him to Tennessee, Alabama, Georgia, and South Carolina—were invariably steadfast, kind, and hospitable. Flag-waving crowds were often to be seen, and there was "perfect unanimity." Every southerner believed that secession had been provoked by the North, with its political dominance, tariffs, and stridency on the slavery question. The author visited a plantation where the slaves were healthy, happy, well-dressed, properly cared for, loyal to their master (who said he had no fear of a servile insurrection), and probably in a better condition than any laboring population in the world. The author affirmed that the South would in time free the slaves. For the present, though, British people ought to be swayed most not by their opposition to slavery but by an equally proper admiration for a nation struggling to be free.[8]

Hope thought that the course of the war made starker the differences between northerners and southerners. After enjoying early successes, southerners had since had to endure defeats, yet they were showing "gallant resistance" and "persistence" with "moderation." The South was not trying to invade or coerce the North but wanted only to have its right to self-government acknowledged. Early in the war, the Confederates might have sacked Washington but held back. Northerners, in contrast, had shown themselves to be bloodthirsty and barbaric; their armies in the field were an extension of the mobs that played so large a role in U.S. politics. They were vain and ambitious, set on punishing the South. They wanted to conquer, not negotiate. When Hope visited Europe, he met northerners who spoke to him in this manner, and he encountered the same sentiments among northerners who lived in London. The northern newspapers that arrived in Britain every week carried the same "atrocious language." If the North restored the Union by force, what could southerners expect? They would be mere "subjects." This was why they were fighting. They had been invaded. They had no choice but to defend themselves, their property, and their independence. Hope commended the tone of southern public life and claimed that southerners trusted in God, loved their country, accepted the responsibilities that came with nationhood, and knew that it would be wrong to submit to oppression.[9]

In this, they were like the English. They had the same blood, spoke the same language, and evinced the same hatred of tyranny.[10] Early in 1863, Hope again took up the theme that the South was similar to England (and more deserving of sympathy than the North). Southerners, he thought, exhibited "the clearest marks of English feelings." The "family likeness" was "authentic." The South resembled eighteenth-century England and might be considered *a part of* England, indeed, whereas the North could not: "The English element in the North has been especially vitiated within the last fifteen years by the peculiar kind of emigration roused by the misgovernment of continental Europe, much of which has . . . acted with most mischievous effect upon America." British people disliked extremism. Liberals were mostly conservative and Conservatives quite liberal in attitude. Across the Channel in Europe were legions of revolutionaries and reactionaries. When repression prompted emigration to America, it tended to be the revolutionaries who left, groups with no understanding of British-style constitutionalism and common law. All this made the North, to which the vast majority of Europeans resorted, even more unlike the South. If the North grew in power and boldness, who could deny that the benign influence of "Englishness" would be destroyed? "The best defense is for our brethren of the South to win their independence, and by embarking upon the gradual liberation of their slaves, to place themselves in full accord with English feeling while in their progressive reforms they steadily keep in view the old family model." The South embraced free trade and individual rights. The North did not and would never be Britain's friend, but the independent Confederacy, if treated well, could be. Hope agreed with the British government's rejection late in 1862 of a French proposal for mediation in the American war not because he was worried about offending the North but because he feared losing the confidence of the South.[11]

He saw an increasing number of British people taking up the Confederate cause. They were not moved by political ideas or economic interest, he thought. Rather, they sensed a cultural unity and spiritual bond with southerners. "The large majority of the respectable opinion of England inclines on their side by an overwhelming instinct."[12] The South was fighting to uphold *British* values of ordered liberty, self-determination, and constitutional government. How could this not find favor in the home country? The Italians had engaged in a similar war against Austria and won their independence, and many in Britain had supported them and welcomed their victory. Perhaps there had been misgivings about certain aspects of the Italian struggle, but these were forgotten in celebration of the outcome. "If we made allowances for Italy, should we not be willing to make equal allowances for our own flesh and blood . . . who are trying to raise up a new English nation?" Italian leaders Camillo Cavour and Giuseppe Garibaldi were respected as patriots and heroes. Even more might Stonewall Jackson, Robert E. Lee, and Jefferson Davis be lauded as personifications of courage and honor. They were the offspring of Britain, and on their lips was "the language of British independence." The North had produced no such figures. As much as southern leaders were to be admired, in fact, northern leaders were to be condemned in the same degree. Hope fixed upon the "unscrupulous, brutal, foul-mouthed" Gen. Benjamin Butler, U.S. commander in occupied New Orleans from May to December 1862, as representative of the northern character.[13]

When addressing a meeting in Maidstone in January 1863, Hope was no less explicit. Common heritage and shared interests meant that the South must be helped to win its freedom. According to reports, his remarks were cheered, though there was also some audible dissent. The *Standard* stated that he had a good reception, the *Bury and Norwich Post* that the audience "was by no means unanimous."[14] Hope's speech at the Liverpool Southern Club in October 1863 accentuated again the special historic ties between England and the South. They were members of a single family. Hope said that his goal was to promote "the consolidation of the kindly feeling and the good understanding which had grown up between England and those most ancient British colonies, her dearest and oldest children, Virginia and the Carolinas." The meeting was followed by a banquet, at which Hope was among the speakers. James Spence, the Liverpool merchant who, as an unofficial southern agent in Britain, was active in propaganda and fundraising efforts during the war (and was known to be "S," who wrote to the *Times* in favor of the South), spoke of "men of our race" and defined a southerner as "simply an Englishman born on the other side of the Atlantic." Spence proposed a toast to "the army and navy of the United Nations—of the Southern States and Great Britain."[15] Hope, Spence, and other pro-southerners would give financial as well as rhetorical backing to their idea of transatlantic family with the "Southern Bazaar for Wounded Confederate Prisoners," held in Liverpool in October 1864.[16]

Many southerners considered themselves "English." Above all, though, they prided themselves on the fact that they were not the same as the people of the North. Yet Hope's insistence that the South was more English than the North ran counter to a tendency among some British commentators to repudiate categorical claims. In his investigation of "race thinking" in Britain, Hugh Dubrulle indicates a reluctance to divide white Americans into separate groups. British observers worried that to do this would be to damage Britain's ability to influence the United States (as Dubrulle puts it, classifying southerners as "Anglo-Saxon" and northerners as "mongrels" would place millions of Americans "outside Britain's cultural empire"). These observers preferred to treat white Americans as part of a shared transatlantic connection, and they desired Britain and the United States to be close after the war.[17]

Another difficulty with Hope's argument was that many of the English who lived in the North did not find it so strange and uncongenial that they could not fit in. If the North really was less English than the South, this seems to have made little difference to them. Indeed, some enlisted to fight for the Union (though recruits from other immigrant groups were more numerous). English militia units were formed in the South, but it appears that this only happened when Federal troops approached the local area.[18]

English integration in the North was not straightforward. These immigrants still had a relationship with their homeland, and previous disputes between Britain and the United States and current tension over the *Trent* crisis and other incidents complicated matters. But America's civic nationalism allowed for flexible identities and facilitated adaptation on the part of immigrants, and when the United States made the Civil War a war about slavery, the English in the North could better prove their loyalty by backing emancipation. The St. George's Societies, which performed important cultural and charitable roles and gave expression to English residents' opinions, were well placed to do this. The English could stress the things they had in common with the host community.[19] Many of them came to feel comfortable in the North. They were untroubled by allegations that the South was more English and England and the North incompatible.

Nevertheless, Hope was far from alone in stressing the distinctions between North and South. Visitors to America before the war reported that North and South were different. To some extent, Hope's readers and listeners in Britain were already primed. From 1861, he increased the stridency, detail, and purchase of the commentary. This ties in with Peter O'Connor's analysis of the travel books, fiction, newspapers, and personal impressions that shaped British attitudes toward America. The British were familiar with American sectionalism and interpreted secession and war in the light of preexisting notions. O'Connor shows that British observers tended to differentiate regions in America, and the apparent lack of cohesion prepared them for the possible disintegration of the Union.[20] Secession did not come as a surprise, agrees Hugh Dubrulle, but if there was a wide acceptance that the South really was "a nation," the more important question was about "whether or not Confederate nationality was worth supporting."[21] Hope thought it was.

People in Britain were ready to receive what Hope had to tell them, and in the South, a separatist ideology was already deeply entrenched. James McPherson refers to the invention of a nationality, a racial and ethnic as well as cultural and ideological endeavor. Descent from noble Normans and seventeenth-century Cavaliers was increasingly assumed and asserted. Northerners did not have the same blood or rank, it was thought, and though this southern national theory was spurious, McPherson advises that its power should not be underestimated. Here was an ethnic nationalism that departed from the civic identity created after the American Revolution. Meanwhile, civic nationalism was reinforced in the North by commitment to the Union and the war to preserve it.[22]

Other historians have shown how influential southern "race mythology" could be. William Taylor points out that discussion of the differences between North and South made them more significant. Few Americans doubted by the 1850s that their country was fundamentally split between "a democratic, commercial civilization and an aristocratic, agrarian one." Each section had "its own ethic," "a different spirit," and "a distinctive racial heritage," and in the South, one of the favorite markers was the Cavalier. Taylor argues that by indulging in these "legends," the South cut itself off from the progressive forces operating in the wider world. Ritchie Devon Watson's study of books and periodicals delineates "the myth of the South's aristocratic and chivalric Norman racial inheritance." Since southerners were from noble Norman stock, northerners must hail from inferior Saxon peasants, or so these publications would have it. In the South, the prevalence of such notions, in Watson's view, lasted into the postwar years.[23] Robert Bonner suggests that they faded earlier, during the war, as questions were raised about racial groupings and their social and religious repercussions.[24]

That there was a white southern race was taken for granted, argues Bonner, and the tendency to categorize people racially, the primary division being between white and black, was intensified by anger against the North so that whiteness ceased to be a unifying identity. Ethnic descent, patterns of settlement, and national character gained increasing attention and gave to southern ideology a strongly separatist inclination, pushed along by the "Cavalier pedigree" and Norman-Saxon dichotomy. But Bonner reveals a change after 1863: "An identity claimed from an invented primordial past became far less popular and useful once the Confederacy generated its own history of collective action to sustain a common purpose." Southern ideology was rearranged on the basis of a new symbol ("a peculiar compound"), the "Roundheaded Cavalier," mainly because of the need to make secession consistent with the defense of authority and because the Cavalier heritage was not sufficient. The "aristocratic" bias of those who had popularized the Cavalier theme was queried, and southern evangelicals pointed to aspects of the Puritanism associated with British struggles of the seventeenth century that were to be admired, not rejected. The Roundheaded Cavalier synthesis was also shaped by the heroism of Stonewall Jackson, for a time the South's most successful general and a devout Presbyterian. Reservations about racial tropes added to the mix. Disapproval was expressed, for example, about the way European powers had for many years used racial claims to plunder the rest of the world, and southern clergymen, especially Presbyterian and Episcopalian, eschewed notions about separate "creations" for difference races (there was only one Creation in the Bible), which discouraged explanation of secession and war in these terms.[25]

Among southern critics, novelists, poets, economists, theologians, academics, and philosophers—mostly urban, well educated, and linked through travel and friendship with each other and with international intellectual currents—there was awareness of changing identities as the empirical, cultural, and chosen gave way to the sentimental, historical, and biological. Michael O'Brien shows that southern writers and thinkers interacted more with their British counterparts than with those of the North. There were shared misgivings about modernity, and in the South, a wish for stability led to a reliance on tradition.[26] Taking a long-term perspective, O. Vernon Burton's investigation of southern customs exposes an unmistakable consciousness of being different.[27]

Southerners mentally separated themselves from the North. Goals and values previously associated with America were altered so that they became specifically southern. The defense of slavery became more vigorous and organized, and there were other causes around which southerners could unite: economic self-sufficiency, a southern literature, churches and schools released from northern influence, and territorial expansion and racial mission. John McCardell seems not to think of southern nationalism as a response to stress or danger, which in some respects it was, for the North was clearly changing, but the South was too. The key issue for southerners was possibly, as O'Brien would have it, how to contain or guide this change. If they saw their society—orderly, courteous, chivalrous—endangered by materialism and competition, they were more likely to blame their problems on an "other," the North. Marc Egnal has linked secession to a struggle within the South, between progress and tradition. The traditionalists got their way, seeking not only to defy a hostile North but also to block modernizing forces in the South. Michael Bernath suggests that the rise of a separate southern mentality (to which slavery was not necessarily central) ended in confusion rather than clarity. There might not have been a thoroughly positive expression of distinctiveness.[28] Perhaps this was why, up until almost the last moment, there were southerners who did not wish to secede.[29]

Even so, many southerners before the war had no doubt that they differed from northerners, and northerners, too, saw the South as different, usually in a negative way, as an obstacle to democratic freedom and economic development. Contrasts were easy to emphasize. The white population of the South was less cosmopolitan and more ethnically homogeneous. Southern values had more to do with kinship, hierarchy, deference, rural routines, and masculine codes of honor, while northern culture seemed impersonal, bureaucratic, meritocratic, urbanizing, commercial, mobile, and rootless. Southerners felt threatened, concludes James McPherson, and they were defensive about slavery because slavery affected almost every aspect of southern life. A competitive, capitalist, free labor, egalitarian future was not desired.[30] There was a strong religious element, as noted by Drew Gilpin Faust. Southerners thought of themselves as God's people and their war for independence as righteous duty. (The downside of this was that defeat had to be borne as God's judgment.)[31]

In particular parts of the South, separatism could take a conspicuously robust form. In the South Carolina Low Country, where there were large plantations and slaves vastly outnumbered the white population, the priority was to uphold authority. Most whites in this region were yeoman farmers who headed small households, some of which included a few slaves. Being masters in a slave society made them similar to the wealthy planters because they had control over dependents. When the North challenged slavery, it was challenging the privileges of *all* masters, all of whom were jealous of their rights as property owners and conscious of their influence over and responsibilities toward others.[32]

Plenty of contemporary and subsequent commentators have agreed that there was a distinctive southern identity, but now—as then—there is disagreement on details. O. Vernon Burton recognizes that not all southerners were fighting to preserve slavery and not all northerners to end it. Most of the combatants, on both sides, were probably motivated by the same things: "Often in war the reason for conflict is political, and often the reason soldiers enlist is cultural. Both Northern and Southern soldiers enlisted on behalf of their community, neighborhood, state, and with their family and friends." This might tell against the distinctiveness of the South. Furthermore, many southerners were pro-Union in sentiment, and some fought for the Union.[33]

Identities were somewhat in flux in the nineteenth century, owing to a series of wars and rebellions in pursuit of nationalist ideals, the 1848 revolutions in Europe, the unification of Italy (in stages, 1859–61, 1866, 1870–71) and Germany (completed in 1870–71), the Irish campaign for home rule, and such events as constitutional reform for Canada (which became a Confederation in 1867), America's acquisition of Alaska from Russia (also 1867), and major risings against imperial authority in India (1857–58), Mexico (1862–67), and Cuba (1868–78). Assumptions about nationhood, governance, blood, and borders were bound to be affected by these developments. Paul Quigley thinks that change in the Atlantic world, as civic nationalism was challenged by "romantic" or ethnic nationalism, led some southerners to rethink their distinctiveness. Those who saw in European models a linkage between national self-expression and revolutionary chaos decided that southern nationality should be shielded from such connotations and that one could be southern but also American because southern identity had American roots. In this spirit, southerners could assert their own version of American history and the Union, encompassing states' rights and slavery, and secession solidified the idea of a nation resting less on political arrangements than on shared values, ethnicity, culture, and history.[34]

So the South was more "American" than "English"? Fluctuating identities made for uncertainty. Quigley has also shown that the movement of people across borders and oceans promoted a concept of citizenship as individual choice. In time, expatriation and naturalization had to be settled collectively, and U.S. leaders pushed for "volitional citizenship" because it accorded with their interests and wartime experience.[35] Some historians have emphasized a "crisis in nationalism," with common problems (including rebellions) having to be addressed simultaneously on either side of the Atlantic. This is a useful reminder of the *limits* of nationalism.[36]

The racial version of southern nationalism was reinforced by what was happening close by, in Mexico. Andre Fleche explains that southerners saw in Mexican instability the evils of multiracialism and expected French (that is, white European) control over Mexico to bring change for the better. They had to believe this because their own vision of nationhood relied upon racial subordination.[37]

To the extent that the southern self-image rested on a supposed homogeneity, it was on shaky ground. There was no white Anglo-Saxon, ethnically pure South to confront a "mongrel" North. At the same time, however, most of the people of the South joined in rebellion whatever their background. Though foreign-born residents in the Confederacy formed only a small proportion of the total population, Ella Lonn has noted concentrations of English, Scots, Irish, Germans, French, and Swiss in particular towns and districts, some of which had immigrant churches and other institutions and even foreign-language newspapers.[38] In these places, ethnic diversity, not uniformity, was the reality. Some of the foreign-born left the South because of the war, and some claimed exemption from war service, but Lonn shows that most assisted the war effort, and many took up arms. Some units in the Confederate army were entirely foreign-born, and immigrants also served in local defense. The navy included foreign-born officers and crews. Lonn points to ethnic and cultural variety in the South, which did not prove to be a serious weakness during the war.[39]

Other historians have pursued these lines of inquiry, highlighting, for instance, pro-northern as well as pro-southern commitments on the part of Germans and Irish in America.[40] Native and adopted identities gave rise to a complex set of relationships. Immigrants in the South might have had reservations about southern nationalism, and in some cases, loyalty to the South was more evident after the war than during it. In addition, the likelihood of easy English integration in the North must be balanced against the known difficulties. Charlotte Erickson's argument about "invisible immigrants"— that the English found America so similar to what they were used to that they could conform to their new surroundings quickly and smoothly—has been questioned. David Gerber stresses their wish to preserve continuity in their lives, through personal and family communication and emotional bonds with their places of origin back in Britain. They were conscious of the distance between America and Britain, and once they had direct experience of American society, they found it had unattractive features. There was homesickness. There were complaints that Americans were not very welcoming and that, contrary to expectation, America was not similar to Britain. The individual testimonies explored by Gerber do vary, but it appears that group identity weakened and personal relationships came to matter more to the English than a wider ethnic affiliation. This may have been the most effective way to maintain bonds and counteract the sense of disconnection. Erickson explains the relatively small English involvement in formal ethnic institutions as a result of easy integration: American society made few demands of English settlers, so they could join in or preserve elements of separateness more or less at will. But Erickson recognizes that experiences were mixed.[41]

While adjusting to American conditions, the British also retained some of the cultural values and economic practices they brought with them, and William Van Vugt argues that if the immigrants had to change, so did Americans. The receiving society was modified by the incomers. Van Vugt points out that easier integration compared to other groups did not preclude these settlers from behaving "ethnically." As time passed, a rising proportion of British returned home, and those who stayed became more Americanized. For a majority, assimilation was rapid. It also seems that in some locations the English, Scots, and Welsh tended to unite, probably in response to the number and influence of the Irish.[42] Another pattern is that most of the English going to America were from rural and agricultural backgrounds, but from the 1860s, the number from towns and cities increased. In part, this reflects accelerating social and economic change in England.[43] Van Vugt's position—relatively easy integration but retention of some distinctiveness—is a departure from the invisible immigrants thesis, but other scholars go further. They see the English in America as a self-conscious ethnic group with a clear identity. The St. George's Societies asserted this identity across class divides and sometimes engaged in ethnic and sectarian conflict.[44] Racial ideas and rhetoric—especially those rooted in Anglo-Saxon superiority—were relied upon after as well as before the American Civil War.[45]

Preserving "Englishness" in America had more impact in the South than in the North. Many southerners remained proud of their English ancestry. Visitors to the Confederacy during the war attested to this. Conventional wisdom was that the early colonists came to America to create an alternative to Britain, especially in New England, whereas Virginia was an *extension* of England. An English pattern was preferred in religion, law, and politics, and the sons of wealthy southerners were sent to be educated in England.[46]

All this did not necessarily make the South "English," for Englishness could be defined in different ways. It was not a fixed or agreed signifier. Some of the English in the North integrated without much difficulty; some fought for the Union. Substantiating the argument that the South was English might not have been as straightforward as Hope and other pro-southerners in Britain presumed. One of the problems was that Britain headed a large empire, had commercial and strategic interests all over the world, and indeed had sent its people out to live in and shape—and be shaped by—that world. Ideas about the British nation and its global role shifted, as Duncan Bell makes plain in his study of proposals for imperial federation.[47] In these proposals, appeal was often made to the example of the American Union because it could be presented as modern and progressive, and the North's victory in the American war was used to argue that federalism had proven itself. But bringing America in could also cause controversy. After all, among the rival world powers about which Britain was most uneasy was the

United States, and the type of patriotism endorsed by imperial federation's supporters—who prioritized duty to the state, rejection of materialism, and the simple and virtuous rural life associated with the colonial frontier— pointed more to the South than the North. Imperial federation did not come to fruition, but it furthered the inquiry into national, cultural, and racial identities and interests, just as Hope did with his description of southerners as English. His opinion was hardly likely to remain uncontested.

Hope was employing, but also pushing further, some of the statements that southerners were making about themselves. The most serviceable ideas, symbols, and definitions could be altered to suit British opinion. Hope had not visited the South, though, and did not know what it was really like. He relied on information gathered from friends and on what he read and heard about America from other sources. He was primarily interested in what was politically useful. Whether his ideas about the South and how he depicted it for readers of his publications and audiences at his speaking engagements were accurate or not was beside the point. His goal was to move others to support the South, in pursuit of which he peddled a version of separatist ideology. This was an attempt to manage perceptions, a careful selection of arguments (factual or otherwise) that seemed most likely to achieve the desired end.

Northern commentators dismissed Hope's assertions about Anglo-southern social and cultural bonds as strange and unconvincing, but they were worried enough to attack him personally (and would not have done so had he not been on to something). In March 1863, for instance, the *Living Age*, a literary weekly published in Boston, claimed that Hope's influence was limited because he had connected himself too closely with the Confederacy. "Like the chameleon he assumes the hue of the nutriment on which he feeds," and he had so overdone it that his own identity had changed. The "flamboyant" Hope was not recognizably English anymore but pure Confederate.[48]

Hope did not relent. During and after the war, he continued openly to adhere to the position taken by the *Saturday Review* in May 1863 that there were stark differences between North and South and that these differences accounted for British preferences. The reason why British people took such a close interest in the American war was because they admired southerners and disliked northerners. Northerners did nothing to change the situation, so it was their own fault. The South's generals, chiefly Stonewall Jackson, and statesmen, chiefly President Davis, had no equals in the North. Their individual superiority was also a national one, for southerners tended to be more virtuous, kind, hospitable, patriotic, self-sacrificing, courageous, and religiously devout than northerners.[49] Southerners were a distinctive people. They were an English people.

4

SLAVERY AND EMANCIPATION

New ideas about nation, citizenship, and race were being discussed across the continents, and in an age that saw the abolition of serfdom in Russia (from 1861) and the enfranchisement of workingmen in Britain (1867 and 1884), and as contemporaries employed a broadening vocabulary of rights, it was inevitable that much attention would be given to the question of slavery.[1] Hope and other friends of the Confederacy were loath to admit it, but at the time, and ever since, the American Civil War was thought to be a war about slavery. Many people in America and Britain made this claim when the war broke out. Many more realized that if there had initially been some doubt, the Emancipation Proclamation (announced in a preliminary fashion in September 1862 and implemented in January 1863) brought clarity, though pro-southerners in Britain persisted with their objections.

Among modern historians, Edward Ayers is typical in maintaining that the war had no single leading cause but that slavery was the core problem and affected everything else. Although support for secession did not correspond with local patterns of slave owning and abolition did not emerge as a primary justification for the war until it was in progress, the war cannot be understood without reference to slavery.[2] O. Vernon Burton is adamant that while upholding the Union was a vital concern, the Union was threatened *because of* slavery. As for states' rights, it could be argued that slave owners were looking to the Union to *defend* them against a northern appeal to states' rights since the federal authorities had been pro-South for a long time and the South objected to the "liberty laws" passed in northern states, which were refusing to send back fugitive slaves without a trial. James McPherson also highlights this problem and the long controversy over the legality of slavery in new territories. Burton emphasizes that seceding states made plain their determination to defend slavery and believed they had to leave the Union to that end.[3]

Perspectives were shaped by European, African, and Caribbean developments. Antislavery commitment could strengthen ethnic bonds and national identities, adding to common experiences of unrest and uprooting.[4] Perhaps these experiences balanced, or at least rendered less virulent, the influence of racist and ethnic conceits in the making of identity, and struggles for liberty in Europe might have reinforced pro-northern sentiment in Britain, to the extent that the war was regarded as a conflict about slavery. American abolitionism influenced and was influenced by developments elsewhere. The links between Europe, America, and Africa created an Atlantic world that was both "free" and "unfree."[5]

Tension between free and unfree systems and contacts over land and sea meant that, however distinctive the South might have considered itself, it was brought into wider patterns of change. In Haiti, in 1791–1804, war and revolution had ended slavery, but the economy was ruined, and the British West Indies also saw economic decline following emancipation there in 1833. Cuba, however, enjoyed prosperity *with* slavery, as did Brazil. For many in the South, bloodshed in Haiti was caused by abolitionist agitation, and Lincoln's election made servile insurrection more likely in America by giving abolitionists control over the government in Washington. But there was a more positive prospect. Just as slave labor had brought success to Cuba and Brazil, it would do the same for the South. With a strong economy, the South could support itself as an independent country.[6]

Such ideas boosted southern self-confidence. A growing body of scholarship indicates that the South was modernizing, with towns, industries, and railroads, and that slavery was not an obstacle to diversification and innovation.[7] To most of the optimists, it was cotton that gave the South an assured future. Since there could be no cotton without slavery, slavery had to stay. Southern planters and merchants could look forward to good times, and they also picked up on changing attitudes to abolitionism in Britain. Some abolitionists had made themselves objectionable because of their perceived extremism or because they were hypocritical or inconsistent or because they were seen as too idealistic. Racist assumptions persisted, and paternalists could point to what they deemed to be the improving effects of slavery and the greater cruelty of free labor systems. There were British commentators who regretted emancipation in the West Indies, and in British colonies in Africa, there was coerced production of lucrative staples for export.[8]

Secessionists thought that local and global trends were operating in their favor. They insisted that the South had only joined the Union because slavery was recognized and protected, that the Union was not meant to be permanent, that the North now needed the Union more than the South did, and that the South's prosperity lay not in the Union but in integration with the rest of the world.[9] Historians of southern nationalism emphasize the inseparability of slavery and states' rights, and the centrality of slavery to a cause—independence—around which southerners could unite, and Stephanie McCurry's thesis about "mastery" (inviolable property rights and authority over and responsibilities to dependents) also goes some way toward an explanation of why non-slaveholders were willing to fight for the Confederacy just as slaveholders were.[10]

Even so, a number of scholars have argued that southern identity did not depend primarily on defense of slavery.[11] It is possible that some southern spokesmen defended slavery less frequently once the Confederacy was formed because they no longer had to respond to abolitionist claims, but for others, this need still prevailed. During the war, criticizing the North by attacking abolitionism remained a common pursuit. Differentiating themselves from northerners using racial and ethnic criteria had also become normal for southerners. Blood, ancestry, heritage, and culture, increasingly connected with such symbols as the noble Norman and chivalrous Cavalier and with natural hierarchies, could all be used to defend slavery and explain the sectional conflict (although distinguishing white from white was unpalatable to many in the South).[12] Some opinions about slavery and secession were reinforced by defeat and Reconstruction; after emancipation, there was more racial segregation.[13]

Southerners realized that slavery made them blameworthy in the eyes of outsiders and that there was a strong antislavery lobby in Britain. There was no buckling under this pressure. To their British adversaries, southern writers addressed numerous correctives and rebuttals. The British did not understand southern life; they had been misled by biased northern sources; they should not think of slavery as incompatible with progress; and slave owners were acting as guardians to the ignorant and irresponsible, who were being physically and morally improved. Slave owners liked to discuss the West Indian emancipation and its ill effects. They also declared that slaves in the South were treated better than the laboring poor of Britain. Angered by abolitionism and fearful about its consequences, they could not give way.[14]

British unease about the West Indies would have risen even without southern critiques. But northerners as well as southerners were part of this debate, and the British emancipation could be employed in contradictory ways. The reform of 1833, and slave rebellions that preceded it in the Caribbean and the South, affected the sectional conflict in America. Positive and negative accounts of 1833 were circulated to substantiate claims about what America could expect if its slaves were freed. Northern and southern commentators emphasized or suppressed at will, in order to support a favored position, and slaves in the South were themselves impressed by the British emancipation. By the 1860s, northern abolitionists were looking at Jamaica's instability and drawing conclusions. They held that after emancipation, it was essential to grant political rights to freed slaves and limit the power of their former owners and that problems in the British colonies after 1833 did not mean that cotton production in the South would suffer from a move to free labor.[15]

In Britain, such notions were dismissed by many as unrealistic, if not absurd, and there were wider disagreements after 1833 about slavery and the slave trade, Britain's economic performance and the future of colonial and global commerce, and imperial security and Britain's international role. The sugar duties were controversial. Should slave-grown sugar cost British consumers more than free-grown, or should duties be equalized in accordance with free trade doctrine? There was also controversy over Britain's African Squadron—naval patrols to deter slave traders—because of the cost to the British taxpayer and protests from other maritime nations. Meanwhile, the slave trade to Cuba was thriving, the French wanted to use coerced labor in their colonies, and the expansion of tropical production over a larger area of the world seemed viable. The Indian Mutiny of 1857 added to British concerns about race and power. Above all, perhaps, was the recognition that while the West Indies had faltered economically, the wealth of the American South was growing.[16]

The most contentious subject that prewar British commentators on America had to address was slavery. Even admirers of America regarded slavery as its greatest flaw. One visitor of 1848, when told by a Virginian that the British should not make judgments about the South and that the South would free its slaves if left alone, opined that there would be no emancipation unless the slave owners were forced into it. Some of the British who spent time in America wondered why the question had not been settled long ago, though they also acknowledged the political difficulties involved. Visitors who passed between North and South were struck by the differences between neighboring free and slave states. It was not uncommon for British observers to think that there would eventually be a violent rupture over slavery in America.[17]

Nor was it uncommon for them to be shocked by the uses made of the Bible there. Revivalism and abolitionism overlapped in some parts of America but not in others. In the South, the Bible was employed to defend slavery, and organized antislavery activity declined during the early nineteenth century. In the North, evangelicals who opposed slavery could also eschew militant abolitionism. British observers might be puzzled, but in the prewar years, the biggest American denominations all had slaveholding members. While many in Britain insisted that churches had a duty to promote change, there was also a reluctance to undermine denominational unity by making accusations against the churches or questioning the integrity of American revivals.[18]

Increasingly, people in Britain regarded blacks as inferior by nature, not because they were kept down by slavery and its consequences. This was not unrelated to the disappointment that attended emancipation in the West Indies, which had not brought the expected results. In addition, Christian teachings and humanitarian values and the libertarian and progressive tendencies in British political culture might have been undermined by class consciousness, poverty, and social danger—which hardened attitudes toward the lower orders, with whom blacks were identified—and by such religious changes as the rise of Dissent to influence and respectability, which meant that Nonconformists, no longer outsiders, were less inclined to side with other disadvantaged groups, including slaves. There was still opposition to slavery, but in debate, in literature, and in imagery, blackness had negative connotations, reinforced whenever abolitionists made patronizing remarks about slaves as inferior beings in need of assistance. Sympathy for abolitionism was falling before the outbreak of the American war, argues Hugh Dubrulle, though this is not to suggest that Britain was becoming *more* racist. Rather, the war facilitated expression of existing British racism. By this time, the British were swayed by "contradictory discourses." They read American commentary on slavery, both northern and southern. Another influence was minstrelsy, in which representations of the slave as lazy, sly, and impulsive conflicted with an approving nod toward protest, self-assertion, and the lampooning of authority. Economic considerations also affected British responses to the American crisis, for Britain needed cotton and other products of slave labor to strengthen its trade and industry and serve its geo-strategic interests. Abolitionists generally preferred not to refer to race in case it split their movement or alienated sections of British public opinion. Pro-southerners tended to avoid racial argument, too, because they found it embarrassing or because they genuinely believed that slavery was not a cause of the war.[19]

Though there was moral condemnation of slavery at all levels of British society, there was also racist and anti-abolitionist sentiment even among the most progressive political circles and in working-class groups and publications. This attitude was emerging before 1833 and was strengthened by protests about the compensation given by Parliament to the West Indian planters, using taxpayers' money, and by the impression that leaders of the antislavery movement in Britain cared nothing about social and economic injustices at home. The disadvantaged in Britain became more aware of themselves as "white" and used racist language (demeaning blacks, whether free or bound) to advance their interests.[20]

For British radicals who praised U.S. democracy, slavery was an uncomfortable issue. Some supported the abolitionist cause in America and claimed that America's toleration of slavery brought shame upon its people and institutions, but others thought that time and energy would be better spent on battling "slavery" at home and condemned the antislavery movement in Britain for ignoring the plight of "wage slaves."[21] These spokesmen were challenging abolitionism as a selective response to labor problems. Yet there was no consensus. Greater clarity emerged from the 1840s within a framework that included a view of suffering that was wider than that of the abolitionists, but this stance was not universally adopted.[22] Malcolm Chase has noted racism among British radicals. Equating the labor system in the South with "wage slavery" in Britain's factories was, Chase thinks, a "clumsy association" demonstrating ignorance of the actual condition of slaves in America.[23]

Wage slavery was one of a broader set of ideas about the nature of work.[24] Negative connotations of wage labor were diminished when race was added to the mix. Although white workers complained about low pay, their whiteness was an asset. They had status because they were not black. Economically defined classes existed in the United States by the mid-nineteenth century, but most Americans did not think of themselves primarily in this way, and political parties did not pursue specific class aims.[25] Class allegiances mattered more to the British. While many white workingmen in America could vote and many were actively involved in party politics, these developments came later in Britain. American workers engaged in politics as neighborhood and ethnic groups rather than as an economic class.[26] British workers and American workers did not think the same way about class or about race.

Many British people were troubled less by disadvantages attaching to race than by those relating to class. "Racial inequality was similar to, and directly related to, other forms of social subordination," writes Douglas Lorimer. If the antislavery movement had helped to contain racial prejudice, a change began in line with intellectual and scientific developments and class consciousness. Accustomed to inequality in Britain and wishing to distance themselves from those they thought beneath them, members of the rising professional and commercial middle classes saw native Africans and the black slaves of America as inferior both racially and socially.[27] As Richard Huzzey has shown, many in Britain could condemn slavery while repudiating racial equality.[28]

The growth of prejudice was probably not as quick and complete as Lorimer thinks. It is not clear that there was a rise in discrimination against blacks in Britain, and if class was more important than race, individual blacks might have been treated according to their perceived social status, not their racial character. There were some in America who decided that prejudice was weaker in Britain and easier to overcome.[29] Racist ideology and behavior were more typical of the empire than Britain. Arguments about race were heightened in the multiracial colonies and in relation to Britain's imperial policy. Lorimer hardly mentions the Indian Mutiny, but it affected thinking about nonwhite peoples. Still, Lorimer does establish that racial and class attitudes could merge with and support each other.

British admirers of the prewar United States found it difficult to discuss slavery without contradicting their praise for America. Abolitionism gained adherents, primarily for moral but also for economic reasons (the assumed inefficiency of slave as opposed to free labor), and there was agreement that slavery was evil, but the responsibility for it was sometimes transferred. Since Europeans had started the transatlantic slave trade, guilt could be redirected toward Europe. Slavery could also be romanticized. Conditions for the slaves were far from unbearable it was claimed. This separated both Americans and Europeans from culpability.[30] Whatever the motive or the level of antislavery conviction, few visitors' accounts of America failed to mention slavery and racism.[31]

Matters were complicated by quarrels between British and American abolitionists and by splits within the British antislavery movement, and since "liberty" could be defined in different ways, it is not surprising that slavery was less important to some activists than to others. The debate also touched on the presence in Britain, primarily among the London poor, of former slaves, and the economic condition of Britain's colonies in the West Indies after 1833. Furthermore, America's war for independence had removed from British politics the American lobby that previously defended slavery in alliance with the West Indian planters.[32] All these developments shaped British attitudes, and the shift from one kind of empire to another—from mercantilism, colonies under close control, and the empire as a regulated trading bloc to freer trade and an outward focus—had implications for Britain's own political and economic prospects. American as well as British observers had seen the West Indies go into economic decline, and southern slaveholders had no wish to run that risk. If in some circumstances free labor was *not* more efficient than slave labor, abolitionism would lose one of its main props, and reliance only on moral and humanitarian arguments was insufficient when claims could be made about welfare provisions for slaves in the South, as opposed to the retreat from paternalism of employers in industrial Britain. Racist assumptions were stimulated as commentators tried to explain why Britain's experiment in emancipation had not worked.[33]

Anglophobia in America also played its part. It was easy for people in Britain to attack the prewar United States by focusing on slavery, and in this, there may have been a desire for revenge for the anti-British jibes of some Americans. In America, opponents of abolition made much of the abolitionists' links with the antislavery movement in Britain. Proslavery activism could thus be presented as loyalty to America. Some northerners who favored abolition nevertheless declared that the British had no right to interfere in U.S. affairs, and in the South, there was fear that the ending of slavery in the West Indies (albeit with unimpressive economic results) made the institution more vulnerable in America.[34]

Along with a strong economy, the United States had a growing population that overtook Britain's during the 1840s. America's economic vitality and population growth would in time sap confidence in the ability of Britain and its empire to compete.[35] Meanwhile, British concerns about cotton and sugar, naval spending, transatlantic commerce, slavery, and U.S. influence came together when attention turned to such problems as the fate of Cuba. In America, talk of annexing Cuba increased, especially in the South, and quarrels about Cuba deepened sectional and partisan animosities within the United States.[36] By the late 1840s, there were many southerners who wanted to deny Cuba to Britain (or France), and they were certain that the South would lose influence within the United States if no new slave states were added to the Union.[37]

India's failure greatly to augment its output of cotton meant that Britain's reliance on the South continued. Abolitionist alarm at the prospect of slave cultivation being extended beyond the South did not diminish in these cir-cumstances, and predictions that slavery in the South would eventually dis-appear were not universally accepted.[38] British observers were nonetheless impressed by the potency of the antislavery movement in the United States, and Harriet Beecher Stowe's *Uncle Tom's Cabin*, which became an interna-tional best seller after its publication in 1852, sold more copies in Britain than America. Its description of the slaves' devotion to Christian worship and fortitude in the face of hardship seemed likely to boost popular support for abolition.[39]

Yet some in Britain may have overestimated the strength of the American movement. Even in its northern heartlands, it faced political and cultural obstacles,[40] and critics on both sides of the Atlantic dismissed *Uncle Tom's Cabin* for its alleged exaggerations. To the *Times,* slavery was "less dreadful in practice than in theory," and as a core part of life in the South, it could not be removed quickly.[41] Although the attention given to *Uncle Tom's Cabin* reinvigorated British abolitionists, it is possible that popular sympathy for the slaves soon declined. Richard Blackett's examination of contemporary plays and novels indicates that in the ten years after the publication of *Uncle Tom's Cabin,* more British people came to the conclusion that the lot of the slaves was not so bad, which played into the hands of slavery's apologists.[42] A departure from the favorable image of blacks that had been put forward by the antislavery movement was hastened by racial theories, English ethnocen-trism, disillusionment with the freed slaves of the West Indies who did not improve themselves after 1833, and the status concerns of rising social groups in Britain.[43] British abolitionism did not collapse, though it did become divided. There were arguments, as in the past, about tactics. Cooperation with American abolitionists suited some but not others. Eventually, there was a split over the legitimacy of war as a means to end slavery.

The influence of *Uncle Tom's Cabin* was strongest on antislavery activists of long standing. Harriet Beecher Stowe added to the excitement by visiting Britain three times during the 1850s. She recorded that antislavery opinion in Britain sometimes became anti-American.[44] Indeed, many of those who interested themselves in these matters did so not because they cared about the slaves but because they wanted to condemn America. The reception of *Uncle Tom's Cabin* in Britain was far from straightforward, though southerners were in no doubt that it was an opinion-shaping force there.[45]

During the 1850s, the British and U.S. governments clashed over the patrols off the African coast. Americans complained about Britain's stop-and-search practices. The U.S. government had declared the slave trade illegal in 1808, but Americans were still involved in the lucrative business of carrying slaves to Cuba and Brazil. Officially, the United States was not involved in the slave trade. The focus, rather, was on a principle, freedom of the seas, and when America made a stand on its maritime rights in May 1858, the British gave way. This followed angry exchanges during the Crimean War of 1854–56, when London took exception to pro-Russian activity on Washington's part. There was also tension over Central America, where the United States and Britain were rivals.[46]

Controversy intensified as British commentators decided that having done its duty in 1833, Britain was not responsible for the behavior of other nations and their guilt, if they chose to retain slavery, was their own affair. Britain used its influence against the slave trade but did not press unrelentingly for foreign emancipations, and British consumers were not unwilling to purchase slave-produced commodities. As Richard Huzzey explains, the British saw no moral problem concerning *how* an item was produced, though the decision to buy or not to buy it *was* a moral question.[47] If Britain was responsible only for what happened in areas under its direct control, was it appropriate to offer advice to the South? Peter O'Connor has shown that the British usually criticized American slavery in the abstract and highlighted elements of the southern labor system that they believed compared favorably with the condition of free blacks in the North. Discussion of slavery in national as opposed to sectional terms collapsed the moral boundary between North and South.[48] This made it easier for activists such as Hope un-ashamedly to state their preference for the South above the North. Hope also brought into his writing and speaking the moral standing of Britain as part of the slavery question.

In late 1861, Hope publicly denounced slavery as "an abominable insti-tution." At the same time, he stressed that responsibility for establishing it in America rested with the British. Since the colonial period, slavery had disappeared from some parts of America because the land and climate made it less profitable than free labor. In more tropical conditions, white Euro-peans were unsuited to agricultural work, and there was a need for black Africans. Hope presented all this as incontrovertible fact. It was also unde-niable that the Union had been increasingly divided over slavery. Hope saw racism as more severe in the North than in the South. As for the abolitionist movement, it was strong in New England but weaker elsewhere. Although its most extreme faction was small in size, by its ceaseless agitation it fo-mented disruption and violence. The extremists obstructed because they did not want a calm discussion of slavery. "Abolition, if carried out at once, would be a source of the greatest misery to the blacks themselves, thrown as they would be upon their own resources," but "ultra-abolitionists are . . . opposed to everything like firm government or good order" and "seize upon slavery as the weakest point for attack. By their threatening, the quiet men in the North and the quiet men in the South, who, without emancipating at once all the slaves, would yet educate them up to liberty, are silenced and driven back."[49]

People in Britain were rightly intolerant of slavery, but they had to re-member that slavery in the South was a legacy of colonial rule. It was also important to acknowledge that slavery in the South was not so great an evil as some commentators claimed. Opinion in Britain, Hope declared, should not be swayed by Harriet Beecher Stowe or her younger brother Henry Ward Beecher, the Congregationalist minister "who sells the seats in his church more unblushingly than anybody else in New York and puts godliness up to auction." The fair-minded in Britain knew that slavery was "a curse and a misfortune," but they also knew that many slave owners were kind and generous and that slaves were being educated, Christianized, and raised to levels of happiness and comfort that were unknown back in Africa. It was wrong to assume that the North's priority was to help the slaves. Northern-ers did not want rapid emancipation. Many of them profited from slavery.

New York and Boston traded in slave-produced items and extended loans to southern planters and merchants.[50]

The South had done well to mitigate the "practical" harm of slavery, Hope insisted early in 1862, and the slave trade was explicitly banned under the Confederate constitution. Hope thought that the South would have done more had it not been for northern abolitionism and that, if undisturbed, the South would gradually phase slavery out in a manner that gave every possible advantage to blacks who would have to adjust to a life of freedom. In the North, free blacks were persecuted. Hope stressed that the North shared in the guilt of slavery as well because slavery was a core part of its economic system. Hope saw secession as a guarantee that emancipation would eventually come. Economic logic had led the South to favor free trade, and free trade would open the South to outside influences, especially British, and was incompatible in the long term with unfree labor. Nor did the South need to preserve slavery for reasons of political representation. Leaving the Union released the South from northern dominion. Hope predicted amelioration across the independent Confederacy, leading to a type of "serfdom," or "villeinage," and subsequently to full freedom. He found it instructive that Lincoln had looked into the deportation of freed blacks. Here was another indication that slavery was not the main cause of the war. The real causes were economic and political: northern protectionism impeding the South's economic growth and the election of Lincoln on a minority vote and against the wishes of a unanimous South committed to states' rights.[51]

Lincoln's willingness to put together a scheme for the removal of blacks to a colony outside the United States featured in Hope's *Saturday Review.* The verdict was that the president did not understand political economy or labor systems. There were sound arguments against the continuation of slavery in America, but Lincoln, it seemed, did not know much about them.[52]

Hope discussed slavery at length in his speeches and publications, notably in *England, the North, and the South* of early 1862. The *Observer* dismissed his arguments as "very delusive."[53] But the pamphlet sold well and went into a third edition within weeks.[54] Hope knew of people in Britain who felt unable to side with the South because they believed southerners to be brutal slave masters. His response to them was that slavery was already being reformed in preparation for emancipation and that the true friends of the slave were in the South, not the North. The pamphlet also restated some previous points: that southerners could not be blamed for the existence of slavery since it had been established by the British in colonial times; that its existence could be explained by history, climate, and the nature of work; that northern businessmen and workers made money from slavery; and that blacks were despised and mistreated across the North and much less so in the South. Hope saw more in the Confederate ban on the slave trade than simply a ploy to win over British opinion. He thought the ban would be difficult to reverse because it was constitutionally secured (unlike in the North, where prohibition of the slave trade depended only on the will of Congress).[55]

Hope maintained that many northerners wished for slavery to continue, and they wanted the South to return to the Union because, otherwise, they would lose their investments in and profits from slavery. While it could not be denied that most abolitionists were sincere, Hope thought their methods unfair and unrealistic. Immediate emancipation promised "bloodshed, outrage, destruction of property, and perpetual starvation over the South, by the letting loose of a race half-savage, half-childish, and their transference into a position of freedom for which they are wholly without preparation." Hope feared that as the war went on and northerners were frustrated by the South's spirit and strength, fanatics would rise to the fore and make emancipation their means of destroying the Confederacy. If the U.S. government did declare for emancipation, the aim would be to damage the South, not to serve any higher motives. Northern politicians and generals were inciting anarchy with their pronouncements, and schemes promoted by such writers and orators as Wendell Phillips and William Lloyd Garrison were dangerous and immoral.[56]

Hope continued to argue that an independent Confederacy would free its slaves. Conditions for the latter were being improved, and anyone who knew the South understood that change had to be gradual, not sudden. As Hope put it, it was best to address the problem of slavery without creating other problems. He repeated that the South's interaction with Britain and Europe would have positive effects. He mentioned Mexico and Brazil, both former colonies of European powers. Mexico had abolished slavery and fallen into political turmoil; Brazil retained slavery and enjoyed prosperity and constitutional government. If Britain and Europe could use their influence to encourage emancipation in Brazil, the same was true of the Confederacy. Hope insisted that Britain would gain more through friendship than antagonism. He noted that there had been discussion in British newspapers about the Confederate envoy in London, James M. Mason, a former U.S. senator for Virginia. Much of the coverage was unfavorable on account of Mason's support for the Fugitive Slave Act of 1850. Hope protested that the law, at the time it was passed, was a necessary measure of self-protection for the South. It directed that escaped slaves who reached a free state had to be returned to their masters, but with secession, it was "virtually repealed." There was a wider context: (southern) respect for property rights versus (northern) endorsement of confiscation. Mason deserved British gratitude, moreover, because he had pushed for the refitting and return of HMS *Resolute*—abandoned in the Arctic in 1854, recovered by Americans, and sent back to Britain as a gift in 1856—"the most graceful act of courtesy which the American government has shown England for many years."[57]

In *The Results of the American Disruption*, Hope wrote of the conviction (under a piracy law of 1820) and execution, in February 1862, of Nathaniel Gordon, of Maine, a slave trader who had carried off nearly nine hundred souls, mostly children, from West Africa in August 1860. Gordon's case reflected badly upon the North, Hope thought, but it was only one sign of a corruption that went much deeper. "The North is as deeply tainted with slavery as the South, with the additional element of utter disingenuousness." Though first introduced into the Americas by the Spanish, slave labor was extended under British rule. In 1776, all of the thirteen colonies had slaves. By the early nineteenth century, slavery had been abolished across the North, but this emancipation was a "device" because northerners made money by selling their slaves to southerners. The North reproached the South while playing an "actively hypocritical part." The South's slaves were probably worth about 500 million pounds. In 1833, the planters of the British West Indies had been awarded 20 million pounds for emancipation there. Should the South be compensated, and if so, how much, and who should pay it? These matters needed careful thought. It also seemed high-handed for British commentators to condemn the South when slavery in the British Empire had only been abolished quite recently. Hope believed that most southern slaveholders did not treat their slaves cruelly. They were not as abolitionist propaganda depicted them.[58]

Hope's purpose was to show that slavery gave the British no reason to favor the North over the South. He did not accept that the South had seceded to preserve slavery. In March 1861, just before Lincoln assumed the presidency, the U.S. Congress resolved that there could be no federal interference with the domestic institutions of any state, yet there had been no rush of seceded states back into the Union. To Hope, this proved that a "new nationality" had come into being in the South and also that the North was not fighting to free the slaves since Congress had explicitly accepted slavery.[59]

Hope was intrigued by a proposal discussed in the state legislature of Delaware. Slaves would be freed and compensation paid by the federal government. Hope suggested that if this plan worked satisfactorily, it could be extended to other states, but he did not think it would bring the South back into the Union or end the war. Furthermore, if it was intended as a model for other states, there would be problems: how to cover the cost of compensation and how to deal fairly and consistently with the varying types and numbers of slaves from place to place. Still, the Delaware scheme had more merit than uncompensated emancipation. It was not just the owners who had to be considered but the slaves too. Hope referred to slaves who, despite opportunities to escape, chose to stay with their masters and slaves who might wish for emancipation but would not want it to be hasty and unconditional for they knew they were not prepared for it.[60]

Many in the North thought that freed slaves should be sent out of America, a reminder that northerners had little regard for blacks and did not want to mix with them, according to Hope. He was also suspicious about the establishment of a colony. It would need administrators to run it and troops to defend it. It would provide the North with a foothold overseas, which was probably the whole idea, but for Britain, there could be no yielding to U.S. aggrandizement. Hope asserted that the "ambitious, grasping spirit" of the North was among the causes of the war, and he agreed with what had been said by Earl Russell, Britain's foreign secretary, in a widely reported speech in Newcastle-upon-Tyne on 11 October 1861: that the North fought for "empire" while the South was fighting to be free.[61]

By this time, Hope's speaking and writing about slavery had been noted in American newspapers. The *New York Herald*, a popular Democratic daily, reported that Hope had been well received in the lecture rooms of England. His supporters, it was presumed, would not approve if Lincoln interfered with "slave laws" upheld by the U.S. Constitution. Southern papers also carried Hope's remarks, while the *Boston Daily Advertiser* balanced Hope's idea that southern independence would be in the slaves' best interests with the growing number of claims to the contrary by pro-northerners in Britain.[62]

When Hope spoke in Stoke-upon-Trent in September 1862, he further clarified his position on slavery. "I have privately to the Southerners, and publicly in lectures, denounced that atrocious system," he began. While it was important to remind the South that the British people opposed slavery, however, it was also important to recognize that guilt for slavery was shared by Britain and by the North and that slavery was permitted by the U.S. Constitution. Hope said that an independent South would abolish slavery but had to be allowed to do so in its own way. There was applause when Hope proclaimed the wisest method to be "gradual emancipation from slavery to serfdom, and serfdom to liberty." He questioned the North's commitment to racial justice and damned as "preposterous" the idea—discussed in the U.S. Congress during 1862—of a colony for blacks in "the pestilential marshes" of Panama.[63]

In this speech, Hope also focused on Lincoln's published response, dated 22 August 1862, to a piece written by Horace Greeley, the antislavery editor of the *New York Tribune*. Lincoln stated that his "paramount object" was "to save the Union" and "not either to save or to destroy slavery." To cheers, Hope denounced the "third rate lawyer from the backwoods of Illinois" and "the cynical way in which he says he will preserve slavery, preserve the greatest curse of the human race, or emancipate the slaves, which means the massacre of the whites."[64]

In January 1863, Hope delivered another lecture, soon published as *The Social and Political Bearings of the American Disruption* (which sold at an impressive rate—by mid-March, it was in its third edition).[65] According to *John Bull*'s report of his lecture, Hope thought that until they could be freed, slaves should be educated and their families kept together, "and this he argued the South was willing to do." He "strongly censured" the Emancipation Proclamation, "which turned out the negroes to starve or else to plunder their masters."[66] Hope's negativity was not unusual at the time, for the Emancipation Proclamation was frequently dismissed as a frantic bid for British sympathy.

Hope confirmed that although he opposed slavery, he was willing temporarily to put that aside for a greater good. In his opinion, the Emancipation Proclamation was deplorable. It only freed slaves in areas where the U.S. government had no authority. It could not be implemented. Hope wanted slavery abolished but not by Lincoln. It was not enough for the slaves to be freed. They had to be given a route to prosperity and usefulness. The North was addressing none of their needs, Hope said, because it lacked genuine concern for the slaves. Journalists in attendance noted that the audience mostly approved of Hope's speech, though there was some opposition.[67]

Hope complained that across Britain, there were many people who did not go beyond the simplistic idea that if slavery were just abolished, all would be well. "I would gladly see the blacks as free as anyone," he declared, but first they had to be "educated and Christians" and capable of "earning a good day's wages for a good day's work, and willing to render that work." This was *real* freedom, but it was not what Lincoln had in mind. To him, emancipation was only appropriate for some blacks in some places, places, moreover, that did not recognize the U.S. government, which meant that slaves had to be liberated by force, "against the will of their employers—against their own means of earning a livelihood—against their continuing to reside where they were raised and are living." Pro-northerners in Britain were gushing over Lincoln's morality and statesmanship, but if the president truly wanted to free slaves, why had he not done so in the slave states still in the Union? Hope did not expect the proclamation to have much bearing in the South beyond the areas occupied by U.S. troops. It was "the last, most desperately wicked move in the game of politics, recklessly made by a baffled adventurer."[68]

More impressive than the Emancipation Proclamation, Hope contended, was the pastoral issued by the bishops of the Episcopal Church of the Confederate States late in 1862, which stressed that the South had a responsibility to look after the slaves. Here was the prospect of meaningful reform, with conditions for the slaves continually improving.[69] There were other documents that Hope recommended for perusal, including an antislavery address sent by "a multitude of ladies in England" to the women of America and Harriet Beecher Stowe's response. The address had been composed eight years earlier. (It was known as the Stafford House Address, after the residence of the Duke and Duchess of Sutherland. Lady Sutherland was one of the organizers of the address.)[70] Bound in twenty-six folio volumes and signed by high and low, it had carried more than half a million names. Now, after a considerable delay, Harriet Beecher Stowe had replied on behalf of America's women. She reproached those in Britain who had sided with the South despite their disapproval of slavery. Did she really not understand why they had done so? The *Saturday Review* had the answer. Plenty of British people had enjoyed *Uncle Tom's Cabin*, but they knew it was not "authentic history," and they knew also that blame for the war in America was to be ascribed to "Mrs. Stowe and her fanatical connections." The British saw, too, that although Stowe wrote as if the North and abolitionism were indistinguishable, northerners who shared her way of thinking were outnumbered by those who did not, and that the U.S. Constitution, rightly or wrongly, guaranteed slavery. "It is not that we love slavery or the South more, but that we love the North less," and still the North continued to give offense, with the "rabid hatred and threats" of its statesmen and journalists.[71]

Hope's *Saturday Review* has been identified by Hugh Dubrulle as one of the publications that added to the confusion in Britain concerning slavery because it included arguments about black inferiority that rested both on natural and on environmental factors.[72] Either way, the *Saturday Review* was counteracting abolitionism and attempting to improve the reputation of the South. Alfred Grant sees in the *Saturday Review* a number of Hope's fixations and, in Hope's wartime pamphlets, no genuine desire for abolition, only statements of opposition to slavery that were riddled with qualifications.[73]

Hope argued that there was nothing strange about people in Britain opposing slavery but backing the South and that organizers of the ladies' address should not have made a formal statement on a delicate political subject and entrusted it to a foreign "literary celebrity," especially when the British and U.S. governments were not on the best of terms. Hope believed that those behind the address misunderstood the South's labor system and ignored the fact that the South was already on a path toward emancipation. As for Stowe, she gave the South two options: return to the Union and accept emancipation; or have the slaves freed by force, with no government safeguards against the "consequences." This was no choice for an independent people, Hope commented. Stowe was telling southerners that if they did not give up their right to self-determination, they would suffer atrocities.[74]

Hope advised that people in Britain who had taken their lead from northern abolitionists ought to look again at southern slavery. Statistics were available that indicated a rise in Christian outreach. More religious instruction was being provided, usually at the slave owners' expense, and many slaves were learning how to read and write. Their material needs were also being met. "It is a mistake to suppose that the blacks have no privileges and are mere chattels." In some parts of the Confederacy, slaves had access to the courts, could own property, and enjoyed protection for their marriages and families. In places where they lacked specific legal rights, they could exercise rights de facto. Their situation was improving, and what to British eyes might appear harsh was really for the benefit of the slaves. Rules that stopped them from being freed above and below certain ages, for example, operated like "a self-acting poor law," meaning that masters had to provide for the very old and the very young. The Emancipation Proclamation did none of this, and it bore repeating that racial prejudice was much stronger in the North than in the South. Northern workers feared that blacks would take their jobs, and if the abolitionists had their way, this would become a serious concern as freed slaves moved to the North.[75]

On the level of political participation appropriate for former slaves, Hope assumed that black voting might be possible to a limited extent but eschewed the idea that all freed slaves should be granted political rights. Office holding should also be ruled out. This was linked with the vote. If blacks were deemed to be capable of voting, were they also qualified to sit in Congress or serve as state governor or even run for president? Hope did not want to encourage any such speculations. Though he believed in "the unity of the human family," he also understood that "the cumulative accidents of rolling centuries have endowed some races with greater capacity . . . than others." For blacks to rule whites would be "loathsome" and "unnatural." Emancipation was coming, and Hope looked forward to a time when it would be possible, but "I yet dare, in the face of false philanthropy, to deprecate in the name of Heaven the subjugation of millions of our Anglo-Saxon brethren by a rabble of Negroes let loose." For the vote, most blacks were not ready, and in areas where they outnumbered whites, their enfranchisement would promote the subjection of whites and probably black-on-white outrages. In India, natives were being brought into legislative and judicial roles, but these were "Hindoos and Mahometans, races with a history, a literature, a philosophy, and not Negroes." Conditions in America were different, and it would not be wise to redistribute power there. "Our own success in that way in the West Indies has not been so very brilliant or encouraging."[76]

These reflections raised another question, "What makes a nation?" Hope listed intelligence and experience acquired over many generations, schooling and religion, creativity and knowledge transmitted from parents to children, language and literature, laws and customs, the Bible, prayer—this was "civilization." It existed most obviously in Britain and also in the major European countries and to some degree in their colonial empires. "What share in all this has the Negro got? Where has he been to school? In what alembic has his nature been refined?" Emancipation in the West Indies had been "noble" and "Christian," but mistakes had been made, and that was in a deliberate, well-planned enterprise. Lincoln's policy had little planning or deliberation to it, declared Hope. It was just a war measure to attack the South.[77]

Hope had already connected some of these ideas to the prospect of a future American continent divided into several independent republics. Such a division would be "good for the blacks," he predicted, because slave owners, "unfettered by the intrigues of a large party playing fast and loose with this question, and of another smaller party preaching immediate emancipation," would "for their own self-interest, make such arrangements as would lead to the gradual abolition of slavery," and "there would no longer be any political necessity for extending slavery over territories where it had not even a climatic excuse."[78]

Hope's opinions were rejected by northern papers, including William Lloyd Garrison's *Liberator,* which reported on Hope's lectures and carried a letter condemning his "falsehoods and calumnies" from British abolitionist George Thompson, founder of the London Emancipation Society, who had previously been on speaking tours in America. In a subsequent editorial, Garrison argued that Hope's public defense of slavery made him highly unusual in "anti-slavery Britain." Although the "knavish and ridiculous" Hope did not openly approve of slavery in the abstract, he justified the system as it existed in the South. "He takes slavery as it is . . . and is content with the ameliorations provided or suggested." But the war was being fought to end slavery, Garrison insisted. Southerners wished to preserve it, the North wanted freedom, and most British people were satisfied that they could not love freedom without hating slavery. The *New York Independent* welcomed a series of antislavery meetings across Britain, at which "men of talent and authority" praised the Emancipation Proclamation, and expected Hope and the "pro-slavery party" to be disconcerted by this popular upsurge.[79]

If they were disconcerted, they soon recovered. In August 1863, the Manchester Southern Club issued a prospectus and circular, calling for an end to the American war, recognition of the South's independence, and the gradual emancipation of the slaves. The organ of the British and Foreign Anti-Slavery Society urged that "anti-slavery friends" must "steadfastly resist all arguments which may be advanced, with a view to induce them to unite in the movement, as they may rest assured it cannot tend to promote the interest of the unhappy negro but only to strengthen the hands of his most inveterate enemies."[80]

The *Anti-Slavery Monthly Reporter* had been contacted by an unnamed but "influential" correspondent who was not unwilling to assist the Manchester club and "asks if we will 'try the South.'" No honest opponent of slavery, however, could cooperate with a group that had men such as Hope among its leaders, and it was deceitful of the Manchester Southern Club to promise gradual emancipation while backing the South in the war because the South was fighting to uphold slavery. Peace was desirable, but British recognition of the South would not end the war. The South sought independence only in order to achieve its true goal, the continuation of slavery, and even gradual emancipation was unacceptable to southerners. Emancipation was already proceeding, thanks to the U.S. government, and as for the oft-vaunted section of the Confederate constitution that banned the slave trade, the *Anti-Slavery Monthly Reporter* insisted that this provision would be overturned if southerners, having won their independence, found that obtaining slaves in Africa was more cost-effective than breeding them at home.[81]

Hope was not put off by critics in the British and Foreign Anti-Slavery Society. He addressed a meeting of the Liverpool Southern Club in October 1863 and repeated some of his earlier remarks about slavery. According to press coverage, he focused wholly on *reforming* the institution, not abolishing it. "The sympathies of the majority of the people of England were in favor of the South," he said, but southerners might lose this goodwill unless they "applied themselves to the task of improving the condition of the slaves."[82] Hope celebrated the greater knowledge of the South that British people had acquired since the war's commencement. Old misconceptions had been discarded. People hated slavery but held, as Hope did, that "it should not be made the bone of contention or the means of alienating." Eventually, the slaves *would* be free. In the meantime, "a liberal policy and feeling should be maintained towards those who had inherited their black peasants with the soil, and who for the most part treated them with consideration and kindness."[83]

Hope's speech in Liverpool further antagonized northern journalists. They considered him "silly and bombastic." The *Boston Daily Advertiser* claimed that his "ultra views in favor of the South" had less impact than the well-received speech by Henry Ward Beecher, in the Philharmonic Hall,

Liverpool, on the same day that Hope was speaking across town to a much smaller audience. Boston's *Living Age* characterized Hope as "perhaps the most intelligent and docile of all the disciples whom the Slave States and their able politicians have found in England." He talked like a slave driver. He had even embraced the untenable proposition that differences between the English agricultural laborer and the slave in the South were "theoretical" rather than "practical."[84]

One of Hope's hosts at the Liverpool Southern Club was James Spence, who had himself entered into the slavery debate with vigor. Spence's position annoyed the government in Richmond and its envoys in Britain and Europe because, in their view, he was not sufficiently robust. He did argue that the slaves were treated well and that their racial inferiority meant that slavery could not be considered degrading, but he also favored emancipation, albeit with laws that would enforce employment and obedience. Spence seemed unreliable to Henry Hotze, editor of the *Index*, the Confederate paper established in London in May 1862.[85] The Swiss-born Hotze, who had gone to America in his youth and taken U.S. citizenship in 1855, was another of Hope's circle of Confederate friends. His statements about slavery changed with the course of the war. Initially, there was overt racism. Hotze attempted to overcome British reservations about southern slavery by presenting the subordination of inferior races as appropriate and by linking this with British interests (social hierarchy, imperial power). As the likelihood that the British government would recognize the Confederacy dwindled, he focused more on the disruption that emancipation would entail and suggested that British as well as American experiences might be useful in figuring out how to prepare the slaves for freedom. It is not likely that the *Index* made many converts in Britain. Hotze's racial prejudice was too much even for staunch pro-southerners.[86]

The Southern Independence Association of London (SIA), with Hope as chairman, was established in 1863 to partner with bodies in other towns. Its literature emphasized the need for "revision" of the system of slavery "in accordance with the spirit of the age." There was some mention of the "gradual extinction" of slavery, which the South was entreated to combine with "the preservation of property, the maintenance of the civil polity, and the true civilization of the negro race."[87] The SIA made sufficient progress for its opponents to step up their countermeasures. In January 1865, the *Anti-Slavery Monthly Reporter* argued that the SIA, like the Manchester club and similar bodies before it, was out to trick the enemies of slavery into giving their acquiescence, or even their backing, by separating southern independence from the question of slavery and holding out the empty ambition of "gradual extinction." The SIA's leadership consisted of notorious pro-southern partisans and critics of abolitionism. "How can an association, comprising such elements, be otherwise than actively hostile to the Federal cause; and how can it sympathize, or have any view in common, with those who desire to see Slavery abolished, not only in the Southern States but everywhere?"[88]

By the spring of 1864, Garrison's *Liberator* was confident that most British people, if they had previously disliked northern abolitionism, now looked upon the North with friendly eyes. Perhaps this was an overstatement, and Garrison was choosing to believe what his British contacts were telling him. Still, the *Liberator* was adamant that a change had taken place over the preceding three years, from the time when "Beresford Hope's venomous print, the *Saturday Review*," had insisted that disagreements about slavery would destroy the Union. These were prophetic words but not in the manner intended. Hope and his friends had expected the slave states to go their own way. In 1864, it was clear that the Union would be preserved, without slavery. It would be a new kind of Union. Hope and his friends had been correct in that the Union could not continue to exist with slavery.[89]

At the end of the war and shortly after Lincoln's assassination, the *Saturday Review* accepted that emancipation of the slaves was inevitable, and perhaps even appropriate, owing to the course of the war and political conditions in the North. For all his faults, Lincoln had taken a sensible path (though this only became apparent with the passing of time). His priority was to restore the Union. The Emancipation Proclamation "looked like a crime, and proved to be only a manifesto." Had it become operative "in those unconquered portions of the South to which it was exclusively applicable," Lincoln would have been "justly condemned as the author of an intolerable servile revolution." The slaves did not rise, however, and "the proclamation served the useful and harmless purpose of advertising an inevitable change in the policy and object of the war." Enlistment of blacks to fight in the war was "a more practical step in the same direction, and ultimately the President found himself strong enough to make emancipation an indispensable condition of peace."[90]

If this denoted a softening of Hope's attitude, his enemies were probably not impressed. He kept saying he opposed slavery yet routinely added provisos, and in lectures and writings, he brought in every argument he could to justify its continuation in the South. He denied that the war was being fought to free the slaves. He maintained that northerners were not genuine about emancipation, that they were unconcerned about organizing it properly, that they were more racially prejudiced than southerners. Hope presented a picture of southern slavery in which it was almost harmless. His overriding goal was to increase British support for the Confederacy *despite* slavery. He had to make slavery less of an obstacle. He could not allow it to weaken his pro-southern appeals. But there was strong customary aversion to slavery and a complexity to British opinion about it. Changing ideas about race and class, economic interests, moral imperatives, new intellectual trends, imperial concerns, and problems in foreign policy all had their effect. Hope's exculpatory analysis might or might not have moved many others, but he persevered. He did not change tack even when the course of the war turned decisively against the South.

5

A RELIGIOUS PERSPECTIVE

One of the most important trends in the historiography of the American Civil War has been the investigation of its religious aspects.[1] Yet relatively little work has been done on these aspects *outside* America—that is, on the religious side of the war's internationalization. To the economic and political reasons why the South gained support in Britain, Beresford Hope added a deeper commitment that sprang from a sense of ethnic and cultural affinity (the "Englishness" of the South) and especially from his religious convictions. Religious factors might have done more to shape the pro-southern lobby in Britain than historians have previously realized.

Hope's case underlines the point that "class" and "party" cannot by themselves explain why people in Britain favored the Union or the Confederacy. Hope came from wealth and privilege and believed in aristocratic rule and social hierarchy, and he was politically conservative. But there were many in the governing elite who did not support the South, and in his pro-southern outspokenness, Hope also went much further than other Conservatives. Indeed, the party's leaders in Parliament were strictly noninterventionist, and neither their disapproval of the North's policies nor the antidemocratic elements in Conservative thought changed this.[2]

Hope wrote and spoke as a loyal son of the Church of England. His was a churchman's perspective, and he offered an analysis of the American crisis that prioritized the role and status of the Episcopal Church in America. Separation of that church into northern and southern branches was no less appropriate, he believed, than the political dismemberment of the Union. Hope argued that division of the Episcopal Church was a boon to the global Anglican Communion, and would bolster religious truth itself, because both branches could advance more quickly by themselves, and through benign competition, they would push each other to excel. But he also argued that the church, and indeed Christianity, was stronger in the South than in the North, as evidenced by the South's superior moral standards, social order, and religious observance. The southern church had the wisest approach to the question of slavery, moreover, holding that there existed a duty before God to treat the slaves well and that reforming the institution with a view to eventual freedom was better than immediate emancipation. Hope was sure that the church in the South enjoyed advantageous prospects owing to southern culture; a more stable, conservative, and homogeneous society than in the North; talented bishops to lead; and interaction with Britain. He regarded the northern and southern churches (like the peoples they served) as irreconcilable. Politicization of the northern church turned it away from ecclesiastical matters, while the southern church was an expression of national distinctiveness.

The American church had separated from the Church of England in 1789 so that its clergy would not be required to accept the supremacy of the British monarch. It used a revised version of the Book of Common Prayer from 1789, and, though its bishops were initially consecrated by senior English or Scottish nonjuring clergy, from 1792 they could be consecrated in America.[3] The church was a hybrid. Its Anglican structure and traditions combined with ideas of liberty that were congenial to the American republic. As late as the 1850s, it was necessary to clarify the powers of the bishops because of an attachment to local autonomy dating back to colonial times. By the mid-nineteenth century, there were also difficult debates about doctrine and practice, mainly between High Church and Evangelical wings, as in the Church of England, and matters were complicated by the rise of Tractarianism. There were disagreements about the church's missionary role both abroad and at home on the frontier and among free blacks and slaves. Despite these tensions, the church remained united.[4]

Hope had an abiding interest in the American church. He had American friends, including clergymen, and was notably forthright on various issues concerning the American church: the building of churches and schools; the spiritual care available for Anglicans who left Britain to live in America; the status of clergymen ordained in America who subsequently applied for livings in England; the advantages of denominational and voluntary, as opposed to secular and public, education; and the spiritual damage that might be done when Anglicans habitually shared buildings and resources with non-Anglicans. Hope discussed these matters with, among others, Charles

Blomfield, the bishop of London (1828–56), and future prime minister W. E. Gladstone, and he spoke about them at meetings and in Parliament.[5]

In 1861, the Episcopal Church split into two as a result of the secession of the South. Unlike other large Protestant denominations, the Episcopal Church had not splintered on the issue of slavery, but the establishment of the Confederacy led southern bishops to set up a separate organization because they were now subject to a new government. There was no great hostility toward the northern church, and in the North, there was a desire to maintain the notion of an unbroken church, from which southerners were only temporarily absent. In its constitution, canon law, prayer book, and organization, the southern church remained the same as the northern, except for adjustments reflecting its separate status.[6]

Episcopalians in the South were probably more pro-Confederate than those in the North were pro-Union because they had more to lose if the South was defeated and because the Evangelical party, more "political" than the High Churchmen, was influential in the South. In the North, a moderate tone was employed by bishops who were personally close to southern bishops, and this suited everyone who wanted to avoid alienating the slave states that remained in the Union. While some Evangelicals in the North opposed slavery, the High Church party included critics of abolitionism, which meant that discussion of slavery was avoided whenever possible. Nevertheless, the General Convention of 1862 issued a non-neutral pastoral, and the trend among Episcopalians, both northern and southern—and among Americans of other denominations—was to support their own side in the war and to believe that God was on their side.[7] Southern Episcopalians' loyalty to the Confederate cause was evident at the time, but so was their lack of bitterness toward the North, compared to other denominations, owing to a sense of devotional unity with northern Episcopalians.[8] The tendency to trust in Providence and to explain the war as God's will furthered the "sacralization" of the nation.[9]

Though the Protestant Episcopal Church of the Confederate States was not recognized in the North, Hope was quick to recognize it. Early in 1862, he wrote of the southern church as a new part of the Anglican Communion. There were now two American nations and two American churches. While the Episcopal Church had more communicants in the North than in the South, government and society in the North were corrupt, and "the cause . . . for whose success in the interests of religion, and also of our communion, we ought as English Churchmen to wish, is the cause of the Confederate States." Hope did not see slavery as a stumbling block because he was certain that the South was heading toward emancipation.[10]

Hope admitted that in some parts of the North, the Episcopal Church was thriving. Several of its "orthodox" clergy were excellent scholars, preachers, and leaders, and there had been spiritual progress in New Jersey under Bishop George Washington Doane, 1832–59; in Maryland under Bishop William R. Whittingham, consecrated in 1840; and at the Church of the Annunciation in Manhattan under its rector, Samuel Seabury, who had been appointed in 1838 (and was the grandson of the Episcopal Church's first bishop). But Hope also argued that the church in the North would do better as a separate organization just as that in the South would make advances in an independent Confederacy. The United States had become too large and complex for a single church to prosper, and for many years, necessary measures had been abandoned for fear of exacerbating sectional tension. "There is better hope for the truth in two homogenous National Churches, keeping each other in check and stimulating each other to exertion."[11]

Hope saw an "upward tendency of Churchmanship in the Confederate States." There were fewer clergy there than in the North, but they were having more impact. In New York, the church had failed to combat materialism, vice, and infidelity. In Boston, it was "weak and Puritanized." In Washington, it was doing nothing to resist a tyrannical government. In the North, the Episcopal Church was supposed to be the church of the refined, wealthy, and cultured. To Hope, however, it was not influencing anyone for good. Meanwhile, reports suggested that the southern church was gaining strength, caring for souls, collecting money, and engaging in missionary work. In October 1861, there had been a meeting in Columbia, South Carolina, to discuss a new constitution. Diocesan meetings were set up and triennial councils arranged, beginning in November 1862 in Augusta, Georgia. Soon a prayer book would be issued. "The prospects of the Church are more hopeful in the Confederate States than they were before the great disruption had thrown the Southerners on their own resources."[12]

The meeting in Augusta produced a church pastoral, which Hope discussed in his lectures and writings. "The churches in America have no endowments and are therefore wholly dependent on their flocks, and so this expression of a decided opinion on the part of the clergy may be held to reflect the views of the best men in the country." It was "an authentic document straight from the South and having emanated from a popular, important, and influential religious community." To Hope, the key point about the pastoral was its insistence that southerners had a responsibility to their slaves, who were to be instructed and improved and their families kept together, their health and housing attended to, their labor burdens eased, their welfare promoted. The pastoral might perhaps be queried for its assumption that slavery would continue, but Hope preferred to emphasize its recognition that the institution's most objectionable features must be mitigated.[13]

This recognition was by now freely expressed across the South. A concept of "Christian slavery" offered a way to reconcile Bible-based faith and southern realities, and as Eugene Genovese and Mitchell Snay have stated, the religious defense of slavery and efforts to "humanize" the institution (to ward off abolitionist criticism) affirmed that slavery and Christianity were not incompatible. There was some acceptance of white-black spiritual equality and mutual responsibility.[14] Owners and nonowners of slaves mixed together in their local churches and were regularly exposed to justifications for slavery that reinforced the mind-set of "mastery"—control over dependents.[15] All this came to have religious as well as legal sanction.

Hope had the pastoral printed at the end of his *The American Church in the Disruption* of 1863. By including the pastoral, he allowed British readers to see for themselves what the Episcopal bishops of the South had agreed as their position on slavery.[16] The "solemn fact" was that slaves "are not merely so much property, but are a sacred trust committed to us, as a people, to be prepared for the work which God may have for them to do in the future." To care properly for the slaves was a Christian duty, though the bishops rather excused the institution with the comment that "systems of labor which prevail in Europe . . . are in many respects more severe than ours."[17] Hope found the bishops' acceptance of slavery unsurprising and realistic. "Holding, as we have always done, that the problem of slavery was one which could only admit of the most gradual and cautious treatment, this statement more than comes up to our expectation."[18]

Hope declared that the present generation of southerners—as all "sensible" people knew—could not be blamed for the existence of slavery. The same sensible people also realized that "ultra-abolitionists" were dangerous, with their "Jacobin" political ideas, and hypocritical, for they wanted no personal contact with blacks while posing as their deliverers. They were quite unlike the great moral crusaders of the past—including Puritans and

Evangelicals—and they took their lead not from the Bible but from Voltaire and Paine. Their abolitionism was really a bid for unchecked democracy.[19]

In the prewar years, Episcopalians were acutely aware—and relieved—that their church had not broken apart over slavery as others had. It is ironic that Hope focused on the church to show why secession was appropriate and necessary and why the South deserved British support, and yet of all the major Protestant denominations in America, the Episcopal Church was the *least* divided into northern and southern blocs. Southern exceptionalism was reinforced during the 1840s and 1850s, thinks James McPherson, by the division along sectional lines over slavery of the largest American denominations—the Methodists, Baptists, and Presbyterians—and John McCardell argues that southerners wanted their own religious life, freed from the influence of the North.[20] But southern Episcopalians did not separate themselves from the rest of the American church until the Union was ruptured, which might suggest that they did not see themselves before then as primarily and distinctively southern. Their sense of nationhood increased dramatically as a result of the war, not least because wartime suffering hastened the fusion of Christian faith and southern identity.[21]

The religious element in southern exceptionalism affected thinking about the ethnic and cultural differences between the sections. The Cavalier motif, for instance, had to be altered to take account of southern evangelicals' respect for the Puritans. Southerners who had seen themselves as Cavaliers in some cases began also to favor a "Roundheaded Cavalier" synthesis. "What was ultimately involved," writes Robert Bonner, "was the relevance of a high-church past to an overwhelmingly low-church present." Southerners who claimed to be the offspring of Roundheads as well as Cavaliers were reluctant to engage in criticism of Puritanism. They argued that the form it had taken in the North was a departure from the seventeenth-century English model, so that the separateness of the South was untarnished. This separateness could be explained in nonracial terms, which suited those who denied that there were *two* white races in America, Episcopalian clergy among them. At the same time, slavery, resting on racial subordination, had to be defended. How southerners saw themselves and how they regarded slavery had to be consistent with the premise that true Christian faith was found in the South.[22]

Episcopalians in the South, including clergymen, owned slaves, and a religious defense of slavery had been organized around two propositions:

the Bible allowed it, or did not explicitly prohibit it; and the institution was a social and moral blessing because it imposed a responsibility to improve the slaves. Some Episcopalians in the North, including clergymen, accepted and disseminated these claims, though the Evangelical wing included strident abolitionists.[23] As Gardiner Shattuck has pointed out, white Episcopalians in the South could agree that all races were equal before God, but when faced with the prospect of abolition, they did not expect blacks to be equal within the church.[24]

Hope was disinclined to dwell on the problem of whether or not the Bible permitted slavery (preferring instead to explain why emancipation could best be managed in an independent South). In this, his position was not unlike the one identified by Mark Noll. Reliance on specific Bible verses in discussions of slavery was less common in Britain and Europe than it was in America. The attachment to democracy and individualism in America had weakened respect for corporate and institutional influences—that is, church traditions—allowing for greater choice in interpretations of the Bible and also more literal readings, detached from context. Outside America, Noll notes, there was a small but significant level of agreement with southern proslavery arguments, and sharing the moral values of northern abolitionists did not necessarily entail firm support for the Union.[25]

Slavery was only one of the topics covered by Hope in *The American Church*. He reviewed religious periodicals in Britain and showed that some titles had moved into the southern camp. He saw this tendency in two papers from opposing wings of the Church of England. The *Guardian*, established by Tractarians in 1846, seemed favorable to the South despite the hostile contributions of its Philadelphia correspondent; and the *Record*, established by Evangelicals in 1828, had, "despite its past prejudices," repudiated the "hollowness and worldliness of the Abolitionist religionism of New York and New England." Hope also mentioned a division between the Evangelical Alliance (formed in 1846) and its French affiliate. The French group had issued a pro-northern manifesto, rejected by Alliance chairman Sir Culling Eardley, and this followed a resolution passed by the Alliance's annual conference, which condemned slavery but also condemned "Mr. Lincoln's aggressive war."[26]

Hope had previously stated that although the Episcopal Church had been "numerically and theologically stronger" in the North than in the South, it had been unable to prevent the North from sinking into corruption. In *The*

American Church, he went further: "The Confederate States . . . indicate considerably more Christianity than the United States." The original colonies in the South had been established with "church and state" principles, but when America became independent, revolutionaries such as Thomas Jefferson decided that there must be no privileges or endowments for religious bodies. Thereafter, growth was not easy. The Episcopal Church had thrived nonetheless, and in the new Confederacy, it was set to play a major role.[27]

Hope thought that the church enjoyed influence in the South primarily because the South had been less disrupted by immigration than the North and southern landowners were traditionally minded. Another cause was the high quality of certain bishops, notably William Meade in Virginia, a devout Low Churchman, and Whittingham in Maryland, who had High Church leanings. Despite these advantages, the "new organization of our Communion" in the South faced difficulties, especially in localities where other faiths had more adherents. In the North, Episcopalians were more numerous, but Dissent was dominant. Hope had consulted census figures and the reports of the General Conventions of 1856 and 1859. He found that the ratio of Episcopalian clergy to population was higher in the South, while the North had more communicants. Obviously, the southern population was smaller and more scattered, there were fewer large towns, and it was likely that many slave owners did not bring their slaves to Communion (though Hope wished they would). Helpful as generalizations might be, it was necessary to go deeper. Hope remarked upon the statistics for Virginia, which showed a larger increase in baptisms between 1850 and 1860 than New York and also a larger increase (as a percentage) in the number of communicants. Hope also pointed to missionary work among the slaves, which was likely to add to the strength of the church in the South.[28]

Describing the condition and prospects of the church as better in the South than in the North, Hope suspected that this was true of all Christian denominations. There were more places of worship in the South per head of population, and "the proportion of persons in the South who make no profession at all of Christianity is less than in the North." The South was more resistant to spiritualism, Mormonism, "free love," and other forms of "devil-worship," and the North evinced a lower moral tone, seen in the ease of divorce. According to Hope, the Confederacy exhibited "Churchlike" rather than "sectarian" spirit. By this, he meant "unity of action combined with the regard for particular rights," "recognition of the sacredness of individual liberty and the supremacy of law," the "localizing of allegiance" and "creation, through sufferings, of a patriotic tradition," and "the hatred of democratic excess" and "recognition of the natural leaders of society in places of trust"—all of which would be reinforced by "the direct intercourse which we expect to see springing up between this country and the Confederacy."[29]

Hope argued that secession had boosted "religious earnestness" across the South, helping to make the struggle for independence a "heroic venture." Its "living embodiment" was Stonewall Jackson, the zealous man of God, a holy warrior who was admired even by his foes. Though he was not an Episcopalian (and Hope did not care much for Presbyterians or revivalism), and notwithstanding reports that some northern commanders were also fervent in prayer and encouraged their troops to keep the Sabbath, "such a man as Jackson the North has not yet produced." Robert E. Lee was an Episcopalian. It was fitting that in March 1862, on his deathbed, Bishop Meade of Virginia had sent for Lee, whom he had known for years, and that during the siege of Richmond, Meade's successor, Bishop John Johns, laid hands on the head of Jefferson Davis, another prominent churchman. Leonidas Polk, bishop of Louisiana, had accepted a commission in the Confederate army. Whatever one might think about this, to Hope it further demonstrated "the religiosity of Confederatism." Polk was serving his diocese in the best way he knew, and he understood, as Johns did and as Meade had before him, that if the North won the war, the South would be reduced to "disorder and irreligion."[30]

A future bishop of North Carolina, Joseph Blount Cheshire, who wrote the first history of the southern church, would also emphasize the religious faith of the Confederate army and maintain that it was reflective of the character of the whole people.[31] Hope had tapped into something that not only made the South more appealing to many people in Britain but also shaped southerners' understanding of their own identity and history. With such guides as Hope, those in Britain who wanted to find religious reasons to support the South during the war could do so.

If "religious earnestness" had increased in the South, what had taken place in the North? Hope drew attention to the General Convention of the Episcopal Church in New York in October 1862. Coverage of this event by the *Guardian* correspondent in Philadelphia was, in Hope's view, unreliable, for he was clearly an abolitionist and a supporter of the Lincoln administration, and he had glossed over the opinions of the northern laity. The convention of 1862 was not attended by bishops or clerical and lay delegates from the South. It might have opted for a practical expedient, carrying on with business as usual without mentioning the separation, and Hope thought that the laity favored this course. But the convention could get nothing done. A "bitter Lincolnite minority" interrupted proceedings. Quarrels broke out. The southern church had consecrated Richard Wilmer as bishop of Alabama. In New York, there was an effort to reject this as "irregular, uncanonical, and schismatical," but in the end, no decision was made, much to Hope's satisfaction. The convention had no jurisdiction in Alabama, he wrote, and no right to deprive its people of the bishop they wanted and needed. Less satisfying were the convention's public statements. Some attendees wanted to avoid open condemnation of the South. They were overruled. While wishing for reconciliation in the church, those who shaped the relevant resolutions also wanted to stress their loyalty to the U.S. government, and for that government, they asked the people to pray. They declared that rebellion against properly constituted authority was wrong. Hope complained that the convention had pushed aside ecclesiastical matters to focus on politics.[32]

Charles McIlvaine, bishop of Ohio, secured approval for a pastoral letter that endorsed government policies and disregarded states' rights. Hope regretted that other opinions—like those of Horatio Potter, bishop of New York, who was absent—had not been heard. This was a *political* pastoral, unlike any ever issued by the Episcopal Church. Hope praised the bishop of Vermont, John Hopkins, who had expressed disapproval in the *Church Journal* (a periodical in the Anglo-Catholic tradition published in New York). Hopkins would not submit to McIlvaine, "the petted emissary of a lawless military republic."[33] (Though Hope did not mention their theological differences, Hopkins led the High Churchmen and McIlvaine the Evangelicals.)

One compensation, in Hope's analysis, was that the General Convention in New York had not subscribed to "war at any price," and in none of the public documents was there a demand for abolition (here Hope noted the presence of representatives from slave states that had stayed in the Union). It was likely that the majority of Episcopalians in the North wanted peace. As pressure mounted to end the war and recognize the Confederacy, the church could help to forward this "inevitable and blessed result." The existence of two American nations served the purposes of God: "The break-up of the unwieldy Union—followed, as it must be, by the division of the Church into provinces—would in itself be an unmeasured benefit to the Church, by the creation of a spirit of godly competition between the sections." Even if the North won the war, Hope did not think that the southern church would agree to rejoin the northern church. It was self-sufficient. It had been insulted; outrages had reportedly been committed by invading forces—the imprisonment of Episcopalian clergy who refused to lead prayers for Lincoln, for example, and the use of churches as army hospitals when other buildings were available. Hope's conviction was that ecclesiastical reunion would be even more difficult to bring about than civil reunion.[34]

Peering into the future, he assumed the global preponderance of "English-speaking nations" headed by Britain. What principles should they live by and seek to inculcate? The "consistent Churchman," Hope declared, would prefer the values associated with "hereditary liberty under a limited monarchy, side by side with a hereditary Church," not those of "unchecked and tyrannous democracy resting on the ballot-box and universal suffrage." Hope thought that the Anglo-Saxon race was diverging into "English" and "Yankee" branches, the latter suffering under "bad foreign infusion" and "a thoroughly rotten political and social system." It was the English branch that should shape the world, and the South had more to offer than the North in this respect because it sought to remain like "the old parent country." The North would do well to recognize the Confederacy and accept the eventual division of the American continent into several independent nations. Even better would be the inclination toward "parent country" principles of those American nations, in the manner of "the different provincial organizations into which the Anglican Communion in our colonies has been so rapidly shaping itself."[35]

All this was for after the war. When Hope was writing *The American Church*, in the early part of 1863, it was the immediate situation in America that most concerned him, and he ended his pamphlet by referring back to the southern bishops' pastoral of 1862. He fully accepted the pastoral's self-justification. It explained that the Episcopalians of the South had been "forced by the providence of God to separate ourselves from the Protestant Episcopal Church in the United States." Despite being "cut off . . . from all communication with our sister Churches of the world" and "compelled to act without any interchange of opinion even with our Mother Church," "our organic law," "our Code of Canons," and "those rich treasures of doctrine and worship which have come to us enshrined in our Book of Common Prayer" had been preserved. The southern church had managed "alone and unaided to arrange for ourselves the organization under which we should do our part in carrying on to their consummation the purposes of God in Christ Jesus." Hope argued that the pastoral letter and the many labors in which it was engaged substantiated the claims he had made about the southern church in his previous speeches and writings.[36]

Religious aspects of the American crisis were also explored in Hope's *Saturday Review.* In May 1863, one contribution suggested that if its leaders were any guide, the South had a more vital Christianity than the North. Confederate statesmen and generals were truly men of faith. Above them all was Stonewall Jackson. A Presbyterian, he was not unlike the British hero, Henry Havelock, a Baptist, whose distinguished career in India had been marked by missionary efforts. Jackson's promotion of Bible studies and prayer meetings had other historical equivalents, in the campaigns of such figures as Gustavus Adolphus and the Duke of Marlborough, with chaplains accompanying the troops and devotions offered to God before battles. "It is possible that some memory of this practice, like a good many other old and religious traditions, may survive in Virginia."[37]

When Hope addressed a meeting of the Liverpool Southern Club in October 1863, he discussed the religious and moral aspects of the war and concluded that the South was not in the wrong. Another speaker at the meeting, James Spence, argued that in this, the third year of the war, no nation calling itself Christian could stand aside any longer. The British government must offer to mediate. European powers would join in, Spence insisted, and were just waiting for Britain to act. The meeting was followed by a grand banquet during which Spence proposed a toast to Hope, "in whose praise too much could not be said for the interest he had taken in the Confederate cause when it was not smiled upon by other men." Hope's response prompted "great cheering." He said "he took up the cause of the Confederate States because he found amongst other things a good, devotional, God-fearing, honest people—both men and women—whilst in the North he saw greed, avarice, ambition, and unprincipled lust of empire."[38] Hope, Spence, and their colleagues could again indulge in this rhetoric in Liverpool at the Southern Bazaar for Wounded Confederate Prisoners of 1864. The event, which raised a significant amount of money, was described by some commentators as a Christian endeavor, a living out of the injunction "do unto others." The *Liverpool Mercury* called it "a labor of love."[39]

There were many in Britain who agreed with Hope or at least showed a willingness to treat the American crisis as religious in nature. The pro-southern agitation during the war provided openings for Hope. His writings sold well, which indicates respect for his opinions, and he had regular speaking engagements, though they appear to have fallen off in 1864.[40] Some of his fellow Anglicans appreciated his approach. There are signs of an ideological mingling of Anglicanism and pro-southern activism. For example, one important expression of fellow feeling was the Manchester Southern Club, of which Hope was a vice president. Its prospectus and circular appeared in the press.[41] The general membership included clergymen. Fourteen clergymen were named on the committee list and as signatories to the circular. Of these, eleven can be confirmed as ministers of the Church of England.[42]

But Anglicans were divided on many issues at this time, including the American war. Even among High Churchmen, there was disagreement. A number of Hope's closest friends distanced themselves from his statements about the southern church, including John Mason Neale, who shared Hope's enthusiasm for Anglican ritual and Gothic design and had, with Hope, been one of the founders of the Cambridge Camden Society. Neale, former chaplain at Downing College, Cambridge, and vicar of Crawley, was now warden of Sackville College, an almshouse in East Sussex, and a respected translator and hymn writer. He could not approve of the division of the Episcopal Church of America, and one of his exchanges with Hope, originally published in the *Guardian*, found its way into periodicals in the United States.

In Neale's view, the establishment of the southern church amounted to "unprovoked schism" and was inexcusable. "It surely was the duty of the undivided Church to cling together to the last—to give the one example of peace, to form the one link by which the two parties might have struggled in common to a peaceful separation or a peaceful reunion." The "spiritual revolt" of southern Episcopalians embittered the temporal division and made the church "a partisan in and promoter of war." Hope seemed not to realize that once schism was allowed, there would be no end to it. The American rupture was a humiliation. It only served "the miserable Erastianism which would rend the Church because the State was divided."[43]

Another High Churchman who protested against Hope's opinions was John Eldon Hole, rector of Washford Pyne in Devon. Hole was annoyed by Hope's idea that the South was fighting in a "sacred defensive cause"—for home and hearth—when it was really fighting to preserve slavery, a flagrant sin. Hope had lauded Bishop Polk of Louisiana, but Polk fought as a wealthy slave-owning planter. However kind a master was, his slaves were morally, intellectually, and spiritually degraded. Slavery could have no other effect. If a master looked after his slaves, he did so only to enable them to do more work. Hole also noted Hope's reference to the executed slave trader Nathaniel Gordon. True, Gordon was a northerner, but it was important to ask who had employed him. He was "the miserable tool of Southern avarice."[44]

On various grounds, therefore, Hope had detractors as well as allies in the Church of England when he offered religious reasons for supporting the Confederacy. He was concerned to limit debate to his chosen parameters: hence his reliance on cultural affinity arguments rather than *theological* ones. He realized that High Churchmanship was stronger in the North than in the South, as reflected in church appointments and training. The General Theological Seminary had been established by High Churchmen in New York in 1817, and their rivals had responded by setting up an alternative, the Virginia Theological Seminary, in Alexandria in 1823. Hope must also have known that sectarianism was widespread in the South, but he could not admit it. He attacked the North for encouraging sectarianism, a self-serving tactic. He was out to win sympathy for the South and ready to pass over uncomfortable truths along the way. He was prepared, indeed, to depart from High Church aversion to schism, welcoming the separation of the American church.

Another likely reason for his unwillingness to go deeply into theological questions was his awareness that the High Church party was coming under increasing pressure in Britain. Quarrels about dogma, ornaments and furnishings, rubrics, ceremonies, and vestments would lead to such measures as the Public Worship Regulation Act of 1874. During the American war, Hope was reluctant to bring any of this into his pro-southern arguments in case he gave the High Churchmen's enemies more material to use against them. The High Church party was itself prone to division, underlining the need for caution, not least because Tractarian criticism of the church-state relationship had heightened concerns about theological disputation. Brent Sirota has highlighted a tension between "Anglican catholicity" and "Tory churchmanship." The former emphasized ecclesiology, episcopacy, sacramentalism, a church in touch with its origins, and the difference between the ecclesial and the civil. The latter emphasized "throne-and-altar integralism," with state and church coexisting under a monarch who was both temporal sovereign and Supreme Head of the Church of England.[45] Tractarianism was one expression of Anglican catholicity. Its leaders championed the independence of the church against state interference, a position that was not easily compatible with the doctrine of royal supremacy.

In this context, Hope was wise not to mix his appeals for the Confederacy with religious debates in Britain. It is notable that Hope's pro-southern strategy was not greatly affected by the wider setting. He wished to keep it at a distance, for much was going on that might have hindered him. In the Scottish Episcopal Church, there had been disagreements about church governance, relations with the state, and the difference between Scottish rites and those of the Church of England. A compromise was worked out in the early 1860s. Meanwhile, the Presbyterians had split in 1843, after which groups seceding from the Church of Scotland further divided. In Ireland, agitation for Roman Catholic, tenant, and national rights defied Parliament's efforts to bring peace. The Church of Ireland would be disestablished in 1869, but Catholic leaders still complained about the denial of equality, and Irish demands for reform continued to merge in the campaign for home rule.

In his speaking and writing about the church in the South, Hope simplified matters. He did not bring in much discussion of the complexity of religious life in the South. Partly this was due to ignorance, partly to the overriding desire to make the pro-Confederate case. There was considerable diversity in the religious life of the prewar South, with elements from Britain and Africa as well as America, but conditions did change. With the ending of the slave trade and the growing defensiveness and isolation of the South in the first half of the nineteenth century, variety was lost. European-style evangelical Christianity became the dominant form.[46] If Hope did not appreciate the way in which religious life in the South had evolved, it also seems that southern religion had become *less* cosmopolitan by the time he assessed it. During the war, he was simplifying something that was already simpler than it had formerly been.[47]

Hope was not wrong to suggest that religious life in the North had been complicated by immigration. More immigrants went to the North than to the South. Throughout America, immigration contributed to a constant reshaping of religious observance. Many of the English brought with them a strong religious faith, especially those from rural backgrounds. Of the one million English, Scottish, and Welsh who arrived in America between 1845 and 1860, it has been estimated that two in every three were Nonconformists.[48] Some English immigrant organizations carried on the familiar enmities of former times and places, with their anti-Irish and anti-Catholic activity.[49]

Most Irish went to the North, but some settled in the South, and Irishmen served in both armies during the war. The Roman Catholic Church in the North supported the war effort. Many Irish Catholics there may have thought it appropriate to fight against the Confederacy, though they did not abandon their animosity toward the abolitionists or disapproval of the Emancipation Proclamation.[50]

Hope's account of the American church differed from that published in 1839 by John Henry Newman, who was at that time the charismatic Tractarian leader and divider of opinion in the Church of England and University of Oxford. As an undergraduate at Cambridge, from 1837 to 1841, Hope was influenced by Tractarianism. Newman converted to Rome in 1845. He remained an important figure to the university men who wrote for the *Saturday Review*, and they respected his mind and character, but they also disparaged him as a propagandist.[51] Nevertheless, Hope was quite magnanimous toward Newman and kept up a personal acquaintance with him into the 1880s.[52]

Newman's impressions of the American church in 1839, like Hope's in the 1860s, were mostly secondhand. They both relied on what they read and what others told them. Newman focused on theological and institutional matters.[53] Hope spoke and wrote more about these issues after the war, not so much before or during it.

Newman thought that the American church reinforced Tractarian arguments against the union of church and state. The Church of England had little "freedom" and was cut off "from Christendom" because of its subordination to Parliament, but the church in America was doing well without such "protection."[54] Newman saw fine "Catholic principles" in the American church. It was not a "voluntary" church "in the bad sense of the word." Those who benefited from it willingly offered to support it, meaning that the clergy were not "at the mercy of the people" and did not have to preach only what people wanted to hear. Generosity was also seen in the erection and decoration of churches. Americans were drawn to the Episcopal Church "on the ground of the consistency, definiteness, and stability of its creed," which was remarkable in a society defiled by the "excesses of sectarianism." The situation would be even better with fuller respect for the apostolic succession and less interaction with dissenting bodies. Newman was worried that the church might fail to develop on its strong foundations. The greatest danger was the weight of the laity, which he deemed incompatible with the jurisdiction that ought to be exercised by bishops. Still, the American church "is freer than we are," and Newman was confident that many of the difficulties experienced in the Church of England could be avoided in America.[55]

By the time Newman was writing, the former resentment against Anglicans in America—suspected as allies of British imperialism—had diminished. The Episcopal Church had grown, although it remained outside the religious mainstream shaped by evangelical revivalism. Episcopalians probably preferred to be a little detached (especially the High Churchmen): they could cast off associations with the church as it had been in the eighteenth century and stay out of the disputes that led to secession and war in the nineteenth. Britain remained an important source of personnel and funding. Joseph Hardwick suggests that English-born clergymen found acceptance, despite being "the most English people in the United States." They were known for their English learning, preaching, and manners but integrated themselves into American communities, and American congregations sometimes demanded English ministers.[56] Southern families took pride in their English ancestry if they had it, and this helped to sustain English religious habits. David Gleeson points out that many southerners based their separatist ideology on the different religious history of the North. To look at Massachusetts or New York or Pennsylvania was to look at alien churches.[57]

Members of the nineteenth-century Church of England liked the idea of an English church extending itself abroad, in the colonies as well as America. This global connection would necessarily be multicultural. Indeed, the Lambeth Conferences that began to meet in 1867 recognized variety in Anglicanism. While there was a wish to sustain versions of England overseas, most of the clergy there were not English, and the laity had more power in church institutions.[58] Nevertheless, for all the diversity, there was enough to hold the global church together. Common structures and beliefs and a desire to maximize the church's size and influence internationally brought loose but effective union, and voluntarism and laicization made for more openness to reform.[59]

Hope was ahead of his time in extolling the global Anglican Communion, in which he expected the southern church to take its place. The global concept did not develop until after the first Lambeth Conference, although there had previously been vague suggestions along these lines, including one from Bishop Hopkins of Vermont. When Archbishop of Canterbury Charles Longley invited every Anglican bishop to Lambeth in 1867, 76 of the

144 bishops attended. As these meetings became regular, their deliberations gained more importance.[60]

The reunification of the Episcopal Church in America was effected soon after the end of the war. While some in the southern church argued against it and in the North there was talk of punishing those who had sanctioned rebellion, and though sensitive issues had to be resolved relating to actions taken by the southern church that lacked the approval of the church as a whole, the majority wanted speedy reconciliation because the separation had not been spiritual, only physical. Arranging for reunification proved to be easier than dealing with ritualism, ecumenism, the ministry to freed slaves and Indians, and the challenges posed by social change, science, and "broad church" liberalism. There were lingering resentments after the war, but church leaders did not involve themselves in the political controversies of the Reconstruction period. The church expanded. In 1860, the ratio of population to communicants had been 209 to 1, but by the 1890s, it was 102 to 1.[61]

All the southern dioceses had rejoined the national church by May 1866. Within the Church of England there was a reluctance to say or do anything that might complicate the reunification process. Affection for the American church was verbalized at the Church Congress held in York in October 1866. Speakers refrained from going much further, Hope among them. In York, he spoke about missionary work in America and elsewhere—which "ought to be diverse, suiting itself to the peculiar nature of the peoples to whose evangelization it directed itself"—and about the need for diocesan synods. His remarks were endorsed by one of the Americans present, the bishop of Illinois, Henry Whitehouse.[62] Hope and Whitehouse had a connection. The bishop had High Church inclinations and during the war had been openly sympathetic toward the South.

Hope continued to write and speak about the American church.[63] Most of his activity was of a kind that evinced pro-southern sentiment and High Church partisanship. For example, in 1876 he supported the bishop of Tennessee, Charles Todd Quintard, who arrived in London to raise money for Sewanee, the University of the South, originally established in 1857 by ten southern dioceses. Construction had been halted during the war, and the university was a symbol of southern separatism. Fundraising in Britain for this "Episcopalian university" was reported in American as well as British newspapers.[64] Hope was awarded honorary degrees by Sewanee and by another prestigious southern institution, Washington and Lee University in

Virginia.[65] As for his collaboration with members of the High Church party in the Episcopal Church, Hope was much more open about this than he had been before the war. The survival of the southern church would have been his first choice. That possibility having passed, the next best thing was a re-united Episcopal Church in which an appropriate style and order prevailed.

In July 1868, Hope was joined on the platform at London venues by Rev. James DeKoven, warden of Racine College, an Episcopalian college founded in Wisconsin in 1852.[66] DeKoven, a celebrated preacher, defended High Church doctrine and ritual,[67] but Hope knew that most American bishops were not of this ilk. As a member of the Ritual Commission, appointed by a Conservative government in 1867 as pressure was building for a reform of Church of England rubrics, Hope had read the protest against ritualism sent by American bishops (later published as part of the commission's offi-cial report).[68] Nevertheless, he encouraged High Churchmen in the United States as and when he could. He urged that they be represented on a com-mittee formed in London in November 1882 to commemorate the life and work of Edward Pusey, the influential Tractarian leader and Regius Profes-sor of Hebrew at Oxford for more than fifty years, who had recently died.[69] Further examples of postwar interaction with High Churchmen in America included meetings and communications during the 1870s with, among oth-ers, Bishop Whittingham of Maryland, on the subject of the "Old Catholic" movement in Europe, which had fellow travelers in both the Church of En-gland and the American church.[70] Hope disliked Evangelical assertiveness in the Episcopal Church, as may be seen from his comments on the case of Stephen Higginson Tyng, a minister in New York, who believed in the unity of all Protestants and had preached in a Methodist chapel and invited a minister of another denomination to speak in his own church. Tyng had contravened church canons, and, Hope gratefully declaimed, met with "the great disapprobation both of his Bishop and of the community to which he belongs."[71]

Hope's conduct did not go unnoticed in America. Several papers re-ported his election as MP for Cambridge University in 1868. The *New York Independent* described it as a victory for tradition and ritualism: "Once Cam-bridge was the champion of Low Church principles; but Mr. Beresford Hope has just been elected there by a triumphant majority of clerical graduate votes, in opposition to an evangelical candidate. This is looked upon as om-inous of the increase of Tractarian principles in the university." Hope's remarks about the Tyng affair and his wish for "more discipline" in the American church led the *New York Observer and Chronicle* to argue that, if anything, the rules should be relaxed, and pulpits opened because restrictions would hamper the spread of the Gospel. Hope was worried about what might be taught in Anglican places of worship, but his was an unhelpful and outmoded perspective.[72]

Hope welcomed indications that the Episcopal Church was moving forward. This was in stark contrast, he stressed in March 1871, to Roman Catholicism, "which has recently been rocked to its center by the novel assumption of Papal infallibility," and to "Dissenting bodies" in Britain and Europe as well as America, "which, as all men know, have often been tried with anxious conflicts within the circles of their own membership."[73] In fact, a number of Evangelicals did not wish to remain in the Episcopal Church. Fearing what they took to be a looming subjection to ritualists, they set up the Reformed Episcopal Church in 1873 as a fusion of evangelicalism, episcopacy, and ecumenism. There was no mass defection from the Episcopal Church and no rush by Dissenters to leave their own churches for an inclusive Protestant national denomination.[74] The Episcopal Church confirmed its opposition to Anglo-Catholicism and to anything that was contrary to the Bible and Prayer Book, but otherwise, it would respect local wishes and not insist on complete uniformity.[75] This was a solution that satisfied Hope, who had been promoting the same arrangement in the Church of England for years.[76] Hope's role in discussions about Anglican doctrine and practice was noted in several American newspapers.[77]

Hope repeatedly stressed the importance of the Episcopal Church to the global Anglican Communion. He made this point to American representatives at the Lambeth Conference in the summer of 1878.[78] The growth of the Episcopal Church was celebrated at a service in St. Paul's Cathedral in November 1884. Hope was in attendance, along with other prominent Anglican laymen and senior clergy from all parts of Britain and the empire. Three bishops were among the American delegation: Henry Whipple of Minnesota, William C. Doane of Albany, and J. H. Hobart Brown of Fond du Lac. The service marked the centenary of the consecration of the first American bishop, Samuel Seabury, who had served as bishop of Connecticut from 1784 to 1796 and presiding bishop of the Episcopal Church from 1789 to 1792.[79]

The first Episcopalian cathedral in the United States, All Saints' in Albany, New York, was dedicated in 1888, after Hope's death, but one of the gifts he had made to friends in the American clergy featured prominently in the ceremony. He had presented to Bishop Doane of New Jersey, a High Churchman, a pastoral staff made of twelve hundred–year–old oak, taken from beams in the refectory of St. Augustine's, Canterbury, the Anglican missionary college founded in 1848 of which Hope was the principal bene-factor. The staff passed to All Saints' Cathedral through Doane's son, the bishop of Albany. It was among the cathedral's most prized artifacts, which would have pleased Hope, and the "English Gothic" design of All Saints' is also likely to have met with his approval.[80]

Hope had been a friend of the Episcopal Church. Yet he welcomed its division in 1861, and during and after the war, he focused on the south-ern church as both consequence and cause: it arose largely as a result of the stronger Christianity and higher moral standards of the South com-pared to the North, and it promised to promote—building on what already existed—a national and social coherence in the South that would be re-markable for its longevity and vigor. This, at least, was how Hope judged it. Therefore, he paid special attention to the church when making a case for British recognition of the Confederacy as an independent sovereign entity. On some points, he was mistaken: the postwar reunification of the church, for instance, was not more difficult than civil reunion. Nevertheless, Hope's position demonstrates the influence that religious beliefs could have in shap-ing opinion for the South and against the North during the American crisis. Hope saw that the Union and southern secession had a religious dimension, and for him, this was represented primarily by the Episcopal Church.

6

AMERICAN WAR AND
BRITISH CONSEQUENCES

Beresford Hope kept up a running commentary on American events and invariably attached to them a pro-southern interpretation. In this, he was not alone, for other British commentators reacted to developments in the same way, although Hope was certainly among the most persistent and unequivocal of the Confederacy's British apologists. He spoke and wrote at length about what was happening in America and how it might have an impact on Britain. He made suggestions about what Britain should do in response to particular events. He cooperated with other pro-southerners and defended his ideas and conduct when assailed. His consideration of the effects of the war extended into the 1880s.

If economic interests and constitutional questions were the main reasons for the secession of the South, Hope saw a political event—the election of Lincoln—as the decisive stimulus. Lincoln had gained the support of only a minority of American voters on 6 November 1860 (less than 40 percent) and failed to carry a single southern state. To Hope, he was unsuited to the presidency, and that Republican promises to treat the South fairly were worthless was shown by the Morrill Tariff and the attempt to reinforce Fort Sumter. In Hope's opinion, the Confederate attack on the fort was provoked by the North, whose leaders, pushed and emboldened by the mob, were set on a confrontation. The Lincoln administration then erected an economic blockade, created a huge army, and restricted individual rights. Northern actions betrayed an astounding want of principle.[1]

The course of the war up to the end of 1861 indicated that both sides had made mistakes. Northerners may have expected the slaves to rise and bring the Confederacy down. Southerners may have expected northern Democrats to induce Lincoln to make a swift peace. The first major engagement, at Manassas (or Bull Run) on 21 July 1861, also defied the expectations of many.

A resounding southern victory, it made the North anxiously scramble for more men and money and prompted the U.S. Congress to pass a series of drastic war measures. As 1861 drew to its close, Hope expressed doubts about the North's ability to conduct the war effectively. Northern politicians and generals seemed incompetent, and public opinion succumbed to the swings that Hope believed must always blight a democracy. The administration and its underlings were desperately clinging to power, suspending "the ancient constitutional privileges won after so many struggles by the English race."[2]

Hope's remarks about Lincoln were condemned as excessive and disrespectful, but he persisted. Republican wire-pullers had used him to alienate the South. Lincoln himself was also to blame. Known for his brief spell in the U.S. Congress as "the standing buffoon of the House and teller of indecent stories," he realized that it would be better for America if a more qualified man became president but went ahead regardless.[3] Another objection was that this "unbaptized Republican autocrat" had politicized religion in the North and was not a carrier of Anglican truth and tradition.[4]

Hope was sure that the Union could not be restored. Though the South had fewer resources, he considered it more united and determined and expected disunity and corruption to sap the North's strength. Taking comfort from a lesson of history, he wrote that three hundred years earlier, in the Dutch Revolt, the odds against an independent Holland holding out against the might of Spain had been even longer, but the Dutch had succeeded, and so would the Confederacy.[5]

The points Hope made in print and on the lecture circuit were also being discussed in British newspapers. From March 1861 to April 1862, experienced war correspondent William Howard Russell was in America, writing for the *Times*. He arrived as a celebrity and was courted by northerners and southerners alike. His reports appeared in many British publications. Though he opposed slavery and expected the North eventually to win the war, Russell also reproached the North. He thought that the *Trent* affair was the North's fault, for instance, and accused northern newspapers of creating anti-British sentiment. He had little respect for U.S. generals. He approved of British neutrality. Russell became the target of northern resentment and had to leave. After his criticism of U.S. forces at First Manassas, the idea that he was pro-southern, and that the *Times* was too, took firm root.[6]

In late 1861 and early 1862, like many British commentators, Hope focused on the *Trent* affair. Confederate envoys James M. Mason and John

Slidell were bound for Europe on a British mail packet, the *Trent*, which was stopped on 8 November 1861 by a U.S. Navy vessel, and the envoys were removed as contraband of war. When news reached Britain, there was a storm of protest. Hope accused the North of a "lawless and piratical outrage" and railed against its leaders' "stubbornness and stupidity" as the matter was resolved.[7] The affair had lasting ramifications. It made more necessary an international consensus on maritime issues.[8] More immediately, relations between the British and U.S. governments had to be brought back from breaking point. On the British side, the wish to avoid a final rupture was strengthened by the realization that there were other problems to attend to in Europe, the empire, and elsewhere, and Seward, for all his threats and complaints, was also conscious of the need for prudence. He wanted to stand up to Britain, not least for domestic reasons, but he cared about how his country was seen abroad.[9]

During the *Trent* controversy, the Conservative *John Bull* welcomed the publication of Hope's *Popular View of the American Civil War,* based on an earlier lecture ("It will probably be more popular, though not more true, now than when it was delivered"), and even the Liberal *Observer,* no ally of Hope, considered his original address "very able." *John Bull* noted that several Liberal MPs had been in their constituencies, speaking against British recognition of the Confederacy. Among friends of the South, none was doing more than Hope to counter these activities.[10] There was a long piece in the *Times* about Hope's lecturing in January 1862. Hope trusted that most people who knew of Fort Sumter, "the great scamper of Bull's Run," the North's effort to close up southern ports, and "the gross insult which had been offered to our flag in the affair of the *Trent*," would be inclined to think more kindly of the South than the North.[11]

Meanwhile, items in the *Saturday Review* in July and December 1861 advocated a peace settlement on the basis of southern independence and warned the North about its offensive conduct toward Britain (and thereby assisted Hope's agenda).[12] Tokens of official approval for Charles Wilkes, the U.S. captain who had stopped the *Trent,* suggested a willingness to run the risk of pushing Britain too far. Yet vigorous British retaliation "will put an end to all hopes of reconquering the seceded States." Britain was not seeking war, but if it happened, there could be no "self-reproach."[13]

Assessing the situation in America in August 1862, the *Saturday Review* repeated that the Union could not be restored. The Federals had failed to take Richmond. Stalemate was likely. Neither side could make the decisive breakthrough, the Confederates because they lacked resources and the North because it had "second rate leaders." The North itself did not have unlimited means, moreover. One day, it would have to negotiate if it was to avoid bankruptcy.[14] Many British observers agreed that the cost of the war would eventually cripple the North, though this turned out to be one of the arguments of pro-southerners that was not well-founded.[15]

The news reaching Britain affected public opinion and sometimes, within just a few weeks, could create the impression that North or South had experienced a dramatic reversal of fortunes. Hope acknowledged this, but as he remained constant in his sympathy for the Confederate cause, he urged people not to be unduly swayed by the latest reports. When he gave two lectures in November 1861, Confederate forces appeared to have the upper hand. By 20 March 1862, when he was writing the postscript for *The Results of the American Disruption*, the South had suffered several defeats. Nevertheless, he saw no reason to change his stance.[16]

He encouraged people in Britain to think about the war's possible consequences. While he doubted that the South could be forced back into the Union, he did accept that the North might win the war. If this happened, the Union would be put back together, but Hope insisted that it could not be what it had been. Northerners would not grant southerners equal rights, and this being so, northerners would be unable to keep the South in obedience and order. Southerners were an independent people ("speaking our own tongue, with our own blood running in their veins") and could not be made to feel otherwise. Hope added that by taking on the government of an unruly southern people, the United States would be less able to act strongly abroad. There were some in Britain who expected the South to be readmitted to the Union on an equal basis. Hope regarded this as a "ridiculous" and even "contemptible" proposition.[17]

For many British observers, the Emancipation Proclamation turned the American war into a moral crusade. Hope sought to disseminate a different interpretation, that Lincoln had no genuine concern for the plight of the slaves and was only trying to damage the southern economy and war effort. Hope agreed with a statement in the *Times*: though slavery could not be condoned, British people would not be "tricked," for the war was not about slavery. Emancipation changed nothing. The South had to defend itself against northern aggression.[18]

In responding to American events, Hope also chronicled—and frequently tried to influence—their wider impact in Britain. This led him to make recommendations about the course the British government and people should take and to discuss the likely (or wished-for) short- and long-term effects.

He was typically forthright, for example, about Britain's proclamation of neutrality of May 1861. Britain also recognized the Confederacy's belligerent status, which facilitated its contracting of loans and purchase of supplies abroad and acknowledged its rights as a combatant on the seas. Hope welcomed these steps as "political and necessary." Some northerners professed themselves affronted, yet the North declared a blockade of a country it refused to recognize as belligerent and, even more bizarre, required other countries to respect this blockade. In view of the attempt to impose a blockade, argued Hope, the claim that the crisis in America amounted to no more than a domestic insurrection was untenable.[19]

The blockade raised concerns, not least because of Britain's need for southern cotton. It was thought (and not by southerners alone) that this would give the Confederacy enormous leverage. Hope assumed so, though he denied that the South was abusing its advantage.[20] Early in 1862, he wrote that as a supplier of valuable commodities to Britain and a customer for British products and services, the South had much to offer. Its commitment to free trade was to be applauded.[21] In 1863, Hope emphasized that the North was jealous of Britain's power and wealth, while the South wished for commerce and cooperation.[22]

Hope's view on British intervention in the war, at the end of 1861, was that it was unnecessary. There were complaints about the interruption in the supply of cotton, but reports in several British newspapers indicated that demand for cotton manufactures was falling because markets were already satisfied. Hope did not think that the government or people of Britain wished for direct involvement in the American crisis. At the same time, however, they were perfectly entitled to express their opinions about it. They could see the North falling deeper into anarchy, while the South was proving itself a nation.[23]

Hope thought that the successful outcome of the *Trent* affair—the release of Mason and Slidell—would boost British pride and marginalize the few outspoken pro-northerners who had misjudged or ignored the people's instincts.[24] If the South won the war, he told an audience (to cheers and applause) in January 1862, one could envisage the gradual abolition of slavery, a sound constitution "growing up out of unbridled democracy," free trade "with a boundless expanse of the richest soil, from which English mills and vessels might reap a golden harvest," European civilization "pervading a people prepared for its influence," and "a true ally tied to us by the bonds of common interest." If the North won, Hope expected anti-British tariffs and danger to Canada. The United States would become incorrigible, with "Federal bankruptcy, a prolongation of internecine strife, the shackles of the slave riveted more firmly than ever, or else slavery swept away in one universal tempest," and with "the worst passions of an unchained democracy let loose to work out its dream of universal insult and promiscuous conquest, or else a military despotism setting its iron yoke upon an enslaved people and employing their energies in outrage and aggression."[25]

Hope presumed that many in Britain were asking themselves whether they had good reason to wish success to either side. He insisted that they did and that it was the cause of the South that had most merit. The South was the victim of aggression, and lasting peace, which would suit the British as well as the Americans, would be more likely if the South established itself as an independent nation. Hope had no doubt that the British government could recognize the Confederacy without irreversibly damaging relations with the United States. He did not deny that Britain needed U.S. friendship, but he also highlighted the advantages of closer links with the South.[26] Hope knew that some of the people who heard him speak or read his writings would think him biased. He wanted to assure them that he was trying to weigh up the qualities of North and South in a reasonable manner. Evidence and experience had led him to favor the South and to believe that its separation from the North was inevitable.[27] He was convinced that the Union should not be restored, even if it became a possibility, because separation was best for both sections and would bring wider benefits. Southern independence indicated a move toward the division of the American continent into several nations, countering each other so that peace and courtesy would prevail.[28]

Americans themselves wanted British intervention to end the war. Some wrote to Hope, having read his publications. He included two of these letters, dated 13 December 1861 and 3 February 1862, from a northerner who signed himself "Octogenarian," in *The Results of the American Disruption*.

The first letter described the war as unnecessary and illegitimate and urged that Britain must help to end it for humanitarian reasons and in line with British honor, duty, and national interest. Octogenarian argued that although the U.S. Constitution did not expressly permit secession, neither did it grant the power to coerce states to remain in the Union if they wanted to leave, and it respected state sovereignty. Secession and slavery were linked, to be sure, but if there was to be emancipation, it had to be carried out peacefully and in consultation with the slave owners, and it was an international question because most of the world consumed the products of slave labor and some countries still traded in slaves. The second letter discussed the destruction of some southern ports and blocking the entry to others with sunken vessels and suggested that eagerness to injure the South also accounted for the northern "plunder" and "swindling" that had caused the war in the first place. Many northerners opposed the war and were ready for British mediation.[29]

From the summer of 1861, Hope was commended to the government in Richmond as a friend. He was often in the company of the top Confederate representatives in Britain, notably the envoy James M. Mason and publicist Henry Hotze. Mason and Hotze both enjoyed Hope's hospitality, and he helped them with introductions, organized and hosted meetings, arranged funding, and provided whatever other support he could. According to Hotze, such endeavors had effect. In Frank Owsley's account, Hope's partiality toward the South arose mainly from "fear and hatred and jealousy" of the North, which is too dismissive, but Owsley is right about the money and effort that went into the campaigns for both the Union and the Confederacy in Britain.[30]

The *Times*, in an editorial of 12 June 1862, argued for European mediation, to put an end to the war and allow America to heal.[31] Hope responded at once: "The opinion which you express . . . has steadily been gaining strength in the minds of thinking people in this country of every condition. It has been my occupation for some time past to feel the popular pulse upon the matter. Rich and poor, High Tories and Conservatives, Whigs and advanced Liberals, Churchmen, Dissenters, Roman Catholics, have all expressed the same desire to me in the strongest language." Hope had recently addressed "several hundreds of the inhabitants of a wealthy town of between 20,000 and 30,000 inhabitants," including "the leaders of the two political parties in the place." He found the meeting "unanimous and enthusiastic in its support of a very outspoken argument for Southern independence." Since that time, "the growing distress in Lancashire has . . . intensified public opinion," as had the offenses committed by the North, notably by "Proconsul" Butler in New Orleans.[32]

Hope insisted that the southern people—who preferred to destroy their crops rather than have them taken by the enemy and whose patriotic womenfolk had been so insulted by Butler, who had responded to assaults on occupying U.S. soldiers with a general order, dated 15 May 1862, to the effect that women engaging in such behavior would be treated as prostitutes—"are not likely to be wooed back into Republican Union." Hope believed that "all over the North there is a party . . . which hates the war, and which accepts (whether liking it or not) the future independence of the South as an irreversible fact." This sensible position had been well expressed by Edward Everett of Massachusetts, a former U.S. minister to Britain (1841–45) and U.S. secretary of state (1852–53). Everett had been the vice presidential candidate for the Constitutional Union Party, which advocated Union with slavery in an effort to avert southern secession, at the 1860 election.[33]

Hope's letter to the *Times* ended with a declaration of Britain's responsibility to act. The French were ready to assist. The North would not welcome an offer to mediate, but Britain had been through the *Trent* affair, when firmness paid off, and Hope expected Washington to condemn before accepting an overture from London and Paris. "At all events, the trial should be made, or Europe, by its silence, will be drifting into complicity with the horrors of the war."[34]

By this time, Hope was notorious in the United States. He was seen by some northerners as an arch-enemy. Horace Greeley of the *New York Tribune* singled him out for his secessionist lecturing and for the pro-southern statements appearing in the *Saturday Review*, "one of the ablest and among the bitterest and most constant of our detractors." Hope had established the *Saturday Review* in 1855, and Greeley thought him "its leading editor." (In fact, although as proprietor he did influence its editorial line, Hope did not seek to control the *Saturday Review*, and it included items over the years that he personally disliked.)[35] Greeley was satisfied that whatever Hope might think, northern armies were having more victories than defeats. A contributor to the *New York Independent* suggested that Britain's leading pro-southerners were not necessarily firm in their negativity toward the North, except for Hope. This writer, "W," dismissed Hope as "a feeble-minded and wealthy political and religious fanatic."[36]

Such material did not deter Hope from advocating mediation, and before long, he was going further and arguing for formal acknowledgment of the Confederacy's independence while the war was still in progress. In the summer of 1862, Napoleon III pressed for Anglo-French intervention (he had domestic reasons for this, notably France's reliance on the South for cotton, and overseas ambitions, especially in Mexico). The British government took three months to deliberate before finally deciding against the move. Hope approved of this decision. As he later explained, his main reservation was that an attempt at mediation might jeopardize relations with the South. Nevertheless, he was still eager for more vigor on Britain's part. He now preferred not mediation but the straightforward recognition of the Confederacy as an independent nation "on its own merits." In the spring of 1863, Hope argued that Britain's should be the first government to act because hesitation would allow the French to get in first and enjoy the benefits.[37]

Another tendency strengthened during the war was for Hope to stress his own consistency as a pro-southern activist. Early in 1863, he said he was gratified that so many others were joining him because they had come to see that the South was fighting for "the cause of true English feeling" and "the cause of those principles of constitutional government which we desire to see prevailing all over the world." In recent times, this very cause had been at stake in Italy. Just as British people had backed the Italians in their fight for independence, so it was appropriate to wish for the South to succeed.[38]

When Hope had spoken in Stoke-upon-Trent in September 1862, as the Conservative candidate in a parliamentary by-election, he made similar statements about his consistency and about Britain's options in dealing with "the American contest." No recent convert, Hope said he had been "a Southerner" from the outset.[39] He had long "distrusted and repudiated the hypocritical claims of the North." As for the motion of William Schaw Lindsay, the (pro-southern) MP for Sunderland, debated in the Commons in July 1862 and designed to prompt British mediation in America, Hope was glad it had been withdrawn. He agreed with Lord Palmerston, who had argued that Parliament should allow for flexibility and not tie the government to any specific course. Hope thought that July 1862 had not been the time for a motion such as Lindsay's but that circumstances were likely to change.[40] His spoken words at Stoke tallied with his printed address to the voters of the constituency.[41]

During 1862, the distress in industrial Lancashire and Yorkshire began more directly to affect British opinion. Some blamed the U.S. blockade, thinking that hunger and unemployment would cease if the supply of southern cotton rose to its former level. In April, Hope's wife, Lady Mildred Beresford Hope, wrote to the *Times* to call for the efficient organization of relief. Soon a London fund was established, and the Hopes were among its supporters. There was also a Central Relief Fund for "the cotton districts," with Lord Derby as chairman and a committee consisting of MPs and other public men. In December 1862, a list of subscribers had Hope as one of the most generous givers (£800). Linked with the central committee were regional bodies that were collecting money.[42]

If anyone in Britain was still harboring doubts about the merits of the South in comparison with the North in 1863, Hope recommended another look at the two national characters. Useful insight could be gleaned from the behavior of representative figures (Jackson, Lee, and Davis versus Butler, Seward, and Lincoln).[43] Hope also claimed that there had been a flood of conversions to the Confederate cause in Britain. Previously, affection for the South had "required more courage to express than it would do at present," as Hope could personally testify, but now "the large majority of the respectable opinion of England" was pro-southern. It was remarkable that of the ten daily newspapers in London, only two, in Hope's view, could be classed as pro-northern: the *Daily News*, catering to the "philosophic radicals," and the *Morning Star*, organ of "Manchester School" radicals and the militant Nonconformists of the Liberation Society. Both of these titles were abolitionist. The other eight papers, ranging from strongly Conservative to ardently radical in political complexion, reflected the preference for the South in British society. They included the "church and state" *Standard*, the Palmerstonian and moderately High Church *Morning Post*, the *Times*, which generally occupied the political center, and the more "advanced" *Daily Telegraph*.[44]

Following one of Hope's speeches, in January 1863, *John Bull* summarized and approved of his position. He had "avowed himself a decided Southerner, and declared that the names of Davis and Jackson would go down to posterity side by side with those of the greatest heroes of other lands." He did not hold slavery against the South but "strongly censured" the Emancipation Proclamation, and "he contended that the South had fairly won its freedom, and called on England to recognize it."[45]

Developments in America were still discussed frequently in Hope's *Saturday Review*. One contribution of May 1863 focused on the differences between northern and southern statements about the Battle of Chancellorsville. Lee's Army of Northern Virginia had soundly defeated Hooker's much larger Army of the Potomac. Yet Hooker maintained that his campaign had enhanced northern pride and honor. All the "brag" and self-promoting deceits were on the northern side, it seemed, while all the honesty and endurance were on the southern.[46]

Support for the Confederacy became more organized. One expression of this was the Manchester Southern Club. Its prospectus and circular appeared in the press in September 1863. The president was a wealthy manufacturer and local magistrate, Daniel Lee, and the vice presidents included, along with Hope, his brother-in-law Lord Robert Cecil, MP for Stamford (the future Marquess of Salisbury), and other Conservative MPs James Whiteside (Dublin University), Sir Edward Kerrison (Eye), G.W.M. Peacocke (Maldon), and W. H. Gregory (County Galway). Liberal MPs were also among the vice presidents: W. S. Lindsay (Sunderland), J. T. Hopwood (Clitheroe), and Frederick Peel (Bury). Two other vice presidents were the independently minded MP for Sheffield, John Arthur Roebuck, and Sir Coutts Lindsay, artist, playwright, and veteran of the Crimean War. The executive committee was led by Manchester men. R. G. Beesley, a factory master, served as chairman. The vice chairman was oil merchant Mark Elliott, and the treasurer was James Armstrong, manufacturer. Members of the club were drawn mainly from the textile region of south Lancashire, north Cheshire, and west Yorkshire, but other parts of Britain were represented (including London, Oxford and Cambridge, Llandudno in Wales, Queenstown in Ireland, and Edinburgh and Glasgow in Scotland). The membership fee of one shilling was optional.[47]

The Manchester club was one of the affiliates of the Central Association for the Recognition of the Confederate States. The vice presidents were common to all the local bodies, each of which had an executive committee to take care of everyday business. Information about the Central Association was included in the material published in September 1863. The "general constitution" was dated 10 August 1863. "This Association was formed in April 1863, to counteract the mischievous violations of neutrality by agitators in the Northern interest . . . and to advocate the just claims of the Confederate States." Branch clubs were responsible for their own "local management, rules, and financial affairs" but would unite with one another and the Central Association "in a sympathy and similarity of objects, assisting each other by frequent interchange of information, publications, lecturers, and

such other means as may be found practicable." Clubs had already been established in thirty towns, including London, but the committee of the Central Association wanted specifically to gain "the countenance and support of
the merchants and manufacturers of Lancashire, whose large property is so
seriously endangered, and the welfare of whose workpeople is so grievously
damaged by the present crisis." A circular letter recommended "a friendly
joint mediation of the European Powers, preceded by fair and equal recognition of the South as a contracting Power": "In the interest of distracted
America, North and South alike—in the interest of our own guiltless, suffering people—in the interest of the unhappy negro, and of common humanity, we ask you to join us in this earnest attempt to check the social, moral,
and political ruin which protracted civil war must bring upon both parts of
the once prosperous Republic."[48] The *Anti-Slavery Monthly Reporter* declared
that the Manchester Southern Club and connected bodies were not serious
about emancipation. What they had established was a "Southern Slaveholders' Aid Society." While it was an admirable thing to press for an end to
the American war, the only way to bring peace was to persuade southerners
"to make their submission to the Government against which they have re-
belled." Was the new movement likely to do this? Its solution—end the war
by recognizing the South—made no sense. The South's objective was *not*
independence: "It is fighting for the right of perpetuating Slavery, independence being only a means to this end." Another problem was that the Manchester Southern Club wanted to do gradually what Lincoln and the U.S.
military were already doing "forthwith," and gradual emancipation, if overseen by the Confederate government, could be delayed for decades because
each state in an independent South would have control over its own internal
concerns.[49]

It was reported in October 1863 that the Manchester Southern Club and
the Central Association had arranged formally to merge. A new body, the
Southern Independence Association, would henceforth coordinate the activities of British friends of the South.[50]

On 16 October 1863, Hope addressed a meeting of the Liverpool Southern Club. Much of his speech related to the "Laird rams" and the demand
from the North, and pro-northern spokesmen in Britain, that the British
government should prevent vessels constructed in British yards—ordered
surreptitiously (though it was now no secret) by southern agents—from put-
ting out to sea to join the Confederate navy. One possibility was to extend

the Foreign Enlistment Act of 1819. The act had been designed to restrain British subjects from fighting in wars in which Britain was not involved, and it prohibited the building and equipping of warships in any British territory without the proper authorization. Hope reminded his audience that in recent times, Russell, now foreign secretary, had been applauded for his stand against the making of policy at the behest of a foreign government. Russell had opposed the Conspiracy to Murder Bill in an impressive Commons speech of 9 February 1858 (Hope, at that time MP for Maidstone, spoke in the same debate). The bill had been introduced by the Palmerston ministry, which was under pressure from the French following an attempt on the life of Napoleon III, a conspiracy developed on British soil. Palmerston was accused of submitting to the French. The bill was lost, and he had to resign. Hope regarded all this as salutary.[51]

As Hope understood it, the "steam rams" had been ordered by a French company. Where was the evidence to disprove this? Allegations from the United States and from northern sympathizers in Britain had to be dismissed in the absence of evidence, and the idea that mere supposition was "likely to lead to a change in the system of our international law" was ridiculous. The British people would not allow it, and Palmerston had surely learned a lesson in 1858. "Truckling to the Northern cause" would bring "shame and humiliation" to all concerned.[52]

The meeting was followed by a banquet addressed by Hope, by James Spence, and by Capt. James D. Bulloch, a former naval officer, born in Savannah, Georgia, who was the Confederacy's chief agent in Britain. (From his base in Liverpool, he operated blockade-runners and commerce raiders, negotiated sales of southern cotton, and arranged for the delivery of armaments and supplies to the South.) The meeting and dinner were widely reported in the press, with prominent members of the Liverpool Southern Club clearly identified: apart from Spence, a tin and metal merchant, the most notable were club president Victor Pontz, a cotton importer; Charles Marshall, a merchant, shipbroker, and agent; Henry Coulborn, a confectioner; Edward Lawrence and P. B. Hughes, both merchants with premises in Brown's Buildings, where the club also had rooms; Charles K. Prioleau, banker and merchant from Charleston, South Carolina, who did a great deal financially for the Confederacy; and Charles Livingston, J. B. Spence, and Alfred Cowie, all cotton brokers.[53]

On visits to Liverpool, Hope became better acquainted with Spence and other pro-southerners there. Spence wrote letters to various newspapers, including the *Times*, and two books, *The American Union* (1861) and *On the Recognition of the Southern Confederation* (1862). As Hope was doing, he highlighted Britain's natural links with the South and rivalry with the North. Spence was involved in the Erlanger Loan of 1863, an effort to market Confederate bonds backed by cotton through the French banking house of Emile Erlanger and Company. Being in favor of abolition, Spence also attempted to minimize the significance of slavery as a cause of secession and war. (Confederate envoy to France John Slidell later criticized Spence for his failure to defend slavery. Spence's father had been a plantation owner in Jamaica and freed his own slaves, without compensation, before 1833.) Spence continued his pro-Confederate campaigning into 1865 and after the war contributed money for the education of Jefferson Davis's children. Spence was close to another of the Liverpool activists, Prioleau. They had probably become friends through Spence's wife, who, like Prioleau, was of American-born Huguenot background. Prioleau was a senior partner in the Liverpool shipping and trading concern Fraser, Trenholm, and Company. Naturalized in England in 1863, he was one of the main financiers of blockade-runners during the war and, in effect, unofficial banker to the Confederate government. Prioleau worked closely with Bulloch. His firm extended generous credit to help Confederate agents make their purchases.

Hope was happy to cooperate with local leaders in different parts of the country when it furthered the common cause. Such was his prominence that pro-northern lecturer Washington Wilkes made Hope his special study for a series on "Pro-Southern Englishmen." In November 1863, Wilkes, who frequented radical and Nonconformist circles in London and was a member of the London Emancipation Society, took his presentation to the Whittington Club in the Strand. His other subjects were W. S. Lindsay, J. A. Roebuck, and Charles Mackay (who was based in New York, from 1862 to 1865, as correspondent of the *Times*).[54]

The possibility that Britain would recognize the Confederacy depended on the course of the war, and it shrank to all but nothing after the Battle of Gettysburg and the fall of Vicksburg in July 1863. The U.S. and British governments still quarreled with each other, not least over the Laird rams, but that difficulty was eased in October 1863, when foreign secretary Russell ordered that the vessels should be stopped.[55] Some members of Palmerston's cabinet had favored recognition of the Confederacy, but they realized that overextension in America would weaken Britain's resistance to challenges in other parts of the world. Russian pressure, antagonism between Prussia and Austria, instability in Italy and Poland, disputation over the Danish duchies, French involvement in Mexico, and Napoleon III's talk of the Rhine as France's eastern border all induced the government in London to watch and wait.[56] The reasons for its reluctance to involve itself in the American crisis were perhaps not fully appreciated by Hope and other pro-southerners in the final months of 1863.

At the end of 1863, a long statement was issued by the Southern Independence Association of London. Hope was chairman of the SIA, and its meetings would usually take place at his house in Connaught Place. The treasurer was his brother-in-law Lord Eustace Cecil. There were eighteen members of the committee, including Hope and Lord Eustace Cecil. Five had also been named as vice presidents in the material previously published by the Manchester Southern Club and Central Association: Hope, Lord Robert Cecil, Peacocke, Gregory, and W. S. Lindsay. James Spence was also on the London committee. There were three Conservative nobles—the Marquess of Lothian (author of *The Confederate Secession*, published in 1864), the Marquess of Bath, and Lord Wharncliffe—and a Liberal peer, Lord Campbell; and among the MPs were Conservatives William Vansittart (Windsor) and T. C. Haliburton (Launceston) and Liberals C. W. Fitzwilliam (Malton), William Scholefield (Birmingham), and Fulke Greville (County Longford). The London committee was completed by Edward Akroyd, a wealthy Yorkshire worsted manufacturer and former Liberal MP for Huddersfield, and lawyer Robert Bourke, son of the Earl of Mayo and a future Conservative MP for King's Lynn.[57]

The SIA statement began with an overview of the (putative) change in British opinion since the beginning of the American crisis. People had become more "enlightened" about "the long-widening and now insuperable divergence of character and interests between the two sections of the former Union." British confidence in the North was in rapid decline owing to its "governmental tyranny, corruption in high places, ruthlessness of war, untruthfulness of speech, and causeless animosity towards Great Britain," while most observers now agreed that the South was ready for its independence. British and European intervention was surely appropriate, and the SIA had been formed to promote a settlement based on recognition of the South as a sovereign country. It was time to do justice to "a brave people sprung from ourselves, speaking our language . . . and claiming recognition in accordance with those principles of British policy which have always been more inclined to help the oppressed than to justify and abet the oppressor." The precedents of Belgium, Greece, and Italy "exist as modern instances to show that Great Britain is always ready to acknowledge, rather than to resist, a national uprising," and when change had come to these three countries, not one of them had been "as well organized for self-government as the Confederate States have now been for nearly three years." The SIA would campaign accordingly, but it would also take care to explain to southerners that the institution of slavery must be altered "in accordance with the spirit of the age."[58]

This statement, in its phraseology and arguments, was so close to Hope's lectures and pamphlets that he probably wrote it. The SIA's appeal was strongest among those who were already favorable to the South. There do not appear to have been many new converts during 1864, and though its leaders communicated (between May and July 1864) with other groups and even with Palmerston for British mediation to end the American war, these conversations came to nothing.[59] Nevertheless, its activity annoyed such opponents as the British and Foreign Anti-Slavery Society, and it was attacked by name in January 1865 in the *Anti-Slavery Monthly Reporter*, which claimed that the SIA had dishonestly separated southern independence from the question of slavery. The truth about the SIA was to be gleaned from the identity of its chairman, Hope, and its committee members, such as Spence, the "paid advocate of the Southern slaveholders," and W. S. Lindsay, who was "more than any other man responsible for the depredations of piratical vessels such as the notorious *Alabama*."[60] Commentators in the United States also condemned the SIA.[61]

Of all the events organized by friends of the South, one of the most impressive was the Grand Southern Bazaar of 1864, held in St. George's Hall, Liverpool, commencing on 18 October and running for four days. Months in the planning, it was hailed by *Bell's Life* as "sumptuous and vast." Thousands attended, and the sum of twenty-two thousand pounds was raised for the Southern Prisoners' Relief Fund. There were twelve stalls, each named after a Confederate state and each under the charge of the wives and daughters of prominent pro-southerners, including Hope's wife, Lady Mildred.[62]

The full list of "Lady Patronesses" reveals a mix of British, French, and American connections and political affiliations. Lady Wharncliffe, the Marchioness of Lothian, the Marchioness of Bath, Lady Mildred Beresford Hope, Lady Rosa Greville, Mrs. Elizabeth Akroyd, and Lady Eustace Cecil were all on the list. It also included Princess Caroline Murat, the American-born granddaughter of former king of Naples Joachim Murat; the Vicomtesse de Dampierre, whose husband was a French general; the American-born Baroness de Longueuil; the Marchioness of Ailesbury, whose husband was a Liberal politician and former official in Queen Victoria's household; Lady de Hoghton, wife of a Lancashire baronet; the American-born Marquise de Montmort; Lady Anson, wife of the chairman of the Society for Promoting the Cessation of Hostilities in America and daughter-in-law of the Earl of Lichfield, a Liberal; the Countess of Chesterfield, wife of a Conservative peer; Lady Eardley, wife of a Hertfordshire baronet; Mrs. Sophia Horsfall, whose husband was Conservative MP for Liverpool; Mrs. Elizabeth Laird, of the Birkenhead shipbuilding family; Countess Paulina Bentivoglio, widow of an American diplomat and mother of a Confederate army officer; Lady Georgiana Fane, from a Conservative family, aunt of the Earl of Westmorland; Mrs. Hannah Callender, whose husband was a Manchester manufacturer and Conservative; and Mrs. Flora Collie, whose husband, a merchant and agent, handled the commercial affairs of North Carolina in London. According to an announcement of July 1864, "many ladies, in addition to those named, have promised their active aid."[63] Subsequent announcements stressed that the event was actuated by "sympathy for the great sorrows and sufferings that now affect a people of our own race."[64]

Along with the goods offered for sale, there were auctions and raffles, refreshments, musical entertainments, and a number of remarkable items on display, including a printed "Eulogy" to Stonewall Jackson, a portrait of Jackson at prayer before the Battle of Chancellorsville, and a fine sword that was to be sent to Robert E. Lee as a memento. Chief among the public figures who attended were Hope, Sir Henry de Hoghton, the shipbuilder and Conservative MP for Birkenhead John Laird, cotton merchant and Palmerstonian MP for Manchester James Aspinall Turner, Lord Wharncliffe, and Lord Campbell. Local civic dignitaries participated, including Liverpool's mayor, Charles Mozley, a banker with heavy investments in cotton. Mason, the Confederate envoy to England, was also present. A significant charitable exercise, the Grand Southern Bazaar was, equally, an opportunity for the Confederacy's friends to meet and socialize together, talk tactics, and evaluate the latest news about the war.[65]

The *Liverpool Mercury* (a Liberal paper and pro-southern) rated the event a wonderful triumph.[66] There was detailed coverage in the London and provincial press.[67] None of this made any difference to the course of the war in America, though, and within six months the war was over. In April 1865, the South's defeat was a disappointment but hardly a surprise to its British adherents.[68]

"With the exception of passionate partisans," asserted the *Saturday Review*, "foreigners will view with a certain regret the failure of a heroic resistance." Meanwhile, northern leaders continued to disgrace themselves, calling for Jefferson Davis to be hanged and making new threats against Canada. The North's behavior in victory gave another reminder of the unwholesomeness of American democracy.[69]

Hope had often been scathing in his assessment of Lincoln, but the *Saturday Review*'s response to Lincoln's assassination was not unkind. It wanted those responsible for this "atrocious" crime to be punished as soon as possible. While his improbable rise to the presidency and the mistakes he made in that office could not be ignored, Lincoln had imposed himself on events. Honest and determined, he learned from experience. His recent turn to peacemaking was admirable. But equally, was it not a vile falsehood for northern politicians and their friends in Britain to say that the assassination was part of a southern plot? Such "malignity" might lead to outrages against the South.[70]

If British verdicts on Lincoln before his assassination were mostly negative, there was a shift after the spring of 1865. Now he was praised as hero and martyr. A positive image of Lincoln was employed to push for parliamentary reform in Britain, and by the end of the nineteenth century, British commentators were also influenced by Lincoln's role as a consensual symbol for Americans. After Reconstruction, he was not as unpopular in the South as he had formerly been. Lincoln was elevated in British discourse as a more appealing figure, if still a divisive one.[71]

Hope and other British detractors of Lincoln had not fully appreciated his achievements. Retrospectively, there was more understanding of his methods and of the competing concepts of Reconstruction with which he had contended. Lincoln had tried to make restoration of the Union as easy as possible.[72] After his death, Reconstruction became chaotic. Had they understood him better, British pro-southerners might have deemed his removal all the more regrettable, for they wished the South to be treated leniently. For years, this proved not to be the case.[73]

Hope returned to the Commons in 1865 as MP for Stoke-upon-Trent. There was a general election in July. Hope's printed address, dated 23 June, made no mention of American affairs.[74] This was in stark contrast to his speech in Stoke in 1862, when he had contested a by-election there. That pro-southerners had no choice but to resign themselves to the consequences of the American war was driven home by the demise of the *Index*, the Confederacy's London newspaper. It ceased publication in August 1865. Hope had been a friend and collaborator of its editor, Hotze, who had also worked with the SIA.[75]

Documents issued by the SIA, some marked "confidential," came into the possession of the U.S. government and appeared in northern papers with suggestive interjections about "how British sympathy with rebellion was manipulated." Meetings were shown to have taken place in Hope's London residence, and there were items bearing his signature, along with a copy of the SIA's constitution, a committee list, and a list of persons who had funded the SIA.[76] Publication of this material was designed to add to northerners' sense of being wronged and to ensure that blame was attached to certain targets, primarily Hope.

He was also embroiled in the "Confederate Loan" controversy. At the beginning of October 1865, citing a telegram from Washington dated 18 September, the *Manchester Guardian* disparaged those who had bought into the loan and published "an estimate" of the loss suffered by each person.[77] London gossip gave the story added momentum, and American papers taunted the *Times* and the *Morning Post*, "whose editors . . . are supposed to have had a strong pecuniary interest in advocating the cause of the South as long as it had a chance of success." J. T. Delane of the *Times* was on the list, having allegedly invested ten thousand pounds. M. R. Sampson, who edited the City News section of the *Times,* was included, with a sum of fifteen thousand pounds, and W. J. Ridout, proprietor of the *Morning Post*, with four thousand pounds.[78]

Hope was on the list (£40,000), but he was not among the largest investors, who were Sir Henry de Houghton (£180,000), London army contractors Isaac Campbell and Company (£150,000), the ship-owner Thomas Sterling Begbie (£140,000), London agent and shipper D. Forbes Campbell (£80,000), the Marquess of Bath (£50,000), and James Spence of Liverpool (£50,000). Other leaders of the "Southern Independence movement" were on the list, including W.S. Lindsay (£20,000), Sir Coutts Lindsay (£20,000), George Peacocke (£5,000), Lord Wharncliffe (£5,000), W.H. Gregory (£4,000), Edward Ackroyd (£1,500), and Lord Campbell (£1,000). Other notables were London stockbroker George Edward Seymour (£40,000); the shipbuilder John Laird (£20,000); John Saunders Gilliat, a director of the Bank of England (£10,000); the Earl of Donoughmore, who had been a member of the Conservative government of Lord Derby in 1858–59 (£1,000); Evelyn Ashley, son of Lord Shaftesbury, private secretary to the prime minister Palmerston (£500); and chancellor of the exchequer Gladstone (£2,000). The list also included Liverpool merchants and ship-owners Fernie Brothers and Company (£30,000); merchants and agents of Manchester and London Alexander Collie and partners (£20,000); Fleetwood, Patten, Wilson, and Schuster, directors of the Union Bank of London, which had an extensive overseas business (£20,000); Lady Georgiana Fane (£15,000); and Lord Richard Grosvenor, Liberal MP for Flintshire, son of the Marquess of Westminster (£1,000).

In a letter to the *Times,* Hope called the list "a fabrication." Reports from America contained "not even a basis of truth." "I never held a farthing of the Loan, nor ever embarked a farthing on blockade-running. The sympathy which I all along felt for the Southern States in their struggle for independence was wholly of a public and political nature."[79] *Bell's Life* defended Hope. It complained that the loan, "which, for business purposes and to the loss of many individuals, has almost become a thing of the past," had been made "the means of wounding reputations." Was the list of bondholders even genuine? Hope, in particular, was right to protest. He was "a person who, without the slightest blame, might have held the stock during the war, for he then possessed no public office." Now that he sat in Parliament, the country had to be sure that his private concerns would not interfere with his public duty, and this was why his enemies had tried to blacken his name. Others on the list had also confirmed that they did not hold any stock. The imputation against Delane, "editor of the most known and highest placed paper in England," appeared to be part of a wider attack on the British press. Indeed, American politicians and journalists were not reluctant to make claims "with the disgraceful purpose of irritating American feeling against England." No less appalling was the policy of British newspapers that had been pro-northern during the war and now besmirched other British papers "without any inquiry or any hesitation."[80] The *Observer* refused, unlike the *Manchester Guardian,* to assume that the list of bondholders was accurate. Only W. S. Lindsay had admitted to holding Confederate stock, "but even he expressed deep indignation at being set down as a loser of £20,000 instead of £2,000."[81]

A correspondent of the *Times* provided further particulars, having conversed with the U.S. secretary of state a few days before the list of bondholders was published. The story told by Seward was that the list had been taken from a Confederate agent in Paris, and with the list was an account of a meeting of pro-southerners at Hope's house in Connaught Place. The correspondent and an unnamed British MP who was also present looked over the material in Seward's possession and told him it was spurious. Seward did not go into authenticity, though he indicated that he trusted his source (probably the U.S. minister to France, John Bigelow).[82]

American newspapers discussed the allegations and denials for some time. Several of them, while refusing to forgive British sympathy for the South during the war, conceded that the list was false. Some maintained that if there had been the claimed level of investment, it was done on principle and not for personal profit.[83] The *New York Times* was more severe. It agreed that there were inaccuracies but added that the list was not "invalidated" by them. Even if the named individuals had not invested such large sums, they supported the end in view, which was to help the South win the war.

> It may be true enough that Mr. Beresford Hope and others were not, as they protest, subscribers to the loan. But it does not follow that their relations with the Confederate agents were not such as to justify the use of their names, made by these agents to give credit to the loan in the London market. Mr. Beresford Hope had given, as a public journalist, all the influence which the *smartest* weekly journal in England possessed to make a national character for the Davis insurrection, and to discredit the bare possibility of the United States continuing to exist as an independent power. Mr. Beresford Hope was, at the same time, the confidant and adviser of the Confederate agents in London. He attended their meetings. He sat in their councils. He spent his means to maintain an organ for them. And if they used his name to bolster up their financial operations without his direct permission, they certainly did not presume to any unpardonable extent on his disposition and good will. All the influence he possessed as a public man was theirs beforehand.[84]

The *New York Times* went on to provide more coverage, including material from British papers that were quarreling with each other over the list.[85] Other northern commentators joined in. Now it was obvious why Hope and his friends had wanted the southern rebellion to succeed: they faced financial disaster if it failed.[86] The *Boston Daily Advertiser* vilified Hope as "completely sold out."[87]

The name of "Sir Beresford Hope" cropped up again early in 1866, in the *Chicago Tribune*, in relation to a plot to damage U.S. credit abroad, but the report was not substantiated.[88] Discussion of the Confederate Loan went on, meanwhile, as northern papers disagreed about whether information recovered from the financial department of the former Confederate government proved the list of bondholders to be correct.[89] In 1883, New York sources alleged that surviving bondholders were about to press for compensation. Here was an excuse to republish a list of names, including Hope's, but as one commentator put it with remarkable understatement, "there is a bare possibility . . . that this report is false."[90]

Hope denied any participation, but fortunes *could* be made doing wartime business with the South, though it was not without risk.[91] Some Confederate economic and financial measures were not ineffective. The principal foreign undertaking, the Erlanger Loan, only raised about half of the expected amount. Yet the Confederate government's credit in Europe was better at the end of 1864 than in the spring of 1863, when the Erlanger Loan was arranged.[92] It made sense commercially for interested parties in Britain to continue trading with and investing in the South into 1865 and all the more so if they wished the South well for other than business reasons.

Despite the irritation of the Confederate Loan controversy, Hope continued to involve himself in American affairs in the postwar period. He was especially interested in the Episcopal Church, as he had been during the war. He read and wrote about the issues it was facing after its reunification, and there was regular personal interaction with some of its members, clerical and lay, and engagement in common endeavors.

Hope did not change his views about "democracy" in America. He warned about the dangers posed by any approximation to it at home. Following the extension of the parliamentary franchise in 1867, which Hope opposed, other electoral reforms were discussed. In July 1868, during a Commons debate on the Election Petitions and Corrupt Practices at Elections

Bill, Hope said that safeguards were needed to promote "electoral purity" and "cheapness and simplicity in the machinery of contests" and, even more, to prevent improper manipulation of voters through the "histrionic electioneering" that had "attained its climax in America."[93] Of the ballot, Hope remained an uncompromising foe. He told the Commons in February 1871 that voting by ballot had not benefited the United States. It would not benefit Britain either, for there was no guarantee of secrecy or of deterring intimidation.[94] Hope subsequently argued that if MPs really cared about the freedom and independence of the voter, then the ballot was not the method to employ. He read out evidence from South Carolina to illustrate "unbounded" electoral corruption. Was this to be desired for Britain? "There would be a gradual weakening of moral obligations, and gradually, not after one election but after two or three, the people would reach the low level of the electors of the United States."[95]

Hope was a hostile observer of certain practices in the U.S. Congress, notably the "cloture" (or "guillotine"), which brought an end to deliberations so that an immediate vote could be taken. A similar thing was suggested for the Commons in March 1882, when new rules of procedure were being debated. "The cloture may advance some divisions," Hope said, but "its inevitable tendency is to multiply the wrangles which go much further to protract the Session than any solid serious debate, however lengthy." Congress had the cloture, and it also had "filibustering," which was "obstruction brought up to its most scientific form."[96] The need to use available time more effectively prompted other proposals. One idea was to allow standing committees to do more of Parliament's business. Hope did not see how government by committee would end delay. Appealing to the American system for support was pointless, he declared, because Britain's constitutional history was different. Strong committees in Washington reflected America's own political development.[97]

Some American newspapers took exception to Hope's criticisms. In their view, the offenses he had committed during the war—his insults, ill will, and misunderstandings—extended into the postwar years. A London correspondent of the *New York Times* offered the mitigation that Hope was a good character with bad politics.[98]

The debate about democracy in Britain was, according to Brent Kinser, "a kind of pressure valve for social unrest." It helped to ensure that political change came without the violence seen elsewhere. Reform was implemented (as in 1867) without endangering stability, and the willingness to reform kept that stability going because there were self-correcting mechanisms within the British system. There was no shift from British- to American-style institutions. Britain did move toward more democratic forms after the American Civil War, but Kinser points to "forces that kept the progress of democracy to a non-revolutionary pace."[99] Hope's speaking and writing on America were of this tendency.

His name continued to feature in American periodicals. He took an interest in the impeachment of President Johnson, prompted by irreconcilable differences over how to treat the postwar South, and one of the managers of that impeachment took an interest in Hope. This was John A. Logan, an Illinois Republican who had served as a U.S. general in the war (and would go on to be a vice presidential candidate in 1884). Logan had one of his speeches about the president printed and sent to Britain, where copies were distributed to public figures, including Hope. As reported in Washington's *Daily National Intelligencer*, the other British recipients were the Prince of Wales, the bishops of London and Oxford, Conservative prime minister Benjamin Disraeli, and the *Times* and the British Museum.[100]

Hope was not alone in thinking of Reconstruction in America as a failure. Its punitive aspects annoyed British pro-southerners and prompted them to repeat their earlier argument that even if it lost the war, the South could not be conquered. Taking a longer-term view, historians have expressed varying opinions about Reconstruction. An international perspective on the causes and consequences of the war brings in other considerations, but again, there is disagreement about whether "a modern concept of rights" was consolidated or faith in democracy strengthened.[101]

Diplomatic relations between Britain and the United States were overshadowed after the war by the *Alabama* claims. Hope took a dim view of the manner in which this dispute was resolved, for he thought that the British government, led from 1868 by W. E. Gladstone, made too many concessions. The Treaty of Washington of March 1871 arranged for the *Alabama* claims to be settled by international arbitration. Britain paid damages in 1872 and, while admitting no guilt, apologized for the destruction of U.S. shipping by British-built Confederate vessels during the American Civil War. Hope spoke against these transactions, as in November 1872, when he addressed his Kentish friends and neighbors at the annual dinner of the Goudhurst Agricultural Association.[102]

The *Alabama* dispute had created serious tension between the two governments, and the settlement of 1872 at least brought some closure.[103] But the affair could still on occasion revive strong feelings because the American war was interpreted in different ways and became a polemical device in later quarrels, as was strikingly demonstrated in the 1980s, when it was announced that a replica of the *Alabama* would feature in a regeneration scheme for Birkenhead on the Mersey (where the original had been built, in the Lairds shipyard). The plan was to redevelop the dockland area, create jobs, and boost tourism, but the *Alabama* replica was eventually left out of the project.[104] During and after the war, allegations were made—by U.S. politicians and newspapers and by pro-northerners in Britain—about conspiracies involving statesmen and civil servants, arms manufacturers, financiers, shipbuilders, and merchants who colluded with Confederate agents and created the environment within which events like the escape of the *Alabama* were allowed to happen. The recriminations did not cease with the settlement of 1872.[105] Hope was close to some of those behind the construction of the *Alabama,* and though he was not directly involved, there is a slight possibility that it was his niece who launched the vessel.[106]

Another issue that complicated British-U.S. relations was Irish home rule. Many Irishmen had fought in the American war, and some used their military experience to aid the nationalist cause, joining such organizations as the Fenian Brotherhood. Fenian leaders crisscrossed the Atlantic, raising money, setting up terrorist cells, and publishing propaganda. There were raids in Canada, bombings in England, and violent acts of resistance to British authority in Ireland. Some captured Fenians claimed U.S. citizenship. This problem, and the fact that anti-British activities were being planned on U.S. soil, prompted heated exchanges between London and Washington, and meanwhile, the constitutional campaign for self-government for Ireland, with "Home Rulers" increasing their numbers in Parliament and obstructing its business, made for further difficulty. (Home rule stopped short of the full Fenian separatist agenda.) Hope approved of the legislative union between Britain and Ireland and opposed most of the proposals designed to appease the Irish and reconcile them to British rule (disestablishment of the Irish church, for example). He and others were struck by the ways in which the American war—especially its lessons about secession, federalism, and national unity—could be used in these quarrels.[107]

Hope was still keeping up with American news and communicating with transatlantic friends, and he was acquainted with Americans in London, including Edwards Pierrepont, the U.S. minister to Britain, 1876–77.[108] In 1878, Hope was awarded an honorary degree by Washington and Lee University in Lexington, Virginia. The LLD diploma was presented in a ceremony at his London residence in the spring of 1879. (Many of the university's students had served under Stonewall Jackson. After the war, Robert E. Lee was the university's president, until his death in 1870, when he was succeeded by his son George Washington Custis Lee.) The ceremony was attended by several notable figures, including the U.S. minister to Britain (1877–79), John Welsh, a Philadelphia businessman; and Alfred Green, a manufacturer of Hamilton, Ontario, who represented the St. George's Union of English expatriates. Welsh introduced the university's deputation. He spoke of Virginia, "founded by the gallant Cavaliers of England," and said he was pleased to be present "to honor a gentleman whom he regarded as the friend of the reunited American people." Green "had pleasure in testifying to the high respect felt for Mr. Beresford Hope by Anglo-Americans in Canada and the United States." In his response, Hope said that "on some questions there had been differences of opinion in this country, as on the other side of the Atlantic," but he was glad that "Americans, who prided themselves on their own independence, were ready to honor independent thought and action in others." He wished Virginia well, and he wished America well, and "it was gratifying to him to know that he had many kind friends both in the North and the South. Blood is thicker than water, and Englishmen and Americans were friends and brothers."[109] Several American newspapers reported the presentation to Hope.[110]

Alfred Green's presence at the degree-awarding ceremony is instructive. Hope was familiar to English-born residents in Canada and the United States who came together to form the North America St. George's Union, originally conceived as a benevolent undertaking (and an umbrella organization for all the local St. George's Societies that had previously been formed in America by English immigrants). Its officers had called a general meeting in Petersburg, Virginia, in 1877 to mark Queen Victoria's birthday (24 May) and invited Hope to attend.[111]

Hope's "blood is thicker than water" formulation shows that there were circumstances in which he put aside his former Confederate associations and took up a more conciliatory interpretation of the war and its consequences. This was in line with a late Victorian tendency, noted by Nimrod

Tal, to think of the war as a purging process, leading to the rise of a stronger, prosperous, reunified America and to greater respect between the British and U.S. governments and peoples.[112] Hugh Dubrulle has also emphasized the rise of a more favorable attitude toward the United States after the war, linked with the weakening of the "postcolonial" air of British superiority and a willingness to treat Americans as equals.[113] Hope was influenced by these developments, but fundamentally, he was still the same. He did not give up his pro-southern preferences. He does not fit the pattern described by Tal and Dubrulle.

Hope's southern connections were strengthened when his eldest son, Philip, married Evelyn Frost, daughter of a former Confederate general, Daniel Marsh Frost of St. Louis, Missouri. The wedding took place in London in August 1883. Reports appeared in British and American papers.[114]

Hope forged other links with the South. He was a friend of former U.S. vice president, Confederate general, and Confederate secretary of war (for three months in 1865) John C. Breckinridge. He offered property and income to Robert E. Lee. He enjoyed a long acquaintance with former Confederate president Jefferson Davis.

After the defeat of the South, Breckinridge spent time in England, and Hope got to know him well.[115] When Breckinridge, who had returned to the South, died in 1875, Hope was the grateful recipient of some of his effects. In a letter that appeared in several American papers, he called Breckinridge a "much-honored and greatly regretted friend." Breckenridge had stayed with the Hopes both in London and at Bedgebury Park, their estate in Kent.[116]

Hope's relationship with Lee was not so close. After the war, Lee sought a dignified retirement from public life, turning down commercial opportunities, posts in foreign armies, and numerous gifts, including English property. Hope put together a committee in London that "offered him a splendid estate in any part of England which he might select." He would have five thousand pounds a year for the rest of his life. Lee politely declined.[117]

Davis was imprisoned without trial after the war. Eventually released, he lived for a time in Canada. Then, after an extended stay in Britain, he returned to the South. Hope urged him to visit in a letter of June 1867. The two were finally able to meet when Davis reached London in September 1868. From this time onward, they maintained a correspondence until Hope's death in 1887. Davis and his family enjoyed Hope's hospitality in London and in Kent. One transatlantic exchange dates from August 1881, when Hope thanked Davis for sending him a copy of *The Rise and Fall of the Confederate Government*. Hope wrote a piece on Davis's book for the *Saturday Review*. He made a gift to Davis of one of his novels. A letter to Davis was among the last Hope wrote, on 10 July 1887.[118]

Hope's piece in the *Saturday Review* in 1881 showed that he was no less a pro-southerner than he had previously been. He began by recalling just how much the war in America had fascinated—and divided—people in Britain. While "condemned, prejudged, unheard" by those who had embraced the "liberty" promoted by the French Revolution, the southern cause received a "candid consideration" from "constitutional Englishmen" who understood that real liberty was "the growth of positive law, of solemn compact, of respect for property, for tradition, and for reciprocal confidence." Studying American history, these "constitutional Englishmen" realized that the United States consisted of sovereign communities that retained independent control over their internal affairs while passing authority over common concerns to a federal government. The book published by Jefferson Davis, Hope thought, clarified the South's position and the right and policy of secession "with much pathetic dignity." Many in Britain had opposed the South because they opposed slavery, but others took the more sensible line that slavery was not the main cause of the war and that southerners, who were not responsible for the existence of slavery, were genuinely trying to improve the condition of their slaves. British opinion was also affected by the actions of the North and especially the *Trent* affair. But even more than the clear basis for secession, the South's intentions regarding slavery, and the wrongdoings of the North, Hope argued that the Confederacy gained British sympathizers because of "the heroic deeds of leaders." These influences combined to make British people favor the South, a partiality that withstood the pleadings of northern politicians and writers.[119]

Hope's review of *The Rise and Fall of the Confederate Government* demonstrates the fixity of his opinions about the American Civil War. His previous commitments were not undermined by time and circumstance. Indeed, his disappointment with events at home increased his contempt for things he associated with the North and its victory in the war. He maintained that British people had sided with the South for sound reasons relating to economic and political conditions, constitutional questions, slavery and emancipation, southern religiosity, and social and cultural bonds between the South and Britain. Hope's respect for the South was undiminished. In the review of 1881, though, he did place more emphasis than he had during the war on "the heroic deeds of leaders." He had hailed these acts of heroism on many occasions but more as one among several promoters of pro-southern sentiment, not as the main motivating force. By the 1880s, he had concluded that of all the influences at work among British people during the American war, it was a sense of southern heroism that was probably most telling.

II

Stonewall Jackson, British Hero

───◦◦◦───

$$\frac{7}{}$$

STONEWALL JACKSON AND
BRITISH OPINION

Victorian Britain was fascinated by "heroes" and heroic character. Heroes lived up to "ideals of conduct." They were courageous, selfless, and steadfast. Zeal for heroes may have increased because of a perceived lack of heroism in public life and because of the cultural power of notions of personal decency, but there were disagreements about what constituted heroism, and it was argued repeatedly that heroic individuals might be unknown as well as famous since fame had no necessary connection with the best values and behavior. Historian and philosopher Thomas Carlyle, who did so much to encourage interest in great men with his opinionated edition of the letters and speeches of Oliver Cromwell in 1845, maintained that a hero could be noble but silent.[1] Nevertheless, Carlyle focused on heroes who rose from ordinary beginnings to become extraordinary. In lectures and publications, he encouraged people to think about what the world might look like if the most powerful and inspired had the influence he thought they merited.[2]

Confederate general Thomas Jonathan "Stonewall" Jackson became a British hero during the second year of the American Civil War. He was not British by birth, and his heroism was displayed not in Britain but in a foreign war zone, but his character and accomplishments had impact nonetheless. The creation and maintenance of his reputation occurred at a distance—physically and ideologically—and depended heavily on secondhand information. The amount and frequency of that information varied, and owing to the nature of communication in the mid-nineteenth century, developments in America involving Jackson could prompt only a delayed reaction in Britain. The transatlantic cable was not operational until 1866. During the war, it usually took ten or eleven days for news to pass from America to

Britain, and vice versa, by steamship. The movement of news within Britain and America rested on their internal communications.[3]

Stonewall Jackson rapidly went from obscurity to celebrity in Britain. Nobody knew or cared about him before the war.[4] He established his reputation with the Valley Campaign of spring 1862. The Shenandoah Valley was of huge strategic importance: it was a source of food and other resources, and for the Confederates, it offered a route into the North. With each successful action in the Valley, Jackson's fame grew in Britain as well as America. In a campaign that prioritized surprise and maneuver, his force of seventeen thousand marched about 650 miles in forty-eight days, gaining impressive victories over a combined force of more than fifty thousand. Jackson had obliged the North to keep forces at Washington and in the Valley that would otherwise have been sent to participate in the Federal offensive against Richmond.[5]

Jackson's victories were the cause of jubilation across the South and in pro-southern circles in Britain. British newspapers noticed that even the fall of New Orleans at the end of April 1862 did not greatly damage morale, and southern papers that reached Britain at this time were optimistic and defiant.[6] As increasing attention was given to Jackson's efforts and they compensated for disappointments elsewhere, his reputation—while merited—also became a political and psychological device. Southerners needed a hero, and so did their sympathizers in Britain.

Several British papers carried items taken from the antislavery and Republican *New York Tribune*, which was pushing an "on to Richmond" agenda. At the time, it was the best-selling daily in the whole of America. It insisted that Jackson could accomplish nothing in the Valley and that his campaign mostly consisted of running and hiding. Reports from New York dated 3 and 4 June 1862 suggested that Jackson was too afraid to face his pursuers "in a fair fight." British newspapers passed on these reports with the proviso that they came from the North and had not been verified.[7]

American news arriving in late June made more details available, and several British papers emphasized Jackson's talent for speed and effectiveness. He could advance and retreat, concentrate and disperse, feint and parry, all with apparent ease.[8] Items from southern newspapers were used to illustrate the sensation caused in the Confederacy by Jackson's exploits.[9] Piecing together what could be gleaned from official and unofficial testimony, the *Essex Standard* stated that Jackson's primary purpose was not to raid into the

North or even control the Valley but to prevent the Federal armies there from joining Gen. George B. McClellan and the Army of the Potomac outside Richmond. Jackson had done enough in this regard, and it was likely that he was moving his army out of the Valley.[10]

The New York correspondent of the *Times* wrote that Jackson would remain in the Valley and that if Federal troops were sent from there to help McClellan, Washington would be vulnerable. Southern sources had McClellan "paralyzed" before Richmond, in contrast to Jackson's "bold dash" and "masterly movements." A letter from Washington dated 17 June 1862, published in the Confederate paper in London, the *Index,* attested to the anxiety caused in the North by Jackson's campaign.[11] The government in Washington decided on 26 June to form a new army, to be led by Gen. John Pope, called the "Army of Virginia," which was composed of the armies that had operated in the Valley and a force that had been defending Washington. Part of McClellan's Army of the Potomac was later added to Pope's command.[12]

"Manhattan," the New York correspondent of the Conservative and pro-southern *Standard,* composed several reports about the situation in the Valley. Manhattan was journalist and novelist Joseph A. Scoville, a Democrat, and clerk of the Common Council of New York.[13] In June, he stressed the mounting frustration in the North and the sense that Jackson had so embarrassed the Federal generals facing him that they *deserved* to be beaten and discarded.[14] These Manhattan letters indicate both the unsettled nature of New York opinion—liable to change with each item of war news—and the recognition that the talented Jackson posed a genuine threat. This contributed to the romance and mystery surrounding Jackson. For many readers in Britain, it was his unpredictable and rapid movements that marked him out.[15]

British interest in Jackson continued to grow. The Federals' Peninsula Campaign was now the focus of attention, especially the Seven Days Battles of 25 June to 1 July. Robert E. Lee had taken charge of all Confederate forces around Richmond. McClellan was slow to advance, Jackson joined up with Lee, and though the Confederates initially suffered heavy losses and could not coordinate their attacks, McClellan ordered a retreat on the evening of 27 June. Jackson's unexpected arrival led McClellan to overestimate the size of the opposing force.[16]

In Britain, eagerness for the latest details intensified. The pro-southern *Blackburn Standard* contended that the war would go on even if Richmond fell: the Confederates could not be conquered, and under such leaders as Jackson, they would pass up no opportunity to strike at the enemy.[17] American news to 1 July was published in British newspapers of 11 and 12 July. Incomplete information about the battles near Richmond was processed and distributed. It seemed that McClellan had failed. Jackson had reportedly led the main attack against the Federal right. To the *Manchester Guardian*, even though it was sympathetic to the North, Jackson's involvement was "another remarkable proof" of his "brilliance." Such comments were echoed in the pro-southern *Westmorland Gazette*.[18]

Among the most prominent pro-southern organs, the *Manchester Courier* declared that McClellan had gone down to "hopeless defeat." In Britain and Europe, there was more talk of mediation to facilitate a peace treaty. Jackson's movements "have been attended with the most complete success," according to the *Liverpool Mercury*. In the Valley, Jackson had been able to "baffle" and "defeat" a string of Federal commanders. The Lincoln administration had merged all the forces there together under Pope in order to contain him, but rendering them useless, Jackson "suddenly crossed the mountains" and helped to push McClellan back to a "precarious" position away from Richmond.[19]

Northern sources maintained that McClellan had retreated for sound strategic reasons, and there were some British commentators who endorsed this. Others predicted that McClellan would be trapped.[20] The *Sheffield Independent* expected the Confederate victories before Richmond to lead to a relentless offensive that would win the war for the South and joined in the growing praise of Jackson.[21]

As more American news arrived, comment tended to reinforce the themes already taking shape.[22] But the *Dundee Courier*, one of the few papers willing to commend McClellan and deny Jackson a success, contended that the Federals were *not* retreating and that the "hot-headed" and "stupid" Jackson had erred in attacking a section of McClellan's army that was going to be repositioned anyway, whatever the Confederates did.[23]

A small number of British papers noted—if only to reject—a rumor that Jackson was dead. His demise was mooted in New York, according to a correspondent of the *Morning Star*, the pro-northern, radical London daily that championed free trade and peace in association with Richard Cobden and John Bright.[24] When American news up to 10 July arrived by steamer in the Mersey on 19 July, plenty of pro-southerners ridiculed the claim that Mc-

Clellan had executed a "masterly retreat." The typical response was that "McClellan could not make up his mind to undertake this beautiful piece of strategy until it was so very forcibly and clearly illustrated to him by the redoubtable Jackson."[25]

By now, further particulars were available from American newspapers (mainly northern), military dispatches, telegrams, correspondence, and other sources. Favorable remarks about Jackson multiplied.[26] In a letter to the *Times,* subsequently reprinted in other papers, "A Virginian" welcomed the growing interest in Jackson outside America: "I feel pride in saying that he, Thomas Jefferson Jackson, is a native of Clarke County, Virginia, born of excellent Anglo-Scotch stock, a graduate of the Military Academy at West Point, New York; he served in the Mexican War with distinguished gallantry, and has been ever since 1851 the Professor of Military Tactics at the Virginia Military Institute at Lexington. He is a most devout member of the Presbyterian Church, and an accomplished modest gentleman and delightful companion. He is between forty and forty-six years old."[27] Here was but one among what, before long, would be many examples of inaccuracy, as writers sought to satisfy the burgeoning demand for information about Jackson, claiming knowledge they did not have but nevertheless adding to Jackson's fame (and probably hoping to gain something—for the southern cause if not for themselves). It is not likely that A Virginian knew Jackson personally. He had his middle name incorrect, and Jackson's place of birth was not Clarke County but Harrison County, now in West Virginia, of which Clarksburg is the county seat. Jackson did go to the Virginia Military Institute in 1851, but his was a newly created post (he was professor of natural and experimental philosophy and instructor of artillery), and in July 1862, Jackson was thirty-eight years old.

There was no shortage of other messages from America that disparaged McClellan and praised Jackson, including a communication from Manhattan dated 8 July.[28] The Saturday satirical magazine *Fun* asked if Jackson, since McClellan had been called "Young Napoleon," should be dubbed "Young Wellington."[29]

With Richmond relieved, what would Jackson do next? Pope's Army of Virginia pushed south, and the expectation was that Jackson would block his way, rather than circle behind him to menace Washington. Some had no doubt that "the boaster" Pope would be defeated. Others envisaged a victory for Pope. The *Leeds Mercury,* while describing Jackson as "again the terror of the Federalists . . . playing his old tricks with the view of keeping back reinforcements from McClellan," reported that popular support for the war across the North was fading.[30] Updates from America did not establish beyond doubt what Jackson intended.[31] American news up to 26 July arrived on 6 August and was transmitted around Britain by "magnetic telegraph" (as was trumpeted by those newspaper editors who wished to emphasize the speed with which they could furnish readers with the latest information). Apparently, Jackson aimed either to draw off some of McClellan's troops or to clash with Pope in the Valley.[32] There was also speculation that he would cross into Maryland, where many people preferred the Confederacy to the Union.[33] In a letter to the *Times,* subsequently published in other papers, pro-southern activist James Spence opined that Jackson would certainly beat Pope in the field.[34]

Some British papers corrected another erroneous report of Jackson's death and stated that he was on his way to fight Pope.[35] But there was still uncertainty about his movements.[36] Anecdotal evidence summarized in the *Leeds Times* showed that there was alarm in Washington, and indeed in other northern cities, owing to gossip that the "daring" Jackson was approaching.[37] Soon there were more confident affirmations that Jackson would confront Pope.[38] A report from Boston dated 5 August suggested that Jackson could not withdraw and that Pope had to defeat him in order to continue the Federal advance.[39] The *Standard,* as usual, expected Jackson to win; the *Derby Mercury* passed on a rumor that Jackson had already attacked.[40]

The Battle of Cedar Mountain, on 9 August 1862, was the first important engagement in Pope's campaign in Virginia. Jackson decided to strike before the whole of Pope's army could join together close to his position.[41] A full picture was not available in Britain until the first week of September.[42] In the meantime, early accounts of Cedar Mountain were short on detail, which encouraged plenty of guesswork.[43] The battle was thought by some to have been inconclusive because Jackson had retreated south and the Federals had also been obliged to pull back.[44] That Pope was pursuing Jackson was denied.[45] The *Westmorland Gazette* stressed Pope's reputation for exaggeration and vanity. How could his version of the battle—in which Jackson had been defeated—be accepted?[46]

Northern sources, as featured in the *Freeman's Journal,* argued that Jackson's prestige had been damaged.[47] But the theory that Jackson had "fled . . . under cover of the night" was ridiculed by the *Standard,* and the *Liverpool*

Mercury suggested that if the battle was a draw, the Confederates were in a better position to renew the fighting when it suited them.[48] Pointing to the withdrawal of McClellan's army from the Peninsula, many British commentators surmised that the Federals had lost the initiative. Jackson's victory at Cedar Mountain was taken as further proof.[49] In the *Liverpool Mercury,* a comparison was made with the Battle of Bussaco, on 27 September 1810, during the Peninsular War, when Wellington, occupying high ground, defeated the French on the plain below and retreated to strong defensive lines in good order. It appeared that Jackson had done the same.[50] Admiration for his "daring enterprise and successful valor" was spreading, even into British India.[51] A contrary view was taken by papers favorable to the Union.[52]

As was normally the case after Jackson fought a battle, British newspapers contributed to his mystique by discussing his options. Different reports had him in different places. The *Belfast Newsletter* remarked that "the secrecy and celerity of his movements are almost a guarantee of his success when he comes to strike the next blow."[53] It emerged that Lincoln had ordered the Army of the Potomac to reinforce Pope's Army of Virginia. Pro-southerners declared that Pope and McClellan, together or apart, did not have the beating of Jackson. The *Manchester Courier* predicted a major battle "in which it is not unlikely that Jackson will ... play a conspicuous part."[54] According to the *Bucks Herald,* Jackson would attack Pope before he could be reinforced.[55]

Pope went down to defeat at Second Manassas at the end of August 1862. British newspapers focused on Jackson's role. Some scorned the "dishonest" statements put forth by Pope, the U.S. government, and some northern papers, all designed to hide the magnitude of the Confederates' victory. After claiming that he was about to crush his enemy, declared the *Leeds Times,* Pope had been seen off by "the sleepless and mysterious Jackson."[56] A private telegram received on 9 September by "one of the first commercial men in Liverpool," from New York via Quebec, stated that Jackson was approaching Washington.[57]

More details emerged to solidify Jackson's reputation. He had "swooped down ... like a hawk among a brood of chickens" to capture the supply depot at Manassas Junction. He had "completely outmaneuvered" Pope in the field.[58] Pope was subsequently transferred, and the Army of Virginia merged with McClellan's Army of the Potomac.[59]

After reporting on Second Manassas, British newspapers followed the Confederate advance into the North. Various commentators claimed to discern a plan, though there was no general agreement. Did Jackson mean to take Washington or Baltimore or Philadelphia, or was he out to destroy railroads, or by moving between Federal armies, was he intending to cut off their supplies and communications?[60] Benjamin Moran, secretary at the U.S. Legation in London, was pessimistic. On 17 September 1862, he wrote in his journal: "That dashing fellow 'Stonewall' Jackson has invaded Maryland . . . I am absolutely heart sick. Our men are brave, God knows; but our commanders are imbeciles." Three days later, he wrote of "another ship in with bad news." Jackson was in Pennsylvania. "The effect here . . . is to make those who were our friends ashamed to own the fact."[61]

Differing stories circulated. The pro-northern *Reynolds's Newspaper* anticipated the fall of Washington (a punishment for the error committed by the North at the outset of the war—the failure to abolish slavery).[62] The *Standard*'s correspondent Manhattan wrote that New Yorkers would welcome Jackson if he reached their city.[63] Details emerged about Jackson's victory at Harpers Ferry, on 12–15 September 1862, after which his troops had reportedly displayed the U.S. flag in Maryland and called for restoration of the Union under the "old constitution." The *Morning Post* stated that if this was so, southern leaders were seeking a way to rejoin the Union on favorable terms. Alternatively, they wanted Maryland to secede.[64] The Federals' inability to "catch" Jackson was the subject of jokes in *Fun*, and there were further accounts of panic across the North.[65]

Soon the British public learned of the Battle of Sharpsburg, on 17 September 1862, and the Confederate withdrawal from Maryland.[66] Commentators who were favorable to the North welcomed a "brilliant success" for McClellan, while pro-southern papers emphasized that Jackson and Lee had shown their talents once again, mounting an excellent campaign and proving that they could carry the war to the enemy. Much was made of the Confederates' "remarkably adroit" withdrawal, supervised by Jackson, with wagons and artillery mostly intact and few losses in men and equipment. In these narratives, McClellan did not pursue because he was afraid that Jackson would pounce. Indeed, Jackson *wanted* him to move south. The desire was to draw the Federals into the Shenandoah Valley, where Jackson "knows every inch of the ground."[67] The *Morning Post* published what purported to be a Confederate soldier's eyewitness account of recent engagements, and the *Essex Standard* argued that Jackson's victory at Harpers Ferry was "a brilliant episode in the expedition."[68] *Punch* quipped that nothing on earth was faster than northern troops falling back from an encounter with Jackson.[69]

A correspondent of the (strongly anti-Confederate) *New York Tribune* wrote a report from McClellan's camp, which later appeared in the British press and served to enhance Jackson's reputation as a soldier. Jackson had been in the Confederates' center and, "as usual, did most of the hard fighting, and it will be remembered that the rebel center we did not budge. The right and left we almost annihilated." But the report focused mainly on Jackson's masterly "escape" from Maryland. In the same vein, a letter from Manhattan dated 26 September included a critique of the Union's generals, so consistently outclassed by Jackson. Manhattan envisaged a restored Union in which southern rights were respected and saw in Jackson—"the only hero that this war has produced"—a future president.[70]

As for Lincoln regarding Sharpsburg as a justification for issuing the preliminary Emancipation Proclamation on 22 September, British commentators gave a mixed response. There was also some discussion of the idea that Jackson might be a suitable peace envoy to Washington.[71] It became clear that the Confederate retreat not only allowed Lincoln to seize a political opportunity; it also meant that Britain would not join in a French proposal for international mediation to broker a peace settlement in America.[72] The war would go on. Yet Jackson was not thought to be preparing to cross back into Maryland, and it did not appear that McClellan wished to move south.[73] American news up to 22 October (mostly reports from Boston and New York) confirmed that Jackson had made camp at Bunker Hill, about fifteen miles from the Maryland line, with Lee a short distance to the southeast.[74] Manhattan, in a piece for the *Standard*, described a mood of "disgrace, defeat, and almost despair" in the North. If, as rumored, McClellan was to lose his command, the *Westmorland Gazette* did not expect his successor—whoever he was—to overcome Jackson.[75] McClellan's replacement as general-in-chief of the Army of the Potomac was Ambrose Burnside. British papers highlighted the instability in the U.S. government and high command and assumed that Burnside would be pushed into a rapid offensive. Jackson would probably get behind him and take Washington.[76]

Later reports indicated that Burnside had ordered his forces to concentrate at a bend in the Potomac River, near the town of Fredericksburg, about thirty-five miles south of Washington and sixty miles from Richmond. Jackson's British followers expected him to make one of his "astonishing" appearances. As the *Leeds Times* put it, "There is really no knowing where he may turn up and what damage he may do."[77]

Manhattan wrote from New York on 25 November that Jackson would move on Washington.[78] Still, British newspapers noted "conflicting" reports.[79] Some found it strange that the Federals, surprised by Jackson so many times before, were not trying harder to locate him. The *Liverpool Mercury* stressed that many of Burnside's troops were accustomed to defeat at the hands of Jackson.[80]

The movements of Jackson were assumed to have a bearing on Lincoln's approach to slavery. There was talk of a constitutional amendment and of compensation schemes, but the *Glasgow Herald* argued that the course of the war would determine how, when, and if abolition was implemented. Jackson, not Lincoln, would be the shaper of events. Even if the Union were restored, could Lincoln get individual states to agree to emancipation? This seemed unlikely, not least because of the example of post-emancipation economic decline in the British West Indies.[81]

Reports from North and South made it plain that Confederate forces were massing to deny the Army of the Potomac a path to Richmond. It was still not clear where the "ubiquitous" Jackson was, but it appeared that his most likely course would be to join Lee in shielding Richmond.[82] American news up to 5 December confirmed that the "celebrated" Jackson was definitely with Lee at Fredericksburg.[83] The New York correspondent of the *Daily News* later mentioned Burnside's move to cross the Rappahannock at Port Conway, which Jackson had prevented.[84]

The Confederates won the Battle of Fredericksburg of 11–15 December 1862.[85] American news up to 17 December arrived in Queenstown (Cobh) on 28 December, and transatlantic steamers also reached the Mersey on 27 and 28 December. The larger cities across Britain received news of the battle by special express from Liverpool. Some accounts included Jackson's "narrow escape"—a bullet had missed him by inches—and some emphasized the recriminations in the North following the defeat.[86]

It was suggested that Jackson might attack the retreating Federals on the north side of the Rappahannock and end the war with the "virtual annihilation" of the Army of the Potomac, but most commentators thought that he and Lee would remain where they were, knowing that their defensive line was sound, that Richmond was safe, and that the Federals could do nothing until the spring. In the North, meanwhile, more people were turning against the war, and political confusion increased as the Democratic Party gained strength.[87] In the South, morale was high. One report, from "the Special Southern Correspondent of *The Times*," highlighted the "aura of success" surrounding Jackson.[88] British admiration for him surged again when telegrams arrived via steamer in Queenstown on 10 January 1863. Jackson had taken many prisoners after an "ambuscade" at Stafford, Virginia.[89] The *Bradford Observer*, citing several sources, deemed it significant that Jackson's heroism was acknowledged even by his northern enemies.[90] The *Times* expected that U.S. operations would continue to be hampered because troops had to be kept back to protect Washington from Jackson.[91]

The spring of 1863 was another period for speculation. Many accounts had Jackson remaining near the Rappahannock, and many others advancing along the Shenandoah Valley.[92] At the end of April, it was reported that Jackson had marched north. The *Dundee Courier* expected a drive through Maryland and did not have a high opinion of Joseph Hooker, who had taken command of the Army of the Potomac in January 1863.[93] A report from New York, dated 29 April, appeared in several British newspapers eleven days later to the effect that Jackson had captured a section of the Baltimore and Ohio Railroad. There were sightings of him close to the Pennsylvania state line.[94] The pro-North *Leeds Mercury*, unimpressed by Jackson's "sudden" appearance, asserted that Hooker would take Richmond.[95] But from Dublin, the editor of the *Freeman's Journal*, John Blake Gallaher, announcing that Jackson was "again in motion after a long inactivity," pointed to the alarm he had caused in the U.S. government and high command, where there was furious quarreling about the allocation of Federal troops. Jackson's presence in the borderlands made the idea of a Federal move on Richmond ridiculous, according to the *Lancaster Gazette*.[96]

Hooker did move south, but he was decisively beaten at the Battle of Chancellorsville of 30 April to 6 May 1863. Vastly outnumbered, Lee defied military logic and divided his forces in the face of a larger enemy, with Jackson moving around the Federal army and surprising its right flank, which crumbled in confusion.[97] As reports began to arrive, it appeared that Jackson had been wounded, although the details were not clear. Since in the past, he had "been killed several times by the Northern press," readers were advised to wait for verification rather than jump to conclusions.[98] Soon there was more up-to-date intelligence. American news to 6 May arrived on 16 May, and news up to 7 May arrived on 21 May. Jackson, it could be confirmed, had been wounded during the first three days of the battle. He had led a "bold flank movement" and fell upon the Federal right, "routing" it with a "desperate charge." Hooker had sent in fresh troops to prevent total collapse but not Confederate victory.[99]

To the pro-southern *Dundee Courier,* "Jackson's rush" at Chancellorsville proved once again that he was a fearless and audacious general.[100] The *Nottinghamshire Guardian* mistakenly reported that his injuries were minor. It added: "With so much depending on his safety, it is remarkable that he continues to risk his life in these thundering shocks."[101]

The foregoing summary indicates that most discussion of Jackson in British publications between the spring of 1862 and summer 1863 concerned his talent for soldiering. The coverage was overwhelmingly positive. The majority verdict ran something like this: Jackson had a profound understanding of modern warfare; his tactical flair and grasp of strategy were superb; he saw that success required action and movement, and being keen to attack and destroy, he was not a general who was content to fall back, dig trenches, and call for reinforcements. He had outfought every commander the North sent against him.

A sketch of Jackson in the *New York Tribune* was reprinted in British papers in July 1862, just as news was arriving about the Seven Days Battles. This proved to be a foundational piece, upon which many later descriptions of Jackson were based. The author was John Williamson Palmer, who was rumored to be a Confederate spy.[102] One of its interesting revelations was that Jackson's brilliance as a general was recognized by his own people, the people of the Valley, before it was appreciated by his political superiors in Richmond. But the latter came to value him, too, and in the Valley Campaign, he proved himself to be the best of all the Confederacy's field commanders.[103] Joining Lee in defense of Richmond, he showed his qualities again in the battles that prompted McClellan to retreat. Jackson was "remarkable," "dashing," and "clever."[104] It was a mark of his genius that he managed to keep the enemy unaware of his plans and movements. He was unpredictable and energetic, and the North had to keep troops back to cover any eventuality. He was "the Confederate Cromwell."[105]

If Cromwell was an apt comparison for some, others preferred to laud Jackson by likening him to more recent figures. They deemed his capabilities to be on a par with those of Wellington and Napoleon. He could make "one small army do the work of six," and the North had nobody like him. "All the

Federal commanders are, tried by the European standard, very far beneath mediocrity," while the South had "military leaders worthy of taking rank with those of any country"—not only Jackson but also Lee, Joseph Johnston, and P.G.T. Beauregard.[106] Jackson was the most "aggressive" and "brave and energetic."[107] His role in Second Manassas made his "audacity and genius" even clearer.[108]

There was no stopping this "daring and adventurous" general who was "always the foremost in attack."[109] His greatness rested in part on the way he trained and led his troops. Indeed, his bravery and talent and the character shown by his men helped to explain why so many in Britain hoped that the South would win the war. "Not a few of their exploits partake of the romance and chivalry of an age long gone by." Jackson was "a cross between Cromwell and the First Napoleon—resembling the Puritan general in his eagle-perception of the weak point of his opponent, and the great Corsican in the hidden celerity of his movements."[110]

From September 1862, British readers had access to an account of Jackson's career written by the New York correspondent of the *Times*. Numerous other papers used this account, printing extracts and adding comment (and it served as another foundation for later assessments of Jackson). It mentioned that northerners were fascinated by him, all the more so when they realized he had been in the same year as McClellan at West Point. (McClellan graduated second out of fifty-nine students in the class of 1846, and Jackson was seventeenth, but having overcome early difficulties with unusual industry and dedication, many of his peers believed that had he stayed another year, he would have been top of the class.) This account made much of Jackson's effective partnership with Lee, stated that Jackson's successes would be analyzed by military students for decades to come, and argued that comparisons with Hannibal, as well as Cromwell, were not out of place.[111]

Another comparison made during 1862 was with Italian patriot Giuseppe Garibaldi. The cause of Italian unification had considerable support in Britain, but Garibaldi's march on Rome in August 1862 prompted mixed feelings. The *Belfast Newsletter* suggested that if Garibaldi wanted so much to fight, he ought to go to America and don the Confederate gray. He and Jackson would be an irresistible combination.[112] Over the following weeks, attention centered on Garibaldi but even more on Jackson "because he appears to be the only dashing soldier the Civil War in America has produced."[113] There was a negative response to a letter published in Britain, apparently from Garibaldi to the U.S. consul in Vienna, in which the Italian stated his preference for the North against the South.[114]

The most notable feature of the Maryland Campaign was thought to be Jackson's capture of Harpers Ferry, and there was warm praise for his well-managed withdrawal from Maryland. The "thunderbolt of war" was also cool in retreat, "as good a general in directing a backward march as he is in conducting an advance." It was telling, moreover, that McClellan did not follow.[115] McClellan was simply incapable of beating Jackson, as were Mc-Clellan's replacements.[116] The Jackson legend was furthered by anecdotes, including that concerning a Welshman named Roberts, who had served in the Federal ranks. Roberts confessed that his own commanding officer was scared of Jackson.[117]

This theme—fear of Jackson—became a favorite. Whenever it appeared that a large Federal army was about to move south, invariably there were reports of apprehension in the North lest Jackson circled behind it to attack Washington.[118] As master of the element of surprise, Jackson knew how to create and exploit fear. He used uncertainty as a weapon.[119]

Summarizing accounts of Jackson taken from various sources, the *Nottinghamshire Guardian* stated that the qualities attributed to him might strike some as bizarre. Who could have foretold that this rather slow and modest student at West Point would go on to elicit "universal wonder and admiration"?[120] A writer in the *Army and Navy Gazette*, whose remarks were subsequently carried in other publications, characterized Jackson as "bold aggression."[121] At the end of 1862, several British newspapers published long retrospective pieces that described significant events of the previous year. Jackson's victories were highlighted.[122] Fredericksburg mattered most to some commentators, for it showed the world "true generalship." Burnside had not done the essential thing: he failed to keep a careful check on Jackson's movements.[123]

Many British newspapers made use of the impressions of a "special correspondent" of the *Times*, Frank Lawley, who wrote about Jackson and other Confederate generals in November 1862, when he visited their camps in Virginia. Lawley's account was first published at the end of December 1862, and it provided a basis for later sketches of Jackson by others.[124] Lawley gave an appreciation of Jackson's preferred tactics, as perfected in the Valley. He would send his men, disregarding their inferiority in numbers, into battle with a larger enemy, and "the day is ordinarily half won by the suddenness and desperation of the attack." Then he would withdraw. The Federals' anxiety would give way to relief, and some northern journalists would get ahead of themselves and claim a Federal victory. But soon, at a moment of his choosing, Jackson would attack again. Sometimes, if the enemy forces knew he was coming, they would retreat without fighting.[125] British interest in Jackson—and admiration for his generalship—was kept up by material provided by visitors to the battlefields where Jackson had distinguished himself. One such visitor, in late 1862, was William Carson Corsan, a hardware merchant from Sheffield, whose business interests had prompted him to journey through the South. In 1863, after returning home, he published *Two Months in the Confederate States, by an English Merchant*, sections of which soon appeared in British newspapers.[126]

As more became known about Chancellorsville, some decided it was Jackson's finest hour. He was just as important to the Confederacy, they declared, as Cromwell had been to the parliamentarian cause in Britain in the 1640s. Jackson's tendency to place himself in danger reminded others of Garibaldi. Whether or not he was another Cromwell or another Garibaldi, he was unquestionably a better general than Hooker. Jackson was the bolder and a superior tactician, and he was a more effective leader of men because he understood them, knew their capabilities, and could inspire them to give their all.[127]

For all the praise, however, there was also negative comment. Pro-northern papers could not leave Jackson's British reputation uncontested. In October 1862, for example, *Reynolds's Newspaper* insisted that southern generals were not as talented and successful as was claimed. Jackson was overrated, just like the rest, and all the glamor and fame attaching to him would prove ephemeral.[128]

There were different stories about how he got his nickname. Even the more accurate ones had details incorrect.[129] Still, the name Stonewall was taken to verify both his importance as a warrior and his popularity. In British accounts, he was idolized by the southern people, his own troops loved him, and he was highly respected even in the North.

It was generally understood that the Valley Campaign made Jackson the South's national hero. His victories bolstered the people's willingness to fight on, to make sacrifices for the cause, and to adhere to patriotic duty.[130] To some in Britain, the key to Jackson's success was his ability to inspire the men under his command. He demanded much from them, but they never failed to rise to the task he gave them. They followed him because they trusted him, and while he led them, he also lived like them (and prayed with them). He had no airs. He dressed as they did and ate the same food.[131] Jackson's army demonstrated the merits of "economy," for "a pampered army is not necessarily the most efficient."[132]

One of the most influential and widely quoted pieces that underlined Jackson's hold over his men appeared in *Blackwood's Magazine* in January 1863. Its author was a British officer, Lt. Col. Garnet Wolseley, future commander in chief of the British Army but then on attachment to a unit in Canada, where he had been sent at the time of the *Trent* affair. While in the South, he traveled for a time with newspaper writer Frank Lawley.[133] Wolseley visited the Confederate camps in Virginia during September and October 1862. Extracts from and comments upon his account appeared in many British newspapers, satisfying the demand for more information about Jackson (and no doubt increasing that appetite as well). Wolseley was struck by the special connection between Jackson and his troops. The general had trained them hard and taught them discipline and devotion. They would follow him anywhere. "I believe that, inspired by the presence of such a man, I should be perfectly insensible to fatigue and reckon upon success as a moral certainty."[134]

Even in the North, Jackson was admired. British newspapers frequently made this point. In August 1862, for instance, a story did the rounds illustrating the "despotism" of the Lincoln administration, which was punishing individuals who had openly expressed respect for Jackson.[135] The *Lancaster Gazette* was amused as northern journalists tried in vain to find a hero on the Federal side.[136]

What kind of man was he? Jackson's rapid rise to fame in Britain created a desire for details about him personally. In the early coverage of Jackson in the British press, mention was often made of his religious faith. This added to his appeal, in the minds of many, although there were commentators who denied that his Christian fervor made him a suitable recipient of British admiration. This disagreement reflected contemporary religious, political, and social tensions in Britain. It is not surprising that Jackson's religiosity brought out a range of responses, for Victorian Britain was a place of controversy on matters of faith. Divisions within the Church of England, the growing assertiveness of Nonconformists, the formation of new denominations, the claims of science and new learning, and the pursuit of alternatives to organized Christianity pushed Victorians to accommodate variety in doctrine and practice.

The sketch of Jackson in the *New York Tribune,* reprinted in British papers in July 1862, emphasized that he was a deeply religious man, "the bluest kind of Presbyterian, and extremely strict in his church observances." During his period of residence in Lexington, from 1851, when he accepted a teaching post at the Virginia Military Institute, "he took a very active part in revivals" and "habitually" led prayer meetings.[137] The New York correspondent of the *Times* supplied statements about the general as an overtly devout and prayerful person.[138] In October 1862, some newspapers reported Jackson's appointment (in July) as a life director of the Bible Society of the Confederate States. The *Essex Standard* went on to discuss Jackson's prayers before battle, his habit of invoking God's blessing in his dispatches and attributing his victories to God, and the prayer meetings he organized in camp for his troops.[139]

By the end of 1862, pieces about Jackson in the British press routinely mentioned his strong religious faith, at least in passing. Some writers went further, describing, for instance, his efforts to set a high moral tone among his staff. He liked to be around other devout Christians. One of his chief aides was the Presbyterian pastor and Calvinist theologian Robert Lewis Dabney, a professor at Union Theological Seminary in Richmond. (Dabney, a future biographer of Jackson, was the general's adjutant from April to August 1862.) An article in the *Presbyterian,* a denominational magazine published in Philadelphia, subsequently carried in British periodicals, included Dabney and Jackson in an account of "ministers in the American armies."[140]

Garnet Wolseley's article in *Blackwood's Magazine* in January 1863 reinforced the impression that Jackson was a spiritual stalwart before he was anything else: "He is a person who never loses sight of the fact that there is an omnipresent Deity ever presiding over the minutest occurrences of life."[141] This was repeated in other publications over the following months and years. Jackson had fully entrusted himself to God. He had a stoicism and fearlessness, particularly in combat, and was unconcerned about his own safety.[142] On visiting Jackson's camp, Frank Lawley noted the general's "unaffected earnestness and piety" and related stories about him praying in battle and raising his hands to God. The general's black servant, Jim Lewis, knew when a battle was coming because Jackson would spend the preceding night on his knees in his tent. Reports such as these gave British readers who were ready to think well of Jackson all the more reason for doing so.[143]

The bond became closer as readers learned more about Jackson's visit to Britain in 1856. When Wolseley met him, Jackson "talked most affectionately of England." York Minster and its windows, stonework, and organ so stirred his religious sensibilities that he often spoke about it afterward. Lawley stated that in his conversation with Jackson, "his heartiest and most enthusiastic utterances were in admiration of the cathedral edifices of England."[144]

In March 1863, the *Sheffield Independent* published a letter from an anonymous southern woman, residing in Florida, to friends in England. It is possible that the letter was fictitious and inserted for propaganda purposes since this newspaper was pro-southern. But whether genuine or false, it does show that Jackson was being presented—and that supporters of the South wished him to be viewed—in a way that made the most of his Christianity. The letter described Jackson's religious commitment and emphasized such commitment as one of the main characteristics of the Confederacy, distinguishing it from the North.[145]

Jackson was fastidious as well as fervent. He opposed the carrying of mail on the Sabbath, and when he heard that the Confederate Congress was to consider repealing the law that required mail to be carried on Sundays, he wrote to his friend Col. Alexander Boteler, representative for Virginia's Tenth District and a former member of Jackson's staff, urging him to vote for repeal. This letter, written in December 1862 (a few days before the Battle of Fredericksburg), later appeared in the British press to buttress Jackson's reputation as a man of faith. "I do not see how a nation that thus arrays itself by such a law against God's holy day can expect to escape His wrath," Jackson wrote.[146]

On 9 April 1863, a "very crowded" meeting of the Liverpool Southern Club was addressed by Rev. Moses D. Hoge of the Second Presbyterian Church, Richmond, who was touring Britain to raise money and obtain Bibles and prayer books for Confederate soldiers. During his speech, Hoge described the religious devotion of his friend Jackson (who attended Hoge's church whenever he was in Richmond). In camp, Jackson's influence was such as to reduce vice and immorality in the ranks. He was "as well-known" to his troops as a Christian as he was in the character of a "brave and efficient" commander.[147]

Before Hoge spoke in Liverpool, he was in Manchester, where his remarks were not so effective. At the annual meeting of the local branch of the Religious Tract Society, it had been resolved that any gift of books would have to be accompanied with a formal declaration against slavery. It was not enough for Hoge to emphasize the piety of Jackson, the meeting decided, and whatever was given to the Confederates should also be given to the Federals.[148]

Some British commentators, far from commending Jackson as a faithful Christian, saw him as a hypocrite who colluded in sin. In a widely reported Sunday sermon of 28 December 1862, Rev. George Gilfillan, author, poet, and Presbyterian minister in Dundee, said that there was no excuse for slavery. Jackson made war "in behalf of the one most diabolical plant of hell that existed in this world," and "the sympathy felt for him by many in this country was disgraceful to it."[149] The *Caledonian Mercury* insisted that Jackson could not be a true Christian. He was fighting to defend slavery and thought slavery had God's approval.[150] This was a sticking point for many. At a meeting in Birkenhead in January 1863, speakers who professed to admire Jackson and the South nevertheless assumed that the war was about slavery. The honest Christian, they argued, wished for the North to win.[151] Gilfillan told an audience in Arbroath that Jackson was a blasphemer if he held that the Bible sanctioned slavery.[152]

Jackson appears not to have questioned slavery. He accepted it, probably because he did not find in the Bible an explicit prohibition, but he was not stridently proslavery in sentiment, and he did not regard the war as a conflict over slavery. He wanted slaves to be educated so that they could read the Bible. His household in Lexington during the 1850s included six slaves, and he ran a Sunday school for local slaves.[153]

Admired as a dynamic military genius or an earnest Christian exemplar, or both, the demand for personal information about Jackson did not diminish. Newspapers began to describe his character and appearance. For some, his glory reflected well on Britain. They made much of his ancestry, expressing the pride of association: "The famous Confederate general is of Anglo-Scotch descent."[154] From July 1862, a great many British newspapers reprinted or carried extracts from the account of Jackson first published in the *New York Tribune* by the pro-Confederate J. W. Palmer:

> He looks at least seven years older than he is—his height about 5 feet 10 inches; his figure thick set, high shouldered and decidedly clumsy; his gait very awkward, stooping, and with long strides. He often walks with his head somewhat on one side, and his eyes fixed upon the ground, im-

parting to his whole appearance that abstracted quality which young ladies describe as "absent-minded." A lady who has known him long and
well has told me that she never saw him on horseback without laughing—
short stirrups, knees cramped up, heels stuck out behind, and chin on
his breast—a most unmilitary phenomenon. In society he is quiet, but
cheerful; not loquacious, but intelligent and shrewd.[155]

Another sketch of Jackson, taken from the *Savannah News*, also played its
part in shaping the impression that British readers formed. Its writer, who
claimed to have observed Jackson during the Seven Days Battles, highlighted his "self-command, perseverance, indomitable will . . . without the
least admixture of vanity, assumacy, pride, foolhardiness, or anything of the
kind": "His face expresses courage in the highest degree, and his phrenologi-
cal developments indicate a vast amount of energy and activity. His forehead
is broad and prominent, the occipital and sincipital regions are both large
and well balanced; eyes expressing a singular union of mildness, energy, and
concentration; cheek and nose both long and well formed." In dress and gait,
Jackson had "magnificent plainness." He rose above his fellow officers with
their braided uniforms and military swagger.[156]

Remarks about Jackson by the New York correspondent of the *Times*
were widely repeated, including those that illustrated curious personality
traits—that he had not been a bright student at West Point; that he was
given to hypochondria; that his diet was, by choice, rigid and sparse; and
that, on campaign, he dressed not like a general but like his troops.[157] Some
British newspapers began quite often to mention Jackson's supposed oddi-
ties of character, especially his untidy appearance. He seemed unconcerned
about dress and deportment.[158] None of this could convince Jackson's admirers that he was unworthy of praise. To them, his dress was unimportant. He
did not seek—or have any need—to impress in that way. What mattered was
his inner nobility. The instructive comparison here was with "Beast" Butler,
whose conduct while U.S. military governor in occupied New Orleans in
1862 had scandalized all right-minded observers.[159]

By December 1862, there was enough material available about Jackson
to put together a full portrait. The *Nottinghamshire Guardian* did just that,
encouraging further discussion of Jackson's personality, dress, and manner-
isms. His was the story of an overcomer, for in his younger days, he had
not shown much promise.[160] Yet how well could British people really know

Jackson? There were plenty of errors and misunderstandings. For example, the *Illustrated London News* had his middle name wrong (Jefferson instead of Jonathan) and his date of birth wrong (1825 instead of 1824) and implied that he was married to a northern woman, which had made it difficult for him to join the southern army. In this account, his father-in-law tried to talk him out of it, but Jackson had decided that his duty was to his state, Virginia. In fact, Jackson's first wife, Elinor Junkin, who was originally from Pennsylvania, had died in 1854, and it was in Virginia that the two had met, married, and settled. Jackson married his second wife, Mary Anna Morrison, in 1857. She was from North Carolina. It is true that Elinor's father, George Junkin, a Presbyterian clergyman and theologian much respected by Jackson, opposed secession and moved to the North when war broke out and urged Jackson not to turn against the Union. But the way this was covered in the *Illustrated London News* was only partly accurate, as was the explanation of the Stonewall nickname.[161] George Junkin's association with Jackson made him a figure of some interest to the British public. Manhattan thought it worthwhile to mention in November 1862 that "Stonewall Jackson's father-in-law" had recently preached in New York.[162]

Descriptions of Jackson and anecdotes about him continued to circulate. There were more remarks about his unkempt and muddy uniform and clumsy riding style.[163] The Jackson that emerged from Wolseley's piece in *Blackwood's Magazine* was an engaging, intelligent person. Wolseley found him "very affable, having been led to expect that he was silent and almost morose." In appearance, "he looks the hero that he is; and his thin compressed lips and calm glance, which meets yours unflinchingly, give evidence of that firmness and decision of character for which he is so famous."[164]

There was a similarly positive portrayal from the *Times* correspondent Frank Lawley. Jackson was "the most genial, courteous, and forthcoming of companions." He was "passionately attached" to the Shenandoah Valley, where he was the subject of adulation, and his officers also revered him. But how long could he go on? "Sinewy and wiry as the General seems, it is impossible not to fancy that he is wearing himself terribly by his restless sleepless activity, by his midnight marches, and by the asceticism of his life." Since there had been differing accounts of how he had come by his nickname, Lawley wanted to set the record straight. In order to embolden his own men, hard-pressed at First Manassas on 21 July 1861, Gen. Barnard Bee of South Carolina, in command of a brigade in the Army of the Shenandoah under Joseph Johnston, pointed to Jackson's brigade in formation on a nearby hill and called out: "Look at Jackson's men—they stand like a stone wall! Rally behind the Virginians!" P.G.T. Beauregard, who was Johnston's second-in-command, used a similar phrase in his report of the battle, "and the name has clung to General Jackson ever since." Lawley believed that Jackson, a brave and dutiful patriot, would wish to fight while there was still fighting to be done. Then he would stop. "A most undemonstrative, reticent man, doubtless, in all that regards his vocation as a soldier, there is every reason to think that, when the war is over, General Jackson will be the very first man to bury himself in the deepest obscurity of private life."[165]

Accounts of Jackson sent home by British nationals who had enlisted in the Confederate army were of special interest. There were not many, but to the extent that they commented on Jackson's appearance and character, they backed up the existing pattern of reportage.[166] Jackson's British reputation was also enhanced by numerous pictures, songs, mementos, and artifacts. In September 1862 in London, there was a much-publicized display of portraits, photographs, and artwork showing scenes and celebrities of America, sent from the studio of New York artist and photographer Mathew B. Brady. The London correspondent of the *Sheffield Independent* visited the exhibition and wrote that Jackson's imposing and affecting likeness reminded him of Marshal Ney, the French commander of the Revolutionary and Napoleonic Wars, dubbed by Napoleon "the bravest of the brave."[167] Engravings of Jackson were included in periodicals to broaden their appeal. The *Illustrated Times, Penny Illustrated Paper,* and *Illustrated London News* all attracted patrons in this way.[168] Attention was given to busts and statuettes, though it was some time before these were available in Britain.[169]

Songwriters began to make use of Jackson's name and fame. He was mentioned in the "Serenade to Lincoln," published in the satirical magazine *Punch* and other periodicals from October 1862. The lyrics carried the suggestion that Lincoln would emancipate the South's slaves in revenge for Jackson's victories in battle.[170] Several British papers published a poem, "My Wife and Child," allegedly written by Jackson while he was serving in the Mexican War in 1846–48. It told of a soldier missing his loved ones and asking God to watch over them.[171] Yet Jackson was neither a husband nor a father at the time of the Mexican War. When he received an inquiry about the poem, he denied authorship.[172]

Jackson's profile in Britain was kept up by discussion of persons and objects named in his honor. Pro-southern writers sometimes combined their eulogies of Jackson with excuses for slavery. They were able to do so in part because some slave children had been named after Jackson.[173] As for specific British examples of naming after Jackson, these included an Aberdeenshire pedigree bull, a Blackburn factory engine, a racehorse, and a boat that competed in the Glasgow Royal Regatta of September 1862.[174] Looking back on the cricket season of 1862, the *Sporting Gazette* singled out the batting of E. M. Grace, of Gloucestershire, whose "system of attack and defense is so varied, brilliant, and effective that we must term him the Stonewall Jackson of the cricket field."[175] Several British papers followed the career of the blockade-runner *Stonewall Jackson* (formerly the *Leopard*, a British side-wheel steam packet).[176]

Jackson's name often came up in British political contention as it was affected by the course of the war in America. He featured in quarrels about the causes of the war, the rights and wrongs of secession, and slavery; the propriety of formal recognition of the Confederacy as an independent sovereign nation; the difficult relationship between the British and U.S. governments; British intervention, possibly as part of an international mediation effort; and the impact of the war on Britain, especially the textile districts. Jackson's name was also used at election time and in local politics.

In July 1862, as it became clear that Jackson had helped to push McClellan away from Richmond, it was commonly argued that the North could not win the war and that Britain and the European powers should act to stop the bloodshed.[177] On 18 July, when the House of Commons debated a resolution for British mediation, one of the speakers was Conservative MP for County Galway W. H. Gregory, a landowner and travel writer who had visited "every state in the South" in 1860. That southerners approved of secession, he said, had been proven on American battlefields through "the arguments of that inexorable logician, General Stonewall Jackson."[178] Gregory would be among the promoters of a monument to Jackson in later years.

Claims that the South could not be conquered and that there must be intervention to arrange peace talks were reinforced by the testimony of war correspondent Frank Vizetelly. He wrote for the *Illustrated London News* (the world's first illustrated weekly news magazine when it was established in 1842), which by 1862–63 was selling three hundred thousand copies a week, a huge circulation compared to other British periodicals. Vizetelly composed a much-cited piece in July 1862 in which he reported that in all the places he had been in the South, he found unanimity on the matter of secession. This was why U.S. commanders on campaign in Virginia could find nobody willing to inform them about Jackson's movements.[179] In a letter to the *Morning Post*, "Fair Play" insisted that the Confederacy had the characteristics of an independent nation: a government and an army; a loyal population; a clearly defined territory; a sense of identity; a public life that bore comparison with Europe's; and a national hero, Jackson, one of the "names that will live in history."[180]

By this time, Jackson's heroic status could not be denied. In the Athenaeum Club, Pall Mall, frequented by affluent professionals and men of distinction in science, literature, and the arts, wagers were being made that Washington would fall before Richmond, mainly on the basis that Federal generals were no match for Jackson. This was also the opinion of British visitors to America who had returned home and of Americans who were visiting London.[181] At the Stoke-upon-Trent by-election of September 1862, Beresford Hope was not slow to identify himself with Jackson: "Mr. Hope assured the electors that he was that General Stonewall Jackson who would lead them to victory." To laughter and applause, he likened the other candidates to the northern generals Jackson had defeated.[182] American Civil War names and examples were now part of everyday parlance. These words had clear associations. British people knew what they meant. At a meeting to mark the reorganization of the Brentwood (Third Essex) Volunteer Rifle Corps, there were speeches about making it a "stone wall" akin to the command of Jackson. At the annual dinner of the Colchester Conservative Association (known locally as the True Blue Club) in October 1862, one of the speakers expressed frustration that the Conservatives were still out of office. They had gained seats at the 1859 general election but still trailed Palmerston's governing coalition by more than fifty in the Commons. The Conservative Party had numbers, organization, and wealth but could not quite "cross the Potomac," partly because it lacked Jackson's "brilliant execution."[183]

Growing concern about the "cotton famine" also focused attention on Jackson. The American war had disrupted the supply from the South, and attempts to develop alternative sources were making little difference. Most observers agreed that southern cotton would become readily available if the Confederates won the war. This was where Jackson came in: he was the man to invade the North and force Washington to sue for peace.[184]

In summarizing articles on the American war in the "quality" periodicals (including the *Edinburgh Review* and *Saturday Review*), provincial newspapers were drawn further into discussion of Jackson and what he was fighting for. This raised questions about the guilt of slavery, the nature of northern aggression, and the constitutionality of secession from the Union.[185] Among London papers, the *Standard* regarded slavery as a matter for the individual states. The idea that Jackson was defending slavery, as if he were in the wrong, rather missed the point. Furthermore, while northern policy was "immoral and un-English," the Confederacy was to be admired as "a self-governing nation of English race and English temper," and its best values were personified in Jackson.[186] But "Our London Letter," written by a correspondent of the *Caledonian Mercury* in January 1863, took a different line on Jackson, as did a spoof report in *Fun* about Jackson and emancipation.[187]

During late 1862 and early 1863, there were a number of pieces on "English sympathy with slavery." It seemed to some observers that traditional British hatred of slavery had waned. Another view was that it had not waned. Rather, it coexisted with other sentiments, the most powerful of which were hostile to the North: shock and resentment over the *Trent* affair, for example, and respect for Jackson and "the simple faith of that praying captain." Still, several writers were convinced that a slave system needed a slave trade, as asserted in *The Slave Power* (1862), by economist John Elliott Cairnes, and in war correspondent William Howard Russell's *My Diary North and South* (1863). If this argument proved correct, it would put Britain and the Confederacy at odds.[188]

Pro-southerners were unmoved. When Beresford Hope lectured at the Corn Exchange, Maidstone, in January 1863, he denied that slavery had caused the American war. Hope believed that Jackson had risen to global prominence because he was leading a virtuous struggle.[189] This was not an uncommon position. Sections of the press repeatedly explained that British culture, history, and foreign policy all pointed toward emancipation, but the preference was for moral influence, and approving of Jackson was not the same as approving of slavery ("a character like that of Jackson will always charm a people who delight in gallantry and resolution"). But even if the South *was* fighting for slavery, the North could not count on British support. That northerners had resorted to "fire and sword" to get southerners to adopt their style of living was deplorable.[190] All this was balanced by the arguments of those who believed that Jackson was fighting in a bad cause.[191]

Jackson's British reputation was not greatly damaged by negative statements connecting him with slavery or any other divisive topic. In prosouthern circles, he remained a quintessential hero. American sources that praised him continued to be employed by British newspapers, and these were often merged with home-produced tributes. The *Sheffield Independent* was typical in presenting Jackson as the godly, courageous, and successful warrior and surrounding this material with broader discussion of the South and its prospects.[192]

By the spring of 1863, Jackson had been grabbing the headlines for many months. A witticism repeated in this period was that such was Jackson's celebrity, only the 10 March 1863 wedding of the glamorous Prince of Wales, twenty-one, to Alexandra of Denmark, eighteen, took attention away from him.[193] Jackson's decency and courage were stressed again in British responses to a speech given by Gen. Benjamin Butler in New York in April 1863.[194] Butler accused the British of abandoning their duty toward the United States.[195] The *Westmorland Gazette* and *Belfast Newsletter,* among others, took Butler's speech as indicative of northern arrogance.[196] When it was reported that British people living in the North were telling their neighbors that Britain was on their side, the *Lancaster Gazette* rejected the idea, pointing to the disenchantment that greeted news of Federal successes in battle and the strong expectation that Jackson would shortly seize Washington.[197]

Events took a different course. Wounded at Chancellorsville, Jackson would soon be dead. In London, Henry Adams, the son and private secretary of the U.S. minister to Britain, wrote that Jackson's death deprived the Confederacy of its best general. But such was his popularity in Britain and the strength of the pro-southern lobby that Adams saw an urgent need for a significant Federal victory, the only thing that would give the North influence over the British government and people.[198]

Jackson's British reputation was almost entirely positive. He had heroic status. Respected as a talented and courageous general and a devout Christian, impressive in physical appearance and even more in personal character, the qualities that Jackson was supposed to embody enabled him to strike a powerful chord among the British as they observed from afar the events taking place in America. They were captivated by him because he was a key player in the unfolding drama, and they became interested in him, too, for himself. For some, the fate of the South rested on his shoulders.

At the U.S. Legation in London, Benjamin Moran expressed relief that the results of Chancellorsville were not as bad as he had first thought. The Federals had made a safe retreat, and Jackson was "dead of wounds." But would Jackson's fame die too? "The British people are as sensibly affected by this last news as if the disaster were their own," Moran declared, "and some are already preparing to raise a statue for him." [199]

8

A REPUTATION SUSTAINED

Jackson was accidentally wounded at the Battle of Chancellorsville. He had been scouting ahead of the Confederate line on the evening of 2 May 1863 with a small retinue. As they returned, they were mistaken for Federal cavalry. Confederate soldiers opened fire, and Jackson was hit three times. He was taken to recuperate in a plantation office at Guinea Station, but pneumonia set in, and he died on 10 May. After his death, Jackson still influenced British opinion. There was no weakening of interest in him or falloff of discussion about him. The reasons why he had gained renown in Britain still mattered. If his character and accomplishments were worthy of respect before his untimely end, they remained topical for the rest of the American war.

There was continuing use of Jackson's name in British politics, at meetings, and by organizations in an effort to win approval for or in condemnation of measures and ideas with which he (however tenuously) could be associated. News of Jackson's death reached most parts of Britain on 26 May 1863. There were many manifestations of sorrow, especially in communities where friends of the South were numerous. Flags were flown at half-mast in Manchester and Stockport. In Liverpool, "this calamity has elicited warm sympathy . . . A proposal has been made to get up a testimonial here to his widow." A disseminator of "London Gossip" wrote that "all politics are at a standstill" and "Stonewall Jackson is universally lamented in the City." "Nothing can testify better to the esteem in which he was held than the fact that . . . the Confederate Loan has steadily declined." From across the Channel came an account of "the universal feeling of grief created among the English colony in Paris." Jackson reminded a correspondent of the *Standard* of Henry Havelock, the British general who had died in India in 1857 and was known as a religious man who gave Bibles to his troops and organized study groups and prayer meetings for them. There was more to the "sorrow" over Jackson than a reaction against the "arrogance and boasting" of the North, this writer explained. Support for the South arose mainly because of the quality of the Confederacy's leaders. It was impossible not to admire Jackson. His loss brought out the contrast between North and South, the latter having the advantage in political wisdom, military talent, and moral strength.[1]

Though Britain was neutral, it seemed appropriate to venerate Jackson. Even journals that had opposed secession joined in acknowledging his gallantry and virtue. Jackson's name had become "a household word" in Britain, and "his name has been in all our mouths." To the *York Herald*, "probably no single event since the outbreak of the war in America" had excited a greater response. "Among Englishmen of all opinions," stated *John Bull*, "there was not one who did not feel a regretful sorrow, as for one of our own heroes." This was as it should be, for Jackson was of "our own race."[2]

The sadness of the South was shared by "the vast majority of the people of England" in the judgment of the *Westmorland Gazette*, but it was still likely that the South would win the war. Independent radical MP for Sheffield John Arthur Roebuck intended to propose a resolution in the Commons for British recognition of the Confederacy, and a meeting in his constituency had given the plan warm approval. Was this not a signal of the public mood? Jackson was dead, and his contribution had been "priceless," but there was no reason to despair. As the *Index*—"the able London organ of the Confederate States"—commented, the memory of Jackson's "glorious life" would inspire southerners to fight to the finish.[3]

A number of commentators linked the Sheffield meeting with the course of the American war. The call for peace talks grew louder. The *Exeter and Plymouth Gazette* claimed that only "black republicans" in Britain wanted the war to continue and that their malignant disposition was revealed by the "unseemly exultation" of one of their periodicals over Jackson's death—a reference to the *Leeds Mercury*. This was disgraceful, for Jackson was a hero, "a singular blending of Rupert and Cromwell," and he also bore comparison with Havelock. The *Bury and Norwich Post* regarded him as "one of the very few men who stand out . . . as worthy of the crisis for which they have been born."[4] The Rupert and Cromwell references were common by this time. Amalgamating Cavalier and Roundhead associations solved some of the problems that promoters of southern separatism had experienced when employing their preferred symbols and images. The mourning for Jackson was decisive, for the greatest champion of the Cavalier nation turned out to be a Puritan. Affection for Jackson pushed forward the merging of Cavalier and Roundhead tropes.[5]

To the *Bradford Observer*, Jackson had helped to make a nation, and he was more than a southern hero because his fame was "the common property of the world, warming manly hearts in every clime and age to deeds of patriotism and daring." Like Havelock, he was pious and honorable, but he was a better strategist than Havelock. He resembled Cromwell in religious enthusiasm, inflexible will, and ability to inspire. For all this, the *Leeds Mercury* had censured Jackson for wasting his talents: "We cannot regret that a bad cause has lost an able supporter." The *Bradford Observer*, which opposed slavery, denied that Jackson had favored slavery. It recognized the South's right to independence and held that "the social diseases of a country are not incurable while it continues to be the mother of heroes and the depository of heroic dust."[6] Anger against the pro-North *Leeds Mercury* was also expressed on 27 May 1863, in Huddersfield, when the men of the Second West Yorkshire Yeomanry Cavalry had their annual dinner. One of the speakers, Maj. Thomas Crosland, was applauded when he condemned the *Leeds Mercury* for its "outrageous" response to Jackson's death: "Talk about it being a blessing to have such a man as that taken away—friend or foe he was an honor to his nation, and an ornament to mankind."[7]

The *Leeds Mercury* was in a small minority. If there were commentators who condemned Jackson for fighting in a bad cause, many more included no such reservations in their tributes. To the *Leicester Chronicle*, his death was "a great calamity." The *North Wales Chronicle* trusted that Jackson's death would increase the South's determination to win the war, and this was also the hope of the *Preston Chronicle*. The *Southampton Herald* found the London press "nearly unanimous" in praising Jackson and, turning to the "unenviable notoriety" of the *Leeds Mercury*, wondered how anyone could believe that the removal of Jackson would shorten the war and lead to the emancipation of slaves. This was "the very madness of Abolitionism."[8] Clearly, Jackson's death, and reactions to it, intensified the existing animosity in Britain between pro-southern and pro-northern lobbies.

Beyond partisanship for the opposing sides in the American war, in death Jackson was also brought more directly into domestic British politics. *Reynolds's Newspaper*, for instance, which was pro-North in editorial line and democratic in ideology, used a comparison of Jackson with Havelock to attack the British system of government. They were both successful generals, but Havelock had to wait for his opportunity, as "courtly noodles and aristo-cratic fops" were promoted ahead of him, while Jackson was given command quickly. The explanation was that "Havelock served a monarchy, Jackson served a republic. The English hero pined in the cold shade of aristocracy; the American hero flourished in a soil where court favoritism is unknown."[9] Politicians realized that they could use the departed Jackson's name to charm a crowd. This was accomplished in Liskeard, at the end of May 1863, by the Cornish borough's Liberal MP, Ralph Bernal Osborne: "No one could have seen the career of that great man—alas now no more—Stonewall Jackson (great cheering)—no one could have seen the close of that noble career with-out feeling that a great hero had departed (renewed cheers)."[10]

In many parts of Britain, there were meetings to express regret at Jack-son's death. In Sheffield, the event was chaired by a local alderman, George Saunders, managing director of an insurance company, who had also chaired antislavery meetings. On this occasion, Saunders stated that some in the town might oppose recognition of the Confederacy, but they would surely not object to a mark of respect for Jackson. It was agreed that on behalf of those assembled, Saunders would contact the Confederate commissioner in London, James M. Mason, and arrange to have a message of sympathy for-warded to Jackson's widow and to his troops.[11] At a planning session on 29 May, members of the Liverpool Southern Club engaged in talk of a "lasting and substantial memorial" to Jackson and resolved to call a public meeting. A notice was sent to the press.[12] But soon another notice was published. Since their plan "would be regarded in certain quarters as a political move," leaders of the club "have prudently resolved to abstain from a public demon-stration, and will simply open a subscription list."[13]

Pro-northern meetings in these weeks sometimes descended into disor-der. At that organized by the Union and Emancipation Society in Todmor-den, Yorkshire, there was uproar when it was suggested that Jackson's death should be welcomed.[14] Spontaneous shows of sympathy for the South and declarations of respect for Jackson were numerous, though perhaps in some cases they were not to be taken seriously, as when students chanted Jack-son's name during a visit to Oxford by the Prince and Princess of Wales in June 1863.[15] The undergraduates might have done this only to annoy known supporters of the North among the university's professors and ad-ministrators. A lecture tour by John H. Smith, "A Voice from the South," gave rise to disturbances in Derby and Nottingham as pro-northerners and pro-southerners exchanged insults and used Jackson's name for their own purposes. Though identified in some reports as English-born (a native of Worcester), in others Smith was described as a Mississippian. He eulogized Jackson and promised that many blessings would result as an independent South took its place in an international order based on peace and free trade. But his opponents shouted antislavery slogans and rejected all talk of official recognition of the Confederacy.[16]

Respect for Jackson could not be expressed independently of this wrangling between groups, and controversy intensified, owing to developments in British and European politics. The *Standard* connected the American situation with the Polish Rising of 1863. As Poles sought to cast off Russian rule and there was discussion in Britain about possible intervention, the *Standard* protested that "in Poland there is not secession, but rebellion; not a conflict between distinct Governments, but a rising against the only Government existing"—so why think of intervening in Poland and not in America? The point was underlined with reference to Jackson's "great appeal" in Britain, to whose people he was a blood relation.[17] A similar argument was made by James Spence in one of his letters to the *Times*.[18]

In Parliament, a key event of the time was Roebuck's motion on 30 June that the British government should enter into negotiations with European powers for a collective recognition of the Confederacy. This motion was withdrawn on 13 July, mainly because of uncertainty produced by the course of the war, but another problem was that pro-northerners had brought up a crucial principle in international law: should seceders be recognized before the outcome of their secession could be ascertained?[19] Newspapers favorable to the South dismissed the notion that the Union would be restored with slavery abolished. One of them declared that southerners could hardly overlook the outrages committed against them or depreciate Jackson's martyrdom.[20]

The idea that nonintervention had been vindicated took firmer root when news arrived of the Battle of Gettysburg, which took place from 1 to 3 July 1863, after which the South struggled to recover. A letter from Richmond, dated 15 August 1863, appeared in several London and provincial papers. It stated that southern leaders were grateful to "the people of England, whose sympathy, as evinced on the death of Stonewall Jackson, and in the tone of their respectable presses, is fully appreciated here." Toward the British government, however, there was indignation. The worst culprit was the foreign secretary, Russell, who had refused to receive the Confederate envoy Mason. For pro-northerners, meanwhile, Russell had acted correctly and would do so again when he ordered the stoppage of the Laird "rams" in September.[21]

Pro-southerners did not abandon their efforts to sway government ministers and influence parliamentary and extra-parliamentary opinion. Jackson was still an essential tool. He was mentioned repeatedly by speakers at a meeting and banquet of the Liverpool Southern Club on 16 October. James Spence proposed a toast to Jackson that "will often be heard again amongst men of our race who are capable of appreciating the noblest qualities that can adorn that race." Jackson "was by descent an Englishman . . . And throughout all time the name of that great general will remain an enduring tie between the two peoples." The meeting and dinner were widely reported in the press. There was a full account in the *Liverpool Mercury* and generous coverage in Scottish and Irish papers.[22]

In November 1863, Spence caused a stir in Glasgow, where he gave an address on "Southern Independence." Though frequently interrupted, he stayed on message: the people of the "hero" Jackson were "our kinsmen," and their independence ought to be recognized.[23] Soon there was a quarrel carried on in the pages of the *Glasgow Herald*, prompted by John Nichol, Regius Professor of English Literature at the University of Glasgow, and Goldwin Smith, Regius Professor of Modern History at Oxford. When Nichol and Smith slurred the southern character, Spence wrote a rebuttal, saluting Jackson as an exemplar.[24] Jackson's British admirers were also antagonized at this time by a pro-northern speech of Thomas Milner Gibson, president of the Board of Trade, Liberal MP for Ashton-under-Lyne, and an ally of Cobden and Bright. In the *Standard*, "Vigilans" derided Gibson for excusing all the actions of the United States and refusing to acknowledge that Jackson had exhibited courage and honor while northern generals had disgraced themselves.[25]

These remarks from Vigilans followed an editorial in the *Standard* that explained the war as the outcome of disagreements about the best political, economic, and social arrangements for a people, disagreements that had a British as well as an American dimension. They concerned democracy and reform, trade and tariffs, slavery and free labor, and progress and order. To the *Standard*, Jackson had been fighting not only for the South but for everyone, anywhere, who embraced the values the South represented. Slavery was repeatedly brought up by friends of the North, but it was not really a cause of the war, and in Britain, before the South seceded, "radical organs and orators were remarkably silent on the subject of slavery, nay, they were even disposed to rise up as its apologists, whenever it was made a ground of reproach against their model Republic . . . They have taken to cursing slavery only since slavery has ceased to be identified with the Union." Now they condemned "a people struggling gallantly for independence against enormous odds." Behind all this was love for democracy. Radicals could not tolerate the Confederacy because its existence uncovered the worthlessness of their obsession, and there was a lesson here for the people of Britain. When they looked at Jackson, they could understand the South and give thanks for its stand against northern greed and corruption.[26]

Prominent friends of the North were more bitterly condemned by prosoutherners as the war went in the Union's favor. They included novelist Anthony Trollope, who had visited and written about America.[27] After a lecture of January 1864, there was protest against his "Northern prepossessions." Politically and socially, Trollope thought, the South was "stationary" and "effete," but his critics claimed that in comparing Jackson and other southern leaders with their northern counterparts, one had no difficulty identifying who were the men of vigor and who were the degenerates.[28]

Jackson's fame, a flexible political weapon, was employed on occasion by pro-northerners, including "Gracchus," who wrote for the radical *Reynolds's Newspaper.* (This was probably Edward, younger brother of the proprietor G.W.M. Reynolds.) In September 1864, Gracchus published a defense of the republican form of government, emphasizing that Jackson "was a republican in faith, was reared and educated at a republican military academy, and laid down his life in the service of a republic."[29] A different political point was made by the *Economist,* which, fearing that a minority Conservative government might replace the Palmerston administration, hoped that Conservative leader Lord Derby would be a "Stonewall Jackson." That is, he would not compromise his values and consistency by acting against the good of his country.[30]

For British supporters of the South, Jackson remained a symbol, and while war news grew bleaker, his image and memory shored up morale. Items on display at the Southern Bazaar for Wounded Confederate Prisoners in October 1864 included a "Eulogy" to Jackson and a portrait of him at prayer. Organizers and patrons of this event included all the leading British pro-southerners.[31] These activists were not ready to abandon the cause, and Jackson memorabilia had undiminished potential to inspire.

Jackson's name was still useful. In October 1864, the annual dinner of the Conservative Association in Rochdale, Cobden's constituency, was addressed by Cobden's likely challenger at the next election, barrister William Brett, who praised Jackson and insisted that the great general could not be classed as "a rebel." Jackson had been "a patriot," and his people were "a nation."[32] A few weeks later, Cobden visited the constituency. His speech appeared in various newspapers, including the *Western Times*, which was unimpressed. An admirer of the United States, Lincoln, and republican government, Cobden imagined that pro-Confederate sympathizers in Britain did not understand the questions of slavery and secession. To the *Western Times*, the American war was not about slavery, and Jackson had taken up arms "not for rights to be acquired, but original rights of independence to be maintained."[33]

More than a year and a half after his death and with the South facing defeat, Jackson's name remained a rallying cry. In December 1864, the Bristol Emancipation Society met to approve a congratulatory address to Lincoln on his reelection. The venue was invaded by "a crowd of boisterous Southern partisans." They called out Jackson's name and prevented the meeting from proceeding.[34] Any discussion of America, wherever it might take place, was incomplete without some mention of Jackson. One lecture of January 1865 was delivered in Wokingham by George Russell, a local official. He had visited America, and he argued that the war was being fought by "men of a kindred race, and that race our own." The British were naturally interested in the actions of individuals related to themselves and could be especially proud of Jackson. Russell developed this point to explain that North and South were not the same.[35] That northerners and southerners were separate peoples and that the war had established their disharmony for all time was also the view of Presbyterian cleric and poet George Gilfillan, still active and outspoken in Dundee in the spring of 1865. Whatever one might think about the American crisis, Gilfillan said, it had made famous some remarkable figures. Foremost among them was Jackson.[36]

The Liverpool Southern Club met on 6 April 1865 to hear addresses by two Methodist clergymen, William Bennett of Richmond, Virginia, and Francis Mood of Charleston, South Carolina, who stressed that the Confederacy stood for "free government" and would not give up. James Spence thanked them, adding that "he was glad to see, from the numerous attendance, that the members were not falling away from the Southern cause in the day of its depression and sorrow." The spirit that had animated Jackson would live on, and Spence "could not bring himself to believe that all the heroism displayed in this struggle would be in vain."[37] Less than two weeks later, news arrived in Britain of the surrender at Appomattox on 9 April.

Pro-northerners exulted, but with their joy came sorrow at the loss of one of their leaders, Cobden, who died on 2 April, before the news came through. There was an instant revival of controversy in Rochdale, and beyond, because Cobden's death meant a by-election. As expected, the Conservative candidate was Brett. He issued a "bold and generous appeal for the justice of recognizing the independence of the Confederacy of the Southern States," which by now was quite unusual, with the war in America almost over, and he again brought into service the "heroic Stonewall Jackson." Brett lost the by-election, but he secured more than 43 percent of votes cast. Even in uncongenial times and places, the Jackson reputation still resonated.[38]

The maintenance of Jackson's positive reputation rested largely on information about and comment upon his religious faith. When news arrived of his death, there was much discussion about how he would be remembered. Some writers were in no doubt. They presented Jackson as the "Puritan warrior" and "man of prayer" who had complete trust in God and a readiness to abide by His will. He had been faithful and upright. There was nothing disreputable about him. One commentator described Jackson as austere and devout but not fanatical, unlike some of those who had fought for Parliament in the seventeenth century. Similarity with Cromwell was a recurrent theme, though, and the other frequent comparisons were with Havelock and, to a lesser extent, Sir Henry Lawrence, who had served as a military commander and reforming administrator in India before his death in 1857 and was known for his philanthropic endeavors. Most agreed that Jackson would be remembered around the world for "devout piety, strict integrity, and tender humanity."[39] W. C. Corsan's book, _Two Months in the Confederate States_ was still being reviewed in the British press when Jackson's death was confirmed, and extracts and summaries reinforced the impression of his "unaffected piety."[40]

Many biographical pieces were published in British periodicals after Jackson's death, and most of them accentuated the "Christian hero" aspect.[41]

To some, his life had more Old Testament than New Testament to it. He "found in the Pentateuch proof positive that slavery was ordained of God" and "discovered in the historical books strong precedent for smiting hip and thigh . . . for downright thorough dealing with those who stood in arms against him."[42] Several papers printed extracts from a letter received by Presbyterian minister Moses D. Hoge of Richmond, who was in England from January to October 1863. The letter was from his brother William, a minister in Charlottesville, Virginia, who described a visit to Jackson's camp during the previous winter. William Hoge stressed that Jackson's primary goal in life was to glorify God.[43] A similar line was taken by Frank Lawley of the *Times*. Lawley's Jackson knew blessed assurance. "An ardent predestinarian, accepting with unquestioning faith the issues of life, equal to any and every fortune, he had at the same time an American's tolerance for the doctrines and faith of other men." His death was a tragedy, but the manner of his dying was glorious. He had placed himself in God's hands.[44]

After his death, as before, this devotion was given a negative spin by some writers. The New York correspondent of the *Daily News* wrote that Jackson's faith consisted of rigidity and racism.[45] The *Western Times* called Jackson "a praying hero" but wondered how a "true Christian" could take up arms to settle a dispute, especially one involving slavery.[46] Several newspapers insisted that although Jackson might have had some pleasing personal qualities, he could not be excused for defending slavery.[47] At a soirée of November 1863 in Edinburgh, speakers declared that all good Presbyterians wished for the ending of slavery and that Jackson's position had been offensive to God.[48] There was trouble in Leicester following lectures there by the aforementioned John H. Smith. In one of his talks, he spoke of Jackson's faith. He made a swift exit when he was shouted down as a slaveholder.[49]

Meanwhile, Jackson's admirers went on extolling.[50] In *A Military View of the Recent Campaigns in Virginia and Richmond* (1863), Capt. C. C. Chesney of the Royal Engineers, a professor at Sandhurst (Britain's officer training college), treated Jackson as a Christian as well as a soldier.[51] Clergymen placed Jackson in the top rank of famous military figures who had been devout Christians. In September 1863, a parade by the First Hampshire Volunteers was followed by a sermon in Winchester Cathedral. Rev. Charles Collier, the regimental chaplain, said that devotion to God and country made "good citizens and true soldiers," and in this connection, Jackson was "ever to be lamented."[52] In their end-of-year reviews of the major events of 1863, many British newspapers included Jackson's death. The *Exeter and Plymouth Gazette* regretted the loss of a brave general who was at the same time the epitome of southern dignity, patriotic fidelity, and Christian manhood.[53]

In the spring of 1864, reviews began to appear of a book-length treatment of Jackson published in London at the end of 1863. *"Stonewall" Jackson, Late General of the Confederate States Army,* dedicated to prominent pro-southerner Sir Henry de Hoghton, was written by Catherine Cooper Hopley, an English governess, teacher, and author whose travels took her to Ohio, Virginia, and Florida. Her book on "The Christian Hero, Jackson"—the phrase she used to open its introduction—though not without errors and shortcomings, reinforced for readers their sense of Jackson's "humble Christian life." A review in the *Standard* expanded further upon the importance of Jackson's faith. He knew religious awakening; he joined the Presbyterian Church and became an elder; he led Bible classes for blacks as well as whites.[54] For those in Britain who wished to adopt Jackson as their paradigm, the very definition of earnest faith and moral rectitude, there was enough material circulating by 1864 to enable them to do so.

One of the most commonly cited books in this period was Col. Arthur Lyon Fremantle's *Three Months in the Southern States,* published in London in 1863 and in New York and Mobile, Alabama, in 1864. Fremantle had taken a furlough from his post in the Coldstream Guards to cross the Atlantic. He entered the Confederacy through Mexico and attached himself to the Army of Northern Virginia. Fremantle arrived too late to meet Jackson, but in his book, he related some of the things he heard about the general, whose fate had been "universally deplored." Officers who had known Jackson told Fremantle that "he was gifted with wonderful courage and determination, and a perfect faith in Providence that he was destined to destroy his enemy." Fremantle also learned about the moral standards Jackson tried to uphold in camp.[55]

The statements of Hopley and Fremantle supported and were supported by numerous other items in books and periodicals, and all were backed by what could be taken as visual corroboration, not least the special attraction at the Southern Bazaar of October 1864, a portrait of Jackson in his "characteristic" attitude, in prayer, "offering, in the solitude of a wood, his morning orisons at the throne of all grace to the giver of all victory."[56]

Of singular influence was the biography of Jackson written by Rev. Robert L. Dabney, the prominent conservative Presbyterian theologian and pastor who had served as Jackson's chief of staff for five months in 1862. Volume 1 covered Jackson's life up to the end of the first year of the war. The version published in London in 1864 was edited by Rev. William Chalmers of Marylebone Presbyterian Church. In view of his own background and the nature of his relationship with Jackson, it is hardly surprising that Dabney wrote about a man of faith. His wife and Jackson's wife were cousins. Anna Jackson encouraged Dabney to write a biography of her husband and provided material, as did the Confederate War Department. Dabney made his book a religious tract as well as a biography. To S. C. Gwynne, it was "deeply biased." Wallace Hettle shows that Dabney's book "embodied his own values"—he was an ardent southern separatist and defender of slavery—and it was also shaped by a prevalent trend in American biography writing at this time, "a near-obsessive concern with the formation of character."[57]

Dabney described Jackson's religious conversion as a gradual but fundamental shift, beginning in 1847–48, during the Mexican War. He devoted himself to study and meditation. He became "punctilious about the purity of his life" and "listened to no other than a sanctified ambition." In November 1851, by which time he had settled in Lexington to teach at the Virginia Military Institute, he was received into the Presbyterian Church.[58]

Dabney's volume was noticed in many newspapers, including the *Manchester Times,* which appreciated the author's special insight.[59] The book inspired a longer article, which first appeared in the *Leeds Times* in January 1865. It was not unusual to compare Jackson with Cromwell, but this article accepted Dabney's notion that the comparison was inappropriate. Dabney argued that Jackson was the superior, morally and spiritually, and that Cromwell was self-seeking, while Jackson's motives were pure. Dabney also stressed the dissimilarity between Cromwell, the "Puritan Independent" and preacher to his troops, and Jackson, who had a layman's respect for the clergy and would not lead a prayer or give a blessing over a meal if a clergyman or an older Christian than himself was present to do it. In other words, Jackson observed "right order."[60] From the early part of 1865, extracts from Dabney were used increasingly in discussions of Jackson's religious life.[61] The long review of Dabney's book in the *Times* was headed "A Christian Warrior."[62]

Jackson the prayerful paragon: it became difficult to stem this tide, but attempts were made. To the *Christian Observer* (a Church of England monthly) of February 1865, Jackson's "hideous" idea that the enemy should be given no quarter—a matter on which he was overruled by the Confederate government—was at odds with the Christian's duty to show mercy, and since war was God's punishment for national sin, there could be no such thing as a "holy warrior."[63] Robert Mackenzie's *America and Her Army*, a pamphlet published in 1865 by a Scottish writer described as an "extreme partisan of the North," asserted that while the Union army was "sincerely Christian," the southern one was not. The *Dundee Courier* disagreed, pointing to the strong faith and impeccable morality of Jackson.[64] Items about Jackson were included several times in the *Monthly Packet of Evening Readings for Younger Members of the English Church*.[65]

After his death, Jackson continued to be commended not only for his religious character but also as an excellent soldier. Once his death had been confirmed, some British newspapers recycled previous material—from Corsan's *Two Months in the Confederate States*, for example—describing Jackson's military successes.[66] He was undefeated, his campaigns would be the stuff of legend, and though the South had other accomplished generals, he was irreplaceable. The South would still defeat the North, but the task would be more difficult without Jackson.[67] Writers made the familiar comparisons, with Cromwell and Garibaldi, and also mentioned Lord Peterborough, commander of allied forces during the War of the Spanish Succession in the early eighteenth century.[68]

Jackson's British admirers were dismayed by his death, and their regret was all the more painful because of the circumstances. They reflected that Federals could not claim the honor "or the ignominy" since Jackson had been shot accidentally by his own men. He had done more damage to the Federals than all his peers with an army he had created, the most loyal and well-disciplined force in the whole Confederacy.[69]

The superlatives flooded forth as the shock of Jackson's loss set in. He was the Wellington, Ney, and Cromwell of the Confederacy, "steadfast and persistent in defense, and bold and irresistible in attack." The South "could scarcely have suffered a greater calamity," for there was no more inspirational figure for its soldiers and civilians. In the North, people assumed that had Jackson been on their side, they would have won the war long ago. He was "chivalrous," "invincible," and extraordinary in his grasp of tactics and topography and in his influence over his men.[70] He died too soon. But if his career had been cut short, who could deny him his due? "He seems to have been born a general."[71]

For all the positive assessments of Jackson's generalship, the *Era* complained that his importance was being exaggerated, doubted that his death would affect the outcome of the war, and expected the South quickly to recover.[72] Nevertheless, the common opinion was that the South had lost its best general and "there may be no compensation for it." Jackson had astonished the world. To some British observers, his death was no less significant than the death of Nelson at Trafalgar, another victory that came at a huge price. That he was shot accidentally by his own men was a terrible tragedy. As one journalist put it, "The intelligence . . . has fallen as heavily upon the ear of Europe as upon the heart of Virginia."[73]

Numerous commentators argued that it was Jackson's religious zeal that had made him a great commander. Ruthless and uncompromising, he believed he was God's instrument. All he cared about was "hard fighting," and southerners would fight on as he had taught them.[74] This seemed far-fetched to the New York correspondent of the *Daily News*, who, while admitting that Jackson's death was probably the biggest reverse suffered by the South since the beginning of the war, held that his admirers had embellished along the way, giving Jackson an unmerited reputation. Moreover, if Jackson was a hero, he did credit to the American Union. "Whatever the result of this war, the United States will enjoy the honor of having bred and educated him," and "the Puritanism which made him . . . was a hardy Northern plant."[75] It was also suggested that, admired as he was in the North as well as the South, all Americans could be proud of his bravery.[76] Such attempts to make Jackson an *American* rather than a southerner, so soon after his death, conflicted with most British commentary.

Many papers carried a copy of Lee's general order of 11 May 1863 announcing the loss of Jackson, and this was sometimes accompanied by Lee's remark in a note he had sent to Jackson on first hearing that he was wounded, that it would have been better for their country had he been disabled in Jackson's place.[77] As more details about Chancellorsville came through, there was even greater respect for Jackson as a general.[78] His ability to get the maximum performance from his men was emphasized by a Scottish-born soldier in the Stonewall Brigade, whose letter to friends in Glasgow was quickly published. Shortly before his death, Jackson complimented his troops. He had previously said that the name Stonewall belonged to them, not to him.[79]

Could the South win the war without Jackson? Pro-southerners liked to think so. Jackson had brought on other generals, notably Jubal Early, A. P. Hill, and Daniel Harvey Hill (who was married to the elder sister of Jackson's wife, Anna). The hope was that they would carry on where he left off.[80] When discussing Lee's invasion of the North after Chancellorsville, some writers stated that it was Jackson's men—the formations prepared and formerly led by him—who were making the main thrust. The new corps commander, Richard Ewell, had served under Jackson, and it was Jackson's "deathbed request" that Ewell succeed him. Though he was gone, Jackson was still contributing to the South's advances.[81]

In August 1863, the *Morning Post* reviewed Chesney's *Military View of the Recent Campaigns in Virginia and Richmond*. The book and the review enhanced Jackson's reputation as a warrior. Chesney rated Jackson alongside several of the most celebrated soldiers of history. He was a unique combination of prophet and general.[82] But some of the naysayers minimized Jackson's role by arguing that Lee had made all the decisions.[83] In *Three Months in the Southern States*, Fremantle recorded a conversation he had in Richmond with Confederate secretary of state Judah P. Benjamin. Referring to the victories over Pope and Burnside, Benjamin pointed out that "the movements were planned and ordered by General Lee, for whom (Mr. Benjamin said) Jackson had the most 'childlike reverence.'"[84] During a series of lectures in December 1863 in Rhyl, North Wales, speakers argued that Confederate successes were due more to Lee than Jackson because Lee had given the orders and Jackson had merely executed them.[85]

Yet it is striking just how *uncommon* this idea was. Praise for Jackson's military talents was much more prevalent in the British press than praise for Lee or any other Confederate commander. By the end of 1863, an impression was gaining ground that Lee did not have the tactical vision and boldness of Jackson and could not win major battles without him.[86] Some writers argued that had Jackson been at Gettysburg, the Confederates would have triumphed there and the course of the war during 1863 would have been markedly different. Manhattan, the New York correspondent of the *Standard*, wrote on 18 December 1863 of the relief in the North that the South no longer had the services of Jackson. Lee was thought to be overcautious, which gave the North a better chance of winning the war. Many retrospective summaries of the events of 1863 described Jackson's death as a turning point.[87]

Jackson's removal affected the morale of U.S. minister to Britain Charles F. Adams, and his son and secretary, Henry, as they tried to gain more backing for the North. Another of the minister's sons was serving with Federal forces in Virginia, and his letters to London suggested that "the crisis is over." Southerners would not win without Jackson. Lee had been saved from disaster previously by Jackson, "his right hand man," but there was no saving Lee from his errors at Gettysburg—a worse defeat for the South than Fredericksburg had been for the North.[88]

Jackson's standing as a general was upheld by extracts from the first volume of *War Pictures from the South*, published in London in 1863. The author was a Hungarian cavalry officer named Bela Estvàn, who had settled in the South in 1856. Estvàn fought for the Confederacy for about eighteen months, though he disagreed with secession. After reaching the rank of colonel, he resigned on medical grounds and moved to England. The book described Jackson's exploits in the early part of the war, his emergence as a "genius," his absolute reliability, and his humanity. One reviewer thought the book dull, its only redeeming feature being material on Jackson.[89]

Reviews of Catherine Cooper Hopley's *"Stonewall" Jackson, Late General of the Confederate States Army* also emphasized that he had been an excellent soldier. The proposition that "he was more suited to occupy the subordinate position of carrying out the conceptions of others, than himself to initiate the movements of great armies," was dismissed. "When his rapid and mysterious marches, his dashing raids, his sudden surprises and irresistible attacks are remembered, such an assertion may well be doubted."[90]

Assessing Jackson alongside historical figures continued to be a cheering pursuit, although rating Jackson the equal of the greatest British and foreign military heroes struck some observers as facile. In part, this was because they thought that why he fought was as important as how he fought. When Garibaldi visited Britain in April 1864, his devotees argued that his efforts for Italian unification showed him to be an exemplary patriot and unselfish servant of "a great and pure cause." In their view, this was not true of Jackson.[91] To most interested people in Britain, however, such distinctions made no sense. Evidence of Jackson's military talents was too plentiful to be set aside. Readers were impressed by the insights provided by George Augustus Sala, special correspondent of the *Daily Telegraph*. (Formerly a clerk in London, Sala had been given his break as a writer by Charles Dickens.) Sala's contributions from America appeared in many British papers. His view was that Jackson had possessed the gift of doing the right thing at the right time. This was the difference between winning and losing a battle and made Jackson's absence from Gettysburg all the more significant.[92] The course of the war was also telling, for "since the death of Stonewall Jackson, nothing but misfortunes have attended the army of General Lee."[93]

More stories were published about Jackson's courage and confidence and how he kept his nerve in battle. He was once isolated in an engagement and the only way of escape was over a bridge, but it was covered by Federal artillery. He concealed his uniform with a cape, rode up to the battery in question, and ordered its commander to take up another position. While it was moving, he was able to cross the bridge to safety.[94] Other reminders of Jackson's exploits came in reports about the fate of those defeated by him in battle.[95]

The rise of Ulysses S. Grant led to suggestions that he might win the war for the North, as Jackson would presumably have done for the South had he lived. The New York correspondent of the *Daily News*, writing in July 1864, remarked that Jackson and Grant both had a special gift. Neither could claim to have been among the top students at West Point, but they had outperformed those students. They had "risen to the highest eminence by the possession of a temperament and of a certain quality of mind which the ordinary college course never calls into play."[96] The *Manchester Guardian* argued at this time that only Jackson's methods could bring victories. Commanders had to take risks, do the unexpected, and focus on aggression, not defense.[97]

A reminder of the panic Jackson had prompted in northerners whenever he was thought to be approaching came in the recollections of Charles Mayo, published in 1864. Mayo, a fellow of New College, Oxford, had gone to America late in 1862. He became a surgeon major and medical inspector in the U.S. Army. Resident for a time in Washington, Mayo was struck more than once by the "big scare" caused by Jackson "making a dash" in the vicinity.[98]

Jubal Early's campaign in the Shenandoah Valley, from June to October 1864, was discussed in many British newspapers. Early was now in charge of Jackson's corps. Even those in Britain who predicted great things for him admitted that it would have been better had Jackson been available to fight in the Valley.[99] Another possible successor to Jackson, in the view of some commentators, had been Ewell, but in the spring of 1864, his performance grew erratic.[100] A Richmond correspondent of the *Times* held out hopes that John Bell Hood or P.G.T. Beauregard might yet match Jackson's achievements.[101]

By the beginning of 1865, a number of papers expected the war soon to be over due to the quality of the North's generals, which was a change from previous claims about all the talent being on the Confederate side. Pro-southern commentators insisted that had Jackson's "black flag" and "no quarter" inclinations been adopted, the North would have surrendered long ago. The Dabney volume seemed to indicate as much, and reviewers used it to highlight Jackson's understanding that the American Civil War was not like earlier wars and that the old rules could not apply. To Jackson, "take no prisoners" was "not only justifiable in principle, but would be in the end the truest humanity, because it would shorten the contest and thus eventually diminish bloodshed."[102] Pro-northern commentators did not accept that the Federals lacked field commanders who were as talented or effective as Jackson had been for the South. Congratulating the North's generals became much easier, of course, toward the end of the war. Philip Sheridan was "the Stonewall Jackson of the Federals."[103] Some pro-southerners were prepared grudgingly to recognize William T. Sherman as the North's "Stonewall."[104] Praising Sheridan or Sherman was a form of tribute to Jackson, for he was the standard by which they were judged. In this way, the Jackson legend continued to grow.

Interest in Jackson's religious commitments and military talents was matched by the continuing fascination with his personal character, appearance, and eccentricities. Extracts from Corsan's *Two Months in the Confederate States* were used to comment on Jackson's personality and appearance. There were also observations from an Englishman serving in the Confederate army, sent from Charleston and dated 4 March 1863. The writer did not know Jackson but had seen him and heard much about him. In this account, the general was most noteworthy for his kindness and prayerfulness.[105]

That Jackson had an unblemished personal character, worthy of approval and emulation, became central to his legend. Pro-southerners were impressed by the way that pro-northern papers in Britain, though they could not approve of the cause in which he had fought, commended Jackson for his faith, courage, honesty, and virtue. Whatever one's opinions about the war, Jackson's honor could not be questioned.[106] An appraisal in the *Satur-*

day Review was used as the basis for articles such as "Superiority of the Men of the South" in the *Westmorland Gazette*. The *Sheffield Independent* asserted that Englishmen were naturally drawn to the South because they knew a hero when they saw one. Comparisons with Havelock were becoming almost obligatory, and the *Cheshire Observer* agreed that Jackson's death was "deeply regretted in England, where he was regarded as a man without fear and without reproach."[107]

After his death, very few published pieces on Jackson failed to mention some admirable personal qualities. Various commentators emphasized his "moral stature" and "high conscience." He had "the pluck that is in a stout heart the offspring of a clear cause," and "it is in this quality that we especially acknowledge and claim 'Stonewall' Jackson as of British blood."[108] There were plenty of recollections and descriptions, some going into detail about his peculiarities—the strange ideas about health and diet, the ungainly style of riding, the slovenly dress, the awkwardness and reticence in social situations. Writers tended to stick to the now familiar outlines of Jackson's rise from obscurity. The slow student at West Point had gone on to show conspicuous bravery in the Mexican War. Later he opted for a quiet life at the Virginia Military Institute, where he was a mediocre professor. He willingly served his country after secession, though he gained no wide reputation before the Valley Campaign of 1862. It was curious that someone could rise to celebrity so quickly, becoming so famous and respected, with relatively little known about him personally. It was assumed that a host of biographers would rush to fill the gap.[109]

Book reviews relating to Jackson began more often to deal with personality traits and physical appearance. These included the *Morning Post*'s review of Chesney's *Military View of the Recent Campaigns in Virginia and Richmond*.[110] Several British papers discussed *The Battlefields of the South, from Bull Run to Fredericksburg, with Sketches of the Confederate Commanders and Gossip of the Camps, by an English Combatant*, which was published in two volumes in London in 1863 and New York in 1864. The author was Thomas E. Caffey, English-born but a longtime resident of the South. Caffey included material on Jackson's character and appearance that further helped to enhance the abiding image of Jackson in the British mind. Here he was wearing a scruffy uniform, riding a sorry-looking horse while leaning over in an unconventional style; solemn and thoughtful, hardly speaking, often going off by himself to plan and reconnoiter; given, on campaign, to sudden and unaccountable actions and always on the move, his aides unable to keep up; pushing his men hard and accepting no excuses from those who failed to do their duty; his cap lowered over his eyes yet nothing escaping his attention; master of the Shenandoah Valley, where he knew all the roads and the distances from place to place.[111]

Reviews of Hopley's *"Stonewall" Jackson, Late General of the Confederate States Army* noted how the book brought out Jackson's humility and courage. Through his childhood and West Point, the Mexican War, and his time at the VMI and on to his period of fame as a Confederate general, he made his own way through strength of character. His parents died. He knew desperate poverty, gained no more than a rudimentary formal education, and had to live with various relatives in the rural northwest of Virginia. He worked hard on his uncle's farm. Though naturally quiet and reserved, deep down there was energy and determination. Reviewers discerned, despite his background, elements of "aristocratic feeling" in his makeup. It had also to be remembered that Jackson's forebears were British: "He was of pure English descent, and his portraits show him to have possessed features of a pure English type."[112] (Actually, his family roots were Scots-Irish.) Writers also used Fremantle's *Three Months in the Southern States* to support their ideas about Jackson's strength of character.[113]

Some writers, though, preferred to focus on Jackson's "peculiarities." Along with his hypochondria before the war and his characterization as a dull professor at the VMI, there was the story that at Fredericksburg, he proposed a surprise night attack on the enemy with troops stripped naked and armed only with daggers.[114] There was considerable interest in this type of material, but it was used to humanize Jackson, to make him more likable, not to assail him. In the hands of his admirers, it did not detract from his greatness.

Jackson the patriot was a figure worth promoting at a time when patriots in Italy and Poland were well regarded in Britain. In August 1864, the *Manchester Courier* suggested that Jackson's finest quality was his "deference to the movements of his native state," which meant that he "scrupulously regulated his own decision by that of the people and government of Virginia."[115] The *Leeds Mercury* preferred to argue that a people could not be judged by looking only at individuals. The South had to be judged as a whole, and the South was for slavery.[116] Some antislavery spokesmen were not quite so unforgiving. George Gilfillan, lecturing in Dundee in the spring of 1865, called slavery abhorrent but also referred kindly to Jackson's "simple-hearted earnestness."[117] Dabney's biography was a boon to those in Britain who wanted to see in Jackson a man of laudable character. From Dabney—and from the many publications that repeated his statements—came more insights into Jackson's ideas about diet and health, his remarkable self-discipline, and how he had overcome the disadvantages of his youth.[118]

Though dead, Jackson continued to feature in British coverage of the war and other published items about America. There was no consensus on the South's ability to recover from the "heavy disaster" of Jackson's death or on the likelihood of a bold Federal offensive to capitalize on his removal.[119] Nor was there consensus on the necessity for British intervention, in cooperation with France, to bring the war to an end.[120] Many papers included detailed and sometimes quite poignant (or intended to be) descriptions of Jackson's final days at Guinea Station.[121] Mostly, they used items lifted from the American press. Relying on Richmond sources, for instance, they reported on Jackson's body lying in state and his well-attended funeral.[122]

Several British commentators were incensed by a poem in the *New York Herald*, "Lines on a Dead Puppy," which "glories in a most disgusting manner over the death of Stonewall Jackson" and "vilifies his memory."[123] There was also much resentment at reports concerning Charles Sumwalt, a former Methodist preacher who had served as a colonel in the U.S. Army. He was arrested in Baltimore "upon the charge of wearing crape as a badge of mourning for 'Stonewall' Jackson."[124] Anger against the North was kept up by further information about the regime erected in occupied New Orleans by "Beast" Butler. The *Liverpool Mercury* carried a letter from New Orleans, dated 20 May 1863, describing the confiscation of property, fines and imprisonments, and the forcible expulsion from their homes of individuals and families. Citizens had also to deal with Jackson's death, which "produced a feeling of melancholy throughout all that depresses our minds beyond anything."[125]

Reports from New York during the summer of 1863 suggested that many of its residents held Jackson in high esteem.[126] For some time, prints of "Stonewall" had been selling extremely well.[127] The *Morning Post* tended to question items that it deemed insufficiently harsh toward the North. This may be seen in its response to Bela Estvàn's *War Pictures from the South*. The reviewer appreciated the useful biographical sketch of Jackson but added that Estvàn had omitted unpleasant facts about the North.[128] As the impression grew that the North was winning the war, pro-southerners claimed that the impact of reverses on the South was being exaggerated and that the old "Stonewall Jackson spirit" was intact. Visitors to the camps found no loss of heart but pride and resilience, and there was hardly any drunkenness or swearing, probably a result of Jackson's influence.[129]

British readers were aware, by late 1863, of the growing unease among southern newspapers about the lack of food, clothing, and supplies for the Confederate armies. There was pressure for a coordinated war strategy designed to affect the U.S. elections of November 1864 and make possible a peace settlement. The key was supposed to be "one signal, Stonewall Jackson campaign."[130] The *Standard*'s correspondent Manhattan hoped for Lincoln's resignation, a general amnesty, a meeting of all state governors North and South, and southern representatives readmitted to Congress, all in advance of the presidential election in November. Southerners would wish to return to the Union with states' rights solidified, Manhattan surmised. The South could not win the war, especially not without Jackson, who had been "invincible to everything, except death." The Union *needed* the South, and since it was clear that the South had no "dashing general of the Stonewall Jackson school" and would not gain independence, its best course would be to return to the Union and rely on the ballot box.[131]

Looking back on the year 1863, when "the death of Stonewall Jackson closed the period of Southern success," the *Bradford Observer* argued that the Confederacy could only prevail by abolishing slavery, while for their part, northerners had to admit that the Union could not be restored by force. The Confederacy bore "the stamp of a separate nationality," and it was simply wrong to set up new governments in seceded states based on only 10 percent of votes cast in the 1860 presidential election (Lincoln wanted quick elections in these states, to restore Union control without delay).[132] Other commentators reiterated that the lack of a Jackson-like figure to lead Confederate forces could prove decisive.[133] Nevertheless, during 1864, there were signs of undiminished British sympathy for the South. For some, the attachment was only strengthened by each blow the Confederates suffered. Regular mention was made of the loss of Jackson, which was brought up when other leading figures died, as happened with Gen. J.E.B. Stuart, who died from wounds suffered at the Battle of Yellow Tavern, north of Richmond, in May 1864.[134] Stuart's death came shortly after the wounding of Gen. James Longstreet at the Battle of the Wilderness (May 5–7). Longstreet was out of action for five months. Though he was "without the heroic impulses and

intuitive quickness of Stonewall Jackson, he had much of that celebrated
commander's dash and ascendancy over his soldiers' mind."[135]

In September 1864, the *Standard* used a speech by U.S. secretary of state
Seward in Auburn, New York, to reflect on the reasons why so many people in Britain had sided with the South against the North. According to the
Standard, these people respected the character and courage that had been
shown by the South. Jackson deserved all the praise he had received, while
northern figures were shamed by comparison. In order to create sympathy
for the North in Britain, it had been argued that the South was fighting for
slavery. This was unconvincing, and now Seward's speech added to the em-
barrassment of the North's supporters in Britain, for he had reportedly said
that slavery was not an obstacle to reunion and did not have to be included
in peace terms.[136]

Several British newspapers covered the Democratic Convention in
Chicago at the end of August 1864, and there was a revival of interest in the
party's presidential candidate McClellan, former commander of the Army of
the Potomac and commanding general of the U.S. Army. He stood as a "War
Democrat," but what most intrigued many British observers—still—was the
fact that he had been at West Point with Jackson.[137]

There was much discussion of the fate of the South during the final
weeks of 1864. The Federals had advanced through the Shenandoah Valley, previously the scene of Jackson's triumphs. According to one jeremiad,
"The choicest troops in the rebel service including the famous corps which
did so much to make the reputation of Stonewall Jackson are now a disor-
ganized, shattered body." Other reports were not so gloomy. They predicted
that Jackson's exploits, far from being forgotten, would inspire a recovery,
but all this had a hollow ring to it.[138]

Firsthand witness statements about Jackson were still highly valued. "A
Visit to the Cities and Camps of the Confederate States, 1863–64," by an
Austrian cavalry officer named FitzGerald Ross, whose background was British (though he had been brought up and educated in Europe), was serialized
in *Blackwood's Magazine* from late 1864. Ross wrote of his conversations with
southern leaders and his travels with the Army of Northern Virginia. He met
the British officer Fremantle. Ross arrived soon after Chancellorsville and
stayed for almost a year. He spoke with Col. Charles J. Faulkner, who had
been on Jackson's staff. Ross understood that Jackson had been "accidentally killed by a shot from one of his own men," but Faulkner pointed out

that this was not quite correct: "He spoke very feelingly of Jackson, and with great admiration of his high qualities. He attributed his death not so much to his unfortunate wounds as to a severe attack on the lungs, brought on by exposure."[139] Another series of articles was published at this time under the title "Adventures of a Dundee Shoemaker," appearing first in the *Dundee Courier* and written by a local man who had been in the South during the early stages of the war. He recalled a visit to Lexington, where he had met Jackson and talked with him about southern policy.[140]

The idea that Jackson's death was the crucial event in the war was by now widely accepted. One book reviewer found it fitting that in a history of America by the Virginia-born Taliaferro Preston Shaffner, a section on the war should end with Jackson's death.[141] The handicap faced by the South— Jackson's unavailability—featured prominently in discussion of continuing Federal advances and especially the peace negotiations at Hampton Roads, Virginia, in February 1865.[142] Jackson was sometimes mentioned by pro-southern commentators when they considered the prospect of emancipation in the South and the incorporation of blacks into the Confederate army. Opposition to the use of blacks as soldiers had been fading for some time, which bolstered the idea that the most likely source of an *effective* policy of emancipation was the South, not the North. Southerners would treat the blacks more generously, and in this respect (as in others), the favorite comparison was between Jackson, supposedly kind and respectful to slaves, and Butler, who as Federal commander in New Orleans had been cruel and overbearing. Runaway slaves had flocked to New Orleans, but Butler did not want to be responsible for finding them food, housing, and employment.[143]

The failed peace talks at Hampton Roads followed the vote in the U.S House of Representatives in favor of a constitutional amendment abolishing slavery. The Conservative and pro-southern *Morning Post* reported meetings across the South where defiance was the order of the day and stated that whatever the outcome of the war, the North could not control hearts and minds: "God never made a race of which Stonewall Jackson is a type . . . to be destroyed."[144] Jackson was invoked again in reports of the adjournment of the final session of the Confederate Congress on 18 March 1865. The Senate issued an address indicating unbroken determination. The *Cork Examiner* was confident that defenses around Richmond would hold: "The voice of Stonewall Jackson has found utterance, and declares, in these words of the Southern address, that his indomitable spirit is still a living flame."[145] When the North finally won the war, Jackson's British admirers had to console themselves with the thought that the defeat of the South was no reflection on him.[146]

Jackson continued to feature in all manner of cultural artifacts, including stories, magazines, lectures, pictures, poems, and songs. There was a burgeoning demand for biographical information, and the correspondent of the *Times* in the South, Frank Lawley, got in early, basing his account on personal knowledge, conversations, and items about Jackson that had already been published. He offered his sketch "in anticipation of a forthcoming 'Life' which the public expects from a competent hand" (probably a reference to Dabney) and because "every incident in relation to 'Stonewall' Jackson cannot fail at this moment to be interesting wherever the English tongue is spoken." Lawley had some details wrong, but he tried to be thorough, and his piece was widely read. Along with Jackson's military victories and religious faith, Lawley described his tour of Britain and Europe in 1856.[147] Individuals and communities liked to claim a special connection with Jackson. People in York, for instance, were proud that he had visited their city and admired their Minster. In May 1863, when news of his death reached Britain, various items of this kind were published in the newspapers. At least one was totally spurious. It was stated "on very good authority" that Jackson was "a Moreton man"—a native of Moretonhampstead, Devon, on the edge of Dartmoor—and had visited the area only a few years earlier. "He was of Devonshire extraction and worthy of his hovage."[148] An earlier claim was that Jackson had been born in Northallerton, Yorkshire.[149]

There were tales about the spell cast by Jackson's name. One appeared, via New York, in British newspapers in October 1863 concerning Presbyterian cleric George Junkin, the father of Jackson's first wife. This story had Junkin visiting a hospital near Gettysburg. He tried to speak to the Confederate wounded there and was ignored until he raised his walking cane and announced that it had been a gift from Jackson. From then on, those present gave him their undivided attention.[150]

Early in 1864, Fremantle's *Three Months in the Southern States* was praised by the *Manchester Courier* as "a welcome and extremely interesting addition to our scanty stores of information."[151] Readers could also refer to *My Diary North and South* by William Howard Russell and to his successor Lawley's letters in the *Times*, but Russell's account ended in December 1862, and Lawley had reported primarily on campaigns in Virginia, whereas Fremantle was a witness to conditions across a large part of the South and could paint a fuller picture. Fremantle passed on absorbing anecdotes about Jackson and made the pleasing revelation that almost all educated persons he encountered expressed fondness for Britain.[152]

Advertisers knew that by mentioning Jackson, they could better market products and services. The manager of a subscription library in Derby expected to do good business by adding a "Memoir of Stonewall Jackson."[153] In the Sheffield Temperance Hall, the "Panorama, North and South" was presented, including readings, music, and illustrations. Of special appeal was the material about Jackson.[154] In late 1863 and early 1864, announcements about upcoming publications promised a new work by John. M. Daniel of Virginia, "who knew the great Confederate general well, served under him throughout his brilliant career, has been assisted in the preparation of his biography by Mrs. Jackson, and had access to all his papers." (In fact, Daniel had not served in the army but was editor of the *Richmond Examiner*. For some time, he was mistakenly thought to be the author of a book on Jackson that was written by John Esten Cooke, who had served on J.E.B. Stuart's staff.) The book had added importance owing to its inclusion of "the most recent portrait of General Jackson."[155] Promoters of Catherine Cooper Hopley's *"Stonewall" Jackson, Late General of the Confederate States Army* made the point that although much of its content was already known to the public, she had been in Virginia and interviewed people connected with Jackson.[156]

Novels set in the American Civil War sometimes mentioned Jackson, in negative as well as positive ways, depending on the authors' purposes and affiliations.[157] Jackson's importance in the emergence of new types of warfare interested a number of experts in the field. He was discussed, for example, in "Railways Strategically Considered," by Capt. H.W. Tyler of the Royal Engineers, a lecture delivered in May 1864 in London to an audience of royals, dukes, generals, peers, MPs, and other public men.[158]

By the end of the war, many people in Britain not only had access to information and opinion about Jackson, but they also had an idea of what he might have looked like. Books, pamphlets, and articles relating to the war often included pictures, and visual representations of war sites and celebrities could be seen in various shows and exhibitions. Revell's Gallery in Leadenhall Street, London, hosted a display in June 1863 of portraits of southern leaders by the American artist Benjamin Franklin Reinhardt. He had made sketches while serving in the Confederate army, but he seems to have relied more on prewar pictures, and his style was more idealistic than realistic. The collection included Jackson. The exhibition moved to the Griffiths Gallery in Church Street, Liverpool, in July.[159] Late in 1864, in the same Liverpool gallery, there was an exhibition of portraits of Jackson and other southern leaders by John Robertson, a member of the Liverpool Academy, who had been in the South and worked "from life."[160] Robertson's work was seen in advance by a number of reporters, and one of them thought that his likeness of Jackson was "perhaps the most characteristic and generally meritorious portrait of the group."[161] In February 1865, there was a "Grand Panorama" exhibition at the Manchester Mechanics' Institute, which included items from pioneering daguerreotype artist Jonas M. Edwards and his associates, covering an expanse of six thousand miles in Canada and America. The main attraction was "a variety of stirring scenes from the present American struggle, in which the siege and the battlefield are vigorously depicted. The figure of the renowned 'Stonewall' Jackson on horseback evokes a general outburst of enthusiasm."[162]

Among all the publications about Jackson available by the end of the war, Dabney's biography was one of the most highly regarded. Before its publication, it was eagerly anticipated, and when the first volume appeared, there was a spate of reviews (though they were not all favorable). The work was widely advertised during late 1864 and early 1865. Many bookshops had it for sale, and sometimes it was advertised alongside guides to American politics and maps of America showing the location of battlefields. Several notices of the book were accompanied by endorsements attesting to its accuracy.[163] The *Morning Post* reviewed Dabney's book in March 1865 and described it as a "permanent record" of "one whose fame filled two hemispheres," and "it will not be the less welcome that the tribute to the memory of Jackson will redound to the benefit of his widow and orphan child, to whom the literary property has been presented."[164] Advertisements and reviews did as much as the book itself to keep Jackson before the British public.

Popular entertainments also played their part. Songs about Jackson featured in the repertoire of professional performers and could be heard in many concert halls, and they were also included in informal and amateur performances in schoolrooms, literary and philosophical societies, mechanics' institutes, temperance halls, and even at "floral and horticultural" fetes.[165] In October 1863, some British papers printed the words of the ballad "Stonewall Jackson's Way," sent by a resident of Boston, who wrote that the original lyric sheet was taken from a Confederate sergeant captured by the Federals in 1862.[166] During 1864, "eminent" vocalists sang of Jackson in several London venues. Concerts by various artistes, including "Christy's Colored Comedians," included the song "Death of Stonewall Jackson." Attention was drawn by advertisers to a "Christy's" concert at the Britannia Theatre in London in July 1864 because it was attended by a "large party of the surviving crew of the *Alabama*," which had been sunk by a U.S. vessel in the English Channel.[167]

There were poems as well as songs. Though he had denied authorship, in May and June 1863, some newspapers expanded their coverage of Jackson's death and funeral by including "My Wife and Child," a poem allegedly written by him during the Mexican War.[168] The anonymous "On the Death of General 'Stonewall' Jackson" also appeared, with stanzas hailing him as "Soldier," "Patriot," and "Christian."[169] In July 1863, the Scottish poet Isa Craig published "In the Dark" in the periodical *Good Words*. Described as "very beautiful," it took Jackson's death as its theme.[170] A "popular author and reciter," T.W.H. Taylor, announced late in 1864 that he intended to compose a new poem about Jackson's life and death.[171]

Jackson became a favorite subject not only for musicians, singers, and poets but also for mediums and mystics. Efforts to communicate with the departed hero were reported in British papers in the summer of 1863, and then, in December, a devotee of "spirit-rapping" named "J.B." (who turned out to be a retired Glasgow businessman and former member of the town council) published a pamphlet in which he claimed to have contacted Jackson. The pamphlet caused a stir, judging by the number of references to it.[172]

Already Jackson was a subject for scholarly study. A graduate paper on Jackson was presented at Queen's College, Belfast, in March 1865.[173] Less edifying was the gossip that he would feature in the anticipated autobiography of Maria "Belle" Boyd, the southern spy–turned–London celebrity, who in May 1862, aged eighteen and at great personal risk, had passed information to Jackson as he approached a Federal force at Front Royal. Imprisoned several times, Boyd eventually arrived in England, where she began a career on the stage and married a former U.S. Navy lieutenant. In February 1865, she was reported to be in London working on her memoirs as, among other things, "aide-de-camp to Stonewall Jackson."[174]

Demand for Jackson souvenirs and gifts was steady by the end of the war. Copies of his picture and signature were offered in the *Autographic Mirror*, a selling point that was stressed by the publishers. A later issue of the *Autographic Mirror* featured several of Jackson's as yet unpublished letters.[175] It was a form of respect (though perhaps this is debatable) that pedigree birds and sports teams were named after him as well as a growing number of racehorses and boats that competed in the Sheerness Regatta of 1864 and at Cowes in 1865.[176]

British newspapers followed the career of the Confederate navy's "formidable" steam-powered casemate turret ram the CSS *Stonewall*, built in France, "ostensibly for Denmark." The government in Washington protested about this apparent violation of French neutrality, which led to accusations against the builders, Lucien Arman, but an official inquiry in the spring of 1865 was hampered because Confederate agents had hidden their tracks. Weaponry was procured from England and added to the *Stonewall* (originally the *Sphynx*) once it left the constructors' yard. There was another diplomatic dispute when a Portuguese fortress mistakenly opened fire on the U.S. vessels that were pursuing it.[177] After the war, the *Stonewall* was seized by the United States. It was sold to Japan in 1869. Shipping news in the *Times* during 1863 and 1864 indicates that a commercial vessel named *Stonewall Jackson* made trips between England and Quebec.[178]

Interest in Jackson extended to his relatives, notably his sister Laura, who had broken with him because she opposed secession. In 1844, Laura had married lawyer and landowner Jonathan Arnold, twenty-four years her senior. She was his third wife.[179] They had a difficult time during the war because the husband, less fervent for the Union than she was, was quoted as complaining that it was impossible "to govern a Jackson." They divorced after the war.[180] According to a Union officer who had met her in West Virginia, Laura Jackson was "a very pleasant and intelligent lady": "When she heard of her brother's death she seemed very much depressed, but said that she would rather know he was dead than to have him a leader in the rebel army."[181] Interest in Jackson also extended to his resting place, in Lexington.[182] There were angry reactions when it was reported that Federal troops had raided the district intending to burn the VMI and desecrate Jackson's grave.[183]

Jackson's British admirers continued to lament his demise and to believe that had his career not been cut short, the South would have won the war. His military talents and successes were still popular talking points, as were his religious faith and his personal character and physical appearance. Though he was dead, his name and example were often used in British political and social discourse, and he featured prominently in war reports and other material about America. Britain's familiarity with Jackson was increased through books and reviews, stories, lectures, songs, and poems. The demand for Jackson souvenirs and visual representations was strong. In the years after his death, Jackson's heroic status in Britain was upheld, his fame enhanced, his appeal maintained. Circumstances changed, but interest in Jackson showed little sign of dwindling. As a soldier, a southern leader, a Christian, a virtuous and courageous exemplar, he had a relevance to large sections of the British public that no other non-British figure of the era could match.

9

STONEWALL JACKSON'S
POSTWAR LONGEVITY

Jackson's British reputation remained positive during the postwar period. There was discussion of his British ties. For his religious fervor, military talents, and successes in battle, there was continuing admiration. Information about his character, appearance, and habits was much sought after, and there was widespread use of his name beyond the turn of the century. He was the subject of songs, lectures, and readings and was often mentioned in material about America and British-U.S. relations after 1865. In different ways, Jackson was kept before the British public. The legend not only survived but flourished. In Britain, the values, behavior, and bearing associated with Jackson ensured that there would be no loss of heroic status.

People in Britain liked to remind themselves of the connection they had with Jackson. His happy memories of his British visit of 1856 were part of his legend. Into the early twentieth century, reference was still being made to the impression made upon him by Britain's mighty religious edifices. Retired field marshal Lord Wolseley published two volumes of memoirs in 1903–4, and among the highlights noted by reviewers was his meeting with Jackson in 1862. In York, it was still a source of pride that Jackson the international celebrity had regarded a local treasure, the Minster, so highly.[1] For Scots, it was equally important that Jackson had spent time in their country. Scottish author David Macrae included a section on Jackson in *The Americans at Home*, published in 1870. The book was based on Macrae's travels in America during 1867–68, but in 1869, seeking more details about Jackson, he corresponded with the general's widow, Anna, and she confirmed that he had recorded his thoughts about Scotland in a journal and that "although he extended his travels to the Continent as far as Rome, he delighted specially in talking of your interesting country."[2]

A biographical notice in the *Standard* in 1866 suggested that Jackson's

time in Europe led him to reflect on the divisions in America. He had concluded that one day North and South would go their separate ways. His
thinking along these lines was solidified by what he learned in Italy about
the despotic Ferdinand II, king of the Two Sicilies (1830–59). An Englishman
who met Jackson in Naples heard him say that "another kind of tyranny . . .
existed in a country which called itself free." Apparently, Jackson in 1856
regarded secession as inevitable: "In the questions at issue, not so much
that of slavery, but that of the right of independence of States, he spoke of
the Southern party as having justice plainly on its side."[3] This rendition of
Jackson's perspective reflected the opinion of the *Standard,* which had favored the South during the war. It was more speculative than verifiable, but
it served its purpose.

Postwar interest in Jackson usually conformed to the previous pattern,
meaning that his religious faith remained a focal point. A detailed account of
his life, based on information from multiple sources that had become available by 1865, was included in William Parker Snow's *Southern Generals.* Snow
had gained some renown as an explorer and travel writer. In *Southern Generals,* one of his more respected works (taken as a whole, his literary career was
not successful), there was no description of Jackson's spiritual conversion or
embracing of the Presbyterian creed, but Snow related all the other familiar
items. He called Jackson "a stern fatalist" and "ready worker in the hands of
destiny."[4] Similar statements were made in the "Reminiscences" published
in British newspapers in November 1865. These were mostly recycled from
American books and articles. Jackson was again depicted raising his arms
in praise or supplication, habitually in prayer, and punctiliously observing
the Sabbath.[5] In January 1866, the *Standard* declared that in serving God,
Jackson felt duty-bound to take up arms for his country. That he was "a true
Christian gentleman" was evident both in his closest relationships and in his
patriotic service to Virginia.[6]

The newspapers continued to take extracts from lengthy biographies.
Some used John Esten Cooke's *Stonewall Jackson: A Military Biography,* published in 1866, which included testimony about Jackson's deep religious
faith.[7] Cooke made his writing as "colorful" as possible, in order to attract
attention.[8] Several reviewers of Robert L. Dabney's *Life and Campaigns of
Lieutenant-General Thomas J. Jackson,* the second volume of which appeared
in 1866, emphasized that the key to understanding Jackson's personality and
career lay in his relationship with God. The *Manchester Times* argued that

Jackson had a sincere selflessness that made people notice "the singleness, purity, and elevation of his aims." His life was a "lesson."[9] The *Glasgow Herald,* well-disposed toward the Presbyterianism espoused by Jackson, nevertheless suggested that Dabney's book might give the wrong idea—as if he was ceaselessly preaching, praying, admonishing others, policing their behavior, verbally invoking the Lord. Really, Jackson was not "obtrusive" or "ostentatious." When he displayed his religiosity in public, it was not for show or to impress but "only such as might beseem a devout and earnest layman of a sect which draws no wide distinction between laymen and ministers."[10]

Is it possible that Jackson joined the Presbyterian Church because he was socially ambitious? Christopher Lawton has implied that though not insincere, Jackson made his creedal choice because he wished for gentlemanly status after settling in Lexington in 1851.[11] There is no hint of any such motive in British accounts.

Jackson's affection for Scotland might have arisen partly from a sense of denominational association, and it was shared (though she had never been there) by his widow. Anna referred in her correspondence with David Macrae to "the dear old land beyond the sea, that land which of all beyond the sea I admire and love the most, good honest-hearted Presbyterian Scotland!"[12] Church of Scotland clergyman Charles Rogers included a biography of Jackson in his *Christian Heroes,* published in 1867.[13]

At the end of the 1860s, Jackson was still being raised up as an exemplar. In him, fear of God and personal courage went together. Along with Cromwell and Havelock, Jackson featured in the literature of the Royal Navy Scripture Readers' Society.[14] It was often suggested that many of the people in Britain who sided with the South during the American war had done so because they were swayed by Jackson's religious faith. This was stated in an obituary for West Country celebrity Adm. Lewis Hole of Barnstaple, who died in 1870. Hole was thought to be the last surviving officer from the Battles of Copenhagen (1801) and Trafalgar (1805). In his post-navy life, he had been an active member of the Evangelical wing of the Church of England. From afar, it seems, Hole had developed an attachment to Jackson, for whom his respect was "often emphatically expressed," and during the American crisis, "though he had a great abhorrence of slavery, his sympathies were enlisted on the side of the Confederates." For Hole, the loss of Jackson was a personal bereavement.[15]

Writings about Jackson usually included some such phrase as "he was often at prayer."[16] People expected this. They wanted to remember Jackson in a certain way. When William C. Corsan's *Two Months in the Confederate States* was reissued in 1870, reviewers again accentuated Jackson's piety.[17] A new book, Macrae's *The Americans at Home*, portrayed Jackson as humble and prayerful. Though tolerant of other beliefs, he was a "Presbyterian of rigid orthodoxy," confident that God would protect him while He had work for him to do, and in his final hours, he accepted death as God's will.[18] Jackson was remembered, too, for trying to promote dignity, rectitude, and self-respect among those under his command. In June 1875, a gunner in the Fourth East Yorkshire Artillery Volunteers deplored the "coarse" language and "rough" behavior of many of his comrades. He encouraged them to become good Christians as well as good soldiers, for "the old Covenanters and Roundheads were not less brave because they feared God and eschewed profanity; nor General Stonewall Jackson less a hero, or fought less trenchantly, because at the dawn of each day he withdrew himself to commune with his Maker."[19]

Victorian Britain respected Jackson's religiosity and took it seriously, unlike some modern historians. Robert Croskery has gently chided those scholars who underestimate the importance of Jackson's religious commitment. To William Davis, it is "the failure to deal intelligently with this aspect of the man" that has led to "the myths that have grown around him as an oddity ... When viewed through the lens of his intense Calvinist faith, his behavior is in fact quite consistent."[20]

Known for his religious enthusiasm, Jackson continued to be praised also for his martial prowess. In the spring of 1865, as the realization set in that the South had lost the war, commentators were quick to state that this did not take anything away from Jackson's achievements. The North's victory was due to its greater economic resources and much larger armies, not to military skill. Jackson's role would never be forgotten.[21] Soon there were further tributes. One of his strengths, it was suggested, was his ability to make the best use of intelligence, as in May 1862 at Front Royal, when the spy Belle Boyd told him about the size and disposition of the Union force in the town, which he then captured.[22] Front Royal also demonstrated Jackson's use of topography and mobility to unite his own forces while dividing those of his enemies.

Snow's *Southern Generals* recognized Jackson for his gallantry, mastery of tactics, speed of movement, and use of deception and surprise. He trained his men well, knew their capabilities, and galvanized them on to success. Snow's Jackson was a modest professional who disliked being lauded above his fellow generals. He respected Lee but did not merely carry out Lee's plans. Snow, disagreeing with those who thought that Jackson had not acted on his own initiative, had no doubt that Jackson deserved to be ranked among the finest generals in history.[23]

The "Reminiscences" published in November 1865 remarked upon Jackson's victories against larger forces and his bond with his men. As a field commander, he was effective because he was a "stern, practical, mathematical calculator of chances." His career revealed not a single "blunder."[24] Jackson the exemplary soldier featured in an essay "What the American War Teaches India," also published in November 1865.[25]

Much was made of the insights of military expert Henry Charles Fletcher, an officer in the Scots Fusilier Guards, who toured the South late in 1862 and published a three-volume *History of the American War* in 1865–66. Jackson's talents helped Fletcher to explain why the Confederates did well in the early part of the war, despite the fact that the North had bigger and better-equipped armies. Jackson was "unsurpassed in enterprise and determination."[26]

Extracts from firsthand accounts of Jackson's campaigning sustained his reputation for personal courage and tactical brilliance. Former Confederate cavalry officer Harry Gilmor published *Four Years in the Saddle* in 1866. He called Jackson "friend and patron."[27] British readers were drawn most to Gilmor's experiences with Jackson in the Shenandoah Valley.[28] Discussing Dabney's biography in October 1866, the *Saturday Review* welcomed the author's coverage of Jackson's movements and victories.[29] To the *Saturday Review*, the extent of Jackson's contribution to the southern cause was shown by what happened after his death. Confederate forces never again had such triumphs. A similar argument was made by reviewers of Snow's *Southern Generals* and of Heros von Borcke's *Memoirs of the Confederate War for Independence*, sections of which were published in *Blackwood's Magazine* before they appeared in book form in 1867 (in two volumes in Britain, then published in Philadelphia as a single volume).[30] Von Borcke, a Prussian lieutenant of dragoons, had arrived in the South in May 1862, looking for adventure and in flight from creditors in his homeland. As a staff officer to J.E.B. Stuart, he got to know Jackson well and referred to him in an affectionate and respectful way throughout the memoirs.[31] At the end of 1866, the *Ob-*

server reviewed all recent publications about Jackson as part of an extended essay on "The Southern States under Defeat."[32] Here was further material for those who wished to see in Jackson the supreme embodiment of a brave and honorable soldier. The republication in 1870 of Corsan's *Two Months in the Confederate States* furthered this trend.[33]

There was annoyance when efforts were made after the war to undermine Jackson's reputation, especially by men who had fought for the North. One of their number would occasionally make a speech or have a letter placed in the newspapers. "Having been terribly afraid of him while he was alive, certain Federal warriors have discovered that Stonewall Jackson dead was only an ass in a lion's skin."[34] For many, Jackson remained the standard by which other protagonists in the American war were judged. In 1869, Raphael Semmes, formerly of the Confederate navy, published *My Adventures Afloat: A Narrative of My Cruises and Services in the "Sumter" and "Alabama."* Semmes had been one of the most effective commerce raiders in history, and British reviewers thought they were paying him a compliment when they called him "the Stonewall Jackson of the seas."[35] Jackson's career was sometimes brought up in quarrels between British officers when they disagreed in print about "the art of war."[36]

In a discussion of Macrae's *The Americans at Home,* the *Morning Post* paraphrased his remarks about Jackson's combination of aggression and surprise and took up the Jackson idea that to give the enemy no quarter would be to end the war more quickly and prevent further bloodshed. To the *Morning Post,* Jackson was harsh and severe but also brilliant, particularly when it came to keeping northern generals guessing.[37] Macrae himself emphasized Jackson's "war look"—the way his eyes blazed in battle—and his determination not to yield. In a piece for the *Glasgow Herald,* Macrae revealed that he was in possession of the coat worn by the general at Chancellorsville. Given by Jackson's widow, it was "to me more precious than its weight in gold."[38] Anna Jackson had received the coat from Robert E. Lee, who retrieved it after Jackson's death.[39] Some southerners considered it a "sacred relic" and wanted it displayed in Virginia, but others were happy for Macrae to show it in British venues.[40]

In Macrae's comparison of Lee and Jackson, Lee was best at defense and Jackson at attack. Lee sought to baffle and weary the enemy, but Jackson aimed to destroy, and Lee was more lenient when it came to army discipline, for Jackson was "stern and remorseless" and only rarely relented in

cases of disobedience by officers or men. Macrae conjectured that Scots
were captivated by Jackson's career because it had all the things they enjoyed most in their own romantic national legends—boldness and bravery,
"unwavering purpose," worthy but doomed struggle—rather like the stories
and songs about John Graham of Claverhouse, Viscount Dundee, the Jacobite leader who died at the Battle of Killiekrankie in 1689, and the "Bonnie
Prince," Charles Edward Stuart, who led the 1745 Rebellion.[41] This Scottish
connection was something Macrae discussed with Lee when the two met
at Washington College (subsequently Washington and Lee University) in
Lexington, where Lee was president. Lee mentioned that Jackson would
sometimes talk of Scotland. Jackson had Scots-Irish ancestry, and Lee told
Macrae, "You will meet with many of your countrymen here" (in "the valley
of Virginia"). "They have the courage and determination of the Scotch, with
the Irish dash and intrepidity. They make fine soldiers."[42]

During the Franco-Prussian War of 1870–71, British observers wondered
if either side had a general of Jackson's caliber and if the tactics he had perfected could bring success in a European setting. Jackson was brought into
reflections on the Prussian advance, the defenses around Paris, the role of
training and study in modern campaigns, and the connection between patriotism and military glory.[43]

British interest in Jackson was extended to encompass officers who had
served under him and benefited from his encouragement and advice. One
such officer was Gen. Raleigh E. Colston, who had commanded a division
at Chancellorsville. In March 1873, it was reported that Colston had taken a
post in the army of the Khedive of Egypt. He was also to teach courses at the
university in Cairo. Colston had formerly been a professor at the VMI with
Jackson, and Jackson had recommended him for promotion several times in
the Confederate army.[44]

The claim that Jackson had acted under Lee's direction and that respect
for Jackson was really due to Lee occasionally resurfaced in the British press.
It was eschewed on the basis that Lee was fully aware of Jackson's talents and
had tended not to give detailed instructions because he knew Jackson would
do all that was necessary. He trusted Jackson to make his own decisions.
Jackson's strengths as a commander were often mentioned in books and
articles by British generals and military experts, the assumption being that
there was much to learn from Jackson's career. It was widely agreed that the
American war would have had a different outcome had Jackson not died.[45]

In 1874, when travel company Thomas Cook announced tours of the United States and an "advance party" sent back endorsements for publication in Britain, the itinerary included places associated with Jackson, the routes he had taken, and the sites of his battles. British travelers wanted to visit the locations where Jackson had made his name.[46] His generalship was still a favorite topic in meeting rooms and lecture halls around Britain, and some commentators maintained that Jackson's soldiering surpassed that of Grant, who was now America's president, having been elected in 1868. Grant had lacked Jackson's "dashing valor and adventurous daring."[47] John Cannon, author of the *History of Grant's Campaign for the Capture of Richmond,* published in London in 1869, could not refrain from praising the "hero" Jackson, even though his book focused on Grant and the final year of the war.[48] Jackson was mentioned in connection with the Russo-Turkish War of 1877–78. A correspondent of the *Manchester Guardian,* for instance, wrote that although in personal character the "amiable and prepossessing" Mehmet Ali Pasha, commander of Ottoman forces in Bulgaria, resembled Jackson, as a general he was not Jackson's equal.[49] The image of the "praying and fighting" Jackson, "ever superior to occasion," was sustained by the recollections of former Confederate general Richard Taylor, published as *Destruction and Reconstruction* in 1879. Taylor, the son of U.S. president Zachary Taylor (1849–50), had served with Jackson, and his book was favorably reviewed in the British press.[50]

Judging by speeches given at regimental dinners and letters and articles published in army magazines, many British servicemen regarded Jackson as a model soldier whom they should try to emulate.[51] Jackson continued to be ranked with the best of Britain's generals, living and deceased, principally Cromwell, Wellington, Havelock, and Sir Charles Napier, a veteran of the Peninsular War, conqueror of Sindh, and commander in chief in India (1849–51). Jackson was also frequently associated with European heroes, particularly Garibaldi.[52] He was respected in Canadian military circles, as may be seen from the book *Modern Cavalry,* published in London in 1868. The author was George T. Denison, commander of the Governor-General's Bodyguard.[53]

On the question of military discipline, Jackson's example was sometimes applied to the British Army. It was thought that he had retained the commitment and obedience of his men through inspiration, not coercion. His approach was brought up when army reforms were debated in Parliament, as in March 1867, when a resolution that flogging should be permitted only in wartime was approved in the House of Commons. According to one writer, the ideal was the army of Jackson, in which there had been a trustful rapport between the commander and his troops.[54] What had been behind it? The *Standard* revisited the matter in its review of von Borcke's *Memoirs*. Von Borcke had observed Jackson at close hand. What came through was the general sharing the "hardships and privations" of his men and his combination of "simple, unaffected manners" and "lion-like courage."[55]

Though it was not its purpose, von Borcke's book helped to explain why so many in Britain had sympathized with the Confederates. It showed their character, courage, and self-sacrifice. They gained support less because of the "abstract justice of their cause" than because "ill-armed, ill-clad, shoeless, and ill-fed," they "beat back splendidly equipped armies of two and three times their own numerical strength." Von Borcke had provided a detailed narrative without offering many of his own opinions. The *Examiner* suggested that von Borcke's account could be profitably read alongside another recent book, Fletcher's "fuller and more sober" *History of the American War*.[56] With works such as these to inform assessments of Jackson, it became easier to identify generals who fell short of his standards. Some were British.[57]

In June 1888, British commentators welcomed the news that a memorial to Jackson had been placed on the spot where he had been wounded at Chancellorsville. The *Times* reported that five thousand people attended the ceremony.[58] Reminders of Jackson's wartime exploits came in vivid fashion in four volumes of essays, maps, engravings, and personal testimony, entitled *Battles and Leaders of the Civil War*, published in New York in 1889 and reviewed in the British press early in 1890. "Friends and enemies appear to be agreed that there was no more striking personality on either side."[59] Jackson's generalship was again extolled—especially his rapidity of decision and movement—when observers of Austro-Hungarian military maneuvers published reports in 1894.[60] War correspondent Frank Lawley wrote a series of short articles in the 1890s about the American conflict, a number of which discussed Jackson.[61]

British people interested in Jackson's religious beliefs and military talents continued also to seek information about his character, appearance, and personal habits. Not all of this material was complimentary. The negative items tended to focus on a familiar problem—a character flaw, it was claimed—that although he had been brave and earnest and talented, he allowed himself to be misdirected. Among the clearest expressions of this point of view came in a lecture in London, just as the American war was coming to an end. The speaker was David Bell, who had recently been in America, "and throughout he was listened to with marked attention." To preserve the Union, Bell asserted, was to uphold constitutional principles and facilitate the abolition of slavery, so that America would be truly free. By opposing this, Jackson had made a terrible mistake.[62]

Nevertheless, there were more than a few favorable pieces about Jackson's personality. Snow's comments in *Southern Generals* were positive, and reviewers of the book insisted that Jackson's fame was based not only on his victories in battle but also on his admirable *character*, for he typified the best qualities of the South. From this, one could gather that some British people had supported the South because they were attracted by Jackson.[63] The "Reminiscences" published late in 1865 described a selfless, dutiful, patriotic man and a devout Christian but added a proviso. Jackson's true personality could not be fully known, and even his admirers had to accept that there was a gap between his image and the reality. While not lessening his greatness, "peculiarities" in his appearance and manner made him a human being and not just a heroic fancy. There was "something absent and abstracted" about Jackson. Some had considered him mad, but though odd and unconventional in his ways, he also had the most laudable of qualities. "Nonsense could not live in his presence." He was "true, kind, brave, and simple."[64]

Jackson's truthfulness was also emphasized by Snow, who cited the formal reports of battles written under Jackson's direction by his staff. Snow included other remarks about personality and appearance. It was suggested that Jackson's early life as a poor orphan "may have somewhat soured his temper, and inclined him to asceticism." Snow repeated stories about his diet and exercise. According to the testimony of one who served under him, the general was "a dry old stick . . . He is solemn and thoughtful, speaks but little, and always in a calm, decided tone; and from what he says there is no appeal." This source also played up the comical element: "His wardrobe isn't worth a dollar; and his horse is quite in keeping."[65] With some artistic license but encompassing all he had heard and read, Snow's depiction of Jackson typified the way his British admirers imagined him: "Cool, calm, stern, and self-collected . . . powerful . . . a true hero."[66]

One of Jackson's quirks was his belief in hydropathy, and there was some discussion that "water treatments" might have contributed to his death. Fascination with Jackson's death and its causes remained strong in Britain. In 1866, when a selection from von Borcke's memoirs was published in *Blackwood's Magazine*, interest was piqued by the accompanying announcement that von Borcke knew the real reason for Jackson's death and had no less an authority than Hunter McGuire, chief surgeon in Jackson's army, to back him up. (McGuire amputated Jackson's arm after he was wounded at Chancellorsville. The two had become friends during the war, and McGuire was one of the pallbearers at Jackson's funeral.) Von Borcke "does not attribute the dauntless Confederate's decease to exhaustion, subsequent upon his wounds," but to "a severe cold caught on the night when he was struck, and which the treatment he insisted on adopting rendered fatal." Against McGuire's advice, Jackson had "insisted on treating his cold by the application of wet blankets."[67]

Tales about Jackson continued to be much in demand. Not thought to have been blessed with a keen sense of humor, he was supposed to have made a joke in public only once.[68] Yet von Borcke's book seemed to show that Jackson "enjoyed the pleasures of life and a harmless joke as much as anybody."[69] Extracts from Cooke's *Stonewall Jackson: A Military Biography* also indicated that Jackson was no intractable, coldhearted Puritan.[70]

That Jackson had not concerned himself with how he looked and was rarely seen in a clean and neat uniform was widely taken in Britain as an endearing quality. The scruffy appearance was by now something for which he was known. A story related by von Borcke strengthened the hold of this image. A smart new coat was sent to Jackson by J.E.B. Stuart. Von Borcke delivered it and "was heartily amused at the modest confusion with which the hero of many battles regarded the fine uniform from many points of view, scarcely daring to touch it." Over Jackson's protestations that it was "much too handsome for me," von Borcke insisted that he must try the coat on, and at once Jackson's men began to gather round, eager to take in a sight they were not used to, their leader in splendid military dress. "The whole of the Staff were in a perfect ecstasy . . . and the soldiers came running by hundreds."[71]

In the summer of 1867, a number of British newspapers debated the question "Was Stonewall Jackson a lunatic?" It was prompted by items in the American press about the early part of the war, before Jackson had made his mark, when some in the senior military staff and government of the Confederacy decided that he was unstable and unreliable. Jackson had wanted to resign and was only prevented by the intervention of his friend John Letcher, governor of Virginia (1860–64).[72] One of the more sensational stories about Jackson—that he had once proposed a night attack by troops stripped naked and armed only with knives—was soon discredited. The *Manchester Courier* pointed out that Jackson had become an almost mythical figure. Truth and falsehood were jumbled together.[73]

The claim about the naked night attack was not new but gained currency when it was included in a piece by Edward A. Pollard in *Putnam's Magazine* of New York in December 1868. Pollard, formerly of the *Richmond Examiner*, was the pro-Confederacy, proslavery author of such books as *The Southern History of the War* (1862–65) and *The Lost Cause* (1866). In *Putnam's*, he wrote that Jackson's readiness "to fight in the most terrible manner" led him to urge the attack because "the novelty and terror of such an apparition would paralyze the enemy."[74] Some southerners thought this defamatory, while in Britain, attention was drawn to a letter in the *New York Herald* signed "A Virginian." It described an episode at Fredericksburg in December 1862. On the last evening of the battle, Confederate commanders expected the Federals to try another attack in the morning. Jackson did recommend a surprise night maneuver and spoke of hand-to-hand combat, using only the bayonet, the southerners stripped to the waist to distinguish them from the enemy. Some preparations were made for this assault under cover of darkness, but it was abandoned (and it proved to be unnecessary because the Federals withdrew).[75] Gen. Jubal Early issued another denial of the story in July 1870. Jackson "could not have made such a proposition as that mentioned by Pollard, because it was a moral impossibility for him to have done it." Even if Christian decency were cast aside, there were practical barriers: it was too cold to strip to the waist, and the Confederates at Fredericksburg were short of knives and bayonets.[76]

What British people knew, or thought they knew, about Jackson was regularly embellished by anecdotes. Southern papers were cited in British publications, and Jackson's character and appearance also featured in widely reviewed books. Selections from these and other items reached a wider readership. Macrae thought of Jackson as a man of war but added that from all he had heard, "off duty Jackson was as modest and unassuming as a child."[77] When Macrae was in the South, "I learnt so much about Jackson . . . that he rises before my mind as clearly as if I had seen him a hundred times myself."[78] Into the mid-1870s, reports still circulated about Jackson's time as a tutor at the VMI, and there were the familiar descriptions of him during the war, awkward in manner and unkempt in appearance.[79] But for all this, he had "nobility of character." The North had not produced a similar figure who "engaged the esteem and affection of foreign observers."[80]

In the postwar years, songs about Jackson continued to be sung at music halls, assembly rooms, and concert venues all across Britain, often in the musical segment of variety shows that included comedy, acrobats, drama, and other attractions. Jackson was the subject of papers read at literary institutes, mutual improvement societies, town halls, masonic lodges, and schoolrooms.[81] It emerged that "The Death of Stonewall Jackson," one of the popular songs of the time, was the work of British composer and harpist Charles Blamphin.[82] Ironically, songs about Jackson were being heard at the very time that news came through of the Confederacy's collapse, at the end of April 1865.[83] In Wrexham in March 1866, during a concert in aid of the local cricket club, "Mr. J. L. Heywood charmed his hearers, especially such as were of Southern proclivities, with the favorite song 'Stonewall Jackson.'"[84] For some, these performances had political meaning, but others just wanted entertainment. Among notable performances of "Stonewall Jackson" was one in May 1869 at the Victoria Theatre, London, by a group of blackface singers. At this time, there were three such troupes on the London stage.[85] The most famous was the Christy Minstrels, who performed in several British cities. "Gallant Stonewall Jackson" was one of their songs on a tour of 1868.[86] *The Australian Melodist,* a songbook published in 1870, included "Stonewall Jackson."[87] Lectures by former war correspondent Frank Vizetelly featured Jackson. One was "Incidents of Campaigning Life," delivered in London in October 1869.[88]

Jackson's name was used to encourage young people to improve themselves. Of all the celebrities who might have been discussed to promote education, good character, and religious faith, speakers clearly thought that the dead Confederate general fit the bill particularly well. The 1866 annual soiree of the Free North Church Sabbath School, Stirling, was addressed by Robert Cuthbertson (who had been a pastor in Dunfermline and later moved to a Congregational Church in Yorkshire). He had a message for the children: Jackson was their guide. His life demonstrated what could be accomplished through "perseverance and determination." Orphaned, poor, a struggling student at West Point, Jackson had gone on to serve God and amaze man.[89]

Jackson's name was also used, as it had been during the war, in political battles in Britain. In June 1866, in Nottingham, a crowd gathered to hear London radical David Faulkner, who had been an unsuccessful candidate at a recent by-election in the borough. Faulkner attacked the prime minister and former foreign secretary, Russell, for a career of failure. What most stirred the audience was complaint about Russell's role during the American Civil War. Many believed that Russell had allowed the U.S. government to bully him. Faulkner also asserted, rather improbably, that Russell could have saved Jackson's life. "A line" from him, "with a man-of-war to carry the letter, would have prevented the death of General Stonewall Jackson" and stopped "rivers of blood" and the "juggernaut of despotism."[90]

Jackson's British admirers were determined that his character and achievements should not be forgotten. Some newspapers, in the "Calendar" they published showing anniversaries, new moons, eclipses, and the like for the coming year, included for May the death of Jackson in 1863. Some included it in their "calendar for the week."[91] Jackson mementos continued to be advertised. In 1866, engravings of Jackson were being offered by J. W. Weir and Company, wholesale stationers of Glasgow.[92] There was unceasing interest in Jackson's "last orders" and "last words" and "last hours." Many accounts were published in Britain, including some written by American correspondents of British newspapers and some lifted directly from American papers.[93]

Items about Jackson's widow, Anna, and daughter, Julia (born 1862), appeared in the British press. From time to time, there were reports that they were "sinking into abject poverty." There were calls to set up a subscription fund. It was also suggested that some of the money collected for the relief of Confederates being held in U.S. prisons could be given to Jackson's family. Another suggestion was that the money raised by "English gentlemen" for a Jackson statue—to be presented to the people of the South at some as yet undetermined time—ought to go instead to the family.[94] The impact of all this was augmented by the many accounts of intense suffering across the South. Some writers sought to use the hardships of Jackson's family to prolong British sympathy for the South. The opportunity was taken to assign blame for the "lamentable" social and political conditions there.[95]

In Britain, the most eager response was associated with the *Standard*. One of its contributors, "Mercator," hoped that readers would agree to relieve the widow "on the ground of the high moral and military character of the husband." The *Standard* put its own weight behind the appeal.[96] Soon Anna Jackson made it known that she and Julia were not in serious need. A letter, sent from the home of Anna's father near Charlotte, North Carolina, appeared in British papers with other items from America, which suggests that readers wished to find out more.[97]

When Jackson's family attended a public event in Richmond in 1866, a report was quickly circulated around Britain. Julia was described as "enchanting," with fair hair and blue eyes, and "the dark-eyed, sad looking lady who followed her in a widow's cap and garb of deep mourning, completed the picture of sunshine and shadow."[98] In 1868, it was suggested that Anna Jackson had received fifteen thousand dollars from sales of "her *Life of Stonewall Jackson*."[99] In fact, she had not yet published any book about her husband (her *Life and Letters of General Thomas J. Jackson* would appear in 1892, and *Memoirs of Stonewall Jackson* in 1895). The reports referred to Dabney's biography, a project with which she had cooperated and from which she had been promised royalties. In 1869, British papers carried another story about Anna and Julia in dire straits. Wade H. Bolton of Memphis, partner in one of the largest cotton firms in the South, being told that all of Jackson's possessions had been sold after the war to pay his debts, left Anna ten thousand dollars in his will.[100] Occasionally, Anna Jackson's movements were reported, as when she went to take the waters at Rockbridge Alum Springs in Virginia, about seventeen miles from Lexington.[101] Her role as "Widow of the Confederacy," a symbol of southern pride and dignity, and her readiness to attend the unveiling of war monuments meant that she remained worthy of press coverage. As the *Times* noted, presidential visits to Charlotte were not complete without her participation. She met Theodore Roosevelt in 1905 and William H. Taft in 1909.[102] There were rumors that Julia Jackson intended to visit Britain. At the end of 1883, she was described as "the American belle *par excellence* for next season in London."[103]

Discussion of his family helped to keep Jackson's memory alive in Britain in the postwar period. This was accomplished in other ways. A public house in Gosta Green, Birmingham, was named after him.[104] So were greyhounds, racehorses, and racing boats.[105] A cargo vessel, the *Stonewall Jackson*, was built in Liverpool in 1865. It was to become notorious through scandal. In March 1867, it was spotted foundering in bad weather off the coast of Ireland. Its master was later accused of slipping a towline to avoid the expense of salvage. He attempted to enter Kinsale harbor, but his ship went down.[106] British newspapers also included updates on the warship *Stonewall*, built in Bordeaux in 1864. By the time it crossed the Atlantic, the American war was over. It passed into U.S. possession and was later, as the *Kotetsu*, the first ironclad in the Japanese navy.[107]

"Stonewall Jackson" had become part of the British vocabulary. The phrase was used in everyday parlance, and people knew what it meant. When a Christmas dinner was laid on for ninety paupers in Bangor Workhouse in December 1865, "the onslaught was of the Stonewall Jackson character, and nothing for a time could stand before it."[108] Assessments of personal worth were made using Jackson's name. To be like him, or unlike him, seems to have mattered.[109] The name of no other American was used so widely in speech or in print in Britain in the years after the war.

Jackson was repeatedly mentioned in British press coverage of American current affairs. Regret at the assassination of President Lincoln merged with denial that responsibility could be attached to the South, which furthered the tendency to present Jackson as representative of southern values. The *Exeter and Plymouth Gazette* scorned "the endeavors of Federal advocates in this country to cast the stigma of a foul murder upon the cause for which Stonewall Jackson died."[110]

There was much speculation about the future of the Union and how events across the Atlantic would affect Britain. The Liberal *Sheffield Independent* called upon British supporters of the South to accept that the war was over and to concentrate on promoting the South's smooth absorption back into the Union. With peace, though, came an obligation for the North to be fair toward the South. Secession, as a policy, had failed, but as a principle— the ability of states to withdraw from a federation into which they had freely entered—it was still valid. Anyone who knew anything about Jackson understood this. The best thing now would be for the abolition of slavery to be accompanied by a proper recognition of the liberties belonging to states and individuals.[111] With the South defeated, its friends in Britain had to focus all the more on the merits of individuals, to mitigate the effects of defeat. They could stress the positive qualities of the South by using Jackson as a personification.

The possibility that former Confederate president Jefferson Davis would be tried and executed prompted further assessments of Jackson, for the purposes of comparison. The radical and pro-northern *Reynolds's Newspaper* considered Davis undeserving of leniency. He was not the same as Jackson, who, though also a rebel, had conducted himself with honor. Other commentators were less severe on Davis and called for clemency, but they added that the respect due to the "brave, conscientious, Christian" Jackson should not extend to Davis.[112] The *Standard,* meanwhile, wary of "the cleverness of the Yankees in falsifying history," warned its readers that northerners would try to control interpretations of the war and lower the reputation of the "immortal" Jackson and other southern leaders.[113]

Reviewers of Snow's *Southern Generals* observed that sympathy for the South rested mainly on respect for Confederate valor. An aura of chivalry surrounded Jackson. He and his colleagues had not sunk to the "outrages" committed by such northern commanders as Butler in New Orleans and Sheridan in the Shenandoah Valley. The British knew that the North won the war not because it had superior social qualities but because of the exhaustion of the economically weaker South. According to Beresford Hope's *Saturday Review,* "There has been no modern war to whose history so much of the zest of personal romance belongs as is attached to the story of the recent American struggle," and there were few in Britain to whom Jackson and the others "are not as familiar and as interesting as the heroes of English history and romance."[114] But to British commentators who wanted and expected Reconstruction fundamentally to change the South, the veneration of Jackson was a distraction and an obstacle. It was not unrelated to President Andrew Johnson's generosity toward the South and the possibility that southerners would gain full power over their own affairs.[115]

There were numerous reports about conditions in the defeated South. Some of the most widely read were those sent by Louis Jennings, the correspondent of the *Times,* who had risen from an impoverished background to make his name as a journalist in India before being sent to America in 1865. Pieces by Jennings appeared not only in the *Times* but also in other London and provincial titles, and Jackson was often mentioned. A tour of the Sharpsburg battlefield, for instance, brought forth an account of Jackson's arrival to reinforce Lee.[116] Jennings moved into the Shenandoah Valley and recorded that Jackson was still idolized there.[117] A "special correspondent" of the *Morning Post* declared that the area in which the "gallant" Jackson had performed "dashing and successful exploits" was "now a waste and a desert."[118]

Several British commentators paid attention to a controversy in the American press regarding Jackson's opinions about secession, slavery, and the giving of "no quarter" to the enemy. The *Standard* argued that long before the war, Jackson had thought secession inevitable.[119] The *Saturday Review* took the matter up in its assessment of Dabney's biography.[120] Provincial newspapers also discussed it. Northern claims that Jackson had been hesitant in his response to secession were rejected, and while his admirers did not deny that Jackson had been a slave owner, they explained that he accepted slavery as a legal institution sanctioned by both the Bible and the U.S. Constitution. As for "no quarter," this seemed appropriate because the invasion of the South was unjustified and unprovoked. Had Jackson's proposal been adopted, the South would not have lost the war.[121] There was continuing discord on these points and on what might have happened had Jackson not died in 1863.[122]

"No quarter" could also be related to the Irish agitation against British rule, which had frequently turned violent. There were Fenian raids in Canada in 1866. Participants included Americans who crossed the border, which complicated British-U.S. relations. In the British press, there was a heated debate concerning leniency for rebels and the similarity (or not) between the Confederate cause and that of the Fenians.[123] The *Westmorland Gazette* dismissed as "preposterous" Seward's contention that Fenian offenses were not deserving of serious punishment. Many in Britain were aware of Jackson's recommendation that no quarter should be shown by Confederate troops, but they were also aware that very rarely in the war had no quarter been given. They maintained, moreover, that the Fenian cause was not the equal of the southern cause and that, toward the South, the North had shown restraint only because of self-interest.[124]

By the spring of 1868, disagreement about how to treat the South had brought the U.S. Congress and President Johnson into headlong collision. Moves were afoot to impeach the president. The *Alabama* claims remained unresolved, and accusations against Britain by northern politicians and newspapers continued. According to the Conservative *Belfast Newsletter*, all this added to the British people's "extraordinary interest" in American affairs, an interest that had been dramatically boosted by the war and the "dash and heroism" of Jackson, who epitomized the courage of the South in what was no mere rebellion but a glorious movement for national independence.[125] This version of recent history was under direct assault from Liberal papers and public figures. The target of their ire was frequently the Conservative *Standard*, which responded in kind.[126] The *Standard* went on to give a warm welcome to Jefferson Davis when he arrived in Britain in 1868 (and was hosted by, among others, Beresford Hope). Davis was greeted as a representative of the cause in which Jackson had died. To publish a friendly assessment of Davis was also a way of continuing the praise and respect due to Jackson. These Confederates still stood for something. For a time, they had headed what the *Standard* called "the critical and decisive contest of the old order against the new, of aristocracy against democracy, of liberty against the despotism of majorities, of Conservatism against political chaos and social revolution."[127]

The *Standard* argued that although Jackson's "countrymen" could not enjoy the "national life" they had fought for, they *would* recover rights and status within the Union in a short space of time, meaning that the real challenges were economic rather than political. The South had lost "the very flower of her youth and manhood," and few were left to restore industry and agriculture. To make matters worse, the manner in which slavery had been abolished was economically disastrous, and it had demoralized the blacks too, as in the British West Indies after the slaves were emancipated there. Still, southerners were "impatient of centralization" and could not be "permanently ruled either by Northern bayonets or by negro votes." The sacrifices made by Jackson and his comrades had not been in vain.[128]

Early in 1870, British papers discussed a claim that Jackson had been killed by Federal troops. This was countered by northern as well as southern sources. Jackson's subordinate, A. P. Hill, who had commanded a division at Chancellorsville, joined in, and a Federal general, Joseph W. Revere, who had also fought at Chancellorsville, confirmed that Jackson was wounded by shots fired by the Eighteenth North Carolina Infantry, part of Hill's division.[129] British commentators noted again that Jackson had been respected in the North as well as the South, and some suggested that this regard would help to moderate the old sectional bitterness.[130]

Hardly any of the British obituary notices for Robert E. Lee, who died on 12 October 1870, failed to mention his reliance on Jackson. In December 1870, when it was announced that the next U.S. minister in London would be Robert C. Schenck, of all the things that might have been written about this congressman, diplomat, and veteran of the American war, British readers appear to have been most interested in the fact that in several battles he had faced Jackson. The same was true of Ambrose Burnside, the postwar governor of Rhode Island, who was in Europe late in 1870 and tried to negotiate a cease-fire in the Franco-Prussian War.[131] The publication in 1873 of a memoir of Lee written by Blanche Lee Childe, the wife of his nephew, prompted yet another repetition of stories about Jackson, "one of the most eccentric and original figures" of recent times.[132]

Jackson's name continued to crop up in discussion of the *Alabama* dispute. British commentators conceded that Britain's failure to stop the *Alabama* from sailing was probably a matter that should go to arbitration, but they complained that what northerners really cared about—Britain's recognition of the Confederacy as a belligerent power—was an unhelpful fixation. The North still resented it, but it had been unavoidable. Now was the time to focus on the natural friendship between Britain and the United States, and when the British praised Jackson, it was asserted, they were expressing admiration for America as a whole, not just the former Confederacy. Expressions of British goodwill were mixed, however, with criticism of the "spoiled child" behavior of northerners.[133]

Arbitrators awarded damages to the United States in 1872, but Britain's negotiator, Chief Justice Sir Alexander Cockburn, dissented from the verdict with regard to British liability. The *North Devon Journal* thanked him for standing up to U.S. allegations and for clearly establishing that the sympathy shown in Britain for the South had been reasonable and sincere and willfully misunderstood by many in the North: "Whatever the cause in which they are exhibited, devotion and courage will ever command respect, and they did so in this instance . . . All the opprobrious terms which might be heaped upon the cause in which he fell could not persuade the world that the earth beneath which Stonewall Jackson rests does not cover the remains of a patriot and hero." Furthermore, in view of past U.S. actions against Canada, Cuba, and Mexico, U.S. support for Russia during the Crimean War, and more recent U.S. encouragement of Fenianism, Washington had no right to complain.[134] A similar position was taken by several London papers.[135]

The Grant presidency (1869–77) offered opportunities to Jackson's British admirers to mention him in their discussion of American politics, as in 1872, when the president stood for reelection. Grant was challenged by Horace Greeley. The *Standard* suggested that Greeley had some questionable endorsements, including that of Nathaniel P. Banks, congressman for Massachusetts (and former governor of the state), who had held several important commands for the North during the war but who was chiefly notable for having been resoundingly defeated by Jackson in the Shenandoah Valley.

Grant won in 1872, but to many British observers, his shortcomings were more apparent than his strengths. The *Examiner* admitted in 1875 that Grant had "steadiness." But he lacked the bold style of Jackson.[136]

After the war, the date on which Jackson died, 10 May, was kept for solemn reflection by many in Virginia. In 1866, there was a firsthand account written by an "Edinburgh gentleman," whose "A Visit to Richmond" appeared in the British press.[137] Across the South, 10 May was a day to honor Jackson and all the Confederacy's fallen. In 1867, it was reported that "the anniversary of Stonewall Jackson's death has been observed in various portions of the South by the ladies visiting the graves of the Confederate dead."[138] British newspapers also noted the plan adopted by VMI alumni to erect a memorial chapel that would include a statue of Jackson and busts of other Confederate generals who had graduated from the college.[139] Over the years, there was frequent reference to the undiminished pride and resilience of the South. Patriotic remembrance was particularly noticeable in Virginia, where, ten years after the end of the war, "almost everyone" was still talking about Jackson.[140] His admirers in Britain continued to speak and write about him as well. Whatever qualities they had attributed to him before and whatever reasons they had for using his name and fame, Jackson still mattered to them and retained relevance and emblematic force.

Jackson had a prominent place in several popular artistic forms—songs, plays, novels—of the late Victorian era. British soldiers were fond of singing about him at their regimental dinners and other social occasions, as at the annual supper of the Thirteenth Suffolk Rifle Volunteers in October 1878, and "Stonewall Jackson songs" continued to feature in the entertainment programs of concert rooms and music halls across Britain.[141] Jackson appeared as a character in dramatic productions, and people who missed these shows could still find out about them in the papers.[142] By the late nineteenth century, a new artistic genre had arisen, the "adventure story" set in the American war and merging together factual detail and a central fictional narrative. Jackson featured in several of these novels. Often they were low-quality fare and sank without trace, but some were popular, at least for a time.[143]

An earlier novel of some renown was *The Coming Race*, a satirical and utopian work published anonymously in 1871 (its author was the politician and man of letters Edward Bulwer-Lytton). One of its themes was struggle as the means to improve the human race, and Jackson was discussed as an exemplary character, a type that only emerged because of war.[144] A novel of 1877 featured a character named Ephraim Gundy, a Confederate soldier who kills himself in remorse when he realizes that in the confusion and darkness at Chancellorsville, it was his gun that brought down Jackson.[145] A novel of 1895 featured a British man who went to fight for the South, rose to the rank of colonel, and had meetings and conversations with the great "Stonewall."[146] Jackson's name cropped up again in reviews in 1899 of Arthur Paterson's *The Gospel Writ in Steel*. As the *Times* put it: "The American Civil War is still wonderfully attractive both to the romancer and to the reader of romances. It lends itself to broad, melodramatic treatment."[147] Tales of Jackson as a charismatic "adventure" figure were included in boys' magazines.[148]

Jackson's positive reputation in Britain was sustained at the end of the century by using the tried and tested device of praise by association—that is, he was often mentioned alongside heroic figures selected from Britain's own history. A recent addition to this pantheon was Gen. Charles Gordon, whose violent death in Khartoum in January 1885, during the Mahdist uprising, occasioned public grief and a wave of memorialization. Both Jackson and Gordon could be seen as noble Christian warrior martyrs.[149] At a prize-giving ceremony of September 1898 at Redhill Farm School (run by the Philanthropic Society as a reformatory for three hundred boys), the speaker, Lord Methuen, a veteran of several wars, told the pupils that of all the great men they should admire and emulate, Jackson and Gordon were the best.[150]

Jackson's name was used to support particular causes in the present. He was taken to represent ideas and values that could legitimately be drawn upon in arguments about current affairs. As in previous years, Jackson's career was brought up in discussions about army reform. In a letter to *Reynolds's Newspaper* of August 1880, "Northumbrian" warned that unless the British Army was placed under the control of real soldiers, rather than royal dukes and aristocratic generals who had never seen combat, the disasters of the Crimea and inefficiencies associated with campaigns against the Afghans and Zulus would be repeated. Northumbrian thought it no accident that America had produced a soldier like Jackson, for America was "free from this cringing to courts and strong in the candor of camps."[151] Jackson's abstemious lifestyle made him a regular in publications that cautioned against the dangers of alcohol. Frederick Sherlock of the National Temperance League included him in a collection of "temperance testimonies of some eminent men" published in 1881.[152]

Albeit infrequently, Jackson's name could be used in negative as well as positive ways. Accounts of religious revivalism in America occasionally brought forth hostility and derision in the British press. One article of 1881 condemned militancy, the mania for collecting money, and other faults of "outward and ostentatious religious observance." As for Jackson and his habit of praying anytime and anywhere, the writer was amused rather than impressed. Was it to be assumed that Jackson won battles because he prayed or, rather, because the Federal generals he faced made mistakes?[153]

Jackson was mentioned in reports, obituaries, and other published items about notable figures of the American Civil War and in accounts of political and social life in the restored Union. Sometimes there was more than a hint of reproof in the coverage. A number of commentators suggested that it was not a good idea to dwell on Jackson and what he might have stood for because sectional reconciliation in America might thereby be impeded. Yet it was also suggested that negative attitudes toward the South would have even worse effects. These problems were addressed by a correspondent of the *Morning Post*—unnamed at first but later known to be the war reporter William Howard Russell—who accompanied the Duke of Sutherland on a tour of Canada and the United States in 1881.[154] Conditions in the South were again discussed in "A Winter Tour in the Southern States," published in installments in the *Times* in 1884. As usual, there was special interest in places associated with Jackson.[155]

Articles about the Republican winner of the 1880 presidential election, James Garfield, who had been a Union general in the war, indicated that he was an admirer of Jackson and had favored severe tactics against the South, much as Jackson had done against the North.[156] In the weeks leading up to the election, the Liberal (and abolitionist and pro-North) *Daily News* reported that Confederate flags had been displayed at Democratic meetings, and the names of southern heroes including Jackson had been used to rally voters. Jackson's principles were on trial, it was claimed. "Vote as he would have voted," advised Democratic leaders across the South.[157] The nomination of U.S. war hero Winfield Scott Hancock as Democratic candidate in June 1880 had prompted British observers to look at his record. He had been on the losing side in important engagements, they found, unlike "Stonewall."[158]

Obituaries of U.S. generals Hooker in 1879, McClellan in 1885, and Hancock in 1886 mentioned their Confederate antagonists, including Jackson, to whom they were widely thought to be inferior.[159] Grant died in 1885. During the war, remarked *John Bull*, "he defeated every leader of the opposite side, except Stonewall Jackson."[160] The death in 1888 of Philip Sheridan prompted the comment that he could not be considered "of the highest order," while Jackson was one of the four all-time greatest military commanders. The others were Alexander the Great, Hannibal, and Michael Skobelev, hero of Russia's war against the Turks in 1877–78.[161] Comparisons were also made between Jackson and William T. Sherman when the latter died in 1891.[162] In an obituary for P.G.T. Beauregard, who died in 1893, it was stated that this "Southern hero" had enjoyed "remarkable and unqualified success" but did not have the stature of Jackson.[163]

By the end of the nineteenth century, the words "Stonewall Jackson" were well established in common conversation. People used sayings that had been attributed to Jackson; his name was employed to indicate meritorious personal qualities; all manner of things were still being named after him. Conservative MP Henry Cecil Raikes, addressing a meeting of his constituents in Chester late in 1879, evoked Jackson's memory when encouraging his supporters to prepare for the next election. From Jackson, they could learn "activity and energy." There would be no breach in *their* stone wall, and they would teach their opponents a lesson in surging to "complete and conclusive victory."[164] Jackson's name conjured up a certain image—the honorable patriot—and it was used as shorthand to describe men of courage and self-sacrifice, as in a letter sent to the *Morning Post* in 1882 in defense of Mustafa Fehmy Pasha, who had been criticized for joining in the recent Arabi Revolt in Egypt. Fehmy had lived for a time in London and was educated there. His former tutor James Robertson Reid described him as "a patriot of the Stonewall Jackson type."[165] In January 1890, when Irish Nationalist leader Charles Stewart Parnell—exposed as an adulterer—was attempting to salvage his political career, he turned on those among his former allies who were deserting him: "In the words of Stonewall Jackson, there are times when the insignificance of the accuser is lost in the ingratitude of the accusation."[166]

Jackson's name had other uses. When a Sunderland football team hosted a team from Darlington in the Durham Cup, the home side put up "as sturdy a defense as Stonewall Jackson."[167] The engine "Stonewall Jackson" continued to drive machines in a large textile factory in Blackburn.[168] Jackson's British admirers were pleased to learn that places in America were being named in his honor.[169] A number of British parents went so far as to name their sons after him, and there were more racehorses and ships.[170] Jackson's name was also used in calls to physical fitness and in warnings against certain medical procedures. An article advocating long-distance walking as a way of staying healthy mentioned Jackson and his "foot cavalry."[171] Jackson featured in an essay on "the destructive practice of bleeding," which argued that he might have survived the wounds suffered at Chancellorsville had his doctors treated him differently.[172]

Publications specifically about Jackson, wholly or in part, continued to appear. In August 1877, when Cassell and Company published the latest volume in its *History of the United States*, reviewers noted that it ended—as all such volumes should—with an important turning point, the death of Jackson, "perhaps the greatest military commander of the Western Continent."[173] Jackson was sometimes mentioned in the series "America as It Is," which appeared in various newspapers and took the form of extracts from a travel journal. One of the essays was about Lexington, where Jackson had resided before the war. His life and career were discussed, and there were remarks about the placing of floral tributes at his burial site ("The sun was scorching hot but the flowers were fresh, for they were daily replaced by the public").[174] Garnet Wolseley's account of his visit to Jackson's camp in 1862 was included in Charles Rathbone Low's *Memoir of Lieutenant-General Sir Garnet J. Wolseley*, published in 1878. Reviewers of Low's book reprinted sections of it for their own readerships, and usually their selection included Wolseley's impression of Jackson's personality, physical appearance, and generalship.[175] Wolseley's piece on "military genius," published in 1888, discussed Jackson and was widely reviewed in the newspapers, keeping his name before the public.[176] Jackson was, as Wolseley put it, "that most brilliant of leaders and of tacticians."[177]

Another publication of the 1880s was written by former Confederate general John D. Imboden. His "Stonewall Jackson in the Shenandoah" first appeared in the New York quarterly the *Century*. It was subsequently discussed in the British press. More than twenty years after the events described, interest in Jackson's career was not fading. Imboden, who had fought under Jackson in the Valley, was now a writer and lawyer in Virginia. He lauded Jackson for his "master mind," attention to detail, and influence over men and circumstances.[178] Accounts of Jackson's religious faith continued to appear, and he was adopted as an inspirational figure by Christian missionaries.[179]

In November 1891 a number of British papers discussed the latest issue of the American *Harper's Magazine*, which carried a "critical sketch" of Jackson by Presbyterian clergyman Henry M. Field, using some of the material that was to feature in a forthcoming book by Jackson's widow. Field was a travel writer and, for many years, owner-editor of the *Evangelist*, a Presbyterian periodical based in New York. His piece on Jackson, thanks to the personal recollections of Anna Jackson, revealed more about the man behind the legend.

It was thirty years since First Manassas and Jackson's emergence as "Stonewall." To Field, Jackson had been a "genius" with "a record of continued success." The rest of the world saw "a man of iron," but what was he to the woman who had been mourning him for so long? Anna Jackson could tell a touching story, and Field was happy to paraphrase it and add comments of his own. "The man of iron is found to be the simplest, the gentlest, and the sweetest of men, who wins our confidence and our strong personal attachment."[180] Field's essay, benefiting from the insights of Anna Jackson, to which no previous writer (except Dabney) had enjoyed such easy access, helped to solidify Jackson's reputation. It enabled his British admirers to remember him and present him all the more vividly as Christian exemplar and good-natured gentleman.

One of the most enduringly influential and important books about Jackson was G.F.R. Henderson's *Stonewall Jackson and the American Civil War*, published in two volumes in 1898. Henderson had been an instructor at the Royal Military College, Sandhurst, and was from 1892 to 1899 the professor of military art and history at the Staff College, Camberley. He had previously served in India and Egypt. His book was very detailed and highly sympathetic toward Jackson. Based on at least eight years of research, it focused heavily on military matters but also commented on Jackson's personality and opinions. Hence, "Jackson's religion entered into every action of his life," and "intimates he had few . . . Still he was not in the least unsociable, and there were many houses where he was always welcome." Henderson highlighted Jackson's "brilliant maneuvers." Jackson possessed not only a sound intellectual grasp of tactics and strategy but also the heart of a fighter, and so "the quiet gentleman of Lexington became, in the estimation of both friend and foe, a very thunderbolt of war."[181]

Many newspapers reviewed Henderson's book, including the *Times*, which had eagerly anticipated its publication and was not disappointed.[182] According to the *Standard*, which had more consistently taken the Confederates' side during the American war, the book was "admirably done" and "most valuable." Henderson had visited American battlefields and spoken with Jackson's family and colleagues, and he was to be commended for clearly establishing something often forgotten "on this side of the Atlantic": that Jackson had been motivated primarily by loyalty to Virginia, his homeland.[183] Less partisan than the *Standard* and conducted by and for the fashionable and well-read gentlemen of London's clubland, the *Pall Mall Gazette* welcomed Henderson's "excellent" book and suggested that his affection for Jackson was an asset rather than a shortcoming. It enabled him better to illustrate Jackson's personality. The book also had a wider importance because the American crisis "may be described as the dawn of modern war." In elucidating the war's causes, Henderson stressed that the states of the South had been self-governing communities, where slavery was legal, and that the U.S. government had not been entitled to intervene in their internal affairs.[184] The Liberal-leaning *Manchester Guardian*, while contending that Jackson's importance in the war was easily exaggerated, described Henderson's book as "a classic."[185]

Stonewall Jackson and the American Civil War was favorably reviewed in *Blackwood's Magazine* by Sir Henry Brackenbury, a senior British Army officer who had served in India and Africa. Formerly the director of military intelligence, Brackenbury was at this time head of the War Office Ordnance Committee. He considered Jackson a "noble" man and "brilliant" soldier and thought that Henderson had done full justice to him.[186] Another discussion of Henderson's work appeared in the *Edinburgh Review* in January 1899.[187] The tone was generally positive: Henderson's book could be recommended "whether as a subject of study for soldiers or as a record fascinating for all readers of one great as a soldier and a man."[188] The book was also noticed in the colonial press.[189]

A second edition was published in 1899. It included an introduction written by Lord Wolseley, now commander in chief of the British Army (1895–1900). Perhaps with Britain in mind, Wolseley declared that the American war had shown how much damage could be done by excessive civilian interference with the army. Wolseley agreed that armies should be under the ultimate authority of elected governments. But when a war broke out, he thought, the generals should be left to fight it. Jackson was the model. He had resigned in January 1862, when the government in Richmond instructed him to change his plans, without consulting him and, what is more, without going through the usual chain of command.[190] He was quickly persuaded to remain in post.

Henderson died in 1903. Obituaries offered a new flurry of compliments about his work on Jackson.[191] It continued to be prominent in booksellers' advertisements.[192] In the summer of 1904, a tablet to Henderson's memory was unveiled at Leeds Grammar School, where he had been a pupil. Speeches were made, and there was a message from Lord Roberts, who until quite recently had been commander in chief (in succession to Wolseley). Roberts stated that Henderson's "fascinating" book on Jackson "cannot be read without instruction and enjoyment."[193] Wolseley referred to it in his memoirs as "delightful and instructive . . . I wish all our officers would read it."[194]

Henderson had been on Lord Roberts's staff when Roberts commanded British forces in the Boer War of 1899–1902. Henderson's book was often referred to during this war. At a time when Britain needed strong leadership and the best available generals, Jackson's relevance was obvious.[195] It was suggested during the Boer War that British forces would benefit from the adoption of tactics associated with Jackson.[196]

Among military experts, there had been a decline in interest in the American conflict as major wars broke out elsewhere, including Europe. But the rise of the United States as a world power, along with the Boer War and the prospect of British involvement in a European war, which might be similar to the American war, made the latter worthy of renewed attention. Though Henderson, Wolseley, and others began to express more respect for northern generals, there was still admiration for Jackson's methods, not least speed and surprise and concentrating forces for a direct attack on the enemy's weak points. Increasingly, Jackson was treated as an *American* rather than a Confederate, in line with conciliatory narratives of the American Civil War. Britain and its empire needed unity just as America did, for stability and influence. Sectional reconciliation in America was therefore to be welcomed, and during the Boer War, it was useful for the British to depict the Boers as nefarious secessionists.[197]

Jackson's name appeared in the British press many times during the Boer War but not only in a manner calculated to encourage British troops and sustain support for the British war effort. It was also used in reports about the most talented Boer generals, more than one of whom were dubbed "the Stonewall Jackson of the war."[198] Jackson's name was kept before the British public in other writings, including Theodore Roosevelt's study of Oliver Cromwell, published in 1900. Roosevelt would soon be a successful Republican candidate for U.S. vice president, but he was already well known as a military hero and popular politician. He wrote an admiring portrait of Cromwell, chiefly for an American readership. A central theme was the resemblance between Cromwell and Jackson.[199]

Newspaper discussion of British military affairs in these years regularly included assessments of Jackson, usually in the belief that he still had something useful to teach the officers and planners of the new generation. Whether it was the regimental system, reconquering the Sudan, the quality of "English military literature," casualty figures as a percentage of forces engaged, an officer's combining of civil and military functions, the need for large and skilled bodies of military engineers, the merits of trusting in young as opposed to old commanders, pacifying Ireland, reforms in the Ordnance Department, or Britain's response to the growing power of the U.S. Army and Navy, Jackson came to mind.[200] Army instructors continued to lecture on Jackson, not only in Britain but also in the empire.[201] In 1901, when American historian William Milligan Sloane reissued his *Life of Napoleon Bonaparte* (originally published in 1896), a review in the *Times* dwelled on the similarities between Napoleon and Jackson.[202] In Parliament, Jackson's career was often brought up to make a point about military matters. Sometimes MPs and peers would quote directly from Henderson's book.[203]

Memories of Jackson did not fade. Wolseley's death in 1913 prompted obituary notices that were in part a recap of his visit to Jackson's camp in 1862 and his subsequent writings about the Confederate general. A statement attributed to Jackson—about honor and freedom—was used in the House of Commons by Conservative leader Bonar Law to validate his party's opposition to the Irish Home Rule Bill. Meanwhile, Henderson's book was still being advertised in the press, and new novels set during the American Civil War continued to feature Jackson—Randall Parrish's *The Red Mist*, for example, published in 1916.[204]

During the First World War, Jackson's military capabilities and religious faith were used to inspire the British people. An obituary of Lord Roberts, who died while visiting troops in France in November 1914, made comparisons with Jackson. Nobody else was mentioned. Roberts had studied and learned from Jackson, and like Jackson, he was "a soldier to the end" and a devout Christian.[205]

That Christian faith would help to see the nation through and that there could be no victory without God were popular assumptions at this time, and many drew inspiration from "famous men of prayer." One writer linked together four such men: the missionary James Gilmour, who died in China in 1891; missionary and explorer David Livingstone, a great Victorian hero, who died in Africa in 1873; seventeenth-century Scottish Presbyterian leader Samuel Rutherford; and Stonewall Jackson, who was included with these British "men of prayer" because he fit the profile so well. Readers were familiar with him, and apparently, the writer thought he could best communicate his meaning to them by discussing Jackson's "fixed habit" of thanking God before he took a drink, asking God's blessing when he posted a letter, commending his cadets to God before he taught a class at the VMI, and submitting himself to God's will when he entered the field of battle.[206]

Although there was no shortage of heroes from Britain's own history who might have served a war-related purpose, Jackson was brought into speeches and ceremonies and incorporated into patriotic imagery by public figures who believed that he still meant something and that, because of his supposed strengths, he could be made useful in a time of national crisis. A striking instance of this tendency occurred in November 1915, with the war into its second year, when the Vicar of Tamworth, Maurice Peel, grandson of the Victorian premier Sir Robert Peel, addressed school pupils on the annual prize-giving day in the town. His topic was sacrificial service. It was always necessary to do one's best, Peel told the schoolchildren, and the supreme ideal of the present time was "the ideal of service with good will, doing service to their country." To illustrate, Peel relied on the Jackson legend.[207]

Reports about the field ambulance service in the spring of 1917 brought up Jackson's wounding at Chancellorsville and the reasons why he had not recovered, and in the following year, when a U.S. hospital was opened in Kensington Palace Gardens, it was noted that one of the wards was named after him. The announcement that the next U.S. ambassador to Britain was to be John W. Davis became all the more interesting when it was learned that Davis hailed from the same district in West Virginia as Jackson. Items associated with Jackson continued to be prized. Auctioneers Sotheby, Wilkinson, and Hodge, of London, made much of the fact that they could offer "autograph letters" of the celebrated general.[208]

In October 1917, Britain's prime minister, Lloyd George, offered thanks to the army that had saved the nation. Speaking of the dreadful combat conditions the troops had endured, he referred to Jackson's campaigns to paint a suitable picture.[209] In January 1918, in the provincial press, under the heading "A Wise Reminder," Jackson was invoked again to show that the best bulwark against "foreign aggression" was the "national character." Henderson's book was cited to substantiate the claim.[210] By this time, there had been another reissue of the book in Britain (1911), and there would be a further four reprints between 1919 and 1937.

Jackson's longevity as a British hero was extraordinary. Famous only during the last two years of his life and foreign-born, he nevertheless retained a hold over the interest and affection of a large section of the people. In part, the unique historical relationship between Britain and America made him seem more familiar. But his appeal had more to it than this because he personified moral standards and had social, religious, and political relevance in a way that other legendary figures did not, and the qualities that British commentators attributed to him—whether or not they had much basis in fact—gave him continuing influence. Beyond all the writings, speeches, pictures, poems, songs, and the use of his name and fascination with his life and the lessons it could teach, British regard for Jackson was given solid material expression. The statue of Jackson unveiled in 1875 in Capitol Square, Richmond, was a British undertaking. Organized by "English gentlemen," promoted in the press, and funded through public subscription, this memorial was a tangible sign of the high esteem in which Jackson was held by British people.

10

"PRESENTED BY ENGLISH GENTLEMEN"

The decision made in 1863 to open a fund for and commission a statue of Stonewall Jackson substantiates the statement made in Beresford Hope's review of 1881 of *The Rise and Fall of the Confederate Government* by Jefferson Davis. Hope recalled that respect for southern heroism was the primary reason why so many British people supported the Confederate cause during the American war. Jackson was by far the most admired and discussed southerner of the period, and his legend was no less potent and fascinating in Britain than it was on the other side of the Atlantic. The Jackson statue and the efforts behind it brought together pro-southern sentiment in Britain, Hope's activism and the ideological and practical contributions he made to wartime and postwar controversy, the heroic and other representations of the war, and Jackson's British reputation.

Hope was one of the leading movers behind the commemoration plan. He publicly expressed his high regard for Jackson in speeches and writings during the war.[1] Jackson's untimely death shocked and distressed pro-southerners, and when Hope was the main speaker and guest of honor at the Liverpool Southern Club, on 16 October 1863, everyone stood in silence when the toast to Jackson was proposed at dinner.[2]

Following Jackson's death, there was a detailed article about him in Hope's *Saturday Review*. In this account, all his strengths were highlighted and the lessons of his life made plain. Jackson had a "striking character," and it was difficult to think of anyone, from ancient times to the Victorian age, who "combined the patriotic and the religious elements" quite as he did. In a short space of time, the British had come to know him well. They were familiar with his courage, his victories in battle, and his personality and appearance. Images of him brought out his "noticeable blue eyes" and the "thin determined lines of his face." Jackson was already a celebrated figure.

"We like his calmness, his sobriety, his gentleness, his charity." He would long be mourned.[3]

News of Jackson's death prompted meetings in many towns, but the one organized in Liverpool was called off because of the intense divisions there over the American war. Instead, it was announced that money would be collected for a memorial to Jackson, to be erected in his home state. The plan was reported in newspapers across Britain.[4]

By July 1863, there was more information. A statue was to be executed "at once" and paid for by public subscription. The Dublin-born sculptor John Henry Foley, of the Royal Academy, had been commissioned to do the work. The cost was estimated at one thousand pounds for a seven-foot marble statue and five hundred pounds for a granite pedestal and incidentals (some early reports mentioned a target figure of two thousand pounds). As for inscriptions, it was expected that a suitable statement of "England's admiration for a truly noble character" would be on one side of the pedestal and on the other Robert E. Lee's order of the day informing the Army of Northern Virginia of Jackson's death. The statue was to be offered to the State of Virginia and would probably be placed near its seat of government in Richmond. The project would be overseen by a committee, formed "for the purpose of obtaining from Britain a recognition of the worth of Gen. Thomas J. Jackson, as a hero and a Christian." Ten names were mentioned initially: Beresford Hope; the Conservative MPs W. H. Gregory, Sir Edward Kerrison, Sir James Fergusson, and G.W.M. Peacocke; the Liberals W. S. Lindsay, MP, and Lord Campbell; Sir Coutts Lindsay; London stockbroker George Edward Seymour; and Liverpool merchant James Spence. "They state that it is not intended that subscriptions to the statue should imply any opinion on the merits of the American struggle."[5]

This assurance was dismissed by numerous commentators. In a letter to the *Daily News,* "Common Sense" protested that the committee's declaration could not be taken seriously: "Erect a statue to a leader of a rebellion, and be silent as to the goodness or badness of the cause in which he was engaged! It is too silly." The "noblemen and gentlemen" of the committee *were* giving an opinion. They were contending that "governments were invented to be the playthings of subjects" and that "slavery is a wise, beneficent, and Christian institution."[6] As the *Leeds Times* remarked, "It is hard to believe that a statue would have been thought of if Jackson had been a successful Federal."[7]

Some newspapers did not go into detail, simply reporting that a fund had been opened. Some had the facts wrong: "A number of English noblemen are collecting a thousand pounds in sixpences, to be sent out to Virginia for the purpose of erecting a monument in honor of General 'Stonewall' Jackson."[8] The most accurate coverage of the committee's activities in the summer of 1863 was in the Conservative *John Bull*, which sometimes used related items from the *Index*, the Confederacy's London paper.[9] The project was fully explained in *John Bull* in mid-July 1863. Promoters of the statue were motivated by the perception "that some general recognition from Great Britain of the worth of General Jackson, by name, by race, and by character related to us, although the citizen of another land, would be a graceful token of friendly feeling from the old country to our kinsmen across the Atlantic." Donations would be held at Coutts Bank in London and would "be taken solely and simply as a recognition of the rare personal merit of General Jackson," not as a sign of partiality with regard to the American war.[10] There followed a list of committee members, who now numbered twenty. To the ten names already published were added the names of Hope's brother-in-law Lord Eustace Cecil; John Gilliat, the head of trading and banking firm with interests in America; Conservative MPs John Laird and W. E. Duncombe, the future Lord Feversham; Conservative peer Lord Donoughmore; Liberal MPs Fulke Greville and C. W. Fitzwilliam; Yorkshire manufacturer Edward Akroyd, a former Liberal MP; Sir Arthur Elton of Clevedon Court, Somerset, another former Liberal MP; and Sir Eardley Eardley of Bedwell Park, Hertfordshire, son of the Evangelical campaigner Sir Culling Eardley. Hope was the committee's treasurer and Gregory its secretary.

By August, the committee had expanded to twenty-three. The latest to join were Evelyn Ashley, son of Lord Shaftesbury and private secretary to the prime minister, Lord Palmerston; Sir Henry de Hoghton, of Hoghton Tower, Lancashire; and Charles Sturt, a Conservative MP.[11] There were also local contacts in different towns who were helping to collect money, including land agent V. J. Flowerdew of Bank Chambers, Norwich. The *Norfolk Chronicle* reported that he was ready to receive subscriptions, "which are desired to be numerous rather than of large amount, as only £1500 will be required." This paper also confirmed that Foley had been commissioned and that the statue of Jackson was intended to be "a recognition from Britain of his valor and worth" and an expression of transatlantic friendship and respect.[12]

A widely reprinted item first published in the Cobdenite *Morning Star* was the clearest statement from the hostile camp. "What Is Truth?" urged people not to forget that in fighting for "the perpetual enslavement of another race," Jackson had to be counted "one of the leaders of a bad cause." Therefore, it was not appropriate to honor him with a statue, still less a statue that would be claimed to represent British opinion. The committee was headed by Hope, hardly an indication of "absolute neutrality as between North and South," for "if any man has been outspoken in his views of American politics, Mr. Hope is that man. His detestation of the North amounts to a monomania." Hope's admiration for Jackson was bolstered by his hatred of Lincoln, "the bare mention of whose name arouses Mr. Hope into foaming fury." Another committee member was Spence, notorious for his "pecuniary connection with the South." Gregory was known to be "a fervid Southern partisan." W.S. Lindsay was one of those who had recently journeyed to Paris "on that mission of honorable neutrality, to induce the Emperor of the French to recognize the Southern Confederacy," and "the opinions of Mr. Peacocke, MP, are no secret; nor has Sir James Fergusson, MP, hidden his Southern flame under any bushel." "What Is Truth?" went on to suggest that the committee was actuated by "aristocratic and class feeling," a reverence for "one who fought the battle of gentlemen and aristocrats against common trading people governed by an ex-rail splitter." The main point was that however the project might be presented in public, in the background were motives that were less than worthy: "We therefore beg to assure the American people, of whatever State, that this movement is not the work of the English people, but that of Mr. Hope and a few friends; and we beg to assure the public of England that it is not a tribute to mere heroism and patriotic ardor in the person of 'Stonewall' Jackson, but a delicate attempt on behalf of some partisans of the Southern cause to entrap Englishmen into an acknowledgment of Southern sympathies."[13]

A letter from "Anti-Slavery" appeared in the *Daily News,* condemning the plan for a statue and insisting that its participants were wasting their time and money. The South would lose the war, and "to entertain for a moment the idea that the North will ever permit the erection of any monument to the memory of a rebel—no matter how great a hero or Christian he may have been—is to suppose something opposed to all the teachings of history." It would be like Frenchmen reviving memories of the bloodshed of the seventeenth century by proposing memorials to Jacobite commanders

Patrick Sarsfield in Ireland and Viscount Dundee in Scotland. The Orange-
men of Ireland and Covenanters of Scotland would never stand for it, and
indeed, the proposal would be totally improper. The Jackson statue was no
different.[14]

Political, social, and religious tensions in Britain were evidently shaping attitudes toward the statue and, more generally, the course of events in
America. Jackson the icon became yet another matter upon which rival lobbies could base their claims for support and their complaints or allegations.
The memorial plan would remain contentious for many years to come.

Opponents of the statue must have been frustrated as money was collected for it at an impressive rate. How could antislavery Britain honor a
man who had fought for slavery? To Richard Blackett, the answer lies in
the decline of British abolitionism. Most of the old campaigners who had
prevailed in 1833 with the ending of slavery in the British Empire were now
dead or retired. By the 1860s, antislavery organizations no longer had the
membership, funding, and energy of earlier times, and there were not many
people who wanted to engage in further agitation, as if there was nothing
more important to them than slavery in America. In addition, Jackson was a
highly influential and malleable propaganda device, a gallant Christian warrior, and of course, one did not have to be proslavery to be pro-southern.
Duncan Campbell has shown that support for the South was rarely "unqualified." Jackson was admired, but some commentators stipulated that it
was his conduct they liked, not his opinions. Blackett suggests that in death,
Jackson was *manufactured* into a hero. Hope and the other promoters of the
statue led this endeavor.[15]

According to reports of September and October 1863, all the money
needed for the statue and pedestal had been collected. Confusion was setting in, however, about what would happen next. The committee had intended to send the statue to the South as soon as possible, but delay seemed
inevitable, at least until hostilities ceased. Different commentators gave different verdicts: the statue would soon be presented to Virginia "on behalf of
the people of England" or "sent to the Confederates after the war" or transported only "when we can get it there." The names of committee members
were routinely mentioned as well, as men to be commended or censured
according to the editorial policy of each publication.[16]

By the following summer, British newspapers had published a letter,
dated 25 April 1864, from the governor of Virginia, William Smith, to the

Confederate envoy in London, James M. Mason, confirming that a suitable place for the Jackson statue would be provided close to the Capitol building in Richmond.[17] Then an advertisement was placed in the *Times* to the effect that Foley "is proceeding" with his commission: "The Committee begs to announce that the subscription is still open to provide a fitting pedestal." Notwithstanding earlier reports, money was still required. Coutts Bank or Hope in his capacity as the committee's treasurer were ready to receive further donations.[18] These details were subsequently given in other newspapers.[19]

During 1864, it emerged that another statue of Jackson was in preparation. This project had been commenced in Virginia, and seven thousand dollars were collected, mostly from soldiers.[20] The statue was to be made by a German, Frederick Volck, who had transferred his operations from Virginia to Bavaria.

Volck had lived in Baltimore and been employed as an illustrator by several periodicals. With the outbreak of war, he moved to Richmond and worked as a draftsman for the Confederate army. He made a death mask of Jackson in May 1863 as the general's body lay in state. He also made drawings and took measurements of the body and obtained boots and a uniform from Jackson's family. A committee chaired by governor of Virginia John Letcher commissioned him to execute a statue of Jackson, to be placed on the campus of the Virginia Military Institute. By the end of 1863, Volck had completed a model. He decided to work in Munich and brought money and materials through the U.S. blockade. In August 1864, it was suggested in several British newspapers that he was making good progress.[21] But lack of funding slowed him down. The statue was unfinished when the American war ended. Volck persevered, and a plaster version was cast in 1866. An engraving of this version was published early in January 1867.[22] There were further efforts to raise money, as in 1873, when the New York Academy of Design produced three portraits of Jackson, from which chromolithographs would be made. It was hoped that the prints would enjoy "an extensive sale."[23] An earlier report, appearing in London papers in August 1870, indicated that Letcher's committee had passed responsibility for the project to the VMI. The envisaged "colossal equestrian statue" was to stand close to the parade area. There was also to be a small Volck-designed figure of Jackson, "which represents him as one of the teachers at the institute." It would be placed in a chapel on the grounds.[24]

After years of work, Volck had to give up on the large statue because he ran out of money. Meanwhile, he used the death mask to make two busts of Jackson (one is now in the Virginia State Library and the other in the Confederate Museum, Richmond). In the 1880s, he made a statue of Jackson for the cemetery in Lexington where the general's body was buried. He planned to make another Jackson statue, but it was not completed, and he sold the death mask to Richmond sculptor Edward Valentine. Volck died in 1891.[25]

Volck's activities were mentioned from time to time in the British press, but they had no discernible effect on Hope and his fellow committee members, who were not deterred from carrying on with their own labors. Clearly, Jackson was considered on both sides of the Atlantic as a proper subject for memorialization, but while the American-financed effort—for a large statue on the VMI campus—failed, the British effort continued. Even with the end of the war and the South's surrender, Hope and his associates decided to persevere. In August 1865, in response to an inquiry, Hope "states that Mr. Foley is at work on the statue."[26] Foley's other engagements and poor health caused the work to be interrupted for long periods, and there was still pressure to abandon it from various commentators, some of them pro-southern. Early in 1866, for example, news from America that Jackson's widow and daughter were sinking into financial hardship brought forth the suggestion that money given for the statue could instead be sent to them.[27] Northern newspapers were less than impressed by the decision to move ahead with the statue.[28]

The subscription list was now a tool for pro-northern and pro-southern polemicists in Britain, rather like the list of supposed investors in the Confederate Loan. Someone with a sense of humor included among the names of supporters of the Jackson statue that of Benjamin Moran, secretary at the U.S. Legation in London.[29]

It was confirmed in August 1870 that Foley would soon make a casting and that all expenses would be covered by the money the committee had collected.[30] This did not go down well with a notable opponent of the statue, "Historicus," who wrote to the *Times*. His letter would be cited and paraphrased in other papers at home and abroad.[31]

Historicus was William Vernon Harcourt, lawyer, writer, Liberal MP, and later home secretary and chancellor of the exchequer under W. E. Gladstone. Harcourt had supported British neutrality and condemned Confederate sympathizers in Britain during the war. Like Hope, he had attended

Trinity College, Cambridge, though they were not there at the same time, for Harcourt was seven years younger.

Historicus was concerned about the American reaction and thought that to persist with the statue was in any case morally wrong. The people of the United States were healing old wounds. They did not wish to be reminded of their "fratricidal struggle" but preferred to live together with "clemency," "tranquility," and "dignity": "And is it at this moment that Englishmen whose names are known and whose follies are remembered are to rush in and awaken the terrible recollection of sleeping resentments, and conjure up the ghosts of buried animosities? I have a great personal regard for Mr. Beresford Hope . . . but this is a subject far too serious to be passed over in silence. I protest against Mr. Hope and the gentlemen for whom he acts being permitted to fling this wanton insult in the face of the American people." Instead of paying for a statue of Jackson, why not use the money for something worthwhile, such as relief for those caught up in the war between France and Prussia? "This traffic in the memories of the dead in order to inflame the passions of the living is alike a desecration of the past and a provocation of the future."[32]

Hope was on the Continent when he read the letter. He replied from Antwerp, deriding the writer's "pomp of language" and pointing out that the decision to proceed with the statue was "an act of the simplest commercial honesty." The notice he had sent to the newspapers was meant to inform, not antagonize: "Certain people in England had subscribed their money for a specific object, the statue of General Jackson—the complete sum having been paid down, and not a fraction of it asked back—and they were anxious to know when they were likely to see that object. Moreover, certain other people in Virginia were getting impatient to have that statue in their own State . . . It was in answer to these appeals that the paragraph was drawn up, in terms carefully selected so as not to wound any American susceptibilities." If the statue was unwanted in America, it would not be sent, and "England will be the richer and America the poorer by one work of art, while those who undertook to spend other people's money for a specified object will have proved themselves honest men." Historicus wanted the money spent on something else, but Hope and the committee had a contract with Foley and could hardly "refuse to remunerate him for the time and trouble which he has devoted to the statue, already nearly ready for the caster's hands." Hope saw nothing strange in memorials to worthy figures. He pointed to Trafalgar Square and the Place Vendôme. People valued their heroes, and respect for heroes crossed national borders: "I shall not be led by 'Historicus' into a discussion upon the rights or wrongs of the intra-American war. It is certain that the victorious North, when it decreed the national monument to Lincoln, did not share his opinions as to the posthumous commemoration of men who achieved greatness by struggling for the cause in which they believed."[33] Historicus was mocked in the *Standard* for "assuming to himself the post of the national conscience-keeper, schoolmaster, and standing counsel." The *Standard* defended Hope and the committee, denied that the statue was an insult to America, and rejected the claim that it did not reflect a significant body of opinion in Britain.[34]

But there was also a piece in the *Pall Mall Gazette* signed "Mutato Nomine" (the pseudonym was taken from an old saying, *mutato nomine de te fabula narrator*, or "with the name changed the same thing applies to you"). This writer described a comparable scenario, a plan to erect a statue of Lord Edward Fitzgerald, the Irish revolutionary who died during the 1798 Rebellion against Britain; the money to be collected by U.S. senator for Massachusetts Charles Sumner, known for his anti-British rhetoric; the statue to be made by American sculptor William Wetmore Story; and the statue to be unveiled in the center of Dublin. Would the United States not be denounced for this hostile meddling in British affairs? The writer turned the situation around and professed to see no difference between the Jackson statue and one of Fitzgerald. The "flummery" from Hope and his friends was unacceptable, and Americans deserved an explanation. Perhaps they could be told that "it is not our habit to take account of the eccentricities of individual Englishmen; that Mr. Beresford Hope does not represent Parliament, or even the Tory section of it, or in truth anybody, and that his act binds nobody." What the statue revealed was "the special incapacity of too many of our aristocracy to enter into the mind of people of another class either at home or abroad, or to understand in what manner their outrecuidance offends at times against decency or dignity." Nonetheless, "however it may satisfy ourselves, such an answer would hardly turn away wrath in others."[35]

The newspapers of Boston, Philadelphia, Milwaukee, New York, and San Francisco reported that the statue was "the object of vigorous protests in the English press," and they carried the letters of Historicus and Hope, and much related material, and themselves questioned the propriety of the Jackson memorial. Of Hope, the *Boston Daily Advertiser* was willing to concede that "in some respects he has the best of the argument," for it was true that "commercial honesty" bound him to use the money for the purpose for which it had been given. In other respects, though, his conduct was reprehensible. "He indulges in unnecessary flings at this country . . . and likens the English monument to a general who was in rebellion against a friendly nation to the national monument to Mr. Lincoln, the rightful head of the government, martyred in the hour of victory." *Frank Leslie's Illustrated Newspaper* was grateful for the comments made by Historicus but complained that "there is in England a class of haters of the American Union, whose animosities have outlived those of our civil war at home, and who would, if they could, arouse again the fell spirit of discord now happily laid." They were led by Hope, "that consummate nuisance—a nuisance at home and abroad." While northerners would not object to a fitting marker at Jackson's burial place in Lexington, the British statue was quite another matter, "a vainglorious monument, raised by foreigners, whose chiefest admiration of the dead is the fact that he aimed his (let us believe misguided) sword at the throat of his country."[36]

Foley died in August 1874. Over the following weeks, there were descriptions in the British press of the Jackson statue he had only recently managed to complete. According to one commentator, this "spirited" work ranked with the finest of Foley's other commissions. For a time, it was on show at the Manor Foundry in Chelsea.[37] In the spring of 1875, it featured in a Royal Academy exhibition in Burlington House, Piccadilly.[38] It was reported that the statue of Jackson, "made for a committee of his English admirers," would in due course be presented to Virginia and that the state legislature had granted ten thousand dollars to pay for a pedestal and for other related arrangements.[39] Great interest was shown in the statue as it was transported across the Atlantic, unloaded, and taken to Richmond, where it was received with full civic and military honors.[40] The statue was of bronze, not the intended marble (to keep the cost down). The pedestal was of Virginia granite.

Opponents of Hope and the committee continued to argue that no good could come from memorializing Jackson in this way. The monument would displease the North and encourage people in the South into a demonstration of antipathy toward the North. It would remind southerners of defeat and hinder their reconciliation with the North.

Once the statue was unveiled in Richmond, the *Times* offered some comments. It acknowledged the "extraordinary display of enthusiasm," the huge crowd of "sympathetic spectators," and the display of "British colors," and it agreed that the heroic Jackson merited the recognition afforded him. Even so, the men responsible for the presentation of the statue were "guilty of extreme indiscretion." Jackson came to fame only because of the war. His triumphs were won, and he was loved in Virginia, as an enemy to the North. "The scene in Richmond was, therefore, nothing less than a political display. It signified that the Virginians still bitterly lament the failure of their attempt to destroy the Union." Their resentment was natural after all they had been through, but far from alleviating it, events like the unveiling in Richmond would exacerbate it. In addition, the statue damaged the British national interest because it reminded northerners that many in Britain had preferred the South during the war. Rather than bring up bad memories, would it not be better to promote cooperation, for the benefit of both Britain and America? "It is peculiarly unfortunate, then, that Englishmen should have gone out of their way to revive half-buried resentments by glorifying the prowess of a Confederate soldier, and by calling forth a display of Southern hatred of the North in the chief town of the Confederacy."[41]

Hope issued a firm response. The *Times* had itself justified the memorial, he wrote. The plan for a statue had been made back in 1863, shortly after Jackson's death, and it was unsurprising that British people "should have been stirred to offer a tribute of sympathy for his loss to his native State at a time when their feelings had been so powerfully moved . . . by the brilliant letters of your Correspondent from the Army of Virginia." The statue did not signify "hatred of the North." It had not been given, or received in any such spirit, and it was important that the full facts should be known: "The money for the statue was collected and the commission entrusted to Mr. Foley within a few weeks after the news of Jackson's death had reached England. The subsequent delay is due to the ill-health, and lately, the death of Foley, the competition of his many other engagements, and his anxiety to perfect the likeness." The war went against the South, and members of the committee had to make a decision: "Either they might court the favor of the more powerful and successful side, by disappointing the defeated and unhappy community whom they had led to expect the gift; or they might keep their word, although those to whom they had pledged it were unfortunate. I cannot conceive gentlemen hesitating for the infinitesimal fragment of a second over the choice."

So the committee quietly carried on its work, out of public view, and

"memory of it had completely faded . . . until it was revived by the contribution of Foley's posthumous statue to last season's Exhibition of the Royal
Academy, when, if ever, the protest against it should have been made."
There were no protests, and the statue was admired by all who saw it. Hope
then wrote to Governor James L. Kemper of Virginia, formally offering him
the statue "to be used at his discretion." Kemper, "the choice of a constituency in which universal suffrage now implies no distinction between white
and black," put the matter to the state legislature, "equally the emanation of
bi-color votes," and the legislature "eagerly voted a large supply to do honor
to the gift." The unveiling ceremony was accompanied by great rejoicing.
Clearly, "the gift was appreciated by grateful recipients." Hope first learned
of the celebrations in Richmond when he read about them in the *Times*. He
was not responsible for what had been said or done there. His duty had been
to have the statue made and delivered, and this duty had been discharged.

> The result shows that it has much gratified a Commonwealth which
> speaks our language, and which still entertains such friendly feelings to-
> wards a country from which it derives its descent, that the Legislature
> last year made an official holiday of the Queen's birthday. I should have
> thought that those who are most eager for international amity would
> have been the first to welcome spontaneous expressions of brotherly love
> between England and a Commonwealth which represents the very oldest
> of all our Colonies, and whose founders were Elizabeth and Raleigh. The
> Southern States of America, though beaten, are not annihilated, and I do
> not understand, either on moral or political grounds, why out of all the
> communities of the earth their friendship alone should not be worth our
> having. Whatever they may be, they are not now Slave States, and the
> white inhabitants of Virginia and the Carolinas are our special flesh and
> blood no less than those of New York and Massachusetts. Equally desir-
> able is the friendship of the Northern States, and no voice of those who
> helped the Jackson statue will, I am sure, be heard against any tokens of
> sympathy passing between those States and England.

Hope ended his letter by mentioning the "Lincoln Tower," a memorial connected with Christ Church, a Congregational chapel in Lambeth, whose
pastor, Christopher Newman Hall, had lectured and written in support of
Lincoln and emancipation during the American war. Hall had raised funds

in the United States as well as Britain for an international tribute to Lincoln, and the Lincoln Tower was to be in Gothic style and part of the redevelopment of the chapel and adjacent buildings. The foundation stone had been laid in 1874 (Lincoln Tower would open on 4 July 1876). As Hope put it, "If the admirers of Stonewall Jackson have given him a statue at Richmond, the admirers of Lincoln have given him a steeple in London, and the hottest partisans of the South have never uttered a complaint."[42]

The unveiling of the Jackson statue in Richmond on 26 October 1875 was widely reported in the British press. Some newspapers offered only the essential details and made little comment beyond noting the "greatest enthusiasm" of the crowd, the "imposing ceremonies" of the day, and the large number of British flags on display.[43] But many involved themselves in the debate about the statue and those who had commissioned and presented it. The Liberal *Leeds Mercury* was struck by the "thoughtlessness" of the "English gentlemen" who had jeopardized British-U.S. harmony—the *Leeds Mercury* was hardly unbiased, having been pro-North and antislavery during the war.[44] The Conservative *Pall Mall Gazette* held that the "solemn lesson" from the *Times* "might well have been spared." Hope was a friend of *Pall Mall Gazette* editor Frederick Greenwood, and Greenwood was a supporter of the Disraeli government appointed in 1874 and an admirer of Hope's *Saturday Review*. To Greenwood, it was foolish to think that northerners would forget British preference for the South during the war, but a distinction must be made between the acts of states and the acts of individuals. This was the cardinal requirement, "and it can scarcely be more completely disregarded than by a formal scolding" of gentlemen who thought it "no harm to contribute towards a monument to a soldier of whom, not North and South only, but the whole English race, whether in the old or the new world, may be justly proud."[45]

The Conservative *Standard* (the London morning paper second only to the *Times* in circulation at this time, owned by James Johnstone and edited by his son) considered it fit and proper that the Jackson statue had been "paid for by English subscribers who, during the American Civil War, took this natural and not ungraceful way of manifesting their sympathy with the South and their admiration for her especial hero." The unveiling ceremony was important also because it demonstrated the pride and dignity of the people of Virginia. Were the *Standard*'s readers not conscious of their bond with Virginians? "The people are English to the core, not Englishmen half-alienated by religious prejudice and passion, nor yet an English race de-Anglicized by a strong admixture of Celtic and German blood . . . but Englishmen whom, save for a few anticipated peculiarities of speech and pronunciation, and a few Republican substitutes for Loyalist phrases, none of us could distinguish from our own countrymen." Virginia's "quiet resolution" and "simple heroism" during the war and its "grand endurance and solid good sense" in defeat "all exhibit the English character in its very highest and noblest type, and show us brethren of whom we may well be proud." The *Standard*, adamant that the statue honored the recipients and did credit to the givers, included in its remarks a recapitulation of Jackson's military exploits, suggesting that he fully deserved his high reputation and his memorial: "It was through him that England learned to admire and honor his country, to love the flag that he upheld, and believe in the cause for which he fought. And for such feelings no American who himself recognizes Jackson as one of the proudest boasts of America can owe us a grudge or bear us malice." The *Standard* did not expect "any political mischief" to result from the presentation of the statue. Virginians would not be provoked by a "Radical press" in the North.[46]

Full particulars about the unveiling ceremony in Richmond and the arrangements leading up to it were later provided in the *Standard*, which included remarks "from our own correspondent" in Washington. This report began by recalling that the statue had been on display at the Royal Academy during the summer of 1875. Rising to seven feet three inches in height, the figure of Jackson was in uniform, his head turned slightly to the right, his left hand resting on the hilt of his sword and his right hand holding a gauntlet. "The attitude is easy. The other details carefully exact. All is simple, homely, heroic, and grand, like the man himself." Originally conceived in a season of genuine sadness at the untimely death of the South's greatest general, the defeat of the Confederacy in 1865 had "changed the aspect of affairs," and for a time, it was not clear what would happen. In 1872, Gen. Fitzhugh Lee, president of the Association of the Army of Northern Virginia (AANV), contacted the English gentlemen responsible for the statue. Some of the relevant correspondence was published, the most important being that between Hope and Gen. Bradley Johnson of the AANV.[47] On a visit to London, Johnson was received by Hope, who introduced him to Foley, and on viewing the work, Johnson was able to recommend changes that would make for a better likeness. He also had a photograph taken of a portrait of

Jackson that was in his Virginia home, which was sent to London along with copies of Confederate buttons and sword buckles.[48]

As the *Standard*'s correspondent put it, "Some delay arose from the fact that the Government of Virginia was for part of the time still in the hands of the aliens and adventurers—carpetbaggers in league with the negroes—but upon the election to be governor of General Kemper, a gallant and loyal officer in the late lost cause, this difficulty vanished. Virginia was Virginia again." Hope wrote to Kemper on 2 March 1875 to ask if Virginia would accept the statue as a "memorial of its distinguished son and tribute of English sympathy." The necessary resolutions were subsequently passed in the state legislature. There would be a grand unveiling ceremony in Richmond—to which Hope was invited, as guest of the state—and all the preparations were entrusted to "a board of commissioners" consisting of the governor, J. L. Eubank (of the Senate), W. B. Taliaferro (of the House), and Jubal Early, all of whom were former Confederate officers.[49] The statue arrived in Baltimore on 9 September 1875 and reached Richmond on 22 September. The next day, it was taken to the Capitol with full honors to be presented by General Johnson to Governor Kemper, and Kemper held it in trust until the unveiling ceremony on 26 October. A granite platform was made, to Foley's design, with an inscription:

> Presented by English Gentlemen as a
> tribute of admiration for the
> soldier and patriot
> Thomas J. Jackson,
> and gratefully accepted by Virginia in
> the name of the Southern People.
> Done A.D. 1875,
> in the hundredth year of the Commonwealth.
> "Look! There is Jackson standing like a stone wall."

The ceremonies on 26 October lasted all day and ended with a "general illumination." The chief marshal was Gen. Joseph E. Johnston, though most of the preparations were made by his assistant, Gen. Henry Heth. The main procession began at 11:00 a.m. It was more than two miles long and included military formations from the State of Virginia and Confederate veterans of the Army of Northern Virginia. There were also cadets of colleges and

groups from volunteer organizations, fire companies, Sunday schools, temperance and benevolent societies, clubs, faculty and student bodies and others, and representatives from such ethnic and national community groups as
the British Association, Caledonian Club, Gesangverein Virginia, and the
Ancient Order of Hibernians. Several bands played music. Many flags were
on display, especially the U.S. flag, and "one Confederate battle flag, being
conspicuous for its solitude, was borne by the Stonewall Brigade."

The *Standard*'s correspondent wrote that "the cheering by the populace
as the procession passed the densest gatherings was deafening; and handsome decorations were seen at every turn. The columns numbered perhaps
ten thousand; and thirty thousand more awaited the arrival at the Capitol grounds, making a concourse of some forty thousand to witness the
unveiling." Among the three hundred who sat on the main platform were
Governor Kemper and the former state governors John Letcher and William Smith; Gens. Joseph E. Johnston, Bradley Johnson, Daniel Harvey Hill,
Henry Heth, and Jubal Early; Bishops David S. Doggett of the Methodist
Episcopal Church and James Gibbons of the Catholic Church; Adm. J. R.
Tucker, formerly of the Confederate and more recently the Peruvian navy;
former Confederate secretary of state and president of the Confederate
Senate Robert M. T. Hunter, now treasurer of Virginia; Robert Ould, one
of the lawyers who had advised Jefferson Davis when it appeared that Davis
would be tried for treason and who had previously served as the Confederacy's agent for the exchange of prisoners of war; the prominent Washington
banker, philanthropist, and art collector William Wilson Concoran; Jackson's biographer and former chief of staff, the Presbyterian clergyman and
theologian Robert L. Dabney; and many U.S. officers and guests from the
North. After a prayer by Bishop Doggett, there were addresses by Governor
Kemper and Moses D. Hoge, the prominent Presbyterian pastor, educator,
and writer, who had been one of Jackson's favorite preachers.[50]

Kemper praised Jackson's admirers across the Atlantic who had presented the statue and suggested that the events of 26 October had a bearing
on North-South relations in America: "Let the spirit and design with which
we erect this memorial today admonish our whole country that the actual
reconciliation of the states must come, and, so far as honorably in us lies,
shall come; but that its work will never be complete until the equal honor
and equal liberties of each section shall be acknowledged, vindicated, and
maintained by both." The spot chosen for the Jackson memorial was just

to the east of a large equestrian statue of George Washington (which had been completed in 1869, the foundation stone having been laid in 1850). In his oration, Hoge said that, like Washington, Jackson was a great Virginian. But Jackson's international standing was unequaled, and it was "a singular and striking illustration of the worldwide appreciation of his character that the first statue of Jackson comes from abroad," from "men of kindred race and kindred heart, as the expression of their good will and sympathy for our people as well as of their admiration for the genius and character of our illustrious hero." The statue was "the visible symbol of the ancient friendship which existed in colonial times between Virginia and the mother country," "a prophecy of the incoming of British settlers," and "a pleasing omen for the future that the rebuilding of our shattered fortunes should be aided by the descendants of the men who laid the foundations of the Commonwealth." After the speeches, the statue was unveiled at 2:40 p.m. Cannon and small arms were fired, and there was "a hearty old-time Confederate shout, repeated, re-echoed, and continued." The hymn "A Castle of Strength Is Our Lord" was sung, and then, amid more cheering, Jackson's daughter, Julia, not quite thirteen years old, was led by Kemper and introduced to members of the Stonewall Brigade.[51]

The *Standard*'s correspondent reported that Richmond's black community had asked to participate in the procession and ceremony and the request was granted. Black leaders changed their minds, however, when their group was assigned a place behind and separate from whites, instead of mixed together. They saw this as an insult. Nevertheless, many blacks did attend as private individuals, and they added to the celebratory mood of the day.[52]

After the ceremony, Kemper sent a telegram to Hope in London: "Statue inaugurated. Assemblage and enthusiasm unprecedented. Likeness surprisingly good." Hope replied on 28 October: "Governor—Delighted. Heartiest congratulations. Deeply regret absence."[53] In their coverage of the events of 26 October, several British publications lifted material directly from southern papers.[54]

As Historicus and others had predicted, some sections of opinion in America did not welcome the presentation of the statue and the unveiling ceremony. Democratic newspapers in the North made matters worse by asserting that the South deserved leniency and respect, which brought out party political as well as racial and sectional discord. American opponents of the statue pointed out that while southerners kept demanding "equality" and "rights," the very fact that the U.S. government allowed the ceremony to go ahead was proof that the South had these things. Commentators also denied that Jackson was to be admired. He had tried to destroy the Union. "Death, that flatterer of humanity, never did so much for a public character as for Stonewall Jackson." The statue was a gift, and it would have been impolite to refuse it, but still, the pageantry and speechifying in Richmond all seemed rather unpleasant. Messages from Britain indicated that people there thought so too. They wanted American friendship. They did not approve of the statue and eschewed the malice and ignorance of the "Anglo-rebels" behind it. One suggestion was that the pedestal should actually read: "This Statue was paid for by a Few Englishmen who Made Money during the Civil War."[55]

The *New York Times* was quite balanced in its coverage. According to its correspondent on the scene, for all the Virginian and British flags displayed on the day of the unveiling, the U.S. flag was "perhaps" even more in evidence. Nevertheless, the evening illuminations did include a notable display of southern pride, the emblem of Virginia beneath thirteen stars representing the Confederacy. This writer also gave a history of the statue and suggested that it had not been presented sooner because the South had lost the war. For years, Virginia had been "prostrate," with its government in the hands of military and civil authorities "who were not supposed to have much veneration for dead Confederates or their effigies."[56]

Another New York title, *Frank Leslie's Illustrated Newspaper*, argued that the whole affair was to be regretted, and that most British people did indeed regret it. ("Frank Leslie" was Henry Carter, an Englishman, born in Ipswich, who had arrived in New York in 1848 and set up an engraving shop.) Appended to these remarks was a sketch of Hope, "the prime mover in the enterprise."[57] Remarks about Hope also appeared in other papers. The *Galveston Daily News* reported that he had sent a photograph of the Jackson statue to Jefferson Davis: "Mr. Hope was an outspoken friend of the South during the rebellion, and it was mainly through his efforts that the money for the statue was raised." Northern and southern papers alike published correspondence relating to the statue, along with illustrations and descriptions of Foley's work.[58]

The controversy in Britain died down. Several newspaper reviews of the year 1875 included the unveiling of the Jackson statue,[59] but most did not. If the statue was discussed, it was treated more as an artistic accomplishment or as an interesting event in the recent past, not as a present political issue or an opportunity to settle old scores from the war years. The *Art Journal* for January 1877 included an engraving of "Foley's powerful statue."[60] Informed commentators thought this engraving the best they had seen.[61]

As British readers continued to be interested in America, remarks about the statue were occasionally included in British publications. One provincial paper, the *Hastings and St. Leonards Observer,* published a series of letters under the title "A Hastings Man in America," sent by a decorator named John Gann, who had become a "flourishing tradesman" in Richmond after emigrating some years earlier. In 1877, he wrote about the visit to Richmond of President Rutherford B. Hayes, whose decision to end Reconstruction and allow "home rule" in the South—though he had little choice, in view of the Democrats' strength in Congress—ensured a friendly reception at the ceremonies he attended. Gann could not leave off his discussion of civic events in Richmond without referring to the Jackson memorial.[62] Ten years later, "A Visit to the States" was serialized in the *Times.*[63] An account of the author's journey "From the Potomac River to the James" appeared in October 1887 (just two weeks before Hope's death) and included an account of conditions in Richmond. It mentioned the Jackson statue and the role played in its history by Hope and other English gentlemen. The author stated that though Virginians honored their heroes, they were ready for sectional resentments to fade. (But was the writer ready? The remarks about the statue were coupled with a negative comment on black suffrage.)[64]

Southern attitudes toward the war and the Jackson memorial were affected by the South's difficult postwar recovery. The recovery was aided by and in turn strengthened southern pride. Retelling the story of the statue was a contributing factor. In June 1896, as people flooded into Richmond for the annual convention of the United Confederate Veterans, this "Assembly to Promote True History and Preserve Holy Memories" was placed in the sequence of commemorative events that had begun in 1875 with the dedication of the Jackson statue, Richmond's "first great Confederate demonstration." Hope and the English committee, Foley, the inscription, and all the other details were revived as a focus of attention.[65]

Jackson would be honored again in Richmond with another statue, dedicated in October 1919, the work of Frederick William Sievers, a northerner who had moved to Richmond as a young man, trained in Rome and Paris, and achieved fame with several Confederate monuments (including the Virginia Monument at Gettysburg). His Jackson statue—sited at the intersection of Monument Avenue and the Boulevard—was cast in bronze, more than seventeen feet high, and placed on a granite pedestal more than twenty feet in height. Jackson was on horseback, facing northward. Jackson's widow, Anna, and daughter, Julia, who were both guests in Richmond for the inauguration of Foley's statue in 1875, attended many such events, actively promoting the Lost Cause movement. Concerned that her husband might not be remembered appropriately, Anna cooperated with one of his earliest biographers, Dabney, and later wrote her own works about him. "Widow of the Confederacy" and president of the United Daughters of the Confederacy, when she died in 1915, she was buried with military honors beside Jackson in Lexington. Julia Jackson unveiled Edward Valentine's statue of Robert E. Lee at Lee's tomb in June 1883. Jackson's granddaughter, Julia Jackson Christian, also participated in Confederate memorialization, as in May 1895 when she unveiled a monument in Raleigh, North Carolina.[66]

These rituals and monuments in the former Confederacy were prompted by what David Blight terms "the despair of defeat and the need for collective expressions of grief." Mark Schantz makes a connection with "heavenly reunions," a belief system that had developed before the war but was greatly intensified through memorials, poems, sermons, and icons, especially those expressing martyrdom. Schantz suggests that mourning for Jackson might have been alleviated by the conviction that he had been granted "heavenly reward."[67]

The South's religious and cultural resources were employed to the full by the Lost Cause movement. The Lost Cause involved self-definition and self-expression, a rejection of northern influence, and a boosting of conservatism. It facilitated recovery from defeat in the war and resilience in the face of postwar social transformation, in a manner that could minimize southern guilt and bitterness. In this construction of "the Confederate tradition," argues Gaines Foster, sensitivity and defensiveness combined with an ongoing sense of southern superiority. But there were also disagreements about whether, or how much, the South should change, and William Blair notes disputes about what exactly should be celebrated and when and how. This lack of consensus did not prevent frequent and widespread memorialization, with an emphasis on visual display. The basic Lost Cause message was nonnegotiable: the South had not been wrong to take up arms and was not discredited by defeat. Jackson was addressing his people from the grave, telling them to take their destiny into their own hands and rebuild their fortunes. Foster shows that it was primarily the veterans who took on "responsibility for speaking for the ghosts of the Confederacy" through their organizations and events. Charles Reagan Wilson rightly stresses the "sacred" and "spiritual" aspects, for without them, the Lost Cause would have lacked power. Jackson's piety made him particularly useful for this reason. There was a "living monument" to him—one that melded piety and history—in the form of the Stonewall Jackson Institute in Abingdon, Virginia, a Presbyterian college that was originally opened in 1866 for girls and young women. It expanded in the 1880s, benefited from scholarships set up by the United Daughters of the Confederacy, and housed a statue of Jackson and other memorabilia. Reestablished in 1917 after a fire, the college continued to operate until 1930, when debt forced its closure.[68]

Part coping mechanism, part proud self-affirmation, David Blight thinks that memorialization became an obligation: "Death on such a scale demanded meaning." Initially, this activity was mainly spiritual, but "very soon, remembering the dead and what they died for developed partisan fault lines." The special dates on which events were held differed from place to place, and in some parts of the South, it was 10 May, the day Jackson died. A crucial breakthrough came in October 1875 with the inauguration of the Jackson statue in Richmond. It was "unprecedented"—the first significant monument to a Confederate hero, the first time Confederate veterans joined in a "major coming-out as a collective force"—and it was effective both as "public ritual" and as "a mass statement of the meaning of Confederate defeat and Southern revival."[69] All this added to what Drew Gilpin Faust calls the "extravaganza of mourning" that had surrounded Jackson's lying in state, funeral journey, and burial in 1863. Perhaps southerners wanted to see in themselves what they saw in Jackson—faith, courage, loyalty. Clearly, in death, Jackson could still inspire. He represented sacrifice. He represented hope. Items associated with Jackson featured in the burgeoning of postwar remembrance. In the spring of 1867, for example, his coat buttons were offered as a raffle prize at a Richmond bazaar, organized to raise money for the care of the Confederate dead.[70]

Over the years, owing to its special connection with Jackson, many commemorative events took place at the Virginia Military Institute. For a full month after his death, officers and cadets wore tokens of mourning. In May 1913, to mark the fiftieth anniversary of his death, a large crowd gathered for the firing of the VMI cadet battery. (This was also the occasion for the decommissioning of the four cannon of the battery. Installed in 1848, Jackson had used them when teaching artillery to his students.) There were speeches, flags, music, a veterans' parade, and a procession to Jackson's grave. The passing of fifty years had not dimmed the desire to honor this idealized Confederate general. His reputation remained high, not least because of his early death. The South had lost the war, but Jackson had died victorious.[71]

Memorialization and iconography were enormously important in the postwar South. The Confederacy survived in widely disseminated lithographs and engravings (most of which, ironically, were produced in the North, where it was quickly realized that money could be made by satisfying demand). There were many prints of Jackson, and they were popular in Britain as well as America. Visual representations became sacred objects—portraits, engravings, and lithographs no less than statues and flags. These objects helped to reconcile southerners to the results of the war but in a way that sustained pride and memory and assured them that their nation, though defeated, would not die. Jackson-related books and articles served the same purpose.[72] The *Confederate Veteran* magazine was established in 1893 and became an influential monthly, with a circulation of twenty thousand by 1900. In 1917, one of its writers remembered Hope as "prominent in the championship of the Confederacy." It was to Hope "that the South is chiefly indebted for the Foley statue of Stonewall Jackson."[73]

Commissioned in 1863, the statue was not unveiled until 1875. Why the long delay? The American correspondent of the *Standard* referred to the Reconstruction regime in Virginia as "aliens and adventurers" and "carpetbaggers in league with the negroes." This terminology suggests that the statue could not have been presented until something like the old order had been restored. Virginia had to be, as conservative whites understood it, "redeemed." Samuel Graber has stressed that Kemper and his party wanted to use the statue as confirmation that they had regained control. They could advertise the return of "true" Virginia and limit the role there of northerners, radicals, and blacks. They could make the most of the British link, without which the statue would not exist, to signify international legitimacy. They could reestablish Virginia as the best representation of Anglo-Saxon culture—the best of America, indeed, and deserving of an appropriate place in the postwar Union. To Graber, "the peculiar politics of the late Reconstruction era, rather than mere nostalgia for a war era connection, brought the British monument to completion."[74]

Graber indicates that delay might have been preferred on the British side, too, for the promoters of the statue shared some of the goals of Kemper and his political allies in Virginia. There was common commitment to a type of "national memory" that buttressed traditional values and institutions. Graber refers to ideas in "transatlantic circulation," so that people in Britain could think of the American war as part of their own history. This reflected tensions that already existed in British politics and society. Traditionalism was a response to modern challenges associated with industrialization and radicalism, and for Hope and his fellow admirers of Jackson and the South, the statue symbolized the things they wanted to protect—their conceptualizations of aristocratic government, hierarchy, religious faith, gentlemanly manners, rural civilization, national cohesion. Although there was a progressive, libertarian side to British identity, in times of unrest the conservative perspective had influence, and during and after the American war, Jackson and the South—in heavily romanticized guise, admittedly—comforted and were commended by those in Britain who prioritized social stability, old institutions, and Anglo-Saxon purity. Jackson came to play a key role, therefore, in "the long struggle over British national memory."[75]

By demonstrating the importance of mnemonic narratives, Graber connects the agenda of Kemper and the Virginian conservatives to the preferences that activated Hope and the promoters of the Jackson statue. The long delay between the commissioning of the statue and its completion, presentation, and inauguration might indeed indicate that the promoters wished to wait until the time was right in order for the statue to do the job they wanted it to do. Still, for Graber, the key determinant was the political condition of Virginia. Richard Blackett also argues that the statue could not have been presented until Virginia's "redeemers" were ready. He attributes the delay to the "tide of war." The project was suspended when it became clear that the South was losing, and it was "shelved" when the war ended in victory for the North. Once Virginia had "home rule," the project was taken up again because leaders of the Association of the Army of Northern Virginia contacted the English committee and made sure that the statue would be completed.[76] Blackett and Graber agree that Virginian circumstances mattered more than the attitude of the statue's British promoters and contributors.[77]

Yet this is not how Hope saw it. In his letter in the *Times* in October 1875, he explained that the delay was mainly down to Foley, who could not focus exclusively on the Jackson statue because he had other projects under way; who wanted to take his time and make the likeness as accurate as possible; and who could not work when incapacitated by illness, leading to his death. Though it was true that the postwar South had been "down on its luck," this fact did not prey on the minds of the gentlemen behind the statue. To them, the matter was simple. Having collected the money for it, they were bound to see the project through. Would they really have decided to wait until Virginia's conservatives had recaptured the state government? How could they have known when that was going to happen? They wanted it to happen, no doubt, but they had no control over its manner and timing. Samuel Graber appears to be more interested in the motivations of Kemper and the Virginians than those of Hope, the English committee, and their pro-southern backers.[78] This allows him to see in the lapse of time between 1863 and 1875 the "embarrassing limits of British sympathy." The enthusiasm behind the statue proposal fell away as the course of the war began unmistakably to favor the North. Commitment faded. British mediation in the war became impossible. Hope and the committee realized that the South would lose the war, Foley turned to other work, and the Jackson project "languished." The commission, Graber contends, was "only revived in the 1870s" because Virginia's white leaders needed the statue as part of their "redemption" bid.[79]

These arguments are not unfounded, but it is easy to exaggerate the strategizing and intentionality behind the statue-related developments of 1863 to 1875. It is not true that the completion and presentation of the Jackson statue owed much more to Virginian initiative than to pro-southern sentiment in Britain. Confederate memorialization, important as it was in the South, was also meaningful to British pro-southerners. There is something to Thomas Sebrell's claim that if the statue commemorated Jackson, it also commemorated the pro-southern stance "of numerous British subjects."[80] That Hope and his friends persisted with the Jackson statue shows that if they thought it worthwhile in 1863, they thought the same way about it in 1875. The values and interests they associated with the Confederacy and the reasons why they had been pro-southerners during the war still mattered. Contemporary British politics were relevant as well (as assumed by Graber, though he does not go into details). By 1875, a Conservative government was in office. For men of Hope's mind-set, this provided opportunities to shore up the established order, urgently necessary in their view because of the unwelcome reforms of recent years, particularly the changes in the electoral system, the centralization and secularization trends in education policy, and the undermining of the Church of England. There was, in addition, among those most closely attached to traditional values and institutions, considerable resentment against what they saw as the weak and vacillating foreign policy of the Liberals, who had been in office from 1868 to 1874. Conservatives wanted and expected British prestige to be restored. They accused Gladstone and the Liberals of giving way to the United States on the *Alabama* claims. Britain paid damages, and Hope was one of the denigrators of that transaction. Meanwhile, his postwar statements about suffrage and the ballot and about certain rules and procedures of the U.S. Congress marked him out as an ardent opponent of the "Americanization" of Britain's government. "It was the fear of democracy," insists Alfred Grant, "that most influenced the ruling class of Britain in its relationship with America during the middle Victorian period."[81]

The Jackson memorial was an expression of opinion that outlasted the American Civil War and did not depend only on the course of that war. Respect for the South did not perish with the defeat of the South. Supporters of the project did not abandon it. Together with the commitment they felt to contributors to the statue fund, it was their continuing regard for the South, their determination to vindicate what they had said and done during the war, and their wish to uphold conservative principles and policies in the present that made them think it was entirely appropriate to present the statue to Virginia (the intention all along) in 1875.

Many statues would be erected in Richmond, but this was the first of a southern war hero, and it was the only one of a Confederate general in Capitol Square. After statue and pedestal costs had been covered, there was a substantial sum left over. With Governor Kemper's blessing, Hope gave this to the Virginia Military Institute, and the money was used to fund the "Jackson-Hope Medals," which are still awarded each year to the top cadets at the VMI. The wording on the medal, in its reference to "the Gift of English Gentlemen," is similar to that on the pedestal in Capitol Square, and Hope was happy to make suggestions about the medal's design. In addition to paying for the medals, the money he sent was put toward scholarships, which continue to be available to VMI students.[82] According to various American newspapers, the sum received from Hope, and invested by the VMI to pay for the medals and scholarships, was $1,344.[83] These papers made no comment, but the fact that so much was left over from the statue fund further attests to the level of commitment in Britain to the plan to memorialize Jackson. The statue kept memory alive just as the medals and scholarships do. If Hope and his colleagues on the committee formed in 1863 intended to make a statement about the American Civil War—that it was not only American in its immediate impact or likely long-term importance—they could not have been more eloquent.

CONCLUSION

D
uring the American Civil War and for decades afterward, Stonewall Jackson enjoyed a favorable reputation in Britain. He was thought to epitomize love of country and fear of God, courage and dash and a talent for modern warfare, gentlemanly manners and family affection, personal discipline and Christian ethics, a will of iron, the overcoming of trials. This was who he was to Beresford Hope and other British prosoutherners, and the southern heroism personified by Jackson was central to the arguments made by Hope to maximize British support for the South, along with the economic, political, constitutional, cultural, social, moral, and religious considerations that Hope also brought forward to this end. Hope sought to paint a positive picture of the South, including conditions for the slaves, and to explain why British values and interests made sympathy for the South natural and necessary. J. H. Foley's statue was a proof of British respect for Jackson and goodwill toward the South. It was no less a testament to British opinion than it was a tribute to an acknowledged hero. What is most remarkable is not that the project was decided upon when news of Jackson's death reached Hope and his friends but that it was pursued for so many years and defended so vigorously whenever it was criticized.

Icons and memorials remain promoters and tools of controversy. They can stir strong feelings. Meanings are attached to them that both gratify and offend, depending on the identity and perspective of whoever makes these connections. Richmond has been affected by such disputes up to the present time. There was a quarrel in the mid-1990s over the proposal to place a statue of Richmond-born black tennis champion Arthur Ashe (1943–93) on Monument Avenue in the former Confederate capital. Objections were raised on the grounds of "heritage preservation" and "historic sensibilities." Many Richmonders, and observers elsewhere, deemed it inappropriate to have Ashe standing alongside Stonewall Jackson and Robert E. Lee. Monu-

ment Avenue was not the right place, they complained. For white southerners, the location is special, but black rights activists also opposed the choice
of Monument Avenue—with its Confederate associations—and made much
of the fact that Ashe had spoken up for their cause. Indeed, he had left Richmond at seventeen because of segregation. Despite protests, the statue of
Arthur Ashe was unveiled on Monument Avenue in July 1996. The affair
was discussed in the British press. So was a related problem: the possibility
of recognizing black heroes while also celebrating Confederate ones. In 1984,
the state government in Virginia agreed that Martin Luther King Day should
be observed on the Monday in January that was closest to King's birthday
(in line with the federal holiday approved in 1983). But this was the same day
as a state holiday that honored Jackson and Lee. By 2000, owing to political
maneuvering and racial tension, a change had to be made. Some Virginians
opposed as disrespectful a move to alter the date of the Jackson-Lee holiday.
They worried that this would make it less important. Nevertheless, it was
moved to the Friday before Martin Luther King Day.[1]

Richmond was again disturbed by a memorialization dispute in 2003,
when it was decided that a statue of Abraham Lincoln should be placed near
the city's Civil War Visitor Center. A spokesman for the Sons of Confederate Veterans called this an "unnecessary slight." There was talk of a plot
to dictate to the people regarding their "monuments, history, heroes, education, and culture." Virginia's Republican politicians, needing the white
vote, were embarrassed and struggled to find a solution. An attempt to prevent the erection of the Lincoln statue on the basis of an old law prohibit-
ing Union markings on Confederate memorials was unsuccessful. This law
did not apply, ruled the state's attorney general (a Republican), because the
statue was to be situated in a park owned by a private corporation. Again,
the quarrel was noticed in Britain.[2]

More recent arguments about preserving statues of Confederate generals
and displaying the Confederate flag demonstrate the power that monuments
and emblems of the American Civil War, or representations of that war, still
possess. Most Confederate memorials date from the 1890s and early 1900s
and reflect the political, economic, and social difficulties of that era in American history, but in later periods of unease, they have been appealed to or condemned by a variety of groups for their own reasons. One British commentator from the political left, David Aaronovitch, opines that "tearing down
statues won't heal America" and that "the potency of monuments can al-

ways be toxic but it's better to explain them than to destroy them."[3] The role and nature of historical symbols change. Though they are familiar and established, they are also amenable for novel uses. In Britain, as well as America, they can be employed for present polemical purposes, even to the extent that a core feature of the Wirral regeneration project of the 1980s and 1990s, for instance, had to be abandoned. The idea of creating jobs and attracting visitors with a replica of the CSS *Alabama* was dropped because of the weight of opposition. Disagreement about statues and symbols is nothing new.

There was a veritable craze for memorials in Victorian Britain. These objects began to multiply in public spaces, parks, town centers, and other sites deemed to be suitable, in the context of social change and urban growth, economic progress, political reform, national ideals, and imperial ambition. In her study of British memorials of the Boer War, Valerie Parkhouse has explored both their diversity (monuments were of varying shapes and sizes, and memorialization was also carried on in newspapers, theaters, and music and poetry) and their function (recording historical events and representing the "collective memory" of the British people and, to some extent, its composition by religion, class, age, and gender). Statues, obelisks, plaques, and other forms of commemoration were fusions of history, culture, and landscape, and when it was a war that was being remembered, monuments expressed awareness of and reactions to that conflict.[4]

Three points made by Parkhouse have particular relevance to the Jackson statue unveiled in Richmond in 1875. The first is that the popular press and rising literacy in Britain meant that opinions about events overseas were readily formed and articulated. The second is that British memorialization respected both sides in the Boer War. This was in line with the pattern seen during the American Civil War, when both sides gathered support. The third is that quarrels broke out over the type of memorials proposed and how they were to be funded. Parkhouse refers to memories of war that were "short" and "selective." People might have liked the idea of statues, but they were reluctant to pay for them, which casts doubt on the strength of commitment to collective memorialization. The manner in which the Jackson statue was paid for becomes more noteworthy in light of this. The target sum was exceeded through public subscription, with the remainder devoted to medals and scholarships at the Virginia Military Institute.

Lincoln statues in Britain have been the subject of quarrels on both sides of the Atlantic, largely because of conflicting narratives propagated and reinforced since the 1860s. Lincoln's reputation in Britain was mixed during the American war, but after his assassination, it improved, and by the mid-twentieth century, he was generally seen as a symbol of "freedom," a victor over adversity, and a strong war leader. Still, there were different versions of Lincoln and different ideas in Britain about what he represented. Early in the twentieth century, closer relations between Britain and the United States encouraged a plan for the exchange of statues: Queen Victoria would go one way, Lincoln the other. The First World War caused a delay, and then there was a danger that British authorities might not accept the American statue of Lincoln that was offered because it was of the "self-made man of the people" style and not the "national leader" they preferred. In the event, *both* images of Lincoln were embodied, in two statues, one in Manchester and one in London, erected in 1919–20. These arrangements underline Nimrod Tal's comment that interested parties in Britain accepted lessons and images "according to their own understandings and needs." British interpretations of the American Civil War were conditioned by the rise to global influence of the United States and the extent to which the government and people of Britain valued U.S. friendship. There were efforts to blur the differences between North and South in a conciliatory version of the war, a war that had brought America together and enabled its rise. Such memorialization was more appealing and useful than depictions of a divided and disintegrating America.[5]

This was a far cry from the claims made by Hope and his pro-southern colleagues during the war and in the postwar years. Hope argued repeatedly that the Union could not be restored and that the United States, and Britain, must recognize the South as independent. Later, though he accepted the North's victory in the war, he could not help but regret it. His preference for the South continued to affect his writing and speaking about America until his death in 1887. During and after the war, many British people shared his attentiveness to, if not his opinions about, America. There was regular coverage in the London papers and in those of the largest British cities, including Birmingham, Bristol, Glasgow, Leeds, Liverpool, and Manchester. Even in relatively small provincial towns, where the circulations of local newspapers were in their hundreds rather than thousands, America was a focus. In much of this coverage, Jackson remained at the forefront.

Jackson's name was still being used well into the twentieth century. Examples from just one source will suffice. The *Economist* has long been among the most highly regarded British publications for its treatment of current affairs. Discussing Britain's alliance with the United States during the Second World War, it noted the "Jackson spirit" that animated the American military, the impressive contribution of officers trained at the VMI, and the lasting affinities between Britain and the South. The South was portrayed as an Anglo-Saxon society that traded with the world, especially Britain, had proud martial traditions, and was the least isolationist part of America. At the war's close, the British people were commended for their resilience in the face of the Nazi menace: whether at home or on the front line, they had fought magnificently. Like Jackson, declared the *Economist*, the British knew how to make war.[6] In items on finance and business in Britain, the *Economist* used the phrase "Stonewall Jackson" to indicate admirable characteristics, as in 1938, when describing investors who refused to panic in falling markets. Those who expected a recovery and by their actions helped to promote it "stood firm like Stonewall Jackson when the battle was going against them." A company chairman who used the press and a shareholders' committee to retain control of his firm when challenged in 1957 had "the tactical timing of Stonewall Jackson."[7] Reviews of military books published in the 1960s mentioned Jackson, as did articles about NATO and nuclear deterrence in the 1980s: "Equality of conventional forces has never guaranteed peace . . . In 1862, Stonewall Jackson never really enjoyed a fight unless he was whacking an enemy twice his size."[8] Jackson was still an exemplary figure. He was still taken to represent laudable qualities. His name and fame had abiding relevance in Britain.

In America, meanwhile, one of Jackson's leading British admirers had fallen into neglect. Though he was more responsible than anyone for the statue in Capitol Square in Richmond, Hope was virtually unknown to Americans of the twentieth century. After his death, he was disregarded. But before his death, the situation was quite different.

Some American commentators seem to have forgiven, if not forgotten, his wartime activism. In May 1869, the *New York Independent* referred to Hope as "an eccentric Tory of great wealth, famous as a builder of gorgeous churches and as the principal proprietor of the *Saturday Review*" but did not bring up his pro-southern record.[9] Nor was it mentioned in reports of December 1873 that Hope, "popularly regarded as the wealthiest commoner in England," had presented twenty-five thousand entomological specimens to the University of Oxford.[10] In May 1879, describing Hope's appointment as a trustee of the British Museum as a significant mark of esteem, *Harper's Bazaar* of New York added a brief biography. His Dutch forebears, inherited wealth, aristocratic relations, famous collection of gems, London villa and "immense mansion" in Kent, munificence and especially his generosity toward projects and institutions connected with the church, eminence in archaeological and architectural fields—all of this featured in the article—but his prominence as a Confederate supporter during the war did not.[11] If it was remembered, it was not necessarily held against him. Pieces about Hope that appeared in American papers during the 1880s also suggest that he was now noted for things other than his wartime activities.[12]

Hope's declining health was reported in the American press, and after his death, there were several appraisals. Specialist publications tended to focus on matters that were of most interest to their readers. They did not hark back to the war. The *American Architect* of Boston emphasized Hope's Gothic tastes. The *Church Review* of New York stressed that he had been a "devoted" and "distinguished" layman who gave unstintingly of his energy, money, and talents to High Church endeavors. Summarizing what had been published in Britain, the *New York Independent* pointed to Hope's strong convictions and his willingness to say unpopular things (though again, it did not refer to the war). Hope, "a benefactor to thought," had been unusual in this "flabby generation, softened out of all manliness."[13] Among other items about Hope after his death, the *Boston Daily Globe* mentioned only that he had been owner of the *Saturday Review*. Several papers were similarly brief. A few added that he was a longtime MP.[14] This limited acknowledgment might indicate that Hope and his words and deeds were no longer of much importance to Americans.

Yet his previous pro-southern activism still mattered greatly to some. The *Chicago Tribune*'s piece about Hope's death was headed "The Confederates' Friend," and in addition to mentioning his family, education, career, and publications, it declared: "The announcement of his death will be received in a large portion of the United States with the profoundest regret and sympathy. Mr. Beresford Hope was an ardent Southerner when the American civil war broke out." For Confederate envoys and agents, Hope's London residence had been "one of the great meeting places or camping grounds." After the war, he was "conspicuous for the delicacy and generosity with which his purse was placed at the disposal of broken-down Confederates, who found their way in swarms to London." The article went on in this vein but without any bitter denunciation of Hope. The writer apparently thought of Hope as a respectable character and one who probably deserved the gratitude that more than a few southerners felt toward him.[15] Another Chicago paper, the *Daily Inter Ocean*, also emphasized Hope's involvement with the Confederacy. He had been its "great friend," chairman of the Southern Independence Association, a generous supporter of southerners during and after the war, and "in 1875 he presented a statue of Stonewall Jackson to the State of Virginia." He was a good person who had erred: "That Mr. Beresford Hope should have felt a great sympathy for an impoverished people is not strange, but that he or any other fair-minded and intelligent Englishman should have championed a cause based upon wrong and fraught with evil for this and future ages is one of the best indications of the extent to which prejudice and self-interest can mislead strong and well-intentioned men."[16] The *Daily Picayune* of New Orleans gave a brief biography of Hope and stated that he would be remembered most, in the South, for the Jackson statue: "His tribute to one of the most heroic characters of modern times is worthy of the donor as well as the subject of his admiration." The *Galveston Daily News* mentioned his pro-southern sympathies and the statue and agreed that Hope's death would be regretted across the South.[17]

Northern opinion of Hope lost its severity as conciliatory interpretations of the American Civil War took hold, and his role in Britain, which had been divisive, also mattered less with the passing of time. But this is not to deny that the war had lasting effects on Britain. Scholars and nonscholars alike have done the research, weighed up evidence, and drawn conclusions, especially on matters pertaining to the big questions: what the war revealed about America, how it affected relations between Britain and the United States, and what British attitudes toward the war and its consequences indicate about Britain's political, social, and economic development. From the outset, British commentators approached these matters in accordance with their own plans and beliefs. They wanted to understand what happened in America and in Britain and to make use of it in their different ways. Through study, travel, communication, films, organizations, and numerous other types of transatlantic exchange, various American and British representations of the war were transmitted and received. Nimrod Tal makes the point that before "transatlantic mass tourism," many in Britain were reliant on "narratives, images, and information" from America, but it is also the case that these were rearranged in line with British preferences. Nor has opinion in the United States been unaffected by British perceptions. For much of the twentieth century, there was a convergence. With America's rise and the cooperation of Britain and the United States to deal with shared concerns, the war was regarded increasingly as the bringer of national unity, a strengthening through crisis, a victory for sound and salutary principles. The alternative southern narrative was marginalized.[18]

Yet the impact of British respect and affection for the South should not be underestimated. It was still shaping British discourse decades after the end of the war. The career of Beresford Hope and the enduring fascination with Stonewall Jackson are but two facets of this. They influenced ideas and affiliations in Britain and connected together wider networks of pro-southern commitment and activity.

NOTES

INTRODUCTION

1. Don H. Doyle, *The Cause of All Nations: An International History of the American Civil War* (New York: Basic Books, 2015), 3, 8, 11.

2. Ian Tyrrell, *Transnational Nation: United States History in Global Perspective since 1789* (New York: Palgrave Macmillan, 2007), 1–9, 84–93. See also *Rethinking American History in a Global Age*, ed. Thomas Bender (Berkeley: University of California Press, 2002).

3. Introduction to *The Civil War as Global Conflict: Transnational Meanings of the American Civil War*, ed. David T. Gleeson and Simon Lewis (Columbia: University of South Carolina Press, 2014), 2.

4. See "Introduction: The Electric Chain of Transnational History," in *The Transnational Significance of the American Civil War*, ed. Jörg Nagler, Don H. Doyle, and Marcus Gräser (Cham, Switzerland: Springer, 2016), 1–12.

5. See, for example, Brian Ward, Introduction to *The American South and the Atlantic World*, ed. Brian Ward, Martyn Bone, and William A. Link (Gainesville: University Press of Florida, 2013), 1–2.

6. There are useful insights in *American Historical Review* 111, no. 5 (2006): 1441–64; and *Journal of American History* 98, no. 2 (2011): 455–89. See also "New Approaches to Internationalizing the History of the Civil War Era," a special issue of *Journal of the Civil War Era* 2, no. 2 (2012).

7. Tal sees a shift from focusing on the political and military lessons of the war to other aspects, such as civil rights and, more recently, depiction of the war in movies and other cultural forms. See Nimrod Tal, *The American Civil War in British Culture: Representations and Responses, 1870 to the Present* (Basingstoke: Palgrave Macmillan, 2015), 2–6, 8.

8. Tal, *American Civil War in British Culture*, 125–26, 129, 148, 154, 162.

9. Tal, *American Civil War in British Culture*, 153.

10. Brent E. Kinser, *The American Civil War and the Shaping of British Democracy* (Farnham: Ashgate, 2011), 1–2.

11. Duncan Andrew Campbell, *English Public Opinion and the American Civil War* (Woodbridge: Boydell Press, 2003), 15.

12. Mary Ellison, *Support for Secession: Lancashire and the American Civil War* (Chicago: University of Chicago Press, 1972).

13. Alfred Grant, *The American Civil War and the British Press* (Jefferson, N.C.: McFarland, 2000).

14. Thomas E. Sebrell II, *Persuading John Bull: Union and Confederate Propaganda in Britain, 1860–1865* (Lanham, Md.: Lexington Books, 2014).

15. For biographical details, see H. W. Law and Irene Law, *The Book of the Beresford Hopes* (London: Heath Cranton, 1925); Gordon Batchelor, *The Beresfords of Bedgebury Park* (Goudhurst: William Musgrave, 1996); and J. Mordaunt Crook's entry in *Oxford Dictionary of National Biography* (Oxford: Oxford University Press, 2004). There is a summary of Hope's wartime activities in Charles Priestley, "Batavian Grace: An Example of English Upper-Class Support for the Confederacy in the American Civil War," *Crossfire* 69 (2002): 18–22.

I. FRIENDLY RELATIONS?

1. Duncan Andrew Campbell, *Unlikely Allies: Britain, America, and the Victorian Origins of the Special Relationship* (London: Hambledon Continuum, 2007), 227.

2. Campbell, *Unlikely Allies*, 221–22.

3. Eugenio F. Biagini, "Introduction: Citizenship, Liberty, and Community," in *Citizenship and Community: Liberals, Radicals, and Collective Identities in the British Isles, 1865–1931*, ed. Eugenio F. Biagini (Cambridge: Cambridge University Press, 2002), 12.

4. Robert Kelley, *The Transatlantic Persuasion: The Liberal-Democratic Mind in the Age of Gladstone* (New Brunswick, N.J.: Transaction Publishers, 1990), 19, 26–29, 53–54.

5. Murney Gerlach, *British Liberalism and the United States: Political and Social Thought in the Late Victorian Age* (Basingstoke: Palgrave, 2001), 17; Kevin Phillips, *The Cousins' Wars: Religion, Politics, and the Triumph of Anglo-America* (New York: Basic Books, 1999), 505–9; *America through British Eyes*, comp. and ed. Allan Nevins (New York: Oxford University Press, 1948), 321–22.

6. Jonathan Parry, *The Politics of Patriotism: English Liberalism, National Identity, and Europe, 1830–1886* (Cambridge: Cambridge University Press, 2006), 22, 24, 272.

7. Daniel T. Rodgers, *Atlantic Crossings: Social Politics in a Progressive Age* (Cambridge, Mass.: Belknap Press, 1998), 21, 26–31, 52–55, 58–64, 70, 72, 74, 77–80; Campbell, *Unlikely Allies*, 235; Kelley, *Transatlantic Persuasion*, 17.

8. Henry Pelling, *America and the British Left: From Bright to Bevan* (London: A. and C. Black, 1956), 50–52, 55, 57, 59–60, 62–64; Gerlach, *British Liberalism and the United States*, 94–101; Tyrrell, *Transnational Nation*, 39–51, 94–117.

9. Stephen Brooks, *America through Foreign Eyes: Classic Interpretations of American Political Life* (Don Mills, Ontario: Oxford University Press, 2002), 3–13.

10. Nevins, *America through British Eyes*, v, 3–4, 8–9, 102.

11. Nevins, *America through British Eyes*, 3, 8, 15, 23, 80, 100, 102, 210.

12. William E. Chace, in *American Historical Review* 50, no. 2 (1945): 353.

13. Howard Temperley, *Britain and America since Independence* (Basingstoke: Palgrave, 2002), 43; Campbell, *Unlikely Allies*, 110; Wendy Hinde, *Richard Cobden: A Victorian Outsider* (New Haven: Yale University Press, 1987), 23; R. K. Webb, *Modern England* (London: Taylor and Francis, 1980), 94; Frank Thistlethwaite, *The Anglo-American Connection in the Early Nineteenth Century* (Philadelphia: University of Pennsylvania Press, 1959), 46, 74; Thomas K. Murphy, *A Land with-*

out Castles: The Changing Image of America in Europe, 1780–1830 (Lanham, Md.: Lexington Books, 2001), 94–95; Eugenio F. Biagini, *Liberty, Retrenchment, and Reform: Popular Liberalism in the Age of Gladstone, 1860–1880* (Cambridge: Cambridge University Press, 1992), 81–82; James Epstein, "'America' in the Victorian Cultural Imagination," in *Anglo-American Attitudes: From Revolution to Partnership*, ed. F. M. Leventhal and Roland Quinault (Aldershot: Ashgate, 2000), 107–23; Peter Mandler, *The English National Character: The History of an Idea from Edmund Burke to Tony Blair* (New Haven: Yale University Press, 2006), 110, 119, 128, 152, 154, 162, 177, 182, 198, 202, 208.

14. Phillips, *Cousins' Wars*, 239; Edward Royle and James Walvin, *English Radicals and Reformers, 1760–1848* (Lexington: University Press of Kentucky, 1982), 15; Lillibridge, *Beacon of Freedom*, xiii–xv, 28; Introduction to Leventhal and Quinault, *Anglo-American Attitudes*, 1.

15. Nevins, *America through British Eyes*, 9–10, 23.

16. Jack P. Greene, "Introduction: Empire and Liberty," in *Exclusionary Empire: English Liberty Overseas, 1600–1900*, ed. Jack P. Greene (New York: Cambridge University Press, 2010), 3–5, 13. See also Tyrrell, *Transnational Nation*, 10–19.

17. Peter S. Onuf, "Federalism, Democracy, and Liberty in the New American Nation," in Greene, *Exclusionary Empire*, 132–59.

18. James Belich, *Replenishing the Earth: The Settler Revolution and the Rise of the Anglo-World, 1783–1939* (Oxford: Oxford University Press, 2009), 21, 23, 51, 88–99, 163, 445–46, 479–82, 548, 555.

19. William E. Van Vugt, *Britain to America: Mid-Nineteenth-Century Immigrants to the United States* (Urbana: University of Illinois Press, 1999), 3; *British Immigration to the United States, 1776–1914*, ed. William E. Van Vugt, 4 vols. (London: Pickering and Chatto, 2009), 1:xliii; Tyrrell, *Transnational Nation*, 20–38, 52–64, 94–117; S. B. Saul, "The American Impact on British Industry," in *Britain and America: Studies in Comparative History, 1760–1970*, ed. David Englander (New Haven: Yale University Press, 1997), 82–99.

20. Belich, *Replenishing the Earth*, 66–68, 70, 165–68, 479–82. See also Simon Morgan, "America, Protectionism, and Democracy in British Free Trade Debates, 1815–1861"; and Edmund Rogers, "Land and Tariffs: The American Economy and British Liberalism, 1867–1914," both in *The American Experiment and the Idea of Democracy in British Culture*, ed. Ella Dzelzainis and Ruth Livesey (Farnham: Ashgate, 2013), 93–106, 147–60.

21. J.C.D. Clark, *The Language of Liberty, 1660–1832: Political Discourse and Social Dynamics in the Anglo-American World* (Cambridge: Cambridge University Press, 1994), 5, 45, 78–79, 194, 261–62, 304–5.

22. Van Vugt, *British Immigration*, 1:xliii.

23. Clark, *Language of Liberty*, 382.

24. Richard Carwardine, *Transatlantic Revivalism: Popular Evangelicalism in Britain and America, 1790–1850* (Westport, Conn.: Greenwood Press, 1978), 32, 42–43, 56, 131, 164, 166–67, 171, 198.

25. Phillip E. Myers, *Caution and Cooperation: The American Civil War in British-American Relations* (Kent, Ohio: Kent State University Press, 2008), 8–34.

26. David P. Crook, *American Democracy in English Politics, 1815–1850* (Oxford: Clarendon Press, 1965), 3, 6–10, 199.

27. Phillips, *Cousins' Wars*.

28. Jonathan Parry, *The Rise and Fall of Liberal Government in Victorian Britain* (New Haven: Yale University Press, 1993).

29. James Vernon, *Politics and the People: A Study in English Political Culture, 1815–1867* (Cam-

bridge: Cambridge University Press, 1993); K. T. Hoppen, *The Mid-Victorian Generation, 1846–1886* (Oxford: Oxford University Press, 1998), chap. 8.

30. Lauren Goodlad, *Victorian Literature and the Victorian State: Character and Governance in a Liberal Society* (Baltimore: Johns Hopkins University Press, 2003), vii, ix, 14, 43.

31. Biagini, *Liberty, Retrenchment, and Reform*; Jon Lawrence, *Speaking for the People: Party, Language, and Popular Politics in England, 1867–1914* (Cambridge: Cambridge University Press, 1998); Malcolm Chase, *Chartism: A New History* (Manchester: Manchester University Press, 2007); Gareth Stedman Jones, "The Language of Chartism," in *The Chartist Experience: Studies in Working-Class Radicalism and Culture, 1830–1860*, ed. James Epstein and Dorothy Thompson (London: Macmillan, 1982), 3–58; James Epstein, "The Constitutional Idiom: Radical Reasoning, Rhetoric, and Action in Early Nineteenth-Century England," *Journal of Social History* 23, no. 3 (1990): 553–74; David Jones, *Chartism and the Chartists* (London: Allen Lane, 1975), 37–40, 64, 186–87; Patricia Hollis, *The Pauper Press: A Study in Working-Class Radicalism of the 1830s* (Oxford: Oxford University Press, 1970), viii, 100, 203–4, 207, 210, 218–58, 286–90, 293, 299, 302.

32. J.G.A. Pocock, "The Limits and Divisions of British History: In Search of the Unknown Subject," *American Historical Review* 87, no. 2 (1982): 311–36; J.C.D. Clark, "Protestantism, Nationalism, and National Identity, 1660–1832," *Historical Journal* 43, no. 1 (2000): 249–76. See also the essays in *Uniting the Kingdom? The Making of British History*, ed. Alexander Grant and Keith Stringer (London: Routledge, 1995); and *A Union of Multiple Identities: The British Isles, 1750–1850*, ed. Laurence Brockliss and David Eastwood (Manchester: Manchester University Press, 1997).

33. Belich, *Replenishing the Earth*, 457–64; P. J. Cain, "The Economics and Ethics of British Imperialism," *Historical Journal* 55, no. 1 (2012): 249–56, 258, 260–61.

34. Linda Colley, *Britons: Forging the Nation, 1707–1837* (New Haven: Yale University Press, 1992).

35. Mandler, *English National Character*, chaps. 2–4.

36. Parry, *Politics of Patriotism*, 2, 4, 35, 73, 387.

37. Max Berger, *The British Traveler in America, 1836–1860* (Gloucester, Mass.: P. Smith, 1964), 183–84.

38. Robert Saunders, *Democracy and the Vote in British Politics, 1848–1867: The Making of the Second Reform Act* (Farnham: Ashgate, 2011), 131–59.

39. Catherine Hall, Keith McClelland, and Jane Rendall, *Defining the Victorian Nation: Class, Race, Gender, and the British Reform Act of 1867* (Cambridge: Cambridge University Press, 2000).

40. Clark, *Language of Liberty*, 382–85.

41. Richard Cobden, one of the most influential of Victorian Britain's reformers, found it difficult to reconcile his respect for the United States with other commitments. Stephen Meardon, "Richard Cobden's American Quandary: Negotiating Peace, Free Trade, and Anti-Slavery," in *Rethinking Nineteenth-Century Liberalism*, ed. Anthony Howe and Simon Morgan (Aldershot: Routledge, 2006), 208–26. See also Anthony Howe, "John Bull and Brother Jonathan: Cobden, America, and the Liberal Mind," in Dzelzainis and Livesey, *American Experiment*, 107–19.

42. Jamie Bronstein, "From the Land of Liberty to Land Monopoly: The United States in a Chartist Context," in *The Chartist Legacy*, ed. Owen Ashton, Robert Fyson, and Stephen Roberts (Rendlesham: Merlin Press, 1999), 147–70; Gregory Claeys, "The Example of America as a Warning to England? The Transformation of America in British Radicalism and Socialism,

1790–1850," in *Learning and Living: Essays in Honor of J.F.C. Harrison*, ed. Malcolm Chase and Ian Dyck (Aldershot: Scolar Press, 1996), 66–80; Ray Boston, *British Chartists in America, 1839–1900* (Manchester: Manchester University Press, 1971), chap. 4.

43. Jon Roper, *Democracy and Its Critics: Anglo-American Democratic Thought in the Nineteenth Century* (London: Unwin Hyman, 1989), 3–16, 18–21, 28, 54–55, 80–83, 109–12, 138–39, 166–68, 193, 212–17. See also Adam Smith, "The 'Fortunate Banner': Languages of Democracy in the United States"; and Joanna Innes, Mark Philp, and Robert Saunders, "The Rise of Democratic Discourse in the Reform Era: Britain in the 1830s and 1840s," both in *Re-Imagining Democracy in the Age of Revolutions*, ed. Joanna Innes and Mark Philp (Oxford: Oxford University Press, 2013), 28–39, 114–28.

44. Saunders, *Democracy and the Vote*, 142–48.

45. Andrew W. Robertson, *The Language of Democracy: Political Rhetoric in the United States and Britain, 1790–1900* (Ithaca, N.Y.: Cornell University Press, 1995), 1–2, 6–7, 11–12, 14–16, 20–21, 68–115, 146–63, 213–14, 216.

46. See, for example, Mary K. Geiter and William A. Speck, "Anticipating America: American Mentality before the Revolution," in Englander, *Britain and America*, 26–47.

47. Joseph Eaton, *The Anglo-American Paper War: Debates about the New Republic, 1800–1825* (Basingstoke: Palgrave Macmillan, 2012).

48. Jennifer Clark, *The American Idea of England, 1776–1840: Transatlantic Writing* (Farnham: Ashgate, 2013).

49. *The Materials of Exchange between Britain and North East America, 1750–1900*, ed. Daniel Maudlin and Robin Peel (Farnham: Ashgate, 2013).

50. Sam W. Haynes, *Unfinished Revolution: The Early American Republic in a British World* (Charlottesville: University of Virginia Press, 2010), chaps. 3–7.

51. Campbell, *Unlikely Allies*, 140–41; and Campbell, *English Public Opinion*, 15.

52. Berger, *British Traveler*; Christopher Mulvey, *Transatlantic Manners: Social Patterns in Nineteenth-Century Anglo-American Travel Literature* (Cambridge: Cambridge University Press, 1990); Richard L. Rapson, *Britons View America: Travel Commentary, 1860–1935* (Seattle: University of Washington Press, 1971).

53. Van Vugt, *Britain to America*, 154–55.

54. Several of the essays in Englander, *Britain and America*, examine these perspectives.

55. Hugh Dubrulle, *Ambivalent Nation: How Britain Imagined the American Civil War* (Baton Rouge: Louisiana State University Press, 2018), 4–6, 30–31.

56. Saunders, *Democracy and the Vote*, 142.

57. Colley, *Britons*, 105, 134–38, 141–45, 148–49, 352–54. But for a different narrative, see Paula E. Dumas, *Proslavery Britain: Fighting for Slavery in an Era of Abolition* (Basingstoke: Palgrave Macmillan, 2016).

58. Tal, *American Civil War in British Culture*, 10–22, 24, 26, 28.

59. Nevins, *America through British Eyes*, 226; Walter L. Arnstein, "The Americanization of Queen Victoria," *Historian* 72, no. 4 (2010): 831–46.

60. Campbell, *Unlikely Allies*, 103, 112; Temperley, *Britain and America since Independence*, 42–43, 45–47.

61. Nevins, *America through British Eyes*, 327–29; Pelling, *America and the British Left*, 4.

62. Brooks, *America through Foreign Eyes*, 3.

2. ECONCOMIC MEASURES AND POLITICAL IDEAS

1. To illustrate his points, Hope sometimes used a large map of America, made by children on his Bedgebury Park estate. Batchelor, *Beresfords*, 111.

2. A.J.B. Hope, *A Popular View of the American Civil War* (London: Ridgway, 1861), 23–24, 27.

3. *London Times*, 17 Jan. 1862.

4. A.J.B. Hope, *Two Years of Church Progress* (London: J. and C. Mozley, 1862), 16. See also Grant, *American Civil War and the British Press*, 97–117, 153–58.

5. British Library, Gen. Ref. 8139 df.17/13, "Mr. Beresford Hope's Address upon the Political Questions of the Day, at Stoke-upon-Trent Town Hall, Tuesday September 9th 1862," 7; *London Times*, 12 Sept. 1862.

6. A.J.B. Hope, *The Social and Political Bearings of the American Disruption* (London: Ridgway, 1863), 32.

7. A.J.B. Hope, *England, the North, and the South* (London: Ridgway, 1862), 18, 21. See also A.J.B. Hope, *The Results of the American Disruption* (London: Ridgway, 1862), 17–18.

8. "The American Civil War," *Saturday Review* 12, no. 297, 6 July 1861, 3.

9. Matthew Karp, "King Cotton, Emperor Slavery: Antebellum Slaveholders and the World Economy," in Gleeson and Lewis, *Civil War as Global Conflict*, 36–55.

10. Brian Schoen, "Southern Wealth, Global Profits: Cotton, Economic Culture, and the Coming of the Civil War," in Nagler, Doyle, and Gräser, *Transnational Significance of the American Civil War*, 69–90. See also Edward L. Ayers, *What Caused the Civil War? Reflections on the South and Southern History* (New York: Norton, 2005), 131–44.

11. Ward, Introduction, 4; and John McCardell, *The Idea of a Southern Nation: Southern Nationalists and Southern Nationalism, 1830–1860* (New York: Norton, 1979), chap. 3.

12. Brian Schoen, *The Fragile Fabric of Union: Cotton, Federal Politics, and the Global Origins of the Civil War* (Baltimore: Johns Hopkins University Press, 2009).

13. See *The Old South's Modern Worlds: Slavery, Region, and Nation in the Age of Progress*, ed. L. Diane Barnes, Brian Schoen, and Frank Towers (New York: Oxford University Press, 2011).

14. *London Observer*, 20, 21 Mar. 1859.

15. Hope, *Popular View*, 3–8. Hope did not go into it on this occasion, but he saw Irish self-determination in the same way. Autonomy for the South was appropriate, while autonomy for Ireland was not. Tal, *American Civil War in British Culture*, 10–18.

16. Hope, *Popular View*, 9–10.

17. Hope's friendship with the bishop is mentioned several times in C. J. Bunyon, *Memoirs of Francis Thomas McDougall, Sometime Bishop of Labuan and Sarawak, and of Harriette, His Wife* (London: Longmans, 1889), 209, 251, 292, 309–10, 342. Kirkland had been a friend of Hope's stepfather, Lord Beresford, and was one of the executors of his will. *Gentleman's Magazine* 41 (Mar. 1854): 314.

18. *John Bull*, 23 Nov. 1861.

19. Hope to Freeman, 3 Mar., 25 June 1861, John Rylands Library, University of Manchester, Freeman Papers, GB133, EAF/1/1/56–57. The book, published early in 1863, was in fact dedicated to Spyridon Trikoupis, the champion of Greek independence.

20. E. A. Freeman, *History of Federal Government, from the Foundation of the Achaian League to the Disruption of the United States* (London: Macmillan, 1863), ix–xii. America and federalism are

discussed in *Making History: Edward Augustus Freeman and Victorian Cultural Politics*, ed. G. A. Bremner and Jonathan Conlin (Oxford: Oxford University Press, 2015). On Freeman's idea that ethnicity and social values were reflected in systems of government, see C.J.W. Parker, "The Failure of Liberal Racialism: The Racial Ideas of E. A. Freeman," *Historical Journal* 24, no. 4 (1981): 825–46.

21. Freeman, *Federal Government*, 2–3.

22. Freeman, *Federal Government*, 91–94, 111–13.

23. Freeman, *Federal Government*, 107, 257.

24. Hope, *Two Years*, 4, 16–17.

25. Hope, *England, the North, and the South*, 1–2; *London Times*, 17 Jan. 1862; Grant, *American Civil War and the British Press*, 37–44, 67–73, 97–117.

26. Hope, *England, the North, and the South*, 4–12.

27. Hope, *England, the North, and the South*, 13–15.

28. Hope, *England, the North, and the South*, 19–23.

29. Hope, *England, the North, and the South*, 24–26.

30. Hope, *Results of the American Disruption*, 3–6.

31. *London Times*, 24 Mar. 1862; Hope, *Results of the American Disruption*, 7–9.

32. Hope, *Results of the American Disruption*, 9–10.

33. Hope, *England, the North, and the South*, 16; and *Social and Political Bearings*, 28.

34. Hope, *Social and Political Bearings*, 32–33.

35. Hope, *Popular View*, 14–16. See also *Results of the American Disruption*, 17–18.

36. Hope, *Popular View*, 16–19; and *England, the North, and the South*, 16–17.

37. Hope, *Popular View*, 21–22.

38. Hope, *Popular View*, 23–26.

39. *British Parliamentary Election Results*, ed. F.W.S. Craig (London: Macmillan, 1977), 290; "Mr. Beresford Hope's Address," 4, 6–8; *John Bull*, 13 Sept. 1862; *London Times*, 12, 24 Sept. 1862.

40. "Mr. Beresford Hope's Address," 16–18; *London Times*, 12 Sept. 1862.

41. *London Times*, 24 Sept. 1862.

42. *Anti-Slavery Monthly Reporter*, 1 Sept. 1863; *Manchester Guardian*, 17 Oct. 1863; *London Times*, 17 Oct. 1863; *John Bull*, 17, 24 Oct. 1863.

43. "The American Civil War," *Saturday Review* 12, no. 297, 6 July 1861, 3.

44. "The English Press and American Opinion," *Saturday Review* 12, no. 321, 21 Dec. 1861, 627–8.

45. "Radicalism in 1862," *Saturday Review* 14, no. 353, 2 Aug. 1862, 125.

46. *London Times*, 13 Jan. 1863.

47. Hope, *Social and Political Bearings*, 33–36.

48. Hope, *Social and Political Bearings*, 36–37.

49. Hope, *Popular View*, 37–38.

50. Hope, *Results of the American Disruption*, 11–12.

51. *New York Times*, 9 Dec. 1861.

52. *New York Times*, 27 Feb. 1863.

53. *Liberator* (Boston), 4 Apr. 1862; *Boston Investigator*, 7 May 1862; *North American and United States Gazette* (Philadelphia), 9 May 1862.

54. *North American and United States Gazette*, 12 Sept. 1862; *Lowell Daily Citizen and News*, 26 Sept. 1862; *Frank Leslie's Illustrated Newspaper* (New York), 18 Oct. 1862.

55. *Liberator,* 4 Apr. 1862, 11 Mar. 1864.

56. "America," *Saturday Review* 19, no. 495, 22 Apr. 1865, 457.

57. Campbell, *English Public Opinion,* 100, 140–52, 194–200, 209, 211–15, 219, 222, 229, 234–35; Robert Saunders, "'Let America Be the Test': Democracy and Reform in Britain, 1832–1867," in Dzelzainis and Livesey, *American Experiment,* 79–91; Joanna Innes and Mark Philp, "Synergies," in Innes and Philp, *Re-Imagining Democracy,* 191–212; Margot C. Finn, *After Chartism: Class and Nation in English Radical Politics, 1848–1874* (Cambridge: Cambridge University Press, 1993), chap. 5.

58. O. Vernon Burton, "Remembering the Civil War," in Gleeson and Lewis, *Civil War as Global Conflict,* 281–83.

59. Leslie Butler, "Lincoln as the Great Educator: Opinion and Educative Liberalism in the Civil War Era," in Nagler, Doyle, and Gräser, *Transnational Significance of the American Civil War,* 49–66.

60. Aaron W. Marrs, "Fulfilling 'The President's Duty to Communicate': The Civil War and the Creation of the *Foreign Relations of the United States* Series," in Gleeson and Lewis, *Civil War as Global Conflict,* 190–210.

61. *William Howard Russell's Civil War: Private Diary and Letters, 1861–1862,* ed. Martin Crawford (Athens: University of Georgia Press, 1992). It has been suggested that Russell's ambivalence "exemplified" British opinion in this period and that he was probably more fair-minded about both Union and Confederacy than other British war correspondents. Dubrulle, *Ambivalent Nation,* 1–2, 47–50, 52, 56–57, 60–61, 68–69, 74, 76–78, 103, 105, 223, 226.

62. Tal, *American Civil War in British Culture,* 67–95; Kinser, *American Civil War in the Shaping of British Democracy,* 163–73; Frank Prochaska, *Eminent Victorians on American Democracy: The View from Albion* (Oxford: Oxford University Press, 2012).

63. Kinser, *American Civil War in the Shaping of British Democracy,* 2–6, 9–11; Dubrulle, *Ambivalent Nation,* 17–18, 45.

64. Gleeson and Lewis, Introduction, 2–3.

65. James M. McPherson, "Antebellum Southern Exceptionalism: A New Look at an Old Question," *Civil War History* 50, no. 4 (2004): 424; Robert B. Bonner, "Roundheaded Cavaliers? The Context and Limits of a Confederate Racial Project," *Civil War History* 48, no. 1 (2002): 55.

66. Adrian Brettle, "1864: The Genesis of a New Conservative World?" in *The Tory World: Deep History and the Tory Theme in British Foreign Policy, 1679–2014,* ed. Jeremy Black (Farnham: Ashgate, 2015), 187–202.

67. Saunders, *Democracy and the Vote,* 142–59.

68. Charlotte Erickson, *Invisible Immigrants: The Adaptation of English and Scottish Immigrants in Nineteenth-Century America* (Coral Gables, Fla.: University of Miami Press, 1972).

69. Alexander Noonan, "'A New Expression of That *Entente Cordiale?*' Russian-American Relations and the 'Fleet Episode' of 1863," in Gleeson and Lewis, *Civil War as Global Conflict,* 116–45.

70. Jeffrey R. Kerr-Ritchie, "Was U.S. Emancipation Exceptional in the Atlantic or Other Worlds?" in Ward, Bone, and Link, *American South and the Atlantic World,* 155–56; Ayers, *What Caused the Civil War,* 131–44.

71. See Schoen, *Fragile Fabric of Union;* and Paul Quigley, *Shifting Grounds: Nationalism and the American South, 1848–1865* (New York: Oxford University Press, 2012).

72. McCardell's *Idea of a Southern Nation* includes no detailed analysis of states' rights ideology, focusing more on other elements in southern nationalism.

73. Peter S. Onuf, "Antebellum Southerners and the National Idea," in Barnes, Schoen, and Towers, *Old South's Modern Worlds*, 25.

3. SOCIAL AND CULTURAL AFFINITIES

1. Hope, *Popular View*, 12–14.

2. Hope, *Two Years*, 18–22; *The Sword of the Lord: A Sermon Preached in the House of Prayer, Newark, New Jersey, on Thursday, September 26, 1861, Being the National Fast Day, by Edward J. Stearns, AM, of the Diocese of Maryland, Minister in Charge* (Baltimore: J. S. Waters, 1861). See also Hope, *Popular View*, 34–35. Stearns had previously published other controversial tracts, including one against abolitionism.

3. Hope, *England, the North, and the South*, 15–17; *London Times*, 17 Jan. 1862.

4. Hope, *England, the North, and the South*, 36–37.

5. "The American Civil War," *Saturday Review* 12, no. 297, 6 July 1861, 3.

6. *Parliamentary Debates*, 3rd ser., 7 June 1861, vol. 163, cols. 762–64.

7. Hope, *Results of the American Disruption*, 18–20.

8. "A Month with 'The Rebels,'" *Blackwood's Edinburgh Magazine* 90, no. 554 (1861): 755–67.

9. Hope, *Results of the American Disruption*, 21–27.

10. Hope, *Results of the American Disruption*, 28; "Mr. Beresford Hope's Address," 7.

11. Hope, *Social and Political Bearings*, 37–41.

12. A.J.B. Hope, *The American Church in the Disruption* (London: J. and C. Mozley, 1863), 3.

13. Hope, *Social and Political Bearings*, 5–8.

14. *London Standard*, 22 Jan. 1863; *Bury and Norwich Post*, 27 Jan. 1863; *Derby Mercury*, 28 Jan. 1863.

15. *Manchester Guardian*, 17 Oct. 1863; *London Times*, 17 Oct. 1863; *Liverpool Mercury*, 17 Oct. 1863; *Birmingham Daily Post*, 19 Oct. 1863; *Caledonian Mercury*, 20 Oct. 1863; *Belfast Newsletter*, 22 Oct. 1863; *John Bull*, 24 Oct. 1863.

16. *Liverpool Mercury*, 19, 20 Oct. 1864; *Manchester Courier*, 20 Oct. 1864.

17. Hugh Dubrulle, "'If It Is Still Impossible to Advocate Slavery . . . It Has Become a Habit Persistently to Write Down Freedom': Britain, the Civil War, and Race," in Gleeson and Lewis, *Civil War as Global Conflict*, 76.

18. David T. Gleeson, "Proving Their Loyalty to the Republic: English Immigrants and the Civil War," in Gleeson and Lewis, *Civil War as Global Conflict*, 114; Ella Lonn, *Foreigners in the Confederacy* (Chapel Hill: University of North Carolina Press, 2002), 496, 498.

19. Gleeson, "Proving Their Loyalty to the Republic," 98–99, 106, 110–11.

20. Peter O'Connor, *American Sectionalism in the British Mind, 1832–1863* (Baton Rouge: Louisiana State University Press, 2017), chaps. 2–3. See also Dubrulle, *Ambivalent Nation*, chap. 1.

21. Dubrulle, *Ambivalent Nation*, 206.

22. James M. McPherson, "'Two Irreconcilable Peoples'? Ethnic Nationalism in the Confederacy," in Gleeson and Lewis, *Civil War as Global Conflict*, 88, 90–91, 94. See also McPherson, *Is Blood Thicker than Water? Crises of Nationalism in the Modern World* (New York: Random House, 1999).

23. William R. Taylor, *Cavalier and Yankee: The Old South and American National Character*

(New York: G. Braziller, 1961), 15; Ritchie Devon Watson Jr., *Normans and Saxons: Southern Race Mythology and the Intellectual History of the American Civil War* (Baton Rouge: Louisiana State University Press, 2008), 17–18.

24. Bonner, "Roundheaded Cavaliers," 36, 50–55.

25. Bonner, "Roundheaded Cavaliers," 34–40, 42, 44–47, 49–51, 54–55, 59.

26. Michael O'Brien, *Intellectual Life and the American South, 1810–1860* (Chapel Hill: University of North Carolina Press, 2010).

27. O. Vernon Burton, "The South as 'Other,' the Southerner as 'Stranger,'" *Journal of Southern History* 79, no. 1 (2013): 7, 12, 16, 31, 34, 48; Ayers, *What Caused the Civil War*, 37–63.

28. McCardell, *Idea of a Southern Nation*, chaps. 3–6; Marc Egnal, "Counterpoint: What if Genovese Is Right? The Pre-Modern Outlook of Southern Planters," in Barnes, Schoen, and Towers, *Old South's Modern Worlds*, 269–87; Michael T. Bernath, *Confederate Minds: The Struggle for Intellectual Independence in the Civil War South* (Chapel Hill: University of North Carolina Press, 2010), chaps. 5–7.

29. Onuf, "Antebellum Southerners and the National Idea," 25–46.

30. McPherson, "Antebellum Southern Exceptionalism," 418–33. McPherson makes the point that objective similarities between North and South did not prevent the rise of separatist sentiment in the South. The North modernized more rapidly, but historians disagree about whether the South should be seen as "backward." William G. Thomas and Edward L. Ayers, "The Differences Slavery Made," *American Historical Review* 108, no. 5 (2003): 1299–1307; Schoen, *Fragile Fabric of Union*; Ward, Introduction, 1–7; and Frank Towers, "The Southern Path to Modern Cities: Urbanization in the Slave States," and William G. Thomas, "'Swerve Me?' The South, Railroads, and the Rush to Modernity," both in Barnes, Schoen, and Towers, *Old South's Modern Worlds*, 145–65, 166–88.

31. Drew Gilpin Faust, *The Creation of Confederate Nationalism: Ideology and Identity in the Civil War South* (Baton Rouge: Louisiana State University Press, 1988). Faust concludes that southern nationalism failed because it had no social unity behind it and the pressures of war brought out its contradictions. James C. Cobb's *Away Down South: A History of Southern Identity* (New York: Oxford University Press, 2005) traces a transformation in race relations and the discarding of a negative and limited self-definition of the South as whatever the North was not.

32. Stephanie McCurry, *Masters of Small Worlds: Yeoman Households, Gender Relations, and the Political Culture of the Antebellum South Carolina Low Country* (New York: Oxford University Press, 1995), 26–29, 81, 84–85, 92, 208–11, 213–14, 225–28, 233–35, 238, 277–88, 290–96, 299–304.

33. Burton, "Remembering the Civil War," 279, 281, 285.

34. Quigley, *Shifting Grounds*, chap. 4.

35. Paul Quigley, "The American Civil War and the Transatlantic Triumph of Volitional Citizenship," in Nagler, Doyle, and Gräser, *Transnational Significance of the American Civil War*, 33–48.

36. See Tiziano Bonazzi, "The United States, Italy, and the Tribulations of the Liberal Nation"; and Enrico Dal Lago, "Nation-Building, Civil War, and Social Revolution in the Confederate South and the Italian Mezzogiorno, 1860–1865," both in Nagler, Doyle, and Gräser, *Transnational Significance of the American Civil War*, 151–68, 169–85.

37. Andre M. Fleche, "Race and Revolution: The Confederacy, Mexico, and the Problem of Southern Nationalism," in Nagler, Doyle, and Gräser, *Transnational Significance of the American Civil War*, 189–203.

38. Lonn's research was first published in 1940, when such findings (not in line with the favorite assumptions of southern historiography) were unlikely to be well received. See William A. Blair's foreword in Lonn, *Foreigners in the Confederacy*, xi–xv.

39. British attitudes are discussed in Lonn, *Foreigners in the Confederacy*, 36, 53–54, 99, 115–16, 188, 408–10, 415–16; and foreigners' service as a whole is summarized in chap. 15.

40. On German allegiances, see Stephen D. Engle, "Yankee Dutchmen: Germans, the Union, and the Construction of Wartime Identity"; and Andrea Mehrländer, "'With More Freedom and Independence than the Yankees': The Germans of Richmond, Charleston, and New Orleans during the American Civil War," both in *Civil War Citizens: Race, Ethnicity, and Identity in America's Bloodiest Conflict*, ed. Susanna J. Ural (New York: New York University Press, 2010), 11–56, 57–98. On Irish allegiances, see Susanna J. Ural, "'Ye Sons of Green Erin Assemble': Northern Irish American Catholics and the Union War Effort, 1861–1865"; and David T. Gleeson, "Irish Rebels, Southern Rebels: The Irish Confederates," both in Ural, *Civil War Citizens*, 99–132, 133–56. For a more thorough treatment of Irish Confederates, see Gleeson's *The Green and the Gray: The Irish in the Confederate States of America* (Chapel Hill: University of North Carolina Press, 2013).

41. See Erickson, *Invisible Immigrants*; and David A. Gerber, *Authors of Their Lives: The Personal Correspondence of British Immigrants to North America in the Nineteenth Century* (New York: New York University Press, 2006).

42. Van Vugt, *Britain to America*; and Van Vugt, "The Hidden English Diaspora in Nineteenth-Century America," in *Locating the English Diaspora, 1500–2010*, ed. Tanja Bueltmann, David T. Gleeson, and Donald M. MacRaild (Liverpool: Liverpool University Press, 2012), 67–83.

43. William Van Vugt, "Relocating the English Diaspora in America," in *English Ethnicity and Culture in North America*, ed. David T. Gleeson (Columbia: University of South Carolina Press, 2017), 8–36.

44. Donald M. MacRaild, "Ethnic Conflict and English Associational Culture in America: The Benevolent Order of the Society of St. George, 1870–1920," in Gleeson, *English Ethnicity and Culture*, 37–63.

45. Tanja Bueltmann, "Anglo-Saxonism and the Racialization of the English Diaspora," in Bueltmann, Gleeson, and MacRaild, *Locating the English Diaspora*, 118–34.

46. David T. Gleeson, "England and the Antebellum South," in Gleeson, *English Ethnicity and Culture*, 139–54.

47. Duncan Bell, *The Idea of Greater Britain: Empire and the Future of World Order, 1860–1900* (Princeton, N.J.: Princeton University Press, 2007).

48. *Living Age*, 7 Mar. 1863.

49. "Stonewall Jackson," *Saturday Review* 15, no. 396, 30 May 1863, 689.

4. SLAVERY AND EMANCIPATION

1. Gleeson and Lewis, Introduction, 3, 7.

2. Ayers, *What Caused the Civil War*, 131–44.

3. Burton, "Remembering the Civil War," 278–80, 283; McPherson, "Antebellum Southern Exceptionalism," 424. See also Thomas and Ayers, "Differences Slavery Made," 1299–1307.

4. Mischa Honeck, "Uprooted Emancipators: Transatlantic Abolitionism and the Politics of Belonging," in Nagler, Doyle, and Gräser, *Transnational Significance of the American Civil War*, 109–26.

5. Andrew Zimmerman, "Africa and the American Civil War: The Geopolitics of Freedom and the Production of Commons," in Nagler, Doyle, and Gräser, *Transnational Significance of the American Civil War*, 127–48.

6. Edward B. Rugemer, "Why Civil War? The Politics of Slavery in Comparative Perspective," in Gleeson and Lewis, *Civil War as Global Conflict*, 14–35. See also Kerr-Ritchie, "Was U.S. Emancipation Exceptional," 150, 152–53, 160, 164–65.

7. Larry E. Hudson Jr., "'A Disposition to Work': Rural Enslaved Laborers on the Eve of the Civil War," Steven Deyle, "Rethinking the Slave Trade: Slave Traders and the Market Revolution in the South," and James L. Huston, "The Pregnant Economies of the Border South, 1840–1860: Virginia, Kentucky, Tennessee, and the Possibilities of Slave-Labor Expansion," all in Barnes, Schoen, and Towers, *Old South's Modern Worlds*, 87–103, 104–19, 120–41.

8. Karp, "King Cotton, Emperor Slavery," 36–55.

9. Schoen, *Fragile Fabric of Union*, 11–21, 146, 197, 245, 257–59.

10. On the inseparability of slavery and states' rights, see, for example, Quigley, *Shifting Grounds*, 13, 46, 52–56, 67, 141. The centrality of slavery to the unifying cause of independence is discussed in McCardell's *Idea of a Southern Nation*. On McCurry's thesis about "mastery," see *Masters of Small Worlds*, chap. 8.

11. See O'Brien, *Intellectual Life and the American South*; and Bernath, *Confederate Minds*.

12. Bonner, "Roundheaded Cavaliers," 42, 54–55, 59.

13. Burton, "South as 'Other,'" 12, 15, 26–27, 42, 48.

14. Matthew Mason, "A World Safe for Modernity: Antebellum Southern Proslavery Intellectuals Confront Great Britain," in Barnes, Schoen, and Towers, *Old South's Modern Worlds*, 47–65. See also Grant, *American Civil War and the British Press*, 25–35, 147–51, 159–71.

15. Edward B. Rugemer, *The Problem of Emancipation: The Caribbean Roots of the American Civil War* (Baton Rouge: Louisiana State University Press, 2008); Nichola Clayton, "Managing the Transition to a Free Labor Society: American Interpretations of the British West Indies during the Civil War and Reconstruction," *American Nineteenth Century History* 7, no. 1 (2006): 89–108.

16. Seymour Drescher, *The Mighty Experiment: Free Labor versus Slavery in British Emancipation* (New York: Oxford University Press, 2004), chap. 11.

17. Archibald Prentice, *A Tour in the United States, with Two Lectures on Emigration* (London: John Johnson, 1849), iv, 4–5, 23, 28, 31, 37–38, 66, 69, 74, 106–7, 112, 116–17, 162–63; Berger, *British Traveler*, 184; Drescher, *Mighty Experiment*, 224.

18. Carwardine, *Transatlantic Revivalism*, 32, 43, 66.

19. Dubrulle, "'If It Is Still Impossible to Advocate Slavery,'" 57–62, 64–65.

20. Ryan Hanley, "Slavery and the Birth of Working-Class Racism in Britain, 1814–1833," *Transactions of the Royal Historical Society* 6th ser., 26 (2016): 103–23.

21. *Power of the Pence*, 16, 30 Dec. 1848, 17 Feb., 14 Apr. 1849; Edward Royle, "The *Cause of the People*, the People's Charter Union, and 'Moral Force' Chartism in 1848," in *Papers for the People: A Study of the Chartist Press*, ed. Joan Allen and Owen Ashton (London: Merlin Press, 2005), 162; Royden Harrison, "British Labor and American Slavery," *Science and Society* 25, no. 4 (1961): 310.

22. Thomas L. Haskell, "Capitalism and the Origins of the Humanitarian Sensibility," *American Historical Review* 90, no. 2 (1985): 350.

23. Chase, *Chartism*, 306–7.

24. Catherine Gallagher, *The Body Economic: Life, Death, and Sensation in Political Economy and the Victorian Novel* (Princeton, N.J.: Princeton University Press, 2006).

25. David Roediger, *The Wages of Whiteness: Race and the Making of the American Working Class* (London: Verso, 1991), contends that in America the benefits of whiteness limited class conflict.

26. Ira Katznelson, "Working-Class Formation and the State: Nineteenth-Century England in American Perspective," in Englander, *Britain and America*, 171–95.

27. Douglas A. Lorimer, *Color, Class, and the Victorians: English Attitudes to the Negro in the Mid-Nineteenth Century* (Leicester: Leicester University Press, 1978), 31, 68, 177, 211.

28. Richard Huzzey, "British Liberties, American Emancipation, and the Democracy of Race," in Dzelzainis and Livesey, *American Experiment*, 121–34.

29. *Black Victorians / Black Victoriana*, ed. Gretchen H. Gerzina (New Brunswick, N.J.: Rutgers University Press, 2003).

30. Murphy, *Land without Castles*, 210–11.

31. Nevins, *America through British Eyes*, 14, 16, 22–23, 88–90, 95–96, 101, 208–9, 213, 216.

32. Drescher, *Mighty Experiment*, 151–53, 166, 173; Royle and Walvin, *English Radicals and Reformers*, 34–35, 186; Greene, "Introduction: Empire and Liberty," 13; Onuf, "Federalism, Democracy, and Liberty," 136, 154–58.

33. Gregory Barton, *Lord Palmerston and the Empire of Trade* (Upper Saddle River, N.J.: Prentice Hall, 2012), 87; Drescher, *Mighty Experiment*, 106–10, 114, 129, 161–63, 171–73, 188–89, 217–18, 221.

34. Haynes, *Unfinished Revolution*, chap. 8.

35. Temperley, *Britain and America since Independence*, 37; Drescher, *Mighty Experiment*, 174.

36. Tom Chaffin, *Fatal Glory: Narciso Lopéz and the First Clandestine U.S. War against Cuba* (Charlottesville: University Press of Virginia, 1996); Robert E. May, *The Southern Dream of a Caribbean Empire* (Baton Rouge: Louisiana State University Press, 1973), chap. 2.

37. Campbell, *Unlikely Allies*, 119, 123–24, 136; Temperley, *Britain and America since Independence*, 38–39; Phillips, *Cousins' Wars*, 347–48.

38. Drescher, *Mighty Experiment*, 115, 126–27, 138–40, 144–45, 151, 153, 162–63, 173–80, 182–88, 190–93, 195–203, 205, 207–14, 216–19, 222, 224, 236.

39. Llewellyn Woodward, *The Age of Reform, 1815–1870* (Oxford: Oxford University Press, 1985), 307; Forrest McDonald, *States' Rights and the Union: Imperium in Imperio, 1776–1876* (Lawrence: University Press of Kansas, 2000), 161–62.

40. William W. Freehling, *The Road to Disunion*, 2 vols. (New York: Oxford University Press, 1990), 2:11–12.

41. *London Times*, 3, 4, 15 Sept., 11 Nov. 1852.

42. R.J.M. Blackett, *Divided Hearts: Britain and the American Civil War* (Baton Rouge: Louisiana State University Press, 2001), 45–46.

43. Lorimer, *Color, Class, and the Victorians*, chaps. 6–7. See also Peter Mandler, "'Race' and 'Nation' in Mid-Victorian Thought," in *History, Religion, and Culture: British Intellectual History, 1750–1950*, ed. Stefan Collini, Richard Whatmore, and Brian Young (Cambridge: Cambridge University Press, 2000), 224–44.

44. Blackett, *Divided Hearts*, 81, 113–14; Howard Temperley, *British Antislavery, 1833–1870* (Columbia: University of South Carolina Press, 1972), 224–28; Temperley, *Britain and America since Independence*, 51; David Turley, *The Culture of English Antislavery, 1780–1860* (London: Routledge, 1991), 103; Campbell, *Unlikely Allies*, 62–64.

45. Sarah Meer, *Uncle Tom Mania: Slavery, Minstrelsy, and Transatlantic Culture in the 1850s* (Athens: University of Georgia Press, 2005), 163; *New Essays on Uncle Tom's Cabin*, ed. Eric J. Sundquist (Cambridge: Cambridge University Press, 1986); John D. Bennett, *The London Confederates: The Officials, Clergy, Businessmen, and Journalists Who Backed the American South during the Civil War* (Jefferson, N.C.: McFarland, 2008), 33.

46. Campbell, *Unlikely Allies*, 137–39; Temperley, *Britain and America since Independence*, 52–53; Robin Humphreys, "Anglo-American Rivalries in Central America," *Transactions of the Royal Historical Society*, 5th ser., 18 (1968): 174–208.

47. Richard Huzzey, "The Moral Geography of British Anti-Slavery Responsibilities," *Transactions of the Royal Historical Society*, 6th ser., 22 (2012): 111–39.

48. O'Connor, *American Sectionalism in the British Mind*, chap. 1.

49. Hope, *Popular View*, 10–11.

50. Hope, *Popular View*, 10–12.

51. Hope, *Two Years*, 15–16.

52. "The President's Message," *Saturday Review* 12, no. 321, 21 Dec. 1861, 624.

53. *London Observer*, 9 Feb. 1862.

54. *London Times*, 7 Feb. 1862.

55. Hope, *England, the North, and the South*, 3–5, 18–19, 23; *London Times*, 17 Jan. 1862.

56. Hope, *England, the North, and the South*, 27–28.

57. Hope, *England, the North, and the South*, 29–32.

58. Hope, *Results of the American Disruption*, 12–14.

59. Hope, *Results of the American Disruption*, 14–15.

60. Hope, *Results of the American Disruption*, 16.

61. Hope, *Results of the American Disruption*, 17–18.

62. *New York Herald*, 5, 7 Dec. 1861; *Weekly Raleigh Register*, 18, 25 Dec. 1861; *Daily Morning News* (Savannah, Ga.), 19 Dec. 1861; *Boston Daily Advertiser*, 31 Jan. 1862.

63. "Mr. Beresford Hope's Address," 4–5; *London Times*, 12 Sept. 1862; *John Bull*, 13 Sept. 1862. References to serfdom were quite topical, owing to reforms taking place in Russia at this time (affecting around 38 percent of the population).

64. "Mr. Beresford Hope's Address," 5; *London Times*, 12 Sept. 1862.

65. *London Observer*, 1, 2 Mar. 1863; *London Times*, 14, 26 Mar. 1863.

66. *John Bull*, 24 Jan. 1863.

67. *London Standard*, 22 Jan. 1863; *Bury and Norwich Post*, 27 Jan. 1863; *Derby Mercury*, 28 Jan. 1863.

68. Hope, *Social and Political Bearings*, 12–13.

69. Hope, *Social and Political Bearings*, 17–21.

70. K. D. Reynolds, *Aristocratic Women and Political Society in Victorian Britain* (Oxford: Clarendon Press, 1998), 122–27.

71. "Mrs. Stowe and the Women of England," *Saturday Review* 15, no. 376, 10 Jan. 1863, 36–38.

72. Dubrulle, "'If It Is Still Impossible to Advocate Slavery,'" 66–67. Efforts to discredit

antislavery material, including *Uncle Tom's Cabin*, would continue into the twentieth century. Tal, *American Civil War in British Culture*, 96–97.

73. Grant, *American Civil War and the British Press*, 16–17, 29, 31, 41, 150.

74. Hope, *Social and Political Bearings*, 14–17.

75. Hope, *Social and Political Bearings*, 22–27.

76. Hope, *Social and Political Bearings*, 28–30.

77. Hope, *Social and Political Bearings*, 30–31.

78. Hope, *Popular View*, 38.

79. *Liberator*, 26 Dec. 1862, 20 Feb. 1863; *New York Independent*, 26 Feb. 1863. There was also coverage in *New York Herald*, 9 Feb. 1863; *North American and United States Gazette*, 17 Feb. 1863 (which referred somewhat derisively to "Mr. Beresford Hope, the millionaire"); and in such southern papers as *Semi-Weekly Raleigh Register*, 14 Feb. 1863; and *Weekly Raleigh Register*, 18 Feb. 1863.

80. *Anti-Slavery Monthly Reporter*, 1 Sept. 1863.

81. *Anti-Slavery Monthly Reporter*, 1 Sept. 1863.

82. *London Times*, 17 Oct. 1863; *Manchester Guardian*, 17 Oct. 1863; *John Bull*, 24 Oct. 1863.

83. *Liverpool Mercury*, 17 Oct. 1863; *Birmingham Daily Post*, 19 Oct. 1863; *Caledonian Mercury*, 20 Oct. 1863; *Belfast Newsletter*, 22 Oct. 1863.

84. *Daily Richmond Examiner*, 12 Nov. 1863; *Boston Daily Advertiser*, 28, 31 Oct. 1863; *Daily National Intelligencer* (Washington, D.C.), 29 Oct. 1863; *Living Age*, 28 Nov. 1863.

85. Dubrulle, *Ambivalent Nation*, 64, 100–101, 108–9, 143, 210.

86. Sebrell, *Persuading John Bull*, 4, 69, 98, 126, 138, 141, 193, 203; Robert E. Bonner, "Slavery, Confederate Diplomacy, and the Racialist Mission of Henry Hotze," *Civil War History* 51, no. 3 (2005): 288–316; Dubrulle, "'If It Is Still Impossible to Advocate Slavery,'" 67–69, 75–77.

87. *John Bull*, 16 Jan. 1864.

88. *Anti-Slavery Monthly Reporter*, 2 Jan. 1865.

89. *Liberator*, 25 Mar. 1864.

90. "President Lincoln," *Saturday Review* 19, no. 496, 29 Apr. 1865, 492.

5. A RELIGIOUS PERSPECTIVE

1. *Religion and the American Civil War*, ed. Randall M. Miller, Harry S. Stout, and Charles Reagan Wilson (New York: Oxford University Press, 1998); Mark A. Noll, *The Civil War as a Theological Crisis* (Chapel Hill: University of North Carolina Press, 2006); Harry S. Stout, *Upon the Altar of the Nation: A Moral History of the American Civil War* (New York: Viking, 2006); George C. Rable, *God's Almost Chosen Peoples: A Religious History of the American Civil War* (Chapel Hill: University of North Carolina Press, 2010).

2. Wilbur D. Jones, "The British Conservatives and the American Civil War," *American Historical Review* 58, no. 3 (1953): 527–43; Donald Bellows, "A Study of British Conservative Reaction to the American Civil War," *Journal of Southern History* 51, no. 4 (1985): 505–26.

3. After the Glorious Revolution, nonjurors, mostly High Churchmen, were those who could not in conscience swear allegiance to the new regime.

4. Colin Podmore, "A Tale of Two Churches: The Ecclesiologies of the Episcopal Church

and the Church of England Compared," *International Journal for the Study of the Christian Church* 8, no. 2 (2008): 124–54; Pierre W. Whalon, "The Tale Needs Re-Telling: A Reply to Colin Podmore's 'A Tale of Two Churches,'" *Theology* 114, no. 1 (2011): 3–12; Noll, *Civil War as Theological Crisis*, 22, 26; Lockert B. Mason, "Separation and Reunion of the Episcopal Church, 1860–1865: The Role of Bishop Thomas Atkinson," *Anglican and Episcopal History* 59, no. 3 (1990): 356; R. W. Albright, *A History of the Protestant Episcopal Church* (New York: Macmillan, 1964), 227, 229–34, 236–37, 245; David Hein and Gardiner H. Shattuck Jr., *The Episcopalians* (Westport, Conn.: Praeger, 2004), 63–76; Robert Prichard, *A History of the Episcopal Church* (Harrisburg, Pa.: Morehouse Publishing, 1999), 137–45; Diana H. Butler, *Standing against the Whirlwind: Evangelical Episcopalians in Nineteenth-Century America* (New York: Oxford University Press, 1996), ix–x, 93–127, 136–62; Robert Bruce Mullin, "Trends in the Study of the History of the Episcopal Church," *Anglican and Episcopal History* 72, no. 2 (2003): 155–60; Edward L. Bond and Joan R. Gundersen, "The Episcopal Church in Virginia, 1607–2007," *Virginia Magazine of History and Biography* 115, no. 2 (2007): 243–50, 252–57, 260–65; William Stevens Perry, *The History of the American Episcopal Church*, 2 vols. (Boston: J. R. Osgood, 1885), 2:269–72, 280, 292, 294–99.

5. Blomfield to Hope, 18 July 1855, Lambeth Palace Library, Blomfield Papers, FP Blomfield 57, ff. 272–73; Hope to Gladstone, 19 July 1857, British Library, Gladstone Papers, Add MS 44213, ff. 310–11; *Parliamentary Debates*, 3rd ser., 20 July 1857, vol. 147, cols. 21–24, 11 Feb. 1858, vol. 148, cols. 1216–17; *Manchester Guardian*, 12 Feb. 1858; *John Bull*, 8 June 1861.

6. Robert Bearden Jr., "The Episcopal Church in the Confederate States," *Arkansas Historical Quarterly* 4, no. 4 (1945): 269–72; Joseph Blount Cheshire, *The Church in the Confederate States* (New York: Longmans, 1912), 8, 14–15, 19–20, 35–37, 39–46, 49–53, 55–62; Mason, "Separation and Reunion," 345–47, 356; Perry, *American Episcopal Church*, 2:328–34; Bond and Gundersen, "Church in Virginia," 265–66; Albright, *Protestant Episcopal Church*, 252–54; Hein and Shattuck, *Episcopalians*, 76–79; Rable, *God's Almost Chosen Peoples*, 40, 48, 59–60.

7. Hein and Shattuck, *Episcopalians*, 78–79; Sydney E. Ahlstrom, *A Religious History of the American People* (New Haven: Yale University Press, 2004), 674–81; Butler, *Standing against the Whirlwind*, 163–67; Rable, *God's Almost Chosen Peoples*, 59–60, 325, 336.

8. Bearden, "Episcopal Church in the Confederate States," 273–74.

9. See especially Noll, *Civil War as Theological Crisis;* and Stout, *Upon the Altar of the Nation.* See also Charles Reagan Wilson, "Religion and the American Civil War in Comparative Perspective," in Miller, Stout, and Wilson, *Religion and the American Civil War*, 395–96, 402–3. Rable, *God's Almost Chosen Peoples*, 390, suggests that acceptance of God's will and the power of providential narratives assisted the later transition to peace. Both sides insisted that God was with them, but the horrors of war eroded the triumphalism to which this belief had given rise.

10. Hope, *Two Years*, 14–16.

11. Hope, *Two Years*, 17–18.

12. Hope, *Two Years*, 18–24.

13. Hope, *Social and Political Bearings*, 17–20.

14. Eugene D. Genovese, *A Consuming Fire: The Fall of the Confederacy in the Mind of the White Christian South* (Athens: University of Georgia Press, 1998), xiv; Mitchell Snay, *Gospel of Disunion: Religion and Separatism in the Antebellum South* (New York: Cambridge University Press, 1993), chaps. 2–3.

15. McCurry, *Masters of Small Worlds*, 6.

16. The pastoral is also cited in Cheshire, *Church in the Confederate States,* 55–68.

17. Hope, *American Church,* 30.

18. Hope, *American Church,* 26.

19. Hope, *American Church,* 4–5.

20. McPherson, "Antebellum Southern Exceptionalism," 424; McCardell, *Idea of a Southern Nation,* chap. 5.

21. See, for example, Quigley, *Shifting Grounds,* 171.

22. Bonner, "Roundheaded Cavaliers," 51–55.

23. Hein and Shattuck, *Episcopalians,* 76–77, 79. On the broader context, see Ahlstrom, *Religious History,* 650–54, 657–68, 671–73; Wilson, "Religion and the American Civil War," 394–95; James H. Moorhead, "The Churches, Slavery, the Civil War, and Reconstruction: A Review Essay," *Journal of Presbyterian History* 78, no. 4 (2000): 285–300.

24. Gardiner H. Shattuck Jr., *Episcopalians and Race: Civil War to Civil Rights* (Lexington: University Press of Kentucky, 2000), 2, 4. See also Cheshire, *Church in the Confederate States,* 106–16, 120, 131–34. To Cheshire, moral responsibility (toward the slaves) and economic profitability (of slavery) went hand in hand.

25. Noll, *Civil War as Theological Crisis,* 95–97, 101–2, 107–8, 111–23. Rable, *God's Almost Chosen Peoples,* 14, points out that some abolitionists stopped using religious appeals altogether because they could not be sure of winning Bible-based arguments.

26. Hope, *American Church,* 3–4.

27. Hope, *American Church,* 4–6.

28. Hope, *American Church,* 6–9.

29. Hope, *American Church,* 10–11.

30. Hope, *American Church,* 11–13. The "religiosity of Confederatism" was personified by the army chaplains, among others. Episcopalian clergymen accounted for perhaps 30 percent of the Confederate army chaplaincy. Pamela Robinson-Durso, "Chaplains in the Confederate Army," *Journal of Church and State* 33, no. 4 (1991): 747–63; Charles F. Pitts, *Chaplains in Gray: The Confederate Chaplains' Story* (Nashville, Tenn.: Broadman Press, 1957); *Faith in the Fight: Civil War Chaplains,* ed. John W. Brinsfield, William C. Davis, Benedict Maryniak, and James I. Robertson Jr. (Mechanicsburg, Pa.: Stackpole Books, 2003); Steven E. Woodworth, *While God Is Marching On: The Religious World of Civil War Soldiers* (Lawrence: University Press of Kansas, 2001).

31. Cheshire, *Church in the Confederate States,* 70–77.

32. Hope, *American Church,* 13–21.

33. Hope, *American Church,* 21–22. Hope's assessment of the convention was heavily influenced by what he read in the *Church Journal.* The formal record is in *Journal of the Proceedings of the Bishops, Clergy, and Laity of the Protestant Episcopal Church in the United States of America, Assembled in a General Convention, Held in St. John's Chapel in the City of New York, from October 1st to October 17th, Inclusive, in the Year of Our Lord 1862* (Boston: E. P. Dutton, 1863).

34. Hope, *American Church,* 22–25.

35. Hope, *American Church,* 25–26.

36. Hope, *American Church,* 26–27.

37. "Stonewall Jackson," *Saturday Review* 15, no. 396, 30 May 1863, 689–90.

38. *Liverpool Mercury,* 17 Oct. 1863; *Birmingham Daily Post,* 19 Oct. 1863; *Caledonian Mercury,* 20 Oct. 1863; *Belfast Newsletter,* 22 Oct. 1863.

39. *Liverpool Mercury*, 19, 20 Oct. 1864; *Manchester Courier*, 20 Oct. 1864.

40. Several of the pamphlets went into third and fourth editions within a few months of their release, judging by newspaper advertisements. A decline in Hope's appearances in meeting rooms and lecture halls is indicated by the small number of press reports about his speaking in 1864 compared to 1861–63.

41. The British and Foreign Anti-Slavery Society (formed in 1839 to campaign for world-wide abolition) published this material in order to condemn it: *Anti-Slavery Monthly Reporter*, 1 Sept. 1863.

42. The identities of these individuals were established by cross-referencing material issued by the Manchester Southern Club with entries in *Crockford's Clerical Directory for 1865* (London: Horace Cox, 1865) and local directories of 1863 and 1867. The eleven Anglican clergymen included a writer of pro-Confederate pamphlets and a former missionary in America.

43. See "The English Clergy and the War," *Living Age*, 31 Oct. 1863.

44. *Living Age*, 31 Oct. 1863.

45. I am grateful to Dr. Sirota (North Carolina State University) for remarks he made about papers I presented in Durham, N.C., in September 2017, and Denver, Colo., in November 2017. Dr. Sirota helpfully expanded on these comments in subsequent exchanges.

46. Jon Sensbach, "Early Southern Religions in a Global Age," in Ward, Bone, and Link, *American South and the Atlantic World*, 45–60.

47. Perhaps Sensbach exaggerates the loss of variety. Some southerners were pessimistic about modernity and retreated into tradition, but others embraced "progress," including religious heterodoxy. See O'Brien, *Intellectual Life and the American South*, chap. 6.

48. These themes are discussed in Erickson's *Invisible Immigrants*; and Van Vugt's *Britain to America*.

49. MacRaild, "Ethnic Conflict and English Associational Culture," 37–63.

50. Ural, "'Ye Sons of Green Erin Assemble,'" 99–132.

51. See, for example, "Dr. Newman on Universities," *Saturday Review* 2, no. 59, 13 Dec. 1856, 733–34.

52. Law and Law, *Beresford Hopes*, 236.

53. "The American Church," *British Critic and Quarterly Theological Review*, no. 52 (Oct. 1839): 281–343, republished as "The Anglo-American Church" in John Henry Newman, *Essays Critical and Historical*, 2 vols. (London: Basil Montagu Pickering, 1871), 1:309–79.

54. Newman, "American Church," 281–86.

55. Newman, "American Church," 288–89, 291, 297–99, 302, 305, 318–19, 321, 323–24, 326–29, 332, 335–37, 339–40, 343.

56. Joseph Hardwick, "The Church of England and English Clergymen in the United States, 1783–1861," in Gleeson, *English Ethnicity and Culture in North America*, 112–38.

57. Gleeson, "England and the Antebellum South," 139–54.

58. Joseph Hardwick, "An English Institution? The Colonial Church of England in the First Half of the Nineteenth Century," in Bueltmann, Gleeson, and MacRaild, *Locating the English Diaspora*, 67–83.

59. Joseph Hardwick, *An Anglican British World: The Church of England and the Expansion of the Settler Empire, 1790–1860* (Manchester: Manchester University Press, 2014), chaps. 1–2.

60. The Dean of Windsor published a record of the early meetings: *The Lambeth Conferences*

of 1867, 1878, and 1888; With the Official Reports and Resolutions, Together with the Sermons Preached at the Conferences, ed. Randall T. Davidson (London: SPCK, 1889).

61. Cheshire, *Church in the Confederate States,* 202–10, 214–17, 239–56; Mason, "Separation and Reunion," 347–65; Bearden, "Episcopal Church in the Confederate States," 273–75; Prichard, *Episcopal Church,* 145–53, 155, 157, 162–63; Hein and Shattuck, *Episcopalians,* 79–80, 85–94, 96–105; Albright, *Protestant Episcopal Church,* 254–68, 270–73, 279–82; Butler, *Standing against the Whirlwind,* 178–214; Shattuck, *Episcopalians and Race,* 7–18; Mullin, "Trends," 162; Bond and Gundersen, "Church in Virginia," 277–88; Ian T. Douglas, "Anglican Mission in Changing Times: A Brief Institutional History of the Episcopal Church," in *Church, Identity, and Change: Theology and Denominational Structures in Unsettled Times,* ed. David A. Roozen and James R. Nieman (Grand Rapids, Mich.: Eerdmans, 2005), 191; Perry, *American Episcopal Church,* 2:339–42, 344, 346–54; Ahlstrom, *Religious History,* 682–97.

62. *John Bull,* 13 Oct. 1866.

63. *John Bull,* 26 Sept. 1865, 13 Oct. 1866, 23 Nov. 1867, 1 Feb. 1868, 18 June 1870, 28 Oct. 1871, 7 Aug., 11, 18, 25 Sept., 2, 9 Oct. 1875, 30 May, 6 June 1885; *Monthly Record of Church Missions,* no. 47 (Mar. 1868), 81–84, no. 110 (June 1873), 187; *Manchester Guardian,* 22 Jan. 1868; *Parliamentary Debates,* 3rd ser., 14, 21 Apr. 1869, vol. 195, cols. 784–86, 1306–11, 27 Apr. 1870, vol. 200, cols. 1927–37, 14 June 1870, vol. 202, cols. 100–24; *London Times,* 15 June 1870, 7 June 1880, 9 Oct. 1885.

64. *John Bull,* 17 June 1876; *Georgia Weekly Telegraph* (Macon), 11 Jan. 1876; *New York Observer and Chronicle,* 6 July 1876.

65. *John Bull,* 17 June 1876, 26 Apr. 1879; *London Times,* 24 Nov. 1885; *The University of the South: Catalogue and Announcements* (Sewanee, Tenn.: University of the South, 1902), 145.

66. *John Bull,* 11, 18 July 1868.

67. DeKoven would lead the ritualists at the General Conventions of 1871 and 1874, and he was denied a bishopric no less than four times during the 1870s, when opponents were able to veto his appointment. Perry, *American Episcopal Church,* 2:354, 357, 359, 361; Hein and Shattuck, *Episcopalians,* 93; Prichard, *Episcopal Church,* 153, 155; Albright, *Protestant Episcopal Church,* 282–86.

68. *London Times,* 10 Sept. 1867.

69. *London Times,* 17 Nov. 1882.

70. *Monthly Packet of Evening Readings for Younger Members of the English Church,* no. 83 (Nov. 1872): 411; *John Bull,* 3 Aug. 1878.

71. *Parliamentary Debates,* 3rd ser., 26 June 1872, vol. 212, cols. 241–50. See also Butler, *Standing against the Whirlwind,* 160–62, 208–9.

72. *Daily Cleveland Herald,* 22 Feb. 1868; *Hawaiian Gazette* (Honolulu), 18 Mar. 1868; *New York Independent,* 26 Mar. 1868; *New York Observer and Chronicle,* 18 July 1872.

73. *Parliamentary Debates,* 3rd ser., 29 Mar. 1871, vol. 205, col. 834.

74. Butler, *Standing against the Whirlwind,* 190–214; Hein and Shattuck, *Episcopalians,* 91–94; Albright, *Protestant Episcopal Church,* 273, 279, 282–94; Prichard, *Episcopal Church,* 147–53; Bond and Gundersen, "Church in Virginia," 278–79; Perry, *American Episcopal Church,* 2:351–64. Allen C. Guelzo, *For the Union of Evangelical Christendom: The Irony of Reformed Episcopalians* (University Park: Pennsylvania State University Press, 1994), treats the Reformed Episcopal Church as a reaction against Anglo-Catholicism, elitism, and anti-modernism.

75. Perry, *American Episcopal Church,* 2:272, 299, 364; Butler, *Standing against the Whirlwind,* 126–27, 137–45, 160–62, 207–14.

76. See Hope's *Hints towards Peace in Ceremonial Matters* (London: Rivingtons, 1874); and *Worship in the Church of England* (London: John Murray, 1874).

77. *Boston Daily Advertiser*, 26 June 1874; *Daily Cleveland Herald*, 30 Oct. 1874.

78. *John Bull*, 27 July 1878.

79. *John Bull*, 22 Nov. 1884.

80. The dedication ceremony was described in *New York Times*, 21 Nov. 1888; *Boston Daily Advertiser*, 21 Nov. 1888; *Chicago Daily Inter Ocean*, 21 Nov. 1888; *New York Christian Union*, 29 Nov. 1888. See also Peter W. Williams, *Religion, Art, and Money: Episcopalians and American Culture from the Civil War to the Great Depression* (Chapel Hill: University of North Carolina Press, 2016), 88–91.

6. AMERICAN WAR AND BRITISH CONSEQUENCES

1. Hope, *Popular View*, 19–20, 23–27; and Hope, *Two Years*, 16.

2. Hope, *Popular View*, 27–35.

3. Hope, *Social and Political Bearings*, 9–11.

4. Hope, *American Church*, 22. Lincoln combined a serious personal piety with elements of skepticism. On whether he was "Christian," there is no scholarly consensus.

5. Hope, *Popular View*, 35–39.

6. Russell's writing on the battle was not meant to humiliate the North, and he was shocked by the hostile reaction. See Crawford, *Russell's Civil War*.

7. Hope, *Popular View*, 39; and Hope, *England, the North, and the South*, 1–2.

8. Robert Bonner, "Free Soil, Free Labor, Free Seas? Civil War Statecraft and the Liberal Quest for Oceanic Order," in Nagler, Doyle, and Gräser, *Transnational Significance of the American Civil War*, 15–31.

9. This affected, for example, the selection of diplomatic material for publication.

10. *John Bull*, 21 Dec. 1861, 18 Jan. 1862; *London Observer*, 8, 9 Dec. 1861.

11. *London Times*, 17 Jan. 1862.

12. "The American Civil War," *Saturday Review* 12, no. 297, 6 July 1861, 3–4.

13. "The President's Message," *Saturday Review* 12, no. 321, 21 Dec. 1861, 624–25. Despite the outrage in Britain over the *Trent* incident, attention was diverted to other events, especially the unexpected death of Queen Victoria's consort, Prince Albert, on 14 Dec. 1861. When Mason and Slidell finally reached Southampton, on 2 Jan. 1862, there was no cheering crowd or reception committee, no public meeting, and no interview with journalists.

14. "America," *Saturday Review* 14, no. 353, 2 Aug. 1862, 124–25.

15. Jay Sexton, "International Finance in the Civil War Era," in Nagler, Doyle, and Gräser, *Transnational Significance of the American Civil War*, 91–106.

16. Hope, *Results of the American Disruption*, 3.

17. Hope, *Results of the American Disruption*, 28–31.

18. Hope, *Social and Political Bearings*, 5, 12–13; *London Times*, 19 Jan. 1863.

19. Hope, *Popular View*, 26–27.

20. Hope, *Popular View*, 28.

21. Hope, *Two Years*, 16.

22. Hope, *Social and Political Bearings*, 39–41.

23. Hope, *Popular View*, 38–39.

24. Hope, *Popular View*, 39; and Hope, *England, the North, and the South*, 1–4.

25. *London Times*, 17 Jan. 1862.

26. Hope, *England, the North, and the South*, 32–36.

27. Hope, *England, the North, and the South*, 36–38; and Hope, *Results of the American Disruption*, 3.

28. Hope, *Results of the American Disruption*, 31–34.

29. Hope, *Results of the American Disruption*, 34–39.

30. Batchelor, *Beresfords*, 114–15; Frank L. Owsley, *King Cotton Diplomacy: Foreign Relations of the Confederate States of America* (Chicago: University of Chicago Press, 1959), 62, 156, 172–74, 176, 193, 219, 221, 545.

31. *London Times*, 12 June 1862.

32. *London Times*, 13 June 1862. See also Grant, *American Civil War and the British Press*, 59–66.

33. *London Times*, 13 June 1862. In fact, as Matthew Mason shows in *Apostle of Union: A Political Biography of Edward Everett* (Chapel Hill: University of North Carolina Press, 2016), 297–301, Everett became a loyal supporter of the Lincoln administration and was angered by Britain's stance during the war.

34. *London Times*, 13 June 1862.

35. Hope had previously written for and put money into the *Morning Chronicle*, and finding that he enjoyed having a regular outlet for his views, he established the *Saturday Review* in 1855. The cofounder was John Douglas Cook, former editor of the *Morning Chronicle*, who brought with him some of its writers. Hope paid the bills but did not insist that the *Saturday Review* should be an exclusively High Church and Conservative organ (though he complained when Cook accepted pieces to which he had objections). Merle M. Bevington, *The Saturday Review, 1855–1868: Representative Educated Opinion in Victorian England* (New York: Columbia University Press, 1941), 7–13, 15–16, 22, 25–28, 31, 33–35, 55, 76–77, 233, 334, 342, 344–46, 373; Hope to E. A. Freeman, 1 Aug. 1855, Freeman Papers, GB 133, EAF/1/1/53; Law and Law, *Beresford Hopes*, 147–48, 214–18, 232–33; Batchelor, *Beresfords*, 42.

36. *New York Independent*, 5 June, 3 July 1862. Other northern papers that commented on Hope's letter to the *London Times* about mediation included the *Boston Daily Advertiser*, 25 June 1862, and the *Daily Whig and Courier* (Bangor, Maine), 25 June 1862. Southern titles also noticed the letter: *Daily Richmond Examiner*, 30 June 1862; *New Orleans Daily Picayune*, 5 July 1862; *Charleston Courier*, 8 July 1862.

37. Hope, *Social and Political Bearings*, 40–42.

38. Hope, *Social and Political Bearings*, 2–6. See also reports in *London Standard*, 22 Jan. 1863; *Bury and Norwich Post*, 27 Jan. 1863; *Derby Mercury*, 28 Jan. 1863.

39. In *Ambivalent Nation*, 128–29, 147, Dubrulle argues that there was a delay in turning against the North because the U.S. government was regarded as legitimate, secession as wrong, and slavery in the South as evil. Yet Hope did not delay. Later, Dubrulle suggests, war weariness in Britain led most people to wish for an end to the American conflict, no matter which side won. Again, Hope represents those who did not adopt this position.

40. "Mr. Beresford Hope's Address," 4–5, 8–9; *London Times*, 12 Sept. 1862; *John Bull*, 13 Sept. 1862; and for Lindsay's motion, see *Parliamentary Debates*, 3rd ser., 18 July 1862, vol. 168, cols. 511–78.

41. *London Times*, 28 Aug. 1862.

42. *London Times*, 24 Apr., 29 July, 20 Dec. 1862.

43. Hope, *Social and Political Bearings*, 6–9; and *American Church*, 24; "Mr. Beresford Hope's Address," 8.

44. Hope, *American Church*, 3.

45. *John Bull*, 24 Jan. 1863.

46. "The Two General Orders," *Saturday Review* 15, no. 396, 30 May 1863, 684–85.

47. *Anti-Slavery Monthly Reporter*, 1 Sept. 1863; *London Index*, 17 Sept., 15, 22 Oct. 1863. Ellison's *Support for Secession* highlights the strength of pro-Confederate opinion in Lancashire, particularly among textile workers.

48. *Anti-Slavery Monthly Reporter*, 1 Sept. 1863.

49. *Anti-Slavery Monthly Reporter*, 1 Sept. 1863.

50. *London Index*, 17 Sept., 15, 22 Oct. 1863; *Public Opinion*, 10 Oct. 1863.

51. *London Times*, 17 Oct. 1863; *Manchester Guardian*, 17 Oct. 1863; *John Bull*, 24 Oct. 1863; *Parliamentary Debates*, 3rd ser., 9 Feb. 1858, vol. 148, cols. 979–1078.

52. *London Times*, 17 Oct. 1863; *Manchester Guardian*, 17 Oct. 1863; *John Bull*, 24 Oct. 1863.

53. *Liverpool Mercury*, 17 Oct. 1863; *Birmingham Daily Post*, 19 Oct. 1863; *Caledonian Mercury*, 20 Oct. 1863; *Belfast Newsletter*, 22 Oct. 1863.

54. *London Observer*, 9 Nov. 1863. Wilkes also lectured outside London. See Blackett, *Divided Hearts*, 101, 169–70, 195.

55. Warren F. Spencer, *The Confederate Navy in Europe* (Tuscaloosa: University of Alabama Press, 1997), 80–83, 104–19; Renata Eley Long, *In the Shadow of the "Alabama": The British Foreign Office and the American Civil War* (Annapolis, Md.: Naval Institute Press, 2015), chap. 11; Wilbur D. Jones, *The Confederate Rams at Birkenhead: A Chapter in Anglo-American Relations* (Tuscaloosa, Ala.: Confederate Publishing Co., 1961); David F. Krein, "Russell's Decision to Detain the Laird Rams," *Civil War History* 22, no. 2 (1976): 158–63.

56. Noonan, "'New Expression of That *Entente Cordiale*,'" 116–45; Long, *In the Shadow of the "Alabama*," 128–29; Niels Eichhorn, "The Rhine River: The Impact of the German States on Transatlantic Diplomacy," in Gleeson and Lewis, *Civil War as Global Conflict*, 146–71.

57. See committee list in the *London Index*, 14 Jan. 1864; *John Bull*, 16 Jan. 1864; *Saturday Review*, 16 Jan. 1864.

58. *John Bull*, 16 Jan. 1864.

59. Palmerston only received a deputation of pro-southerners as a political ploy: he needed the votes of the MPs among them to maintain other parts of his foreign policy. Sebrell, *Persuading John Bull*, 181–84; Long, *In the Shadow of the "Alabama*," 139–40.

60. *Anti-Slavery Monthly Reporter*, 2 Jan. 1865.

61. *New York Independent*, 31 Dec. 1863; *San Francisco Daily Evening Bulletin*, 4 Feb., 4 Mar. 1864; *Liberator*, 4 Dec. 1863.

62. *Bell's Life in London*, 22 Oct. 1864.

63. *Manchester Guardian*, 23 July 1864.

64. *Manchester Guardian*, 20 Aug., 24 Sept., 1, 15 Oct. 1864.

65. *Liverpool Mercury*, 19, 20 Oct. 1864; *Manchester Courier*, 20 Oct. 1864.

66. *Liverpool Mercury*, 22 Oct. 1864.

67. *London Standard*, 18, 19 Oct. 1864; *Sheffield Independent*, 18, 20, 25 Oct. 1864; *Dundee Courier*,

20 Oct. 1864; *Manchester Courier*, 19, 20, 21 Oct. 1864; *Westmorland Gazette*, 22 Oct. 1864; *Newcastle Guardian*, 22 Oct. 1864; *Huddersfield Chronicle*, 22 Oct. 1864; *Caledonian Mercury*, 25 Oct. 1864; *Blackburn Standard*, 26 Oct. 1864; *Newcastle Journal*, 26 Oct. 1864; *Preston Chronicle*, 27 Oct. 1864; *Jackson's Oxford Journal*, 29 Oct. 1864; *Bucks Herald*, 29 Oct. 1864.

68. The belligerent rights of the Confederacy were partially withdrawn on 11 May 1865 and terminated by the British government on 2 June.

69. "America," *Saturday Review* 19, no. 495, 22 Apr. 1865, 457–58.

70. "President Lincoln," *Saturday Review* 19, no. 496, 29 Apr. 1865, 491–92.

71. Lawrence Goldman, "'A Total Misconception': Lincoln, the Civil War, and the British, 1860–1865," in *The Global Lincoln*, ed. Richard Carwardine and Jay Sexton (New York: Oxford University Press, 2011), 107–22; Tal, *American Civil War in British Culture*, 67–95; Grant, *American Civil War and the British Press*, 175–86.

72. Louis P. Masur, *Lincoln's Last Speech: Wartime Reconstruction and the Crisis of Reunion* (New York: Oxford University Press, 2015), 7–11, 34–35, 39, 51–53, 57–58, 60–61, 66–68, 74, 80, 82–85, 93, 97, 101, 105–7, 110, 114, 124, 140–43, 145–47, 151, 155, 157, 162–65, 174, 185–87.

73. Tal, *American Civil War in British Culture*, 97–102.

74. *John Bull*, 1 July 1865.

75. Sebrell, *Persuading John Bull*, 9, 57, 130–31, 141, 198–200.

76. *New York Times*, 2 Oct. 1865; *North American and United States Gazette*, 2 Oct. 1865.

77. *Manchester Guardian*, 2 Oct. 1865.

78. *Bell's Life in London*, 7 Oct. 1865.

79. *London Times*, 4 Oct. 1865.

80. *Bell's Life in London*, 7 Oct. 1865.

81. *London Observer*, 8 Oct. 1865.

82. *London Times*, 3 Nov. 1865 (the correspondent's message was dated 21 Oct.); *Manchester Guardian*, 4 Nov. 1865. Different lists were in circulation, one of them transmitted to Seward by Benjamin Moran, secretary at the U.S. Legation in London.

83. *New York Albion*, 23 Sept. 1865; *Chicago Tribune*, 23 Oct. 1865.

84. *New York Times*, 19 Oct. 1865.

85. See, for example, *New York Times*, 20 Oct. 1865.

86. *Boston Daily Advertiser*, 19, 20, 21 Sept. 1865; *North American and United States Gazette*, 22 Sept. 1865.

87. *Boston Daily Advertiser*, 26 Sept. 1865.

88. *Chicago Tribune*, 15 Feb. 1866.

89. *North American and United States Gazette*, 2 Oct. 1865; *Frank Leslie's Illustrated Newspaper*, 28 Oct. 1865; *Boston Daily Advertiser*, 17 Nov. 1865; *San Francisco Daily Evening Bulletin*, 3 Jan. 1866; *Hawaiian Gazette*, 20 Jan. 1866.

90. *Los Angeles Daily Times*, 9 Aug. 1883.

91. Michael Clark, "Alexander Collie: The Ups and Downs of Trading with the Confederacy," *Northern Mariner* 19, no. 2 (2009): 125–48. See also Stephen R. Wise, *Lifeline of the Confederacy: Blockade-Running during the Civil War* (Columbia: University of South Carolina Press, 1989); and Thomas Boaz, *Guns for Cotton: England Arms the Confederacy* (Shippensburg, Pa.: Burd Street Press, 1996).

92. Richard C. Todd, *Confederate Finance* (Athens: University of Georgia Press, 2009), chap.

2; Jay Sexton, *Debtor Diplomacy: Finance and American Foreign Relations in the Civil War Era, 1837–1873* (Oxford: Clarendon Press, 2005), 162–74, 182–83, 187–88, 227–28; Owsley, *King Cotton Diplomacy,* chap. 11; Richard I. Lester, *Confederate Finance and Purchasing in Great Britain* (Charlottesville: University Press of Virginia, 1975), 3–57; Richard Burdekin and F. K. Langdana, "War Finance in the Southern Confederacy," *Explorations in Economic History* 30, no. 1 (1993): 352–376; Judith F. Gentry, "A Confederate Success in Europe: The Erlanger Loan," *Journal of Southern History* 36, no. 2 (1970): 157–88; Marc Weidenmier, "The Market for Confederate Cotton Bonds," *Explorations in Economic History* 37, no. 1 (2001): 76–97; William O. Brown Jr. and Richard Burdekin, "Turning Points in the American Civil War: A British Perspective," *Journal of Economic History* 60, no. 1 (2000): 216–31. Douglas Ball, *Financial Failure and Confederate Defeat* (Urbana: University of Illinois Press, 1991), argues that the South lost the war because it pursued the wrong financial policies but goes on to make excessive claims about how different measures would have changed the course of the war.

93. *Parliamentary Debates,* 3rd ser., 24 July 1868, vol. 193, cols. 1715–32.

94. *Parliamentary Debates,* 3rd ser., 20 Feb. 1871, vol. 204, cols. 554–55.

95. *Parliamentary Debates,* 3rd ser., 26 June 1871, vol. 207, cols. 593–604, and 14 July 1871, vol. 207, col. 1762.

96. *Parliamentary Debates,* 3rd ser., 23 Mar. 1882, vol. 267, cols. 1704–11.

97. *Parliamentary Debates,* 3rd ser., 25 Feb. 1884, vol. 284, cols. 1920–21.

98. *New York Times,* 1 Apr., 2 Aug. 1867; *Milwaukee Daily Sentinel,* 5 Apr. 1867; *American Law Review* 2, no. 1 (Oct. 1867): 170; *Chicago Tribune,* 9 May 1869; *San Francisco Daily Evening Bulletin,* 22 May 1869, *Boston Daily Advertiser,* 2, 17 Apr. 1867, 22 June 1870, 14 Aug. 1877; *Lowell Daily Citizen and News,* 30 Oct. 1873; *Washington Post,* 29 July 1883.

99. Kinser, *American Civil War in the Shaping of British Democracy,* 163–68, 171–72. On postwar connections between British and U.S. politics, see also Saunders, *Democracy and the Vote,* 10–11, 61, 126, 131–32, 142–59; Parry, *Politics of Patriotism,* 22, 24, 272, 281, 340–42, 388, 394–95; Gerlach, *British Liberalism and the United States,* 5–6, 8–10, 12, 14–17, 19–20, 23–24, 27–28, 40, 45–46, 49–55, 94–101; Temperley, *Britain and America since Independence,* 69–71, 74–75, 82, 84–86; Campbell, *Unlikely Allies,* 200–209, 216–22; Pelling, *America and the British Left,* 8–10, 12–23, 29, 36, 39, 43–47, 50–52, 54–55, 57, 59–60, 62–64; Phillips, *Cousins' Wars,* 461–64, 494–95, 502–3, 505–9; Lillibridge, *Beacon of Freedom,* 105–10; Nevins, *America through British Eyes,* 312–16, 321–22; Robertson, *Language of Democracy,* chaps. 8–10; Kelley, *Transatlantic Persuasion,* 4, 6–8, 17, 19, 26–29, 53–54; Rodgers, *Atlantic Crossings,* 21, 26–31, 52–55, 58–64, 70, 72, 74, 77–80.

100. *Daily National Intelligencer,* 8 May 1868.

101. Eric Foner, *Reconstruction: America's Unfinished Revolution, 1863–1877* (New York: Harper and Row, 1988); Burton, "Remembering the Civil War," 284–85; Burton, "The South as 'Other,'" 15–16, 42, 45; Joseph P. Reidy, "The African American Struggle for Citizenship Rights in the Northern United States during the Civil War," in Ural, *Civil War Citizens,* 213–36; Clayton, "Managing the Transition to a Free Labor Society," 89–108; Kerr-Ritchie, "Was U.S. Emancipation Exceptional," 152–53, 155–56, 160, 164–65; Gleeson and Lewis, Introduction, 3–5.

102. *London Times,* 11 Nov. 1872.

103. See Campbell, *Unlikely Allies,* 182–88; Myers, *Caution and Cooperation,* 248–54; William Mulligan, "Mobs and Diplomats: The *Alabama* Affair and British Diplomacy, 1865–1872," in *The Diplomats' World: A Cultural History of Diplomacy, 1815–1914,* ed. Markus Mosslang and Tor-

sten Riotte (Oxford: Oxford University Press, 2008), 105–32. For more detailed accounts, see Adrian Cook, *The "Alabama" Claims: American Politics and Anglo-American Relations, 1865–1872* (Ithaca, N.Y.: Cornell University Press, 1975), and Frank J. Merli, *The "Alabama," British Neutrality, and the American Civil War*, ed. David M. Fahey (Bloomington: Indiana University Press, 2004).

104. Anti-racist groups complained of insensitivity and presented the American Civil War as a conflict over slavery. Other groups complained of an insult to the Lancashire working classes on the basis that they had been pro-North during the war. Tal, *American Civil War in British Culture*, 145–48, 153–54. One of the more hysterical responses to the replica proposal came from the political left. See "The Flag of Slavery Must Not Fly in Merseyside," *Workers' Hammer*, 109 (Sept. 1989): 6–7, 10.

105. Long, *In the Shadow of the "Alabama,"* 1–3, 5–6, 35, 39, 46, 53–56, 68–69, 84, 88–94, 99, 102–8, 135–36, 146–47, 151–52, 158–59, 161, 164–65, 184–85.

106. Long, *In the Shadow of the "Alabama,"* 75. Hope's niece was called Henriette, similar to *Enrica*, the name of the ship before it was the *Alabama*, and it was launched on 14 May 1862, her twentieth birthday. Henriette sometimes participated in fundraising activities for the Confederacy, and Hope himself was a friend of Bulloch, the agent responsible for ordering the *Alabama* and throwing U.S. spies and British officials off the trail.

107. Hope told MPs in 1869 that "he thoroughly disliked and repudiated the whole scheme" of Irish church disestablishment, and he declared in 1884 that devolving power over Irish affairs "would be to break up that principle on which their great Parliament rested—namely, that local prejudices should be tempered by the general common sense." *Parliamentary Debates*, 3rd ser., 22 Apr. 1869, vol. 195, col. 1390, and 25 Feb. 1884, vol. 284, col. 1919. On the linkages between the American Civil War and approaches to the Irish question, see Brian Jenkins, *Fenians and Anglo-American Relations during Reconstruction* (Ithaca, N.Y.: Cornell University Press, 1969); and Tal, *American Civil War in British Culture*, 12–18, 24, 26, 28.

108. See, for example, *John Bull*, 29 July 1876.

109. *John Bull*, 26 Apr. 1879.

110. *New York Independent*, 4 July, 26 Sept. 1878; *St. Louis Globe-Democrat*, 8 July 1878; *Frank Leslie's Illustrated Newspaper*, 27 July 1878, 10 May 1879; *Congregationalist* (Boston), 31 July 1878; *Washington Post*, 23 Apr. 1879; *Chicago Tribune*, 8 May 1879.

111. *San Francisco Daily Evening Bulletin*, 18 Apr. 1877.

112. Tal, *American Civil War in British Culture*, 7.

113. Dubrulle, *Ambivalent Nation*, 14–15, 81–83, 155–56, 230–32.

114. *John Bull*, 14 July, 4 Aug. 1883; *Ladies' Monthly Magazine*, 1 Aug. 1883; *London Times*, 4 Aug. 1883; *Raleigh News and Observer*, 7 July 1883; *Washington Post*, 8 July 1883; *Daily Arkansas Gazette* (Little Rock), 25 July 1883; *New York Times*, 3 Aug. 1883; *St. Louis Globe-Democrat*, 3 Aug. 1883; *Frank Leslie's Illustrated Newspaper*, 11 Aug. 1883.

115. William C. Davis, *Breckinridge: Statesman, Soldier, Symbol* (Lexington: University Press of Kentucky, 2010), 564.

116. *St. Louis Globe-Democrat*, 20 Nov. 1875; *Daily Rocky Mountain News* (Denver), 25 Nov. 1875; *Georgia Weekly Telegraph*, 30 Nov. 1875.

117. *Fayetteville Observer and Gazette*, 1 July 1886, citing New York sources.

118. *Jefferson Davis: Private Letters, 1823–1889*, ed. Hudson Strode (New York: Harcourt, 1966), 293, 304, 510, 550–51; *The Papers of Jefferson Davis*, ed. Lynda Crist, Suzanne Gibbs, Brady Hutchin-

son, and Elizabeth Smith, 12 vols. (Baton Rouge: Louisiana State University Press, 2008), 12:xl-viii, 209, 219, 316–17, 360, 363–64, 384, 496; William J. Cooper Jr., *Jefferson Davis, American* (New York: Knopf, 2001), 623; Law and Law, *Beresford Hopes*, 207; Batchelor, *Beresfords*, 114.

119. "Mr. Jefferson Davis's Rise and Fall of the Confederate Government," *Saturday Review* 52, no. 1340, July 1881, 19–20.

7. STONEWALL JACKSON AND BRITISH OPINION

1. Walter Houghton, *The Victorian Frame of Mind, 1830–1870* (New Haven: Yale University Press, 1957), 122, 171, 197, 305, 326, 328; Mark Girouard, *The Return to Camelot: Chivalry and the English Gentleman* (New Haven: Yale University Press, 1981), 78, 83, 229; Gertrude Himmelfarb, *Victorian Minds* (London: Weidenfeld and Nicolson, 1968), 254, 264, 268; Juliette Atkinson, *Victorian Biography Reconsidered: A Study of Nineteenth-Century "Hidden" Lives* (Oxford: Oxford University Press, 2010), chap. 2.

2. Thomas Carlyle, *On Heroes, Hero-Worship, and the Heroic in History* (London: Chapman and Hall, 1840); A. L. Le Quesne, "Carlyle," in *Victorian Thinkers*, ed. Keith Thomas (Oxford: Oxford University Press, 1993), 69–72.

3. Joel H. Wiener, *The Americanization of the British Press, 1830–1914: Speed in the Age of Transatlantic Journalism* (Basingstoke: Palgrave Macmillan, 2011), 1, 4–5, 24, 30–31, 33, 55–57, 63–67, 72, 75, 80–93; Temperley, *Britain and America since Independence*, 61.

4. On Jackson's childhood and education, his early army career, marriages, and period as an instructor at the Virginia Military Institute, see James I. Robertson Jr., *Stonewall Jackson: The Man, the Soldier, the Legend* (New York: Macmillan, 1997), chaps. 1–6; S. C. Gwynne, *Rebel Yell: The Violence, Passion, and Redemption of Stonewall Jackson* (New York: Scribner, 2014), 104–9, 111–34, 136–39, 141–48, 152–54, 341–47.

5. Scholarly verdicts on the campaign are not uniform: Robertson, *Stonewall Jackson*, 323–457; Donald A. Davis, *Stonewall Jackson: A Biography* (New York: Palgrave Macmillan, 2007), 75–104; Gwynne, *Rebel Yell*, 212–327; David J. Eicher, *The Longest Night: A Military History of the Civil War* (New York: Simon and Schuster, 2001), 208–12, 257–67; John Keegan, *The American Civil War: A Military History* (New York: Knopf, 2009), 143–45; Robert G. Tanner, *Stonewall in the Valley* (Mechanicsburg, Pa.: Stackpole Books, 1996), 430, 433; Peter Cozzens, *Shenandoah 1862: Stonewall Jackson's Valley Campaign* (Chapel Hill: University of North Carolina Press, 2008), 3.

6. *London Morning Post*, 13 May 1862; *Manchester Times*, 17 May 1862; *Westmorland Gazette*, 17 May 1862; *Derby Mercury*, 21 May 1862.

7. *Glasgow Herald*, 5 June 1862; *Leeds Mercury*, 16 June 1862; *Sheffield Independent*, 16 June 1862; *Huddersfield Chronicle*, 21 June 1862; *Manchester Times*, 21 June 1862. On 9 June 1862, the secretary at the U.S. Legation in London greeted news of another Jackson victory in the Valley with dismay. *The Journal of Benjamin Moran, 1857–1865*, ed. Sarah A. Wallace and Frances E. Gillespie, 2 vols. (Chicago: University of Chicago Press, 1948), 2:1018.

8. *London Times*, 26, 28 June 1862; *Liverpool Mercury*, 26 June 1862; *Belfast Newsletter*, 27 June 1862; *Sheffield Independent*, 27 June 1862; *Freeman's Journal*, 27 June 1862; *Essex Standard*, 27 June 1862; *Manchester Courier*, 28 June 1862; *Westmorland Gazette*, 28 June 1862; *Southampton Herald*, 28 June 1862; *Northampton Mercury*, 28 June 1862; *Norfolk Chronicle*, 28 June 1862; *Manchester Times*,

28 June 1862; *London Examiner,* 28 June 1862; *Bristol Mercury,* 28 June 1862; *Worcester Journal,* 28 June 1862; *London Observer,* 29 June 1862.

   9. *Belfast Newsletter,* 30 June 1862.

   10. *Essex Standard,* 2 July 1862.

   11. *Liverpool Mercury,* 30 June, 1 July 1862; *Sheffield Independent,* 1 July 1862; *Dundee Courier,* 1 July 1862; *Cork Examiner,* 2 July 1862; *Westmorland Gazette,* 5 July 1862; *Reynolds's Newspaper,* 6 July 1862; *London Index,* 3, 10, 17 July 1862.

   12. *London Times,* 11 July 1862; Eicher, *Longest Night,* 318; Keegan, *American Civil War,* 163–64.

   13. Scoville had briefly been private secretary to John C. Calhoun, the U.S. senator for South Carolina (and former secretary of war, vice president, and secretary of state). As "Manhattan," he embarrassed the Lincoln administration but was not removed from office, probably because the administration was wary of involvement in New York politics. There is an obituary in *Gentleman's Magazine* 17, no. 217 (Aug. 1864): 258.

   14. *London Standard,* 28 June, 1, 5, 9 July 1862.

   15. *Newcastle Guardian,* 12 July 1862; *Manchester Courier,* 12 July 1862.

   16. Jackson's role in these engagements has had mixed reviews: Keegan, *American Civil War,* 146–51; Eicher, *Longest Night,* 280–97; James M. McPherson, *Embattled Rebel: Jefferson Davis as Commander in Chief* (New York: Penguin, 2014), 90–92; Davis, *Jackson,* 106–20; A. Wilson Greene, *Whatever You Resolve to Be: Essays on Stonewall Jackson* (Knoxville: University of Tennessee Press, 2005), 35–74; Judkin Browning, *The Seven Days' Battles: The War Begins Anew* (Santa Barbara, Calif.: Praeger, 2012), 32–33, 37–39; Gwynne, *Rebel Yell,* 348–82; Robertson, *Stonewall Jackson,* 458–512.

   17. *Blackburn Standard,* 9 July 1862.

   18. *London Times,* 9, 11, 15 July 1862; *Royal Cornwall Gazette,* 11 July 1862; *York Herald,* 12 July 1862; *Dundee Courier,* 12 July 1862; *Sheffield Independent,* 12 July 1862; *Morpeth Herald,* 12 July 1862; *Nottinghamshire Guardian,* 11 July 1862; *Manchester Guardian,* 11 July 1862; *Westmorland Gazette,* 12 July 1862; *John Bull,* 12 July 1862; *Bell's Life in London,* 13 July 1862; *London Observer,* 13 July 1862.

   19. *Manchester Courier,* 12 July 1862; *Liverpool Mercury,* 12 July 1862.

   20. *London Examiner,* 12 July 1862; *Newcastle Guardian,* 12 July 1862; *Reading Mercury,* 12 July 1862.

   21. *Sheffield Independent,* 12 July 1862.

   22. *Glasgow Herald,* 14 July 1862; *Sheffield Independent,* 15 July 1862; *Leeds Mercury,* 15 July 1862; *London Morning Post,* 15 July 1862; *Liverpool Mercury,* 16, 17 July 1862.

   23. *Dundee Courier,* 18 July 1862; *Caledonian Mercury,* 18 July 1862; *Leeds Times,* 19 July 1862; *Westmorland Gazette,* 19 July 1862.

   24. *Birmingham Daily Post,* 19 July 1862; *Manchester Guardian,* 19 July 1862; *Leeds Times,* 19 July 1862.

   25. *Reynolds's Newspaper,* 20 July 1862; *Liverpool Mercury,* 21 July 1862; *London Morning Post,* 21 July 1862; *Sheffield Independent,* 21 July 1862.

   26. *Bury and Norwich Post,* 22 July 1862; *Sheffield Independent,* 23 July 1862; *Leeds Mercury,* 23 July 1862; *Cork Examiner,* 25, 30 July 1862; *Newcastle Courant,* 25 July 1862; *John Bull,* 26 July 1862; *Reynolds's Newspaper,* 27 July 1862; *Bucks Herald,* 26 July 1862.

   27. *London Times,* 21 July 1862; *Glasgow Herald,* 23 July 1862.

   28. *Belfast Newsletter,* 22 July 1862; *London Standard,* 22 July 1862.

29. *Fun*, 9 Aug. 1862; see also "Two Dispatches of General McClellan" in the issue of 6 Sept. 1862.

30. *London Times*, 30, 31 July 1862; *Manchester Guardian*, 30, 31 July, 5 Aug. 1862; *Cork Examiner*, 29 July 1862; *London Daily News*, 30 July 1862; *Hull Packet*, 1 Aug. 1862; *Essex Standard*, 1 Aug. 1862; *Royal Cornwall Gazette*, 1 Aug. 1862; *Anti-Slavery Reporter*, 1 Aug. 1862; *Westmorland Gazette*, 2 Aug. 1862; *Reading Mercury*, 2 Aug. 1862; *Nottinghamshire Guardian*, 1 Aug. 1862; *Northampton Mercury*, 2 Aug. 1862; *John Bull*, 2 Aug. 1862; *Lady's Newspaper*, 2 Aug. 1862; *Leeds Mercury*, 30 July 1862.

31. *London Observer*, 3 Aug. 1862; *Manchester Guardian*, 4 Aug. 1862; *Liverpool Mercury*, 4 Aug. 1862; *London Morning Post*, 4 Aug. 1862; *London Standard*, 4 Aug. 1862.

32. *London Times*, 6, 7 Aug. 1862; *Liverpool Mercury*, 7 Aug. 1862; *Dundee Courier*, 7 Aug. 1862; *Glasgow Herald*, 7 Aug. 1862; *Newcastle Journal*, 7 Aug. 1862; *London Daily News*, 7 Aug. 1862; *London Morning Post*, 7 Aug. 1862; *Manchester Guardian*, 7 Aug. 1862.

33. *London Times*, 8 Aug. 1862; *Manchester Courier*, 9 Aug. 1862.

34. *London Times*, 1 Aug. 1862; *Westmorland Gazette*, 9 Aug. 1862.

35. *Westmorland Gazette*, 9 Aug. 1862; *Preston Chronicle*, 9 Aug. 1862; *London Observer*, 10 Aug. 1862; *Bell's Life in London*, 10 Aug. 1862; *Caledonian Mercury*, 11 Aug. 1862; *Liverpool Mercury*, 11 Aug. 1862; *Belfast Newsletter*, 11 Aug. 1862; *Newcastle Courant*, 15 Aug. 1862.

36. *Leeds Mercury*, 9 Aug. 1862; *John Bull*, 9 Aug. 1862; *Lady's Newspaper*, 9 Aug. 1862; *London Observer*, 10, 11 Aug. 1862; *Sheffield Independent*, 11 Aug. 1862; *Glasgow Herald*, 11 Aug. 1862; *London Morning Post*, 11 Aug. 1862; *Manchester Guardian*, 11 Aug. 1862; *Morpeth Herald*, 16 Aug. 1862; *Manchester Courier*, 9, 16 Aug. 1862.

37. *Leeds Times*, 9 Aug. 1862.

38. *Liverpool Mercury*, 14 Aug. 1862; *Dundee Courier*, 14 Aug. 1862; *Glasgow Herald*, 14 Aug. 1862; *Manchester Guardian*, 14 Aug. 1862; *Nottinghamshire Guardian*, 15 Aug. 1862; *Newcastle Courant*, 15 Aug. 1862; *London Times*, 16 Aug. 1862.

39. *London Daily News*, 18 Aug. 1862.

40. *London Standard*, 20 Aug. 1862; *Derby Mercury*, 20 Aug. 1862.

41. Robertson, *Stonewall Jackson*, chap. 18; Gwynne, *Rebel Yell*, 394–407; McPherson, *Embattled Rebel*, 95, 97; Eicher, *Longest Night*, 318–22; Davis, *Jackson*, 123–25; Keegan, *American Civil War*, 163–64.

42. *Newcastle Journal*, 1 Sept. 1862; *Westmorland Gazette*, 6 Sept. 1862.

43. *London Standard*, 21 Aug. 1862; *Liverpool Mercury*, 21 Aug. 1862; *Glasgow Herald*, 21 Aug. 1862.

44. *Leicestershire Mercury*, 23 Aug. 1862; *Manchester Guardian*, 23 Aug. 1862; *Manchester Courier*, 23 Aug. 1862; *John Bull*, 23 Aug. 1862; *Lady's Newspaper*, 23 Aug. 1862; *Bell's Life in London*, 24 Aug. 1862; *London Observer*, 24 Aug. 1862; *Leeds Mercury*, 25 Aug. 1862.

45. See, for example, *Leicester Chronicle*, 23 Aug. 1862.

46. *Westmorland Gazette*, 23 Aug. 1862.

47. *Freeman's Journal*, 25 Aug. 1862; *Lady's Newspaper*, 30 Aug. 1862.

48. *London Standard*, 25 Aug. 1862; *Liverpool Mercury*, 25 Aug. 1862.

49. *London Times*, 23, 25, 29 Aug. 1862; *Glasgow Herald*, 27 Aug. 1862; *Stirling Observer*, 28 Aug. 1862; *Nottinghamshire Guardian*, 29 Aug. 1862; *London Standard*, 29 Aug. 1862.

50. *Liverpool Mercury*, 27 Aug. 1862.

51. See, for example, *Friend of India* (Calcutta), 4 Sept. 1862.

52. *London Daily News*, 25 Aug. 1862.

53. *Sheffield Independent*, 1, 3 Sept. 1862; *London Standard*, 1, 3 Sept. 1862; *Belfast Newsletter*, 1 Sept. 1862; *Caledonian Mercury*, 1 Sept. 1862; *Liverpool Mercury*, 3 Sept. 1862; *Leeds Mercury*, 3 Sept. 1862; *London Daily News*, 3 Sept. 1862; *Glasgow Herald*, 3 Sept. 1862; *Manchester Guardian*, 3 Sept. 1862; *London Morning Post*, 3 Sept. 1862.

54. *Southampton Herald*, 6 Sept. 1862; *Manchester Courier*, 6 Sept. 1862.

55. *Bucks Herald*, 6 Sept. 1862. Charles F. Adams, the U.S. minister to Britain, received a letter from Washington at this time (from his son, also named Charles) that emphasized the northern generals' unwillingness to work together. *A Cycle of Adams Letters, 1861–1865*, ed. Worthington Chauncey Ford, 2 vols. (Boston: Houghton Mifflin, 1920), 1:179–80.

56. *Leeds Times*, 13 Sept. 1862.

57. *London Daily News*, 10 Sept. 1862; *Dundee Courier*, 10 Sept. 1862; *Cork Examiner*, 10 Sept. 1862; *Caledonian Mercury*, 10 Sept. 1862; *Sheffield Independent*, 10 Sept. 1862; *Liverpool Mercury*, 11 Sept. 1862; *Birmingham Daily Post*, 10, 11 Sept. 1862; *Bradford Observer*, 11 Sept. 1862; *York Herald*, 13 Sept. 1862.

58. *London Times*, 13, 15, 17 Sept. 1862; *London Daily News*, 16 Sept. 1862; *Liverpool Mercury*, 16 Sept. 1862; *Caledonian Mercury*, 16 Sept. 1862; *Lloyd's Illustrated Newspaper*, 14 Sept. 1862; *Cork Examiner*, 18 Sept. 1862; *Newcastle Journal*, 18 Sept. 1862.

59. Eicher, *Longest Night*, 324–34; Davis, *Jackson*, 128–36; Greene, *Whatever You Resolve to Be*, 75–112; McPherson, *Embattled Rebel*, 97; Keegan, *American Civil War*, 164–65; Gwynne, *Rebel Yell*, 411–46; Robertson, *Stonewall Jackson*, 546–77.

60. *London Times*, 16 Sept. 1862; *London Morning Post*, 17 Sept. 1862; *London Standard*, 15, 18 Sept. 1862; *Birmingham Daily Post*, 18 Sept. 1862; *Liverpool Mercury*, 18 Sept. 1862; *Sheffield Independent*, 18 Sept. 1862; *Leeds Mercury*, 18 Sept. 1862; *Manchester Guardian*, 18 Sept. 1862; *John Bull*, 20 Sept. 1862.

61. *Journal of Benjamin Moran*, 2:1072–73.

62. *John Bull*, 20 Sept. 1862; *Lady's Newspaper*, 20 Sept. 1862; *Manchester Courier*, 20 Sept. 1862; *Sheffield Independent*, 20 Sept. 1862; *Bristol Mercury*, 20 Sept. 1862; *London Examiner*, 20 Sept. 1862; *Huddersfield Chronicle*, 20 Sept. 1862; *Birmingham Gazette*, 20 Sept. 1862; *Liverpool Mercury*, 20 Sept. 1862; *Reynolds's Newspaper*, 21 Sept. 1862; *London Observer*, 21 Sept. 1862; *Manchester Guardian*, 22 Sept. 1862.

63. *London Standard*, 22 Sept. 1862; *London Morning Post*, 23 Sept. 1862; *Liverpool Mercury*, 23 Sept. 1862; *Sheffield Independent*, 23 Sept. 1862; *Caledonian Mercury*, 23 Sept. 1862; *Birmingham Daily Post*, 23 Sept. 1862; *Leeds Mercury*, 23 Sept. 1862.

64. *London Times*, 23, 27, 30 Sept., 2 Oct. 1862; *Liverpool Mercury*, 22, 26 Sept. 1862; *Manchester Guardian*, 26, 27 Sept. 1862; *Essex Standard*, 26 Sept. 1862; *Glasgow Herald*, 26 Sept. 1862; *Cork Examiner*, 26 Sept. 1862; *London Examiner*, 27 Sept. 1862; *Nottinghamshire Guardian*, 26 Sept. 1862; *John Bull*, 27 Sept. 1862; *Manchester Courier*, 27 Sept. 1862; *Lady's Newspaper*, 27 Sept. 1862; *London Observer*, 28 Sept. 1862; *Bell's Life in London*, 28 Sept. 1862; *London Standard*, 29 Sept. 1862; *London Morning Post*, 27, 29 Sept. 1862; *Blackburn Standard*, 1 Oct. 1862; *Sheffield Independent*, 3 Oct. 1862.

65. *Fun*, 27 Sept. 1862. For other accounts, see, for example, *Liverpool Mercury*, 30 Sept. 1862.

66. On the Maryland Campaign, see Robertson, *Stonewall Jackson*, 584–623; Gwynne, *Rebel Yell*, 451–81; Keegan, *American Civil War*, 167–69; Eicher, *Longest Night*, chap. 12.

67. *Manchester Guardian,* 29, 30 Sept., 1 Oct 1862; *Freeman's Journal,* 1 Oct. 1862; *London Standard,* 1 Oct. 1862; *Anti-Slavery Reporter,* 1 Oct. 1862; *Leeds Mercury,* 1 Oct. 1862; *Belfast Newsletter,* 1 Oct. 1862; *Devizes and Wiltshire Gazette,* 2 Oct. 1862; *Stirling Observer,* 2 Oct. 1862; *North Devon Journal,* 2 Oct. 1862; *Bradford Observer,* 2 Oct. 1862; *London Times,* 4 Oct. 1862; *London Daily News,* 4 Oct. 1862; *London Morning Post,* 1, 4 Oct. 1862; *John Bull,* 4 Oct. 1862; *London Examiner,* 4 Oct. 1862; *Manchester Courier,* 4 Oct. 1862; *Huddersfield Chronicle,* 4 Oct. 1862; *Leeds Times,* 4 Oct. 1862; *York Herald,* 4 Oct. 1862; *Lady's Newspaper,* 4 Oct. 1862; *Bell's Life in London,* 5 Oct. 1862; *London Observer,* 5 Oct. 1862; *Reynolds's Newspaper,* 5 Oct. 1862; *Era,* 5 Oct. 1862; *Sheffield Independent,* 1, 6 Oct. 1862; *Liverpool Mercury,* 2, 7 Oct. 1862; *Friend of India,* 16, 23, 30 Oct. 1862.

68. *London Times,* 4 Oct. 1862; *Leeds Times,* 4 Oct. 1862; *York Herald,* 4 Oct. 1862; *Leicester Chronicle,* 4 Oct. 1862; *London Morning Post,* 10 Oct. 1862; *Derby Mercury,* 8 Oct. 1862; *Nottinghamshire Guardian,* 10 Oct. 1862; *Essex Standard,* 3, 8 Oct. 1862.

69. *Punch,* 4 Oct. 1862.

70. *Lloyd's Illustrated Newspaper,* 12 Oct. 1862; *London Standard,* 11 Oct. 1862; *Nottinghamshire Guardian,* 17 Oct. 1862.

71. *Bradford Observer,* 16 Oct. 1862; *Liverpool Mercury,* 13 Oct. 1862; *Westmorland Gazette,* 18 Oct. 1862; *John Bull,* 18 Oct. 1862.

72. Campbell, *English Public Opinion,* 177–79; Keegan, *American Civil War,* 169–71; and on the background, see Howard Jones, *Union in Peril: The Crisis over British Intervention in the Civil War* (Chapel Hill: University of North Carolina Press, 1992), chaps. 8–10; Doyle, *Cause of All Nations,* chaps. 9–10; Sebrell, *Persuading John Bull,* chaps. 5–6.

73. *London Examiner,* 18 Oct. 1862; *John Bull,* 18 Oct. 1862; *Dundee Courier,* 20 Oct. 1862; *Caledonian Mercury,* 20 Oct. 1862; *Newcastle Courant,* 24 Oct. 1862; *Leeds Mercury,* 18 Oct. 1862; *Liverpool Mercury,* 20 Oct. 1862.

74. *London Times,* 16, 18 Oct., 3, 6 Nov. 1862; *Glasgow Herald,* 20 Oct. 1862; *Sheffield Independent,* 30 Oct., 3 Nov. 1862; *London Observer,* 2 Nov. 1862; *Bell's Life in London,* 2 Nov. 1862; *London Morning Post,* 3 Nov. 1862; *London Daily News,* 3 Nov. 1862; *Liverpool Mercury,* 3 Nov. 1862; *Stirling Observer,* 6 Nov. 1862; *Lady's Newspaper,* 8 Nov. 1862; *Western Times* (Exeter, Devon), 8 Nov. 1862; *Bucks Herald,* 8 Nov. 1862.

75. *London Times,* 30 Oct. 1862; *London Standard,* 15 Nov. 1862; *Westmorland Gazette,* 8 Nov. 1862.

76. *London Times,* 20, 22, 24, 28, 29 Nov. 1862; *Manchester Guardian,* 20, 22, 28 Nov. 1862; *Cork Examiner,* 19 Nov. 1862; *London Morning Post,* 20 Nov. 1862; *Liverpool Mercury,* 20 Nov. 1862; *Newcastle Journal,* 20 Nov. 1862; *Caledonian Mercury,* 20 Nov. 1862; *Glasgow Herald,* 21 Nov. 1862; *John Bull,* 22, 29 Nov. 1862; *York Herald,* 22 Nov. 1862; *Cheshire Observer,* 22 Nov. 1862; *Hereford Journal,* 22 Nov. 1862; *Era,* 23 Nov. 1862; *Sheffield Independent,* 20, 26 Nov. 1862; *Bell's Life in London,* 23, 30 Nov. 1862; *Blackburn Standard,* 26 Nov. 1862; *Essex Standard,* 26 Nov. 1862; *Derby Mercury,* 26 Nov. 1862; *London Standard,* 20, 26 Nov. 1862; *London Observer,* 23, 24, 30 Nov. 1862.

77. *London Examiner,* 29 Nov. 1862; *London Standard,* 29 Nov., 1, 2, 3 Dec. 1862; *London Morning Post,* 29 Nov., 1, 4, 5 Dec. 1862; *London Daily News,* 29 Nov., 4 Dec. 1862; *Sheffield Independent,* 29 Nov., 6, 9 Dec. 1862; *Manchester Courier,* 29 Nov. 1862; *Manchester Times,* 29 Nov., 6 Dec. 1862; *Manchester Guardian,* 29 Nov., 3, 9 Dec. 1862; *York Herald,* 29 Nov., 6 Dec. 1862; *Birmingham Gazette,* 29 Nov. 1862; *Belfast Newsletter,* 29 Nov., 11 Dec. 1862; *Glasgow Herald,* 29 Nov., 1, 5 Dec. 1862; *Leeds Times,* 29 Nov., 6 Dec. 1862; *Leeds Mercury,* 29 Nov., 1, 9, 11 Dec. 1862; *Westmorland Gazette,* 29 Nov., 6 Dec. 1862; *Liverpool Mercury,* 29 Nov., 1, 3, 4 Dec. 1862; *Bristol Mercury,* 29 Nov. 1862;

Lloyd's Illustrated Newspaper, 30 Nov. 1862; Cork Examiner, 2 Dec. 1863; London Times, 2, 3, 9, 10 Dec. 1862; Bradford Observer, 4, 11 Dec. 1862; John Bull, 6 Dec. 1862; London Observer, 7, 8 Dec. 1862; Era, 7 Dec. 1862; Bury and Norwich Post, 9 Dec. 1862; Freeman's Journal, 9 Dec. 1862; Blackburn Standard, 10 Dec. 1862; Birmingham Daily Post, 10 Dec. 1862; Derby Mercury, 10 Dec. 1862; Stirling Observer, 11 Dec. 1862; Dundee Courier, 9, 11 Dec. 1862; Newcastle Journal, 11 Dec. 1862; Hull Packet, 12 Dec. 1862; Nottinghamshire Guardian, 12 Dec. 1862; Huddersfield Chronicle, 13 Dec. 1862; Worcester Journal, 13 Dec. 1862.

78. London Standard, 10 Dec. 1862.

79. Manchester Courier, 13 Dec. 1862; Leeds Mercury, 13 Dec. 1862; Bristol Mercury, 13 Dec. 1862; Reynolds's Newspaper, 14 Dec. 1862.

80. Leeds Times, 13 Dec. 1862; Glasgow Herald, 10 Dec. 1862; Liverpool Mercury, 11 Dec. 1862.

81. Glasgow Herald, 17 Dec. 1862.

82. Bucks Herald, 20 Dec. 1862; Reynolds's Newspaper, 21 Dec. 1862; Dundee Courier, 22 Dec. 1862.

83. London Times, 16, 17, 20, 23, 27 Dec. 1862; Cork Examiner, 16 Dec. 1862; Freeman's Journal, 16 Dec. 1862; London Standard, 17, 20 Dec. 1862; Newcastle Journal, 17, 20 Dec. 1862; Devizes and Wiltshire Gazette, 18 Dec. 1862; London Morning Post, 16, 20 Dec. 1862; London Examiner, 20 Dec. 1862; Sheffield Independent, 17, 20 Dec. 1863; Southampton Herald, 20 Dec. 1862; Reading Mercury, 20 Dec. 1862; Leicester Chronicle, 20 Dec. 1862; Preston Chronicle, 20 Dec. 1862; Birmingham Daily Post, 17, 20 Dec. 1862; Birmingham Gazette, 20 Dec. 1862; Westmorland Gazette, 20 Dec. 1862; York Herald, 20 Dec. 1862; Liverpool Mercury, 18, 20 Dec. 1862; Dundee Courier, 20 Dec. 1862; Glasgow Herald, 16, 20 Dec. 1862; Hereford Journal, 20 Dec. 1862; Bristol Mercury, 20 Dec. 1862; Western Times, 20 Dec. 1862; Leeds Times, 20 Dec. 1862; Huddersfield Chronicle, 20 Dec. 1862; Caledonian Mercury, 20 Dec. 1862; Lancaster Gazette, 20 Dec. 1862; Leeds Mercury, 16, 20 Dec. 1862; Manchester Guardian, 20 Dec. 1862; John Bull, 20 Dec. 1862; London Observer, 21 Dec. 1862; Bury and Norwich Post, 23 Dec. 1862; Derby Mercury, 24 Dec. 1862; Bradford Observer, 24 Dec. 1862; North Devon Journal, 25 Dec. 1862; Royal Cornwall Gazette, 19, 26 Dec. 1862; Nottinghamshire Guardian, 19, 26 Dec. 1862; Essex Standard, 19, 24, 26 Dec. 1862; Bucks Herald, 27 Dec. 1862.

84. London Daily News, 27 Dec. 1863.

85. Keegan, American Civil War, 171–72; Eicher, Longest Night, 395–405; Greene, Whatever You Resolve to Be, 113–40; Gwynne, Rebel Yell, 491–503; Robertson, Stonewall Jackson, 647–64.

86. London Observer, 28 Dec. 1862; London Times, 29 Dec. 1862; Liverpool Mercury, 29 Dec. 1862; Caledonian Mercury, 29 Dec. 1862; Sheffield Independent, 29 Dec. 1862; Birmingham Daily Post, 29 Dec. 1862; Newcastle Journal, 30 Dec. 1862; London Morning Post, 30 Dec. 1862; Aberdeen Journal, 31 Dec. 1862; North Devon Journal, 1 Jan. 1863; Essex Standard, 31 Dec. 1862, 2 Jan. 1863; Chelmsford Chronicle, 2 Jan. 1863; Cheshire Observer, 3 Jan. 1863; Bucks Herald, 3 Jan. 1863; Manchester Courier, 3 Jan. 1863; Huddersfield Chronicle, 3 Jan. 1863; Hereford Journal, 3 Jan. 1863; Westmorland Gazette, 3 Jan. 1863; Reading Mercury, 3 Jan. 1863; Preston Chronicle, 3 Jan. 1863; Lloyd's Illustrated Newspaper, 4 Jan. 1863; Stirling Observer, 8 Jan. 1863; Glasgow Herald, 9 Jan. 1863; Royal Cornwall Gazette, 9 Jan. 1863; Reynolds's Newspaper, 4, 11 Jan. 1863; Friend of India, 15 Jan. 1863.

87. London Observer, 27 Dec. 1862; Belfast Newsletter, 27, 29 Dec. 1862; Leeds Times, 3 Jan. 1863.

88. Sheffield Independent, 29 Dec. 1862; Dundee Courier, 29 Dec. 1862, 5 Jan. 1863; Glasgow Herald, 29 Dec. 1862; Cork Examiner, 29 Dec. 1862; London Times, 1, 3 Jan. 1863; Westmorland Gazette, 3 Jan. 1863; Bury and Norwich Post, 6 Jan. 1863.

89. *London Observer*, 11 Jan. 1863; *London Standard*, 12 Jan. 1863; *Manchester Guardian*, 12 Jan. 1863; *Sheffield Independent*, 12 Jan. 1863; *Newcastle Journal*, 12 Jan. 1863; *London Morning Post*, 12 Jan. 1863; *Caledonian Mercury*, 12 Jan. 1863; *Cork Examiner*, 13 Jan. 1863; *Liverpool Mercury*, 12, 13 Jan. 1863; *Blackburn Standard*, 14 Jan. 1863; *Aberdeen Journal*, 14 Jan. 1863; *North Devon Journal*, 15 Jan. 1863; *Bradford Observer*, 15 Jan. 1863; *Devizes and Wiltshire Gazette*, 15 Jan. 1863; *Western Times*, 16 Jan. 1863; *Nottinghamshire Guardian*, 16 Jan. 1863; *Preston Chronicle*, 17 Jan. 1863; *Leicester Chronicle*, 17 Jan. 1863; *Leicestershire Mercury*, 17 Jan. 1863; *Huddersfield Chronicle*, 17 Jan. 1863; *Leeds Intelligencer*, 17 Jan. 1863; *Cheshire Observer*, 17 Jan. 1863; *Wrexham Weekly Advertiser*, 17 Jan. 1863.

90. *Bradford Observer*, 26 Feb. 1863.

91. *London Times*, 16 Feb. 1863.

92. *London Daily News*, 12 Mar. 1863; *Sheffield Independent*, 12, 14 Mar. 1863; *Liverpool Mercury*, 12 Mar. 1863; *Freeman's Journal*, 12 Mar. 1863; *Dundee Courier*, 12 Mar. 1863; *Caledonian Mercury*, 12 Mar. 1863; *Bradford Observer*, 12 Mar. 1863; *Western Times*, 12 Mar. 1863; *Birmingham Daily Post*, 12 Mar. 1863; *Newcastle Journal*, 12 Mar. 1863; *London Standard*, 12, 13 Mar. 1863; *London Morning Post*, 13 Mar. 1863; *Leeds Mercury*, 12, 13 Mar. 1863; *Exeter and Plymouth Gazette*, 13 Mar. 1863; *Hull Packet*, 13 Mar. 1863; *Nottinghamshire Guardian*, 13 Mar. 1863; *Leicestershire Mercury*, 14 Mar. 1863; *Leicester Chronicle*, 14 Mar. 1863; *Lancaster Gazette*, 14 Mar. 1863; *Southampton Herald*, 14 Mar. 1863; *Preston Chronicle*, 14 Mar. 1863; *Westmorland Gazette*, 14 Mar. 1863; *Leeds Times*, 14 Mar. 1863; *London Observer*, 15 Mar. 1863; *Bury and Norwich Post*, 17 Mar. 1863; *Blackburn Standard*, 18 Mar. 1863.

93. *Dundee Courier*, 30 Apr. 1863.

94. *London Times*, 11 May 1863; *Liverpool Mercury*, 11 May 1863; *Belfast Newsletter*, 11 May 1863; *Caledonian Mercury*, 11 May 1863; *Newcastle Journal*, 11 May 1863; *Freeman's Journal*, 11 May 1863; *Leeds Mercury*, 11 May 1863; *Derby Mercury*, 13 May 1863; *Essex Standard*, 13 May 1863; *Exeter Flying Post*, 13 May 1863; *Hampshire Telegraph*, 16 May 1863; *Bristol Mercury*, 16 May 1863; *Huddersfield Chronicle*, 16 May 1863; *Hereford Journal*, 16 May 1863; *Lancaster Gazette*, 16 May 1863; *Leeds Times*, 16 May 1863.

95. *Leeds Mercury*, 11 May 1863.

96. *Freeman's Journal*, 11 May 1863; *Lancaster Gazette*, 16 May 1863.

97. Robertson, *Stonewall Jackson*, 701–36, 744, 757; Gwynne, *Rebel Yell*, 519–45; Keegan, *American Civil War*, 179–86; Eicher, *Longest Night*, 473–89.

98. *London Times*, 18 May 1863; *Era*, 24 May 1863.

99. *Worcester Journal*, 16 May 1863; *Cork Examiner*, 16, 19 May 1863; *John Bull*, 16, 23 May 1863; *London Observer*, 17, 24 May 1863; *Bell's Life in London*, 17, 24 May 1863; *Manchester Guardian*, 18, 22, 26 May 1863; *London Standard*, 22 May 1863; *London Times*, 22 May 1863; *Nottinghamshire Guardian*, 22 May 1863; *Liverpool Mercury*, 19, 22 May 1863; *Birmingham Daily Post*, 22 May 1863; *Leeds Mercury*, 22 May 1863; *Sheffield Independent*, 19, 22 May 1863; *Glasgow Herald*, 16, 22 May 1863; *London Daily News*, 22 May 1863; *Dundee Courier*, 22 May 1863; *London Morning Post*, 22 May 1863; *Nottinghamshire Guardian*, 22 May 1863; *Western Times*, 19, 22 May 1863; *Lloyd's Illustrated Newspaper*, 24 May 1863; *Reynolds's Newspaper*, 24 May 1863; *Caledonian Mercury*, 16, 26 May 1863.

100. *Dundee Courier*, 19 May 1863.

101. *Nottinghamshire Guardian*, 22 May 1863.

102. *New York Tribune*, 27 June 1862. Palmer, born in Baltimore, studied medicine and traveled in Asia before settling in New York. In 1862, he wrote the poem "Stonewall Jackson's Way," which was put to music and became a popular song. Later he was on the staff of John C. Breck-

inridge. See *"Words for the Hour": A New Anthology of Civil War Poetry*, ed. Faith Barrett and Cristanne Miller (Amherst: University of Massachusetts Press, 2005), 389; David W. Gaddy, "John Williamson Palmer: Confederate Agent," *Maryland Historical Magazine* 83, no. 2 (1988): 98–110; Daniel E. Sutherland, "John Williamson Palmer in the Civil War," *Maryland Historical Magazine* 78, no. 2 (1983): 54–66; *Who's Who in America, 1899–1900*, ed. John W. Leonard (Chicago: A. N. Marquis, 1899), 545; Gwynne, *Rebel Yell*, 484–86.

103. *Leeds Mercury*, 17, 19 July 1862; *Freeman's Journal*, 17 July 1862; *Caledonian Mercury*, 18 July 1862; *Manchester Courier*, 19 July 1862; *Leeds Times*, 19 July 1862; *Derby Mercury*, 23 July 1862; *Southampton Herald*, 26 July 1862.

104. *Sheffield Independent*, 12 July 1862; *Liverpool Mercury*, 12 July 1862; *Glasgow Herald*, 14 July 1862; *Caledonian Mercury*, 18 July 1862.

105. *London Times*, 17 July 1862; *Liverpool Mercury*, 17 July 1862; *Derby Mercury*, 23 July 1862; *Bucks Herald*, 26 July 1862.

106. *Leeds Times*, 9 Aug. 1862.

107. *London Daily News*, 18 Aug. 1862.

108. *Caledonian Mercury*, 16 Sept. 1862.

109. *Leeds Mercury*, 18 Sept. 1862; *Liverpool Mercury*, 22 Sept. 1862.

110. *Stirling Observer*, 18 Sept. 1862.

111. *London Times*, 20 Sept. 1862; *Blackburn Standard*, 24 Sept. 1862; *Dundee Courier*, 24 Sept. 1862; *Newcastle Courant*, 26 Sept. 1862; *Essex Standard*, 26 Sept. 1862; *Royal Cornwall Gazette*, 26 Sept. 1862; *Manchester Courier*, 27 Oct. 1862; *Westmorland Gazette*, 27 Oct. 1862; *Caledonian Mercury*, 29 Sept. 1862. The West Point connection is discussed in Robertson, *Stonewall Jackson*, chap. 2; Gwynne, *Rebel Yell*, 340–47; Keegan, *American Civil War*, 144. See also John C. Waugh, *The Class of 1846 from West Point to Appomattox: Stonewall Jackson, George McClellan, and Their Brothers* (New York: Warner Books, 1994).

112. *Belfast Newsletter*, 29 Aug. 1862.

113. *Exeter Flying Post*, 17 Sept. 1862.

114. *London Times*, 25 Sept. 1862; *Cork Examiner*, 26 Sept. 1862; *Blackburn Standard*, 1 Oct. 1862. Negotiations involving Garibaldi are discussed in Doyle, *Cause of All Nations*, 19–26, 229–33, 237–38; Burton, "Remembering the Civil War," 280.

115. *Essex Standard*, 3, 8 Oct. 1862; *Leeds Times*, 4 Oct. 1862; *Manchester Courier*, 4 Oct. 1862; *Huddersfield Chronicle*, 4 Oct. 1862; *Era*, 5 Oct. 1862; *Sheffield Independent*, 6 Oct. 1862; *Liverpool Mercury*, 7 Oct. 1862; *Lloyd's Illustrated Newspaper*, 12 Oct. 1862.

116. *Westmorland Gazette*, 8 Nov. 1862; *London Standard*, 15 Nov. 1862.

117. *North Wales Chronicle*, 15 Nov. 1862.

118. *Leeds Mercury*, 24 Nov. 1862; *Dundee Courier*, 25 Nov. 1862.

119. *Western Times*, 6 Dec. 1862.

120. *Nottinghamshire Guardian*, 12 Dec. 1862.

121. *Manchester Guardian*, 13 Dec. 1862; *Glasgow Herald*, 13 Dec. 1862; *Cork Examiner*, 13 Dec. 1862; *Belfast Newsletter*, 15 Dec. 1862; *Preston Chronicle*, 20 Dec. 1862.

122. *Aberdeen Journal*, 31 Dec. 1862; *London Standard*, 31 Dec. 1863; *Liverpool Mercury*, 31 Dec. 1863.

123. *Sheffield Independent*, 29 Dec. 1862; *North Devon Journal*, 1 Jan. 1863; *Glasgow Herald*, 9 Jan. 1863.

124. See Brian Jenkins, "Frank Lawley and the Confederacy," *Civil War History* 23, no. 2 (1977): 144–60. Lawley was the brother of Lord Wenlock and a former MP. He had been Gladstone's private secretary but moved to the United States after a scandal in the mid-1850s (he tried to pay off gambling debts by using confidential financial information). When the South seceded, Lawley sympathized with the North, but he was offended by northern opinion and mindful of what he took to be Britain's interests, so he began to favor the Confederacy.

125. *London Times*, 30 Dec. 1862. See also *Sheffield Independent*, 31 Dec. 1862; *Dundee Courier*, 31 Dec. 1862; *Cork Examiner*, 31 Dec. 1862; *Caledonian Mercury*, 31 Dec. 1862; *Birmingham Daily Post*, 31 Dec. 1862; *Bradford Observer*, 1 Jan. 1863; *Leeds Mercury*, 1 Jan. 1863; *Devizes and Wiltshire Gazette*, 1 Jan. 1863; *Liverpool Mercury*, 2 Jan. 1863; *Newcastle Journal*, 2 Jan. 1863; *Nottinghamshire Guardian*, 2 Jan. 1863; *Hampshire Telegraph*, 3 Jan. 1863; *Leeds Times*, 3 Jan. 1863; *Preston Chronicle*, 3 Jan. 1863; *Lancaster Gazette*, 3 Jan. 1863; *Bury and Norwich Post*, 13 Jan. 1863; *Jackson's Oxford Journal*, 17 Jan. 1863.

126. See, for example, *Lancaster Gazette*, 9 May 1863. Corsan's book would be reissued in 1870. There is a useful introduction in the 1998 edition: *Two Months in the Confederate States: An Englishman's Travels through the South*, ed. Benjamin H. Trask (Baton Rouge: Louisiana State University Press, 1998), xi–xx.

127. *Dundee Courier*, 19 May 1863; *Nottinghamshire Guardian*, 22 May 1863.

128. *Reynolds's Newspaper*, 5 Oct. 1862.

129. *Sheffield Independent*, 12 July 1862; *Newcastle Courant*, 1 Aug. 1862; *Blackburn Standard*, 27 Aug. 1862. On Jackson's nickname, see Robertson, *Stonewall Jackson*, 262–64; Gwynne, *Rebel Yell*, 88–90, 99–103.

130. *Belfast Newsletter*, 30 June 1862; *Liverpool Mercury*, 12 July 1862; *Westmorland Gazette*, 3 Jan. 1863.

131. *Bucks Herald*, 26 July 1862; *Blackburn Standard*, 24 Sept. 1862; *Dundee Courier*, 24 Sept. 1862; *Newcastle Courant*, 26 Sept. 1862; *Essex Standard*, 26 Sept. 1862; *Royal Cornwall Gazette*, 26 Sept. 1862; *Manchester Courier*, 27 Oct. 1862; *Westmorland Gazette*, 27 Oct. 1862; *Caledonian Mercury*, 29 Oct. 1862.

132. *London Times*, 29 Oct. 1862; *Glasgow Herald*, 31 Oct. 1862.

133. See *The American Civil War, An English View: The Writings of Field Marshal Viscount Wolseley*, ed. James A. Rawley (Mechanicsburg, Pa.: Stackpole Books, 2002), ix–xxxvii, 5–45; Ian F. W. Beckett, *The Victorians at War* (London: Hambledon and London, 2003), chap. 1.

134. "A Month's Visit to the Confederate Headquarters, by an English Officer," *Blackwood's Edinburgh Magazine* 93, no. 567 (1863): 21. See also *London Morning Post*, 1 Jan. 1863; *London Times*, 2 Jan. 1862; *Leeds Times*, 3 Jan. 1863; *Leeds Mercury*, 3 Jan. 1863; *Westmorland Gazette*, 3 Jan. 1863; *Bury and Norwich Post*, 13 Jan. 1863.

135. *London Times*, 18 Aug., 16 Sept. 1862; *Manchester Courier*, 23 Aug. 1862.

136. *Lancaster Gazette*, 13 Sept. 1862.

137. *Leeds Mercury*, 17, 19 July 1862; *Freeman's Journal*, 17 July 1862; *Caledonian Mercury*, 18 July 1862; *Manchester Courier*, 19 July 1862; *Leeds Times*, 19 July 1862; *Derby Mercury*, 23 July 1862; *Southampton Herald*, 26 July 1862. Jackson has been treated as an exemplar in spiritual books and Bible studies: John W. Schildt, *Jackson and the Preachers* (Parsons, W.Va.: McClain Printing, 1992); David T. Myers, *Stonewall Jackson: The Spiritual Side* (Harrisonburg, Va.: Sprinkle, 2003). In Kenneth E. Hall, *Stonewall Jackson and Religious Faith in Military Command* (Jefferson, N.C.: McFarland, 2005), chaps. 1–2, Jackson is a "priestly warrior." On his conversion experience, see

Robertson, *Stonewall Jackson*, 134–39. Gwynne, *Rebel Yell*, 146–47, 154, 156–57, points to an intensification of Jackson's faith in the early and mid-1850s (in this period Jackson knew both depths of grief and heights of joy associated with his first marriage, the death of his wife and child, remarriage, domestic comfort, and settled employment).

138. *Blackburn Standard*, 24 Sept. 1862; *Dundee Courier*, 24 Sept. 1862; *Newcastle Courant*, 26 Sept. 1862; *Essex Standard*, 26 Sept. 1862; *Royal Cornwall Gazette*, 26 Sept. 1862; *Manchester Courier*, 27 Oct. 1862; *Westmorland Gazette*, 27 Oct. 1862; *Caledonian Mercury*, 29 Sept. 1862.

139. *Essex Standard*, 8 Oct. 1862; *John Bull*, 18 Oct. 1862; *Proceedings of the Bible Convention of the Confederate States of America, Including the Minutes of the Organization of the Bible Society, Augusta, Ga., March 19th–21st, 1862* (Augusta, Ga.: Constitutionalist, 1862), 15. On the context, see Keith J. Hardman, *Seasons of Refreshing: Evangelism and Revivals in America* (Eugene, Ore.: Wipf and Stock, 2006), chap. 8.

140. *Nottinghamshire Guardian*, 12 Dec. 1862; *Birmingham Daily Post*, 17 Dec. 1862.

141. "Month's Visit to the Confederate Headquarters," 21; *London Morning Post*, 1 Jan. 1863; *London Times*, 2 Jan. 1862; *Leeds Times*, 3 Jan. 1863; *Leeds Mercury*, 3 Jan. 1863; *Westmorland Gazette*, 3 Jan. 1863.

142. *Reynolds's Newspaper*, 11 Jan. 1863; *Freeman's Journal*, 14 Jan. 1863.

143. *London Times*, 30 Dec. 1862; *Sheffield Independent*, 31 Dec. 1862; *Dundee Courier*, 31 Dec. 1862; *Cork Examiner*, 31 Dec. 1862; *Caledonian Mercury*, 31 Dec. 1862; *Birmingham Daily Post*, 31 Dec. 1862; *Bradford Observer*, 1 Jan. 1863; *Leeds Mercury*, 1 Jan. 1863; *Devizes and Wiltshire Gazette*, 1 Jan. 1863; *Liverpool Mercury*, 31 Dec. 1862, 2 Jan. 1863; *Newcastle Journal*, 2 Jan. 1863; *Nottinghamshire Guardian*, 2 Jan. 1863; *Hampshire Telegraph*, 3 Jan. 1863; *Leeds Times*, 3 Jan. 1863; *Preston Chronicle*, 3 Jan. 1863; *Lancaster Gazette*, 3 Jan. 1863; *Bury and Norwich Post*, 13 Jan. 1863; *Jackson's Oxford Journal*, 17 Jan. 1863.

144. "Month's Visit to the Confederate Headquarters," 21; *London Times*, 30 Dec. 1862; *Jackson's Oxford Journal*, 17 Jan. 1863; *Sheffield Independent*, 2 Feb. 1863.

145. *Sheffield Independent*, 11 Mar. 1863.

146. *Liverpool Mercury*, 4 Apr. 1863; *Caledonian Mercury*, 9 Apr. 1863. The Confederate Congress did not change the law on Sunday mails. Gaines M. Foster, *Moral Reconstruction: Christian Lobbyists and the Federal Legislation of Morality, 1865–1920* (Chapel Hill: University of North Carolina Press, 2002), 20–21. Jackson's respect for the Sabbath was a dominant trait: Robertson, *Stonewall Jackson*, 74, 135–36, 148, 176–77, 180–81, 259, 298, 340, 404, 508, 518, 520, 650; Gwynne, *Rebel Yell*, 18, 145, 216, 511; Hall, *Jackson and Religious Faith*, 6, 24, 58.

147. *Newcastle Journal*, 17 Apr. 1863; *Westmorland Gazette*, 18 Apr. 1863.

148. *Manchester Courier*, 21 Mar. 1863.

149. *Stirling Observer*, 1 Jan. 1863.

150. *Caledonian Mercury*, 10 Jan. 1863.

151. *Cheshire Observer*, 31 Jan. 1863.

152. *Dundee Courier*, 21 Jan. 1863; *Stirling Observer*, 29 Jan. 1863.

153. Robertson, *Stonewall Jackson*, 17, 21–22, 168–69, 191–92, 199, 290–91, 668; Gwynne, *Rebel Yell*, 17, 22, 142, 154–56. See also Moorhead, "Churches, Slavery, the Civil War, and Reconstruction," 285–300.

154. See, for example, *Dundee Courier*, 22 July 1862. Jackson's great-grandfather was from County Londonderry, of Scots-Irish stock. He moved to London, where he was arrested for crim-

inal activity. He was transported to America for a seven-year indenture, as was Jackson's great-grandmother, who had also lived in London, though she was possibly born in Ireland. Jackson's father, Jonathan, married Julia Neale, the daughter of Irish immigrants, in 1817. Robertson, *Stonewall Jackson*, 1–8; Gwynne, *Rebel Yell*, 136–38.

155. *Leeds Mercury*, 17, 19 July 1862; *Freeman's Journal*, 17 July 1862; *Caledonian Mercury*, 18 July 1862; *Manchester Courier*, 19 July 1862; *Leeds Times*, 19 July 1862; *Derby Mercury*, 23 July 1862; *Southampton Herald*, 26 July 1862.

156. *London Times*, 4 Sept. 1862; *Glasgow Herald*, 5 Sept. 1862; *Belfast Newsletter*, 6 Sept. 1862; *Illustrated London News*, 6 Dec. 1862.

157. *Manchester Guardian*, 22 Sept. 1862; *Blackburn Standard*, 24 Sept. 1862; *Dundee Courier*, 24 Sept. 1862; *Newcastle Courant*, 26 Sept. 1862; *Essex Standard*, 26 Sept. 1862; *Royal Cornwall Gazette*, 26 Sept. 1862; *Manchester Courier*, 27 Oct. 1862; *Westmorland Gazette*, 27 Oct. 1862; *Caledonian Mercury*, 29 Sept. 1862.

158. *Sheffield Independent*, 3 Oct. 1862.

159. *London Standard*, 23 Oct. 1862.

160. *Nottinghamshire Guardian*, 12 Dec. 1862.

161. *Illustrated London News*, 6 Dec. 1862.

162. *London Standard*, 10 Dec. 1862; *John Bull*, 13 Dec. 1862.

163. *Dundee Courier*, 25 Dec. 1862; *Sheffield Independent*, 29 Dec. 1862; *Stirling Observer*, 1 Jan. 1863; *North Devon Journal*, 1 Jan. 1863; *North Wales Chronicle*, 3 Jan. 1863.

164. "Month's Visit to the Confederate Headquarters," 21. See also *London Morning Post*, 1 Jan. 1863; *London Times*, 2 Jan. 1862; *Leeds Times*, 3 Jan. 1863; *Leeds Mercury*, 3 Jan. 1863; *Westmorland Gazette*, 3 Jan. 1863.

165. *London Times*, 30 Dec. 1862; *Manchester Guardian*, 31 Dec. 1862; *Sheffield Independent*, 31 Dec. 1862; *Dundee Courier*, 31 Dec. 1862; *Cork Examiner*, 31 Dec. 1862; *Caledonian Mercury*, 31 Dec. 1862; *Birmingham Daily Post*, 31 Dec. 1862; *Bradford Observer*, 1 Jan. 1863; *Leeds Mercury*, 1 Jan. 1863; *Devizes and Wiltshire Gazette*, 1 Jan. 1863; *Liverpool Mercury*, 31 Dec. 1862, 2 Jan. 1863; *Newcastle Journal*, 2 Jan. 1863; *Nottinghamshire Guardian*, 2 Jan. 1863; *Hampshire Telegraph*, 3 Jan. 1863; *Leeds Times*, 3 Jan. 1863; *Preston Chronicle*, 3 Jan. 1863; *Lancaster Gazette*, 3 Jan. 1863; *Bury and Norwich Post*, 13 Jan. 1863; *Jackson's Oxford Journal*, 17 Jan. 1863.

166. *London Times*, 11 May 1863; *Glasgow Herald*, 13 May 1863; *Dundee Courier*, 13 May 1863; *Western Times*, 19 May 1863.

167. *London Times*, 30 Aug. 1862; *Westmorland Gazette*, 6 Sept. 1862; *Sheffield Independent*, 27 Sept. 1862.

168. See advertisements in *London Standard*, 29 Aug., 23 Oct. 1862, 12 Feb. 1863.

169. *London Daily News*, 24 Mar. 1863; *Southampton Herald*, 28 Mar. 1863; *John Bull*, 28 Mar. 1863.

170. *Punch*, 18 Oct. 1862; *Westmorland Gazette*, 18 Oct. 1862; *Manchester Times*, 18 Oct. 1862; *Leeds Mercury*, 18 Oct. 1862.

171. *Westmorland Gazette*, 8 Nov. 1862; *Huddersfield Chronicle*, 8 Nov. 1862; *North Devon Journal*, 13 Nov. 1862; *Birmingham Daily Post*, 20 Nov. 1862; *Leicester Chronicle*, 22 Nov. 1862; *Manchester Courier*, 29 Nov. 1862; *Manchester Times*, 6 Dec. 1862; *Lancaster Gazette*, 6 Dec. 1862; *Nottinghamshire Guardian*, 12 Dec. 1862.

172. *Richmond Enquirer*, 6 Dec. 1862. The poet was another officer who had served in the Mexican War, John R. Jackson of Alabama.

173. *Exeter and Plymouth Gazette*, 6 Feb. 1863.

174. *Aberdeen Journal*, 25 Feb. 1863; *Blackburn Standard*, 25 Mar. 1863; *Racing Times*, 6 Oct. 1862, 2 Feb., 4, 11, 25 May 1863; *Bell's Life in London*, 4, 11 Jan., 3, 17, 24 May 1863; *Sporting Gazette*, 10, 17 Jan., 2, 16, 23 May 1863.

175. *Sporting Gazette*, 3 Jan. 1863.

176. *London Times*, 27 Apr., 2 May 1863; *Sheffield Independent*, 1, 5 May 1863; *Birmingham Daily Post*, 1 May 1863; *Liverpool Mercury*, 2 May 1863; *Belfast Newsletter*, 2 May 1863; *Bury and Norwich Post*, 5 May 1863.

177. *Manchester Courier*, 12 July 1862; *Belfast Newsletter*, 22 July 1862.

178. *Parliamentary Debates*, 3rd ser., 18 July 1862, vol. 168, cols. 511–78; *London Daily News*, 19 July 1862.

179. The provincial papers most likely to carry this piece were those that agreed with its viewpoint: see, for example, *Glasgow Herald*, 30 July 1862. On the *Illustrated London News* and Vizetelly, see *Dictionary of Nineteenth-Century Journalism in Great Britain and Ireland*, ed. Laurel Brake and Marysa Demoor (Ghent, Belgium: Academia Press, 2009), 301–3, 653.

180. *London Morning Post*, 14 Aug. 1862.

181. *Exeter Flying Post*, 17 Sept. 1862.

182. *London Standard*, 18 Sept. 1862; *London Daily News*, 23 Sept. 1862; *Cork Examiner*, 25 Sept. 1862. Moran, of the U.S. Legation in London, had heard Hope speak in Parliament before the war and was not impressed. Hope, then MP for Maidstone, "is a man of talents and education, but was exceedingly personal, and talked like a drunken man." *Journal of Benjamin Moran*, 1:319.

183. *Chelmsford Chronicle*, 24 Oct. 1862; *Essex Standard*, 24 Oct. 1862; *London Morning Post*, 24 Oct. 1862; *London Standard*, 24 Oct. 1862; *London Times*, 25 Oct. 1862; *John Bull*, 25 Oct. 1862; *Belfast Newsletter*, 27 Oct. 1862; *Bury and Norwich Post*, 28 Oct. 1862.

184. *London Examiner*, 27 Sept. 1862; *London Standard*, 26 Nov. 1862.

185. See, for example, *Hampshire Telegraph*, 3 Jan. 1863.

186. *London Standard*, 6 Jan. 1863.

187. *Caledonian Mercury*, 10 Jan. 1863; *Fun*, 10 Jan. 1863.

188. *Preston Chronicle*, 13 Dec. 1862; *Illustrated London News*, 14 Dec. 1862; *Blackburn Standard*, 4 Jan. 1863; *Birmingham Daily Post*, 10 Jan. 1863; *Liverpool Mercury*, 12, 13 Feb. 1863.

189. *London Standard*, 22 Jan. 1863; *Bury and Norwich Post*, 27 Jan. 1863; *Derby Mercury*, 28 Jan. 1863.

190. *Athenaeum*, 17 Jan. 1863; *Glasgow Herald*, 24 Jan. 1863.

191. *Dundee Courier*, 21 Jan. 1863; *Stirling Observer*, 29 Jan. 1863; *Cheshire Observer*, 31 Jan. 1863; *Blackburn Standard*, 25 Mar. 1863.

192. See, for example, *Sheffield Independent*, 11 Mar. 1863.

193. *Chelmsford Chronicle*, 13 Mar. 1863.

194. This speech caused controversy in the North as well. See David Work, *Lincoln's Political Generals* (Urbana: University of Illinois Press, 2009), 215.

195. *Speech of Major-General Butler, New York Academy of Music, April 2nd, 1863* (New York: Loyal Publication Society, 1863), 19–21.

196. *Westmorland Gazette*, 18 Apr. 1863; *Belfast Newsletter*, 21 Apr. 1863.

197. *Lancaster Gazette*, 16 May 1863.

198. *Cycle of Adams Letters*, 2:32–33.

199. *Journal of Benjamin Moran*, 2:1167.

8. A REPUTATION SUSTAINED

1. *Manchester Courier*, 30 May 1863; *Glasgow Herald*, 28 May 1863; *Stirling Observer*, 28 May 1863; *London Standard*, 28 May 1863; *John Bull*, 30 May 1863.

2. *London Times*, 26, 28 May 1863; *Western Times*, 26 May 1863; *Liverpool Mercury*, 29 May 1863; *Belfast Newsletter*, 26 May 1863; *Cork Examiner*, 26 May 1863; *Birmingham Daily Post*, 26 May 1863; *Hull Packet*, 29 May 1863; *Dundee Courier*, 26 May 1863; *Sheffield Independent*, 26 May 1863; *Royal Cornwall Gazette*, 29 May 1863; *Lady's Newspaper*, 30 May 1863; *York Herald*, 30 May 1863; *John Bull*, 30 May 1863.

3. *Westmorland Gazette*, 30 May 1863; *London Index*, 28 May, 4 June 1863; *Nottinghamshire Guardian*, 29 May 1863.

4. *Exeter and Plymouth Gazette*, 29 May 1863; *Bury and Norwich Post*, 26 May 1863.

5. Bonner, "Roundheaded Cavalier," 36, 51–53.

6. *Bradford Observer*, 28 May 1863; *Leeds Mercury*, 26 May 1863.

7. *Huddersfield Chronicle*, 30 May 1863; *London Times*, 29 May 1863; *Leeds Mercury*, 26 May 1863.

8. *Leicester Chronicle*, 30 May 1863; *North Wales Chronicle*, 30 May 1863; *Preston Chronicle*, 30 May 1863; *Southampton Herald*, 30 May 1863; *Royal Cornwall Gazette*, 29 May 1863.

9. *Reynolds's Newspaper*, 31 May 1863.

10. *London Morning Post*, 29 May 1863; *Birmingham Daily Post*, 29 May 1863; *Sheffield Independent*, 30 May 1863; *Westmorland Gazette*, 30 May 1863; *Leeds Times*, 30 May 1863; *Western Times*, 2 June 1863; *Derby Mercury*, 3 June 1863.

11. *Sheffield Independent*, 4 June 1863; *Liverpool Mercury*, 4 June 1863; *Birmingham Daily Post*, 6 June 1863; *Dundee Courier*, 6 June 1863; *London Observer*, 8 June 1863; *Derby Mercury*, 10 June 1863; *Blackburn Standard*, 10 June 1863.

12. *Liverpool Mercury*, 30 May 1863; *Manchester Guardian*, 30 May 1863; *Manchester Courier*, 30 May 1863.

13. *Liverpool Mercury*, 2 June 1863; *London Standard*, 1, 2 June 1863; *Sheffield Independent*, 2 June 1863; *Dundee Courier*, 1 June 1863; *Birmingham Daily Post*, 2 June 1863; *Newcastle Journal*, 3 June 1863; *Chelmsford Chronicle*, 5 June 1863; *Royal Cornwall Gazette*, 5 June 1863; *John Bull*, 6 June 1863; *Preston Chronicle*, 6 June 1863; *York Herald*, 6 June 1863; *Newcastle Courant*, 5 June 1863; *Huddersfield Chronicle*, 6 June 1863; *Leeds Times*, 6 June 1863; *Manchester Courier*, 6 June 1863; *Lloyd's Illustrated Newspaper*, 7 June 1863; *Essex Standard*, 10 June 1863.

14. *Bradford Observer*, 4 June 1863.

15. *London Daily News*, 18 June 1863; *London Standard*, 18 June 1863; *Bucks Herald*, 20 June 1863; *Reading Mercury*, 20 June 1863; *London Observer*, 21 June 1863.

16. *Derby Mercury*, 8 July 1863; *Dod's Peerage, Baronetage, and Knightage of Great Britain and Ireland* (London: Sampson Low, Marston, and Co., 1904), 778; Francis White, *History, Gazetteer, and Directory of the County of Derby* (Leeds: James Ward, 1857), 125, 133, 157; *Nottinghamshire Guardian*, 17 July 1863.

17. *London Standard*, 30 June 1863. U.S.-Russian friendship hampered the northern cause in Britain: Campbell, *English Public Opinion*, 96–100, 109.

18. *London Times*, 29 July 1863.

19. *Parliamentary Debates*, 3rd ser., 30 June 1863, vol. 171, cols. 1771–1841, and 10 , 13 July 1863,

vol. 172, cols. 554–71, 661–73. See also Sebrell, *Persuading John Bull*, 124–27; Campbell, *English Public Opinion*, 168–77; Doyle, *Cause of All Nations*, 252–53; Charles M. Hubbard, *The Burden of Confederate Diplomacy* (Knoxville: University of Tennessee Press, 1998), 142–48.

20. *Westmorland Gazette*, 18 July 1863.

21. *London Standard*, 18 Sept. 1863; *Manchester Courier*, 19 Sept. 1863; *Derby Mercury*, 23 Sept. 1863; *Westmorland Gazette*, 26 Sept. 1863; *York Herald*, 26 Sept. 1863. Britain's policy was ridiculed in *Punch*, 5 Sept. 1863:

> Of course we claim the shining fame of glorious Stonewall Jackson
> Who typifies the English race, a sterling Anglo-Saxon
> But for the cause in which he fell we cannot lift a finger
> 'Tis idle on the question any longer here to linger.

22. *Liverpool Mercury*, 17 Oct. 1863; *Birmingham Daily Post*, 19 Oct. 1863; *Caledonian Mercury*, 20 Oct. 1863; *Belfast Newsletter*, 22 Oct. 1863.

23. *Glasgow Herald*, 27 Nov. 1863; *Post Office Glasgow Directory for 1863 and 1864* (Glasgow: William Mackenzie, 1863), 68; *The Scotch Commercial List, Ninth Year* (London: Seyd and Co., 1877), 27; George Stewart, *Progress of Glasgow* (Glasgow: John Baird, 1883), 12.

24. *Glasgow Herald*, 6, 11 Jan. 1864.

25. *London Standard*, 26 Jan. 1864.

26. *London Standard*, 23 Jan. 1864.

27. Amanda Claybaugh, "Trollope and America," in *The Cambridge Companion to Anthony Trollope*, ed. Carolyn Dever and Lisa Niles (Cambridge: Cambridge University Press, 2011), 210–23.

28. See, for example, *Bury and Norwich Post*, 2 Feb. 1864 (letter from "N.L.B." dated 28 Jan.).

29. *Reynolds's Newspaper*, 18 Sept. 1864.

30. *Economist*, 16 July 1864.

31. *Liverpool Mercury*, 19, 20 Oct. 1864; *Manchester Courier*, 20 Oct. 1864.

32. *Manchester Courier*, 28 Oct. 1864; *Standard*, 29 Oct. 1864.

33. *Western Times*, 29 Nov. 1864.

34. *Bristol Daily Post*, 2 Dec. 1864; *Manchester Guardian*, 3 Dec. 1864; *Derby Mercury*, 7 Dec. 1864; *Nottinghamshire Guardian*, 9 Dec. 1864.

35. *Reading Mercury*, 21 Jan. 1865.

36. *Dundee Courier*, 4 Apr. 1865. See also David Macrae, *George Gilfillan: Anecdotes and Reminiscences* (Glasgow: Morison Brothers, 1891), 49–50, 147–49; David C. Carrie, *Dundee and the American Civil War* (Dundee: David Winter, 1953), 6.

37. *Manchester Courier*, 8 Apr. 1865.

38. *London Daily News*, 14 Apr. 1865; *Manchester Courier*, 15 Apr. 1865; *Westmorland Gazette*, 15 Apr. 1865; *John Bull*, 15 Apr. 1865; W. D. Pink and A. B. Beavan, *The Parliamentary Representation of Lancashire, County and Boroughs, 1258–1885* (London: Henry Gray, 1889), 334–35.

39. *London Morning Post*, 26 May 1863; *Birmingham Daily Post*, 26 May 1863; *Dundee Courier*, 26 May 1863; *Bury and Norwich Post*, 26 May 1863; *Sheffield Independent*, 26 May 1863; *Hull Packet*, 29 May 1863; *Nottinghamshire Guardian*, 29 May 1863; *Royal Cornwall Gazette*, 29 May 1863; *Wrexham Weekly Advertiser*, 30 May 1863; *Reading Mercury*, 30 May 1863; *Southampton Herald*, 30 May 1863.

40. *Newcastle Guardian*, 30 May 1863; *Leeds Intelligencer*, 30 May 1863; *Leicestershire Mercury*, 30 May 1863; *Westmorland Gazette*, 30 May 1863.

41. This was in line with southern reactions to Jackson's death: Daniel W. Stowell, "Stonewall Jackson and the Providence of God," in Miller, Stout, and Wilson, *Religion and the American Civil War*, 187–207. See also Rable, *God's Almost Chosen Peoples*, 38, 107–8, 112, 137–38, 140, 151, 232–33, 261–64; Stout, *Upon the Altar of the Nation*, 64, 73, 103–4, 121–22, 127–30, 132, 135–36, 143–44, 150–51, 210–11, 224–25, 227–29, 252, 254, 288, 329, 367, 401; Noll, *Civil War as Theological Crisis*, 84–88, 105.

42. *Bradford Observer*, 4 June 1863; *Lancaster Gazette*, 6 June 1863; *Hereford Journal*, 6 June 1863; *Westmorland Gazette*, 6 June 1863.

43. *Manchester Guardian*, 30 May 1863; *London Index*, 1 June 1863; *Westmorland Gazette*, 6 June 1863; Peyton H. Hoge, *Moses Drury Hoge: Life and Letters* (Richmond, Va.: Whittet and Shepperson, 1899), chap. 8.

44. *John Bull*, 6 June 1863; *Freeman's Journal*, 12 June 1863; *Cork Examiner*, 12 June 1863; *Westmorland Gazette*, 13 June 1863; *Preston Chronicle*, 13 June 1863.

45. *London Daily News*, 4 June 1863.

46. *Western Times*, 2 June 1863.

47. *Leeds Mercury*, 25 June 1863; *Bury and Norwich Post*, 14 July 1863.

48. *Dundee Courier*, 27 Nov. 1863; *United Presbyterian Magazine*, n.s., 7 (1863): 251.

49. *Leicester Chronicle*, 12 Dec. 1863; William White, *History, Gazetteer, and Directory of the Counties of Leicestershire and Rutland* (London: Simpkin and Marshall, 1863), 142, 236.

50. *Norfolk Chronicle*, 8 Aug. 1863; *Belfast Newsletter*, 18 Aug. 1863.

51. See review in *London Morning Post*, 6 Aug. 1863.

52. *Southampton Herald*, 19 Sept. 1863.

53. *Exeter and Plymouth Gazette*, 1 Jan. 1864.

54. Catherine C. Hopley, *"Stonewall" Jackson, Late General of the Confederate States Army: A Biographical Sketch, and an Outline of His Virginian Campaigns. By the Author of "Life in the South"* (London: Chapman and Hall, 1863), v, 12–13; *John Bull*, 12, 26 Sept., 3, 10 Oct. 1863; *London Observer*, 14 Sept., 4, 11, 12 Oct. 1863; *London Times*, 21 Oct. 1863; *Friend of India*, 12 Nov. 1863; *London Standard*, 26 Mar. 1864.

55. Arthur L. Fremantle, *Three Months in the Southern States* (New York: John Bradburn, 1864), 46, 65, 116–17, 126, 140. For extracts and reviews, see *Westmorland Gazette*, 5 Sept. 1863; *Manchester Courier*, 5 Sept. 1863; *Blackburn Standard*, 9 Sept. 1863; *Exeter Flying Post*, 9 Sept. 1863; *Manchester Guardian*, 11 Sept. 1863; *Bradford Observer*, 17 Sept. 1863; *Belfast Newsletter*, 19 Nov. 1863; *North Devon Journal*, 26 Nov. 1863; *Royal Cornwall Gazette*, 8 Jan. 1864; *Economist*, 18 June 1864; *Devizes and Wiltshire Gazette*, 30 June 1864.

56. *Manchester Courier*, 20 Oct. 1864.

57. Robertson, *Stonewall Jackson*, 759; Gwynne, *Rebel Yell*, 487, 557, 568; Wallace Hettle, *Inventing Stonewall Jackson: A Civil War Hero in History and Memory* (Baton Rouge: Louisiana State University Press, 2011), 47.

58. Robert L. Dabney, *Life of Lieutenant-General Thomas J. Jackson* (London: J. Nisbet, 1864), 1:62–63, 65, 78, 94–95.

59. *Manchester Times*, 31 Dec. 1864.

60. *Leeds Times*, 28 Jan. 1865.

61. *Manchester Times*, 21 Jan. 1865; *Sheffield Daily Telegraph*, 24 Jan. 1865; *London Morning Post*, 2 Mar. 1865.

62. *London Times*, 17 Jan. 1865.

63. *Christian Observer*, n.s., no. 326 (Feb. 1865): 120–28.

64. Robert Mackenzie, *America and Her Army* (London: T. Nelson, 1865), 12–13, 31; *Dundee Courier*, 27 Feb. 1865.

65. *Monthly Packet of Evening Readings for Younger Members of the English Church*, 1 Jan., 1 Mar., 1 Apr., 1 Sept., 1 Oct. 1865.

66. See, for example, *Worcester Journal*, 30 May 1863.

67. *Liverpool Mercury*, 26 May 1863; *Freeman's Journal*, 26 May 1863; *Glasgow Herald*, 26 May 1863.

68. *Belfast Newsletter*, 26 May 1863; *Dundee Courier*, 26 May 1863; *London Morning Post*, 26 May 1863.

69. *Royal Cornwall Gazette*, 29 May 1863; *Hull Packet*, 29 May 1863; *Birmingham Daily Post*, 28 May 1863; *Cork Examiner*, 29 May 1863; *Manchester Guardian*, 12 June 1863; *London Times*, 16, 17 June 1863.

70. *Stirling Observer*, 28 May 1863; *Sheffield Independent*, 26 May 1863; *Isle of Wight Observer*, 30 May 1863; *Leeds Times*, 30 May 1863; *Manchester Courier*, 30 May 1863; *North Devon Journal*, 28 May 1863; *Exeter and Plymouth Gazette*, 29 May 1863; *Norfolk Chronicle*, 30 May 1863; *Northampton Mercury*, 30 May 1863; *Bell's Life in London*, 31 May 1863.

71. *Southampton Herald*, 30 May 1863.

72. *Era*, 31 May 1863.

73. *Devizes and Wiltshire Gazette*, 4 June 1863; *North Devon Journal*, 4 June 1863; *Western Times*, 2 June 1863; *Lancaster Gazette*, 30 May 1863; *Hampshire Telegraph*, 30 May 1863; *John Bull*, 6 June 1863.

74. *Bradford Observer*, 4 June 1863; *Lancaster Gazette*, 6 June 1863; *Hereford Journal*, 6 June 1863.

75. *London Daily News*, 4 June 1863.

76. *Reading Mercury*, 30 May 1863; *York Herald*, 30 May 1863.

77. *London Observer*, 25 May 1863; *Hull Packet*, 29 May 1863; *Exeter and Plymouth Gazette*, 29 May 1863; *Westmorland Gazette*, 30 May 1863; *Norfolk Chronicle*, 30 May 1863; *Leicester Chronicle*, 30 May 1863; *Northampton Mercury*, 30 May 1863; *Newcastle Guardian*, 30 May 1863; *Leicestershire Mercury*, 30 May 1863; *Leeds Mercury*, 30 May 1863; *Jackson's Oxford Journal*, 30 May 1863; *Essex Standard*, 29 May, 3 June 1863; *North Devon Journal*, 28 May, 4 June 1863.

78. *Freeman's Journal*, 12 June 1863; *Cork Examiner*, 12 June 1863; *Westmorland Gazette*, 13, 20 June 1863; *Preston Chronicle*, 13 June 1863; *Dundee Courier*, 18, 19 June 1863; *Worcester Journal*, 20 June 1863.

79. *Manchester Guardian*, 5 June 1863; *Nottinghamshire Guardian*, 5 June 1863; *Lancaster Gazette*, 6 June 1863; *Leeds Times*, 6 June 1863; *Newcastle Journal*, 6 June 1863; *Derby Mercury*, 10 June 1863; *Westmorland Gazette*, 13 June 1863.

80. *Birmingham Daily Post*, 6 June 1863; *Sheffield Independent*, 9 June 1863; *Dundee Courier*, 9 June 1863; *Exeter Flying Post*, 10 June 1863; *Derby Mercury*, 10 June 1863; *Cork Examiner*, 11 June 1863; *Hull Packet*, 12 June 1863; *Leeds Intelligencer*, 13 June 1863; *Preston Chronicle*, 13 June 1863.

81. *Exeter and Plymouth Gazette*, 29 May 1863; *Chelmsford Chronicle*, 29 May 1863; *Newcastle Courant*, 29 May 1863; *Jackson's Oxford Journal*, 30 May 1863; *London Times*, 28 June 1863; *Manches-*

ter Guardian, 29 June, 21 July 1863; *Liverpool Mercury*, 29, 30 June, 7 July 1863; *Westmorland Gazette*, 4 July 1863; *North Wales Chronicle*, 4 July 1863; *Leeds Times*, 4 July 1863; *Lancaster Gazette*, 4 July 1863; *John Bull*, 22 Aug. 1863.

82. *London Morning Post*, 6 Aug. 1863.

83. *Westmorland Gazette*, 18 July 1863.

84. Fremantle, *Three Months in the Southern States*, 106.

85. *Cheshire Observer*, 12 Dec. 1863.

86. *Caledonian Mercury*, 5 Nov. 1863.

87. *London Times*, 1, 20 Jan. 1864; *Westmorland Gazette*, 2 Jan. 1864; *Bury and Norwich Post*, 5 Jan. 1864; *London Morning Post*, 1 Jan. 1864; *Cheshire Observer*, 2 Jan. 1864; *Glasgow Herald*, 1 Jan. 1864; *Leeds Mercury*, 1 Jan. 1864 (citing the *London Times*, 26 May 1863); *London Standard*, 1, 2 Jan. 1864; *Sheffield Daily Telegraph*, 2 Jan. 1864.

88. *Cycle of Adams Letters*, 2:51, 56–58.

89. Bela Estvàn, *War Pictures from the South*, 2 vols. (London: Routledge, Warne, and Routledge, 1863), 1:111–12, 141–42, 156–57, 160–64, 176, 189, 217–18, 221–24; *Friend of India*, 6 Aug. 1863; *London Morning Post*, 13 Aug. 1863; *Manchester Times*, 26 Mar. 1864.

90. *London Morning Post*, 17 Sept. 1863.

91. *Morpeth Herald*, 9 Apr. 1864; *Derbyshire Times*, 9 Apr. 1864.

92. *Westmorland Gazette*, 7 May 1864.

93. *Birmingham Daily Post*, 9 June 1864; *Belfast Newsletter*, 15 June 1864.

94. *Birmingham Daily Post*, 14 July 1864. There were different versions of this story, possibly based on a narrow escape at Port Republic in June 1862. See Elihu S. Riley, *A Thesaurus of Anecdotes and Incidents in the Life of Lieutenant-General Thomas Jonathan Jackson, C.S.A.* (Annapolis, Md.: Riley's Historic Series, 1920), 54–57; Robertson, *Stonewall Jackson*, 430–35; Gwynne, *Rebel Yell*, 312–19.

95. *Sheffield Independent*, 13 Aug. 1864; *Manchester Guardian*, 13 Aug. 1864; *Dundee Courier*, 15 Aug. 1864; *Freeman's Journal*, 16 Aug. 1864; *Glasgow Herald*, 17 Aug. 1864; *Chelmsford Chronicle*, 19 Aug. 1864; *Westmorland Gazette*, 20 Aug. 1864.

96. *London Daily News*, 29 July 1864.

97. *Manchester Guardian*, 24 Aug. 1864.

98. Charles Mayo, "The Medical Service of the Federal Army," in *Vacation Tourists and Notes of Travel, 1862–1863*, ed. Francis Galton (London: Macmillan, 1864), chap. 9.

99. *London Morning Post*, 18 July 1864; *Liverpool Mercury*, 18, 19 July 1864; *London Standard*, 19 July, 26 Aug. 1864; *London Times*, 23 Aug., 8 Oct. 1864; *Leeds Times*, 27 Aug. 1864; *Bucks Herald*, 27 Aug. 1864; *Reynolds's Newspaper*, 28 Aug. 1864; *Manchester Courier*, 6 Sept. 1864; *Belfast Newsletter*, 18 July, 8 Sept. 1864; *Huddersfield Chronicle*, 10 Sept. 1864.

100. *Lancaster Gazette*, 4 June 1864; *Sheffield Independent*, 14 June 1864.

101. *London Times*, 5 Nov. 1864.

102. *Southampton Herald*, 7 Jan. 1865; *London Standard*, 19 Jan. 1865; Dabney, *Life of Jackson*, 1:46–52, 212, 226; *Westmorland Gazette*, 24 Dec. 1864; *Leeds Times*, 28 Jan. 1865; *Huddersfield Chronicle*, 31 Dec. 1864; *Friend of India*, 29 Dec. 1864, 5 Jan. 1865; *Manchester Times*, 31 Dec. 1864, 7 Jan. 1865; *London Morning Post*, 2 Mar. 1865.

103. *Leeds Mercury*, 17 Apr. 1865.

104. *London Standard*, 19 Jan. 1865; *Belfast Newsletter*, 21 Jan. 1865.

105. *Globe*, 25 May 1863; *Manchester Guardian*, 26 May 1863; *Birmingham Daily Post*, 26 May 1863; *Sheffield Independent*, 26, 30 May 1863; *Cork Examiner*, 28 May 1863; *Hull Packet*, 29 May 1863; *Reading Mercury*, 30 May 1863; *Westmorland Gazette*, 30 May 1863; *Newcastle Guardian*, 30 May 1863; *Leicestershire Mercury*, 30 May 1863; *London Examiner*, 30 May 1863; *Lloyd's Illustrated Newspaper*, 31 May 1863.

106. *Stirling Observer*, 28 May 1863; *Leeds Intelligencer*, 30 May 1863; *Wrexham Weekly Advertiser*, 30 May 1863; *Reading Mercury*, 30 May 1863; *Manchester Courier*, 30 May 1863; *Westmorland Gazette*, 30 May 1863; *Royal Cornwall Gazette*, 29 May 1863; *Sheffield Independent*, 26 May 1863.

107. "Stonewall Jackson," *Saturday Review* 15, no. 396, 30 May 1863, 689–90; *Westmorland Gazette*, 6 June 1863; *Sheffield Independent*, 2 June 1863; *Reynolds's Newspaper*, 31 May 1863; *Isle of Wight Observer*, 30 May 1863; *Cheshire Observer*, 30 May 1863.

108. *Lancaster Gazette*, 30 May 1863; *North Devon Journal*, 4 June 1863; *Westmorland Gazette*, 6, 20 June 1863; *Newcastle Journal*, 18 June 1863; *Liverpool Mercury*, 18 June 1863; *Dundee Courier*, 18, 19 June 1863; *Nottinghamshire Guardian*, 19 June 1863; *Newcastle Courant*, 19 June 1863.

109. *Dundee Courier*, 26 May, 9 June 1863; *Nottinghamshire Guardian*, 29 May 1863; *Manchester Guardian*, 4 June 1863; *London Times*, 6, 11 June 1863; *Glasgow Herald*, 6 June 1863; *Birmingham Daily Post*, 6 June 1863; *Sheffield Independent*, 9 June 1863; *Exeter Flying Post*, 10 June 1863; *Hull Packet*, 12 June 1863; *Leeds Intelligencer*, 13 June 1863; *Preston Chronicle*, 13 June 1863.

110. *London Morning Post*, 6 Aug. 1863.

111. *Dundee Courier*, 28 Oct. 1863; *Newcastle Guardian*, 31 Oct. 1863; *Westmorland Gazette*, 31 Oct. 1863; *John Bull*, 31 Oct. 1863.

112. *London Morning Post*, 17 Sept. 1863; *London Standard*, 26 Mar. 1864.

113. *Westmorland Gazette*, 5 Sept. 1863; *Manchester Courier*, 5 Sept. 1863; *Blackburn Standard*, 9 Sept. 1863; *Exeter Flying Post*, 9 Sept. 1863; *Bradford Observer*, 17 Sept. 1863; *Belfast Newsletter*, 19 Nov. 1863; *North Devon Journal*, 26 Nov. 1863; *Royal Cornwall Gazette*, 8 Jan. 1864; *Economist*, 18 June 1864; *Devizes and Wiltshire Gazette*, 30 June 1864.

114. *Leeds Times*, 12 Dec. 1863; *Aberdeen Journal*, 23 Dec. 1863.

115. *Manchester Courier*, 25 Aug. 1864.

116. *Leeds Mercury*, 9 Aug. 1864.

117. *Dundee Courier*, 4 Apr. 1865.

118. *Leeds Mercury*, 19 Dec. 1864; *Westmorland Gazette*, 24 Dec. 1864; *Manchester Times*, 31 Dec. 1864; *London Morning Post*, 2 Mar. 1865.

119. *Devizes and Wiltshire Gazette*, 28 May 1863; *Exeter and Plymouth Gazette*, 29 May 1863; *Newcastle Journal*, 1 June 1863; *Liverpool Mercury*, 1 June 1863; *Era*, 31 May 1863; *Friend of India*, 18, 25 June, 2 July 1863.

120. *Lancaster Gazette*, 30 May 1863; *Leeds Intelligencer*, 30 May 1863; *Leeds Times*, 30 May 1863.

121. *London Daily News*, 26 May 1863; *Caledonian Mercury*, 26 May 1863; *London Standard*, 26 May 1863; *Western Times*, 26 May 1863; *Freeman's Journal*, 26 May 1863; *Bury and Norwich Post*, 26 May 1863; *Birmingham Daily Post*, 26 May 1863; *North Devon Journal*, 28 May 1863; *Bradford Observer*, 28 May 1863; *Exeter and Plymouth Gazette*, 29 May 1863; *Chelmsford Chronicle*, 29 May 1863; *Royal Cornwall Gazette*, 29 May 1863; *Preston Chronicle*, 30 May 1863; *Wrexham Weekly Advertiser*, 30 May 1863; *Norfolk Chronicle*, 30 May 1863; *Leicester Chronicle*, 30 May 1863; *Northampton Mercury*, 30 May 1863; *Leicestershire Mercury*, 30 May 1863; *Hull Packet*, 5 June 1863; *York Herald*, 30 May, 6 June 1863; *Manchester Courier*, 6 June 1863; *Hereford Journal*, 6 June 1863; *Worcester Journal*, 6 June

1863; *Bucks Herald*, 6 June 1863; *Cork Examiner*, 16 June 1863; *Leeds Mercury*, 26, 28 May, 17 June 1863; *Glasgow Herald*, 17 June 1863; *Belfast Newsletter*, 26 May, 17 June 1863; *Sheffield Independent*, 26 May, 17, 18 June 1863; *Newcastle Journal*, 26, 28 May, 18 June 1863; *Liverpool Mercury*, 26 May, 16, 17, 18 June 1863; *Dundee Courier*, 26 May, 17, 18, 19 June 1863; *Nottinghamshire Guardian*, 29 May, 19 June 1863; *Newcastle Courant*, 29 May, 19 June 1863; *Westmorland Gazette*, 20 June 1863; *Leeds Intelligencer*, 20 June 1863.

122. *Manchester Guardian*, 26, 27, 28 May, 1 June 1863; *Exeter and Plymouth Gazette*, 29 May 1863; *Newcastle Guardian*, 30 May 1863; *Morpeth Herald*, 30 May 1863; *Norfolk Chronicle*, 30 May 1863; *Northampton Mercury*, 30 May 1863; *Cork Examiner*, 30 May 1863; *Bristol Mercury*, 30 May 1863; *Lancaster Gazette*, 30 May 1863; *London Examiner*, 30 May 1863; *Jackson's Oxford Journal*, 30 May 1863; *Derbyshire Times*, 30 May 1863; *Hampshire Telegraph*, 30 May 1863; *Lloyd's Illustrated Newspaper*, 31 May 1863; *Anti-Slavery Monthly Reporter*, 1 June 1863; *London Times*, 1, 5 June 1863; *London Morning Post*, 1 June 1863; *London Daily News*, 1 June 1863; *Liverpool Mercury*, 28 May, 1 June 1863; *Glasgow Herald*, 1 June 1863; *Sheffield Independent*, 30 May, 1 June 1863; *Leeds Mercury*, 30 May, 2 June 1863; *Newcastle Journal*, 2 June 1863; *Dundee Courier*, 2 June 1863; *Bury and Norwich Post*, 2 June 1863; *Aberdeen Journal*, 3 June 1863; *Essex Standard*, 29 May, 3 June 1863; *Derby Mercury*, 3 June 1863; *Hull Packet*, 29 May, 5 June 1863; *John Bull*, 6 June 1863; *York Herald*, 6 June 1863; *Southampton Herald*, 6 June 1863; *Huddersfield Chronicle*, 30 May, 6 June 1863; *Reading Mercury*, 30 May, 6 June 1863; *Leicester Chronicle*, 6 June 1863; *Preston Chronicle*, 6 June 1863; *Leeds Times*, 30 May, 6 June 1863; *Manchester Courier*, 6 June 1863; *Hereford Journal*, 6 June 1863; *Leicestershire Mercury*, 6 June 1863; *Worcester Journal*, 6 June 1863; *Bucks Herald*, 30 May, 6 June 1863; *Reynolds's Newspaper*, 7 June 1863; *Friend of India*, 11 June 1863.

123. *Blackburn Standard*, 10 June 1863; *Stirling Observer*, 11 June 1863; *Westmorland Gazette*, 13 June 1863; *Leeds Times*, 27 June 1863.

124. *Sheffield Independent*, 10 June 1863; *Dundee Courier*, 11 June 1863; *Wrexham Weekly Advertiser*, 13 June 1863; *Lancaster Gazette*, 13 June 1863; *Leicester Chronicle*, 13 June 1863.

125. *Liverpool Mercury*, 27 June 1863.

126. *Bradford Observer*, 16 July 1863.

127. *Bury and Norwich Post*, 26 May 1863; *Exeter and Plymouth Gazette*, 29 May 1863.

128. *London Morning Post*, 13 Aug. 1863.

129. *Hereford Journal*, 15 Aug. 1863.

130. *London Daily News*, 2 Nov. 1863; *Manchester Guardian*, 2 Nov. 1863.

131. *London Standard*, 21 July, 1 Sept. 1863, 2 Jan. 1864.

132. *Bradford Observer*, 31 Dec. 1863; Masur, *Lincoln's Last Speech*, 73–74, 80–82, 88, 97–99, 105–6, 110–14.

133. *London Times*, 24 Nov. 1863, 1 Jan. 1864; *Newcastle Courant*, 8 Jan. 1864.

134. *Bucks Herald*, 18 June 1864.

135. *Glasgow Herald*, 23 May 1864; *Leeds Mercury*, 24 May 1864; *Liverpool Mercury*, 25 May 1864; *Bradford Observer*, 26 May 1864.

136. *London Standard*, 21 Sept. 1864. What Seward actually said was that war measures—including those concerning slavery—would automatically cease once the war was over. *The Great Issues: Speech of William H. Seward, Delivered at Auburn, N.Y., September 3, 1864* (New York: n.p., 1864).

137. *London Morning Post*, 17 Sept. 1864; *John Bull*, 17 Sept. 1864; *Liverpool Mercury*, 20 Sept. 1864; *Sheffield Daily Telegraph*, 20 Sept. 1864; *Birmingham Daily Post*, 22 Sept. 1864; *Nottinghamshire Guardian*, 23 Sept. 1864.

138. *Liverpool Mercury*, 11 Oct. 1864; *Birmingham Gazette*, 15 Oct. 1864.

139. "A Visit to the Cities and Camps of the Confederate States, 1863–64," *Blackwood's Edinburgh Magazine* 96, no. 590 (Dec. 1864): 645–70; *Glasgow Herald*, 30 Nov., 3 Dec. 1864. The whole series was published in book form in 1865 and later reissued: FitzGerald Ross, *Cities and Camps of the Confederate States*, ed. Richard Barksdale Harwell (Urbana: University of Illinois Press, 1997).

140. *Dundee Courier*, 3 Dec. 1864.

141. *Sheffield Daily Telegraph*, 7 Jan. 1865; T. P. Shaffner, *History of the United States of America: From the Earliest Period to the Present Time* (London: London Printing and Publishing Co., 1864), 1:i–xxxvi.

142. *Leeds Mercury*, 21 Feb. 1865.

143. *London Standard*, 16 Mar. 1865; *Manchester Courier*, 17 Mar. 1865.

144. *London Morning Post*, 2 Mar. 1865.

145. *Cork Examiner*, 5 Apr. 1865.

146. *Manchester Times*, 15 Apr. 1865; *Sheffield Independent*, 20 Apr. 1865; *North Devon Journal*, 20 Apr. 1865; *Manchester Guardian*, 25 Apr. 1865.

147. *London Times*, 11 June 1863; *Freeman's Journal*, 12 June 1863; *Cork Examiner*, 12 June 1863; *Westmorland Gazette*, 13 June 1863; *Preston Chronicle*, 13 June 1863.

148. *Exeter and Plymouth Gazette*, 29 May 1863; *Western Times*, 26 May 1863.

149. *Manchester Guardian*, 11 Aug. 1862.

150. *Exeter Flying Post*, 7 Oct. 1863; *Manchester Guardian*, 7 Oct. 1863; *Bradford Observer*, 8 Oct. 1863; *Wrexham Weekly Advertiser*, 10 Oct. 1863; *Preston Chronicle*, 10 Oct. 1863; *Manchester Courier*, 10 Oct. 1863; *Leicester Chronicle*, 10 Oct. 1863; *Leeds Intelligencer*, 10 Oct. 1863; *Leeds Times*, 10 Oct. 1863; *Lancaster Gazette*, 10 Oct 1863; *Derby Mercury*, 14 Oct. 1863; *Blackburn Standard*, 14 Oct. 1863.

151. Sections of the book had already been published in *Blackwood's Edinburgh Magazine*. There are notices in *Westmorland Gazette*, 5 Sept. 1863; *Manchester Courier*, 5 Sept. 1863; *Blackburn Standard*, 9 Sept. 1863; *Exeter Flying Post*, 9 Sept. 1863.

152. *Manchester Courier*, 5 Jan. 1864. See also John Hohenberg, *Foreign Correspondence: The Great Reporters and Their Times* (Syracuse, N.Y.: Syracuse University Press, 1995), 26–30.

153. *Derby Mercury*, 6, 20 Jan. 1864.

154. *Sheffield Daily Telegraph*, 14 Jan. 1864.

155. *London Observer*, 8 Nov. 1863; *Manchester Courier*, 8 Feb. 1864; *Leeds Intelligencer*, 13 Feb. 1864. The first chapter of Daniel's book had already been published: *Manchester Guardian*, 6 June 1863. See also John Moncure, "John M. Daniel: The Editor of *The Examiner*," *Sewanee Review* 15, no. 3 (1907): 257–70; Peter Bridges, *Pen of Fire: John Moncure Daniel* (Kent, Ohio: Kent State University Press, 2002).

156. See, for example, *London Standard*, 26 Mar. 1864.

157. *Manchester Courier*, 1 Feb. 1864; *Birmingham Daily Post*, 18 Feb. 1864; *London Morning Post*, 3 Mar. 1864.

158. *London Morning Post*, 17 May 1864; *London Standard*, 18 May 1864.

159. Harold Holzer, "Virginians See Their War," in *Virginia at War, 1862*, ed. William C. Davis

and James I. Robertson Jr. (Lexington: University Press of Kentucky, 2007), 110; Bennett, *London Confederates*, 114; Blackett, *Divided Hearts*, 166; *London Times*, 26 June 1863; *Liverpool Mercury*, 18 July 1863.

160. *Liverpool Mercury*, 1 Dec. 1864.

161. *Belfast Newsletter*, 16 Aug. 1864.

162. *Manchester Courier*, 20 Feb. 1865.

163. *Manchester Courier*, 1 Feb., 22 Nov. 1864; *Christian Observer*, n.s., no. 326 (Feb. 1865): 120–28; *London Morning Post*, 25 Jan. 1865; *Caledonian Mercury*, 25 Jan. 1865; *Stirling Observer*, 12, 19, 26 Jan., 2, 9, 16 Feb. 1865; *London Standard*, 31 Jan., 13 Apr. 1865; *London Daily News*, 19 Apr. 1865.

164. *London Morning Post*, 2 Mar. 1865.

165. *Nottinghamshire Guardian*, 12 Aug. 1864; *London Standard*, 11, 12, 13, 16, 18, 20, 22, 23 July, 9 Aug. 1864, 6 Jan. 1865; *London Morning Post*, 5, 6 Jan. 1865; *Bury and Norwich Post*, 17 Jan. 1865; *Belfast Newsletter*, 27 Jan. 1865; *Northampton Mercury*, 31 Dec. 1864, 28 Jan., 25 Feb. 1865; *Jackson's Oxford Journal*, 25 Feb. 1865; *Era*, 14 Aug., 11 Dec. 1864, 8, 22 Jan., 5 Feb., 5 Mar. 1865; *Sheffield Daily Telegraph*, 1 Apr. 1865.

166. *Nottinghamshire Guardian*, 23 Oct. 1863.

167. *London Times*, 13, 16, 21 July 1864; *London Standard*, 18, 22 July 1864; *Manchester Guardian*, 29 Nov. 1864.

168. *Nottinghamshire Guardian*, 29 May 1863; *London Standard*, 2 June 1863; *Southampton Herald*, 6 June 1863.

169. *Worcester Journal*, 6 June 1863.

170. *Stirling Observer*, 2 July 1863; *Western Times*, 7 July 1863.

171. *Manchester Guardian*, 19 Nov. 1864.

172. *Hampshire Telegraph*, 11 July 1863; *Cheshire Observer*, 11 July 1863; *Western Times*, 14 July 1863; *Dundee Courier*, 14 July 1863; *Westmorland Gazette*, 18 July 1863; *Chelmsford Chronicle*, 24 July 1863; *Glasgow Herald*, 17, 22 Dec. 1863; *Caledonian Mercury*, 7 July, 18, 21 Dec. 1863; *Liverpool Mercury*, 7 July, 21 Dec. 1863; *York Herald*, 26 Dec. 1863; *Stirling Observer*, 31 Dec. 1863; *Sheffield Independent*, 21 Dec. 1863, 9 Jan. 1864; *Birmingham Daily Post*, 19 Dec. 1863, 11 Jan. 1864.

173. *Belfast Newsletter*, 24 Mar. 1865.

174. *London Standard*, 26 Aug. 1864; *Sheffield Daily Telegraph*, 26 Aug. 1864; *London Daily News*, 26 Aug. 1864; *Leeds Intelligencer*, 27 Aug. 1864; *Leeds Times*, 27 Aug. 1864; *Hampshire Telegraph*, 27 Aug. 1864; *Freeman's Journal*, 27 Aug. 1864; *Dundee Courier*, 27 Aug. 1864; *Cheshire Observer*, 27 Aug. 1864; *Belfast Newsletter*, 27 Aug. 1864; *Blackburn Standard*, 31 Aug. 1864; *Bradford Observer*, 1 Sept. 1864; *North Devon Journal*, 1 Sept. 1864; *Devizes and Wiltshire Gazette*, 1 Sept. 1864; *Exeter and Plymouth Gazette*, 2 Sept. 1864; *Essex Standard*, 31 Aug., 2 Sept. 1864; *London Morning Post*, 26 Aug., 12 Oct. 1864; *Sheffield Independent*, 27 Aug. 1864, 28 Feb. 1865; *London Observer*, 11 June 1865.

175. See advertisements in *London Observer*, 19 June 1864; *Leeds Intelligencer*, 25 June 1864; *Sheffield Independent*, 28 June 1864; *Royal Cornwall Gazette*, 1 July 1864; *London Standard*, 21 Nov. 1864; *London Morning Post*, 19 Jan. 1865.

176. *Stirling Observer*, 3 Dec. 1863; *Preston Chronicle*, 16 July 1864; *Sporting Gazette*, 30 May, 20, 27 June, 18 July, 15 Aug. 1863, 18 Feb., 11 Mar., 6 May 1865; *Bell's Life in London*, 31 May, 14, 21 June, 19 July 1863, 2 Jan., 2 Apr., 9 July, 10 Sept. 1864, 11 Mar., 6 May, 23 Sept. 1865; *Racing Times*, 1, 15 June, 20 July 1863; *Sporting Chronicle*, 13 June 1863; *London Times*, 11 June, 14 Aug. 1863; *Manchester Guardian*, 18 July 1863, 12 July 1864.

177. *Manchester Guardian*, 18 Feb. 1865; *Leeds Mercury*, 1, 4 Mar. 1865; *London Standard*, 15 Feb., 3 Apr. 1865; *London Observer*, 2 Apr. 1865; *Sheffield Daily Telegraph*, 3 Apr. 1865; *London Morning Post*, 3 Apr. 1865; *Manchester Courier*, 3 Apr. 1865; *Liverpool Mercury*, 1 Mar., 3 Apr. 1865; *London Daily News*, 3 Apr. 1865; *Caledonian Mercury*, 3 Apr. 1865; *Manchester Times*, 8 Apr. 1865; *Morpeth Herald*, 8 Apr. 1865; *North Wales Chronicle*, 8 Apr. 1865; *Bucks Herald*, 8 Apr. 1865; *Bristol Mercury*, 8 Apr. 1865; *Hampshire Telegraph*, 8 Apr. 1865.

178. *London Times*, 12 Nov. 1863, 3 Mar. 1864.

179. Gwynne, *Rebel Yell*, 140.

180. *Liverpool Mercury*, 24 June 1864; *Sheffield Independent*, 25 June 1864; *Westmorland Gazette*, 25 June 1864; *Birmingham Daily Post*, 27 June 1864; *Freeman's Journal*, 28 June 1864; *Nottinghamshire Guardian*, 1 July 1864.

181. *Leeds Mercury*, 25 June 1863; *Liverpool Mercury*, 27 June 1863.

182. See, for example, *London Times*, 31 Dec. 1863.

183. *London Times*, 23 July, 15 Sept. 1864.

9. STONEWALL JACKSON'S POSTWAR LONGEVITY

1. Lord Wolseley, *The Story of a Soldier's Life*, 2 vols. (New York: Scribners, 1903–4), 2:140–41; *Yorkshire Evening Post*, 16 Nov. 1903.

2. *Glasgow Herald*, 20 Jan. 1870.

3. *London Standard*, 8 Jan. 1866.

4. William Parker Snow, *Southern Generals: Who They Are and What They Have Done* (New York: Charles B. Richardson, 1865), 170, 176–78, 189–90, 192, 197, 201–2, 205, 208, 211. A more recent study of Confederate generals has pointed out that a seeking after righteousness seems not to have moved many of them. Jackson was an exception. Robert H. Croskery, "Religious Rebels: The Religious Views and Motivations of Confederate Generals in the American Civil War" (PhD diss., University of Western Ontario, 2013), 4, 41. On the survival of "Christian nationalist" sentiment in the South, see Edward H. Sebesta and Euan Hague, "The U.S. Civil War as a Theological War: Confederate Christian Nationalism and the League of the South," *Canadian Review of American Studies* 32, no. 3 (2002): 253–83.

5. *Manchester Courier*, 11 Nov. 1865.

6. *London Standard*, 8 Jan. 1866.

7. *Glasgow Herald*, 19 Oct. 1866; *Huddersfield Chronicle*, 27 Oct. 1866.

8. Cooke gave publishers and readers what they wanted, presenting Jackson as a mix of greatness and quirkiness. Hettle, *Inventing Stonewall Jackson*, 53–68.

9. *Manchester Times*, 1 Dec. 1866. Dabney's book was advertised and discussed across the empire: *Friend of India*, 1 Nov. 1866, 6, 13 Feb., 3 Sept. 1868; *Australasian* (Melbourne), 24 Nov., 1 Dec. 1866, 5 Jan. 1867. A report on missionary work in New Zealand stressed the need for a Jackson-like spirit. *Mission Field*, no. 137 (May 1867): 207.

10. *Glasgow Herald*, 27 Oct. 1866.

11. Christopher R. Lawton, "The Pilgrim's Progress: Thomas J. Jackson's Journey toward Civility and Citizenship," *Virginia Magazine of History and Biography* 116, no. 1 (2008): 2–41.

12. *Leeds Mercury*, 6 Aug. 1868; *Sheffield Daily Telegraph*, 7 Aug. 1868; *Liverpool Mercury*, 7 Aug.

1868; *Manchester Times*, 8 Aug. 1868; *Derby Mercury*, 12 Aug. 1868; *Royal Cornwall Gazette*, 13 Aug. 1868; *North Devon Journal*, 13 Aug. 1868; *Chelmsford Chronicle*, 21 Aug. 1868.

13. *London Observer*, 22 Sept. 1867.

14. *Western Times*, 11 June 1869; *Exeter and Plymouth Gazette*, 13 June 1869.

15. *North Devon Journal*, 21 July 1870.

16. See, for example, *Newcastle Courant*, 20 June 1873.

17. See, for example, *Lancaster Gazette*, 6 Aug. 1870.

18. *Glasgow Herald*, 9, 11 Mar. 1869, 8 Mar. 1870.

19. *Hull Packet*, 4 June 1875.

20. Croskery, "Religious Rebels," 9; William C. Davis, *The Cause Lost: Myths and Realities of the Confederacy* (Lawrence: University Press of Kansas, 1996), 169.

21. *Sheffield Independent*, 25 Apr. 1865; *Royal Cornwall Gazette*, 28 Apr. 1865; *Preston Chronicle*, 29 Apr. 1865.

22. See, for example, *Stirling Observer*, 22 June 1865.

23. Snow, *Southern Generals*, 171, 184–91, 193–95, 197–203, 206, 208–11.

24. *Manchester Courier*, 11 Nov. 1865.

25. *Friend of India*, 2 Nov. 1865.

26. *London Morning Post*, 25 Apr. 1866. On Fletcher's book, see also Dubrulle, *Ambivalent Nation*, 69, 162–64, 166.

27. Harry Gilmor, *Four Years in the Saddle* (New York: Harper, 1866), 24, 26–29, 33, 36–43, 62–63.

28. See, for example, *Dundee Courier*, 2 Aug. 1866.

29. "Stonewall Jackson," *Saturday Review* 22, no. 573, 20 Oct. 1866, 488–89.

30. "Southern Generals," *Saturday Review* 20, no. 509, 29 July 1865, 149–51; *Cork Examiner*, 2 Aug. 1865.

31. *Westmorland Gazette*, 11 Nov. 1865, 3 Feb., 12 May 1866.

32. *London Observer*, 2 Dec. 1866.

33. See, for example, *Lancaster Gazette*, 6 Aug. 1870.

34. *Sheffield Daily Telegraph*, 1 Sept. 1868.

35. *London Morning Post*, 25 Jan. 1869; *London Standard*, 25 Jan. 1869.

36. See, for example, *London Times*, 24 Dec. 1868.

37. *London Morning Post*, 20 Aug. 1870.

38. *Glasgow Herald*, 9, 11 Mar. 1869. The coat was later acquired by the Museum of the Confederacy, Richmond

39. *Leeds Mercury*, 6 Aug. 1868; *Sheffield Daily Telegraph*, 7 Aug. 1868; *Liverpool Mercury*, 7 Aug. 1868; *Manchester Times*, 8 Aug. 1868; *Derby Mercury*, 12 Aug. 1868; *Royal Cornwall Gazette*, 13 Aug. 1868; *North Devon Journal*, 13 Aug. 1868; *Chelmsford Chronicle*, 21 Aug. 1868.

40. *Glasgow Herald*, 10 Oct. 1868.

41. *Glasgow Herald*, 27 Jan. 1870.

42. *Glasgow Herald*, 20 Jan. 1870.

43. *London Standard*, 30 Sept. 1870; *Glasgow Chronicle*, 23 Nov. 1870; *Reynolds's Newspaper*, 11 Dec. 1870; *London Daily News*, 24 Nov. 1871; *Pall Mall Gazette*, 28 Nov. 1871; *Exeter Flying Post*, 6 Dec. 1871.

44. *Newcastle Courant*, 21 Mar. 1873; *Preston Chronicle*, 22 Mar. 1873. On Jackson's relationship with Colston, see Gwynne, *Rebel Yell*, 16, 147, 522, 531, 537; and especially Robertson, *Stonewall Jackson*, 117, 123, 126–27, 132, 140, 145, 157–58, 181–82, 199–200, 215–18, 677, 690, 695, 699, 704, 715, 718, 721, 723–24.

45. *Newcastle Courant*, 20 June 1873; *Southampton Herald*, 15 Nov. 1873; *York Herald*, 30 Apr. 1874.

46. See, for example, *Tamworth Herald*, 18 July 1874.

47. *Exeter Flying Post*, 2 Dec. 1874; *London Examiner*, 10 Apr. 1875.

48. *Manchester Guardian*, 7 Apr. 1869.

49. *Manchester Guardian*, 24 Dec. 1877.

50. See, for example, *John Bull*, 12 July 1879.

51. *Derbyshire Times*, 15 Feb. 1868; *Hull Packet*, 4 June 1875.

52. *Liverpool Mercury*, 26 Sept. 1868, 10 May 1869; *Western Times*, 11 June 1869; *Exeter and Plymouth Gazette*, 13 June 1869; *London Standard*, 30 Sept. 1870.

53. *London Morning Post*, 20 Oct. 1868.

54. *Parliamentary Debates*, 3rd ser., 15 Mar. 1867, vol. 185, cols. 1951–91; *Huddersfield Chronicle*, 23 Mar. 1867.

55. *London Standard*, 30 Jan. 1867.

56. *London Standard*, 30 Jan. 1867; *London Examiner*, 1, 15 Dec. 1866.

57. *Glasgow Herald*, 30 July 1868.

58. *London Times*, 15 June 1888.

59. *London Times*, 28 Jan. 1890.

60. *London Times*, 2 Nov. 1894.

61. *Baily's Monthly Magazine*, no. 410 (Apr. 1894): 250–57, no. 412 (June 1894): 380–87, and no. 451 (Sept. 1897): 175–84.

62. *Sheffield Daily Telegraph*, 25 Apr. 1865.

63. See Snow, *Southern Generals*, 169–71, 174–77, 185, 202–4; and reviews in *Saturday Review* 20, no. 509, 29 July 1865, 149–51, and *Cork Examiner*, 2 Aug. 1865.

64. *Manchester Courier*, 11 Nov. 1865.

65. Snow, *Southern Generals*, 177, 184–85, 202–3.

66. Snow, *Southern Generals*, 172

67. *Exeter and Plymouth Gazette*, 8 June 1866; *London Examiner*, 15 Dec. 1866.

68. *Leeds Times*, 9 June 1866.

69. *London Examiner*, 15 Dec. 1866.

70. *Manchester Guardian*, 17 Oct. 1866; *Glasgow Herald*, 19 Oct. 1866; *Huddersfield Chronicle*, 27 Oct. 1866.

71. Heros von Borcke, *Memoirs of the Confederate War for Independence* (Philadelphia: J. B. Lippincott, 1867), 203–4; *Manchester Guardian*, 5 Dec. 1865; *London Standard*, 30 Jan. 1867.

72. *Glasgow Herald*, 10 July 1867; *Stirling Observer*, 11 July 1867; *Bury and Norwich Post*, 23 July 1867; *Newcastle Journal*, 23 July 1867.

73. *Manchester Courier*, 6 Jan. 1869.

74. Edward A. Pollard, "Stonewall Jackson—An Historical Study," *Putnam's Magazine of Literature, Science, Art, and National Interests*, n.s., 2, no. 12 (1868): 733–40.

75. *London Times*, 14 Dec. 1868; *Manchester Courier*, 15 Dec. 1868; *Exeter Flying Post*, 16 Dec. 1868; *Sheffield Independent*, 16 Dec. 1868; *Royal Cornwall Gazette*, 17 Dec. 1868; *Manchester Times*, 19 Dec. 1868; *Hampshire Telegraph*, 26 Dec. 1868.

76. Jubal A. Early, "Stonewall Jackson at Fredericksburg," *Historical Magazine* 8 (1870): 32–35.

77. *Western Mail*, 1 May 1869; *Lancaster Gazette*, 6 Aug. 1870; *Glasgow Herald*, 27 Jan., 8 Mar. 1870.

78. *Glasgow Herald*, 11 Mar. 1869.

79. *Newcastle Courant*, 20 June 1873; *Southampton Herald*, 15 Nov. 1873.

80. *Graphic*, 16 Mar. 1872.

81. *Liverpool Mercury*, 1 May 1865; *Leeds Intelligencer*, 10 June 1865; *Cheshire Observer*, 29 July 1865; *North Wales Chronicle*, 5 Aug. 1865; *Reading Mercury*, 25 Nov. 1865, 6 Jan. 1866; *Chelmsford Chronicle*, 12 May 1865, 26 Jan. 1866; *Nottinghamshire Guardian*, 26 Jan., 23 Feb. 1866; *Norfolk Chronicle*, 7 Apr., 24 Nov. 1866; *Hereford Journal*, 1 Dec. 1866; *Newcastle Guardian*, 6 Oct. 1866, 2, 9 Feb. 1867; *Exeter and Plymouth Gazette*, 1 Mar. 1867; *Wrexham Weekly Advertiser*, 12 May 1866, 12, 26 Jan., 16 Mar., 19 Oct. 1867; *Englishwoman's Domestic Magazine*, 1 Feb. 1868; *Hampshire Telegraph*, 9 Mar. 1867, 22 Feb. 1868; *Sheffield Daily Telegraph*, 29 Feb. 1868; *Bucks Herald*, 21 Mar. 1868; *Southampton Herald*, 29 Apr., 6 May 1865, 16 Feb., 28 Dec. 1867, 2 Jan. 1869; *Worcester Journal*, 26 May 1866, 20 Nov. 1869; *Jackson's Oxford Journal*, 26 Mar. 1870; *Morpeth Herald*, 28 May 1870; *Belfast Newsletter*, 1 Feb. 1866, 21, 23, 24, 26, 27 Apr. 1869, 25, 26 Apr., 21 Sept. 1870; *Hull Packet*, 10 Feb. 1871; *Derbyshire Times*, 25 Feb. 1871; *Bury and Norwich Post*, 2 Jan., 6, 27 Mar., 13 Nov. 1866, 14 Nov. 1871; *North Devon Journal*, 18 Jan. 1872; *Royal Cornwall Gazette*, 26 Mar. 1868, 17 Feb., 25 May 1872; *Era*, 1 May 1870, 17 Aug. 1873; *Western Times*, 1 Mar. 1867, 17 Mar. 1868, 23 Jan. 1872, 18 Nov. 1873; *Ipswich Journal*, 15 Jan. 1870, 21 Feb. 1874; *Northampton Mercury*, 25 Nov. 1865, 21 Dec. 1867, 21 Mar. 1868, 28 Aug. 1869, 28 Feb. 1874; *Sunderland Daily Echo*, 23 June 1874.

82. Blamphin's composition has been cited to show that "interest in the Jackson of legend burned brightly in England." Robert K. Krick, "The Metamorphosis in Stonewall Jackson's Public Image," in *The Shenandoah Valley Campaign of 1862*, ed. Gary W. Gallagher (Chapel Hill: University of North Carolina Press, 2003), 24–42.

83. *Sheffield Daily Telegraph*, 25 Apr. 1865; *Exeter and Plymouth Gazette*, 28 Apr. 1865.

84. *Wrexham Weekly Advertiser*, 10 Mar. 1866.

85. *Era*, 30 May 1869.

86. See, for example, *Hampshire Telegraph*, 3 Oct. 1868.

87. *Australian Journal* (Melbourne), 1 May, 1 June, 1 July, 1 Aug., 1 Sept. 1870.

88. *London Morning Post*, 28 Oct. 1869.

89. *Stirling Observer*, 8 Mar. 1866.

90. *Nottinghamshire Guardian*, 29 June 1866.

91. *Manchester Times*, 6 May 1865; *Essex Standard*, 29 Dec. 1865, 2 Jan. 1867.

92. *Glasgow Herald*, 5 Jan. 1866; *Stirling Observer*, 11 Jan. 1866.

93. *Manchester Courier*, 19 Sept. 1865; *Sheffield Independent*, 20 Sept. 1865; *North Devon Journal*, 21 Sept., 2 Nov. 1865; *Dundee Courier*, 21 Sept. 1865; *Cork Examiner*, 21 Sept. 1865; *Belfast Newsletter*, 21 Sept. 1865; *York Herald*, 23 Sept. 1865; *Newcastle Guardian*, 23 Sept. 1865; *Manchester Times*, 23 Sept. 1865; *Worcester Journal*, 23 Sept. 1865; *London Standard*, 31 Oct. 1865.

94. *Chelmsford Chronicle*, 5 Jan. 1866; *Newcastle Guardian*, 5, 6 Jan. 1866; *Salisbury and Winchester Journal*, 13 Jan. 1866; *Belfast Newsletter*, 18 June 1866; *North Devon Journal*, 4, 18 Jan 1866; *Exeter and Plymouth Gazette*, 19 Jan. 1866; *Leeds Intelligencer*, 20 Jan. 1866.

95. *London Times*, 25, 26 Dec. 1865; *Liverpool Mercury*, 25 Dec. 1865; *Sheffield Daily Telegraph*, 27 Dec. 1865; *Essex Standard*, 27 Dec. 1865; *Freeman's Journal*, 28 Dec. 1865; *Caledonian Mercury*, 28 Dec. 1865; *Bradford Observer*, 28 Dec. 1865; *Hull Packet*, 29 Dec. 1865; *Exeter and Plymouth Gazette*, 29 Dec. 1865; *Westmorland Gazette*, 30 Dec. 1865; *Preston Chronicle*, 30 Dec. 1865; *Birmingham Gazette*, 30 Dec. 1865; *Huddersfield Chronicle*, 30 Dec. 1865; *Manchester Courier*, 27, 30 Dec. 1865; *Reynolds's Newspaper*, 31 Dec. 1865; *North Devon Journal*, 4 Jan. 1866.

96. *London Standard*, 6, 8, 10, 13 Jan. 1866.

97. *Era*, 11 Feb. 1866; *Reynolds's Newspaper*, 11 Feb. 1866; *London Standard*, 26 Jan., 9 Mar. 1866; *Manchester Guardian*, 14 Feb. 1866; *Sheffield Independent*, 14 Feb. 1866; *Manchester Courier*, 14 Feb., 10 Mar. 1866; *Derby Mercury*, 28 Feb. 1866; *Hereford Journal*, 27 Jan. 1866; *Leeds Mercury*, 10 Mar. 1866; *Dundee Courier*, 12 Mar. 1866; *Glasgow Herald*, 13 Mar. 1866; *Blackburn Standard*, 14 Mar. 1866; *Stirling Observer*, 15 Mar. 1866; *North Devon Journal*, 15 Mar. 1866; *Devizes and Wiltshire Gazette*, 15 Mar. 1866; *Chelmsford Chronicle*, 16 Mar. 1866; *Newcastle Guardian*, 17 Mar. 1866; *Cheshire Observer*, 17 Mar. 1866; *Essex Standard*, 23 Mar. 1866.

98. *Dundee Courier*, 12 Apr. 1866.

99. See, for example, *Preston Chronicle*, 28 Mar. 1868.

100. *Liverpool Mercury*, 20 Aug. 1869; *Sheffield Independent*, 21 Aug. 1869; *Sheffield Daily Telegraph*, 21 Aug. 1869; *Blackburn Standard*, 25 Aug. 1869; *Manchester Guardian*, 8 Sept. 1869; *Hull Packet*, 10 Sept. 1869; *Freeman's Journal*, 11 Sept. 1869; *Exeter and Plymouth Gazette*, 17 Sept. 1869; *Chelmsford Chronicle*, 17 Sept. 1869.

101. *Glasgow Herald*, 9 Oct. 1869; *North Devon Journal*, 14 Oct. 1869; *Chelmsford Chronicle*, 22 Oct. 1869.

102. *London Times*, 21 Oct. 1905, 22 May 1909.

103. *Sporting Times*, 8 Dec. 1883.

104. *Birmingham Daily Post*, 13 Mar. 1866.

105. On greyhounds, see *Bell's Life in London*, 2, 23, 30 Nov., 7, 21 Dec. 1867, 22, 29 Feb., 24 Oct., 7 Nov., 5, 19 Dec. 1868, 13 Jan., 3 Feb., 10, 13, 24, 27 Mar., 30 Oct., 6 Nov., 11, 18 Dec. 1869, 2 Apr., 4 June, 23 July, 29 Oct., 5 Nov., 3, 10 Dec. 1870, 21 Jan., 4, 18 Mar., 13 May, 30 Sept., 14, 21 Oct., 4, 18 Nov., 2, 30 Dec. 1871, 13, 20 Jan., 3, 24 Feb., 2, 16, 23, 30 Mar., 12, 19 Oct., 2, 30 Nov., 28 Dec. 1872, 11 Jan., 1 Feb., 8 Mar., 11, 18 Oct., 1 Nov. 1873, 10 Jan., 28 Feb., 5 Sept., 3, 17 Oct., 28 Nov., 5 Dec. 1874, 4 Sept., 9, 30 Oct. 1875; *Sporting Gazette*, 2, 9, 30 Nov., 7, 21 Dec. 1867, 15, 22, 29 Feb., 31 Oct., 7 Nov., 5, 19, 26 Dec. 1868, 16 Jan., 6 Feb., 13, 20, 27 Mar., 29 May, 30 Oct., 6, 20, 27 Nov., 4, 11, 18 Dec. 1869, 1, 15, 22, 29 Jan., 5, 26 Feb., 5, 12, 19, 26 Mar., 2, 9, 16, 23, 30 Apr., 7, 14, 21, 28 May, 11 June, 23, 30 July, 24 Sept., 8, 29 Oct., 5 Nov., 3 Dec. 1870, 14, 21 Jan., 4 Mar., 13 May, 19 Aug., 23 Sept., 7, 14, 21 Oct., 4, 25 Nov., 2, 9, 16, 23, 30 Dec. 1871, 6, 20, 27 Jan., 3, 10, 24 Feb., 2, 16, 23, 30 Mar., 6, 13, 20 Apr., 25 May, 1, 29 June, 5, 19 Oct., 2, 16, 30 Nov., 7 Dec. 1872, 11, 18 Jan., 22 Feb., 14 June, 11, 25 Oct., 1 Nov., 20 Dec. 1873, 3, 10, 17, 31 Jan., 14, 28 Feb., 22 Aug., 3, 10, 17 Oct., 7, 14 Nov. 1874, 28 Aug., 9, 16 Oct. 1875; *Manchester Guardian*, 19, 20, 21 Feb., 4 Dec. 1868, 9 Mar. 1869; *Racing Times*, 24 Feb. 1868. On racehorses, see *Bell's Life in London*, 12 Aug. 1865, 28 July, 18 Aug., 29 Sept. 1866, 1 June 1867, 26 Feb. 1870, 29 Apr. 1871, 27 Apr. 1872; *Sporting Gazette*, 6, 13, 30 May, 3 June 1868, 14 Jan., 11 Mar., 29 Apr., 16 Dec. 1871, 27 Apr. 1872; *Manchester Guardian*, 18 Jan. 1871. On racing boats, see *Bell's Life in London*, 6 Jan. 1866.

106. *Sheffield Independent*, 23 Mar. 1867; *London Standard*, 26 Mar. 1867; *Dundee Courier*, 27 Mar., 18 Apr. 1867; *Leeds Mercury*, 17, 20 Apr. 1867; *London Daily News*, 17 Apr. 1867; *Manchester*

Guardian, 17 Apr. 1867; *Western Times,* 18 Apr. 1867; *Manchester Courier,* 23 Mar., 18, 20 Apr. 1867; *Glasgow Herald,* 21 Mar., 18 Apr. 1867; *Belfast Newsletter,* 18 Apr. 1867; *Newcastle Courant,* 19 Apr. 1867; *Liverpool Mercury,* 19 Apr. 1867; *York Herald,* 20 Apr. 1867; *Salisbury and Winchester Journal,* 20 Apr. 1867; *Reading Mercury,* 20 Apr. 1867; *Norfolk Chronicle,* 20 Apr. 1867; *Manchester Times,* 20 Apr. 1867; *Leicester Chronicle,* 20 Apr. 1867; *Lancaster Gazette,* 20 Apr. 1867; *Illustrated Police News,* 20 Apr. 1867; *Huddersfield Chronicle,* 20 Apr. 1867; *Lloyd's Illustrated Newspaper,* 21 Apr. 1867; *Hampshire Telegraph,* 24 Apr. 1867; *Blackburn Standard,* 24 Apr. 1867; *Nottinghamshire Guardian,* 19, 26 Apr. 1867.

107. *Dundee Courier,* 3 Feb. 1868; *Derby Mercury,* 5 Feb. 1868; *Bradford Observer,* 8 Oct. 1868; *Birmingham Daily Post,* 20 July 1872; *Sheffield Daily Telegraph,* 20 July, 4 Sept. 1872; *Leeds Mercury,* 8 Oct. 1868, 3 Sept. 1872; *Friend of India,* 15 Aug. 1872; *Manchester Guardian,* 3 Sept. 1872; *Reynolds's Newspaper,* 8 Sept. 1872; *London Times,* 7 Oct. 1868, 19 July, 3 Sept. 1872, 5 Apr. 1900, 19 July 1910.

108. *North Wales Chronicle,* 30 Dec. 1865.

109. See, for example, *Punch,* 2 Apr. 1870.

110. *Chelmsford Chronicle,* 28 Apr. 1865; *Manchester Guardian,* 3 May 1865; *Leeds Mercury,* 3 May 1865; *London Morning Post,* 2 May 1865; *London Standard,* 3 May 1865; *Dundee Courier,* 5 May 1865; *Derby Mercury,* 10 May 1865; *Exeter and Plymouth Gazette,* 5 May 1865.

111. *Sheffield Independent,* 13 May 1865.

112. *Reynolds's Newspaper,* 4 June 1865; *Birmingham Daily Post,* 29 May 1865; *Western Times,* 2 June 1865; *Hull Packet,* 2 June 1865; *London Morning Post,* 6 June 1865.

113. *London Standard,* 5 July 1865.

114. "Southern Generals," *Saturday Review* 20, no. 509, 29 July 1865, 149–51; *Cork Examiner,* 2 Aug. 1865.

115. *Spectator,* 28 Oct. 1865; *Sheffield Daily Telegraph,* 3 Nov. 1865.

116. *London Times,* 16 Nov. 1865; *Westmorland Gazette,* 18 Nov. 1865; *Cork Examiner,* 18 Nov. 1865; *Cheshire Observer,* 18 Nov. 1865; *Newcastle Journal,* 20 Nov. 1865; *Bury and Norwich Post,* 21 Nov. 1865; *Friend of India,* 28 Dec. 1865.

117. *London Times,* 16, 23 Nov. 1865; *Cork Examiner,* 24 Nov. 1865.

118. *London Morning Post,* 10 Nov. 1865.

119. *London Standard,* 8 Jan. 1866. The same argument was made in later years—for example, by John Baker Hopkins (journalist and author, former manager of the *London Index*) in the *London Times,* 14 Sept. 1871.

120. "Stonewall Jackson," *Saturday Review* 22, no. 573, 20 Oct. 1866, 488–89.

121. *Westmorland Gazette,* 27 Oct. 1866. On "no quarter" as a combination of ruthlessness and righteousness, see Charles Royster, *The Destructive War: William Tecumseh Sherman, Stonewall Jackson, and the Americans* (New York: Knopf, 1991).

122. *London Morning Post,* 28 Sept. 1866; *Manchester Guardian,* 26 Oct. 1866: *London Times,* 9 Mar., 4, 10, 12 Sept. 1866; *Caledonian Mercury,* 14 Mar. 1866. Some papers mentioned that Dabney's book had been "carefully revised by General Robert E. Lee," which was untrue, but it did make the book more authoritative in the eyes of many. In fact, Lee disliked its strident tone and thought it likely to make northerners more vindictive in their attitude toward the South. In later years, as sectional reconciliation was under way, Dabney was unable to get the work republished because it was not in keeping with the times. See Hettle, *Inventing Stonewall Jackson,* 40, 48.

123. *John Bull,* 10 Feb. 1866, dismissed the idea that Fenian leader James Stephens was an Irish Stonewall Jackson.

124. *Westmorland Gazette,* 17 Nov. 1866.

125. *Belfast Newsletter,* 9 Mar. 1868.

126. *London Standard,* 4 Mar. 1868.

127. *London Standard,* 8 Aug. 1868.

128. *London Standard,* 30 Aug. 1869.

129. *Manchester Guardian,* 6 Jan. 1870; *London Morning Post,* 7 Jan. 1870; *Leeds Times,* 15 Jan. 1870; *Illustrated Police News,* 15 Jan. 1870.

130. *Glasgow Herald,* 27 Jan. 1870.

131. *Exeter and Plymouth Gazette,* 21 Oct. 1870; *Tamworth Herald,* 22 Oct. 1870; *York Herald,* 22 Oct. 1870; *Birmingham Daily Post,* 24 Dec. 1870; *Sheffield Independent,* 27 Dec. 1870; *Dundee Courier,* 28 Dec. 1870; *Graphic,* 10 Dec. 1870.

132. See, for example, *London Times,* 5 June 1873.

133. *Parliamentary Debates,* 3rd ser., 6 Mar. 1868, vol. 190, cols. 1150–98; *Belfast Newsletter,* 9 Mar. 1868; *Liverpool Mercury,* 26 Sept. 1868, 10, 11 May 1869; *London Standard,* 6 May 1869; *Derbyshire Times,* 29 May 1869.

134. *North Devon Journal,* 3 Oct. 1872.

135. *London Standard,* 25 Sept. 1872; *Pall Mall Gazette,* 25 Sept. 1872; *London Morning Post,* 26 Sept. 1872.

136. *London Standard,* 15 Aug. 1872; *London Examiner,* 10 Apr. 1875.

137. *Stirling Observer,* 7 June 1866.

138. *Worcester Journal,* 1 June 1867.

139. *Liverpool Mercury,* 25 Dec. 1866; *Dundee Courier,* 27 Dec. 1866; *Derby Mercury,* 2 Jan. 1867.

140. *Pall Mall Gazette,* 3 June 1875.

141. *Bury and Norwich Post,* 15 October 1878; *Ipswich Journal,* 9 Oct. 1880.

142. *London Daily News,* 21 Feb. 1876; *London Examiner,* 4 Mar. 1876.

143. Among the more notable were two novels by Reginald Horsley, published in the 1890s. *London Times,* 23 Nov. 1895; *Glasgow Herald,* 1 Oct. 1896; *Pall Mall Gazette,* 6 Nov. 1896.

144. *Manchester Guardian,* 21 June 1871.

145. This was *Erema; or My Father's Sin,* by R. D. Blackmore. *London Standard,* 7 Dec. 1877.

146. This was *For Life and Liberty,* by Gordon Stables. *London Times,* 23 Nov. 1895.

147. *London Times,* 6 Jan. 1899.

148. *Boys of England: A Magazine of Sport, Sensation, Fun, and Instruction,* 23 Nov. 1877; *Our Young Folk's Weekly Budget,* 30 Mar. 1878; *Boys' Own Paper,* 31 Dec. 1881.

149. *London Standard,* 29 Oct. 1875; *London Morning Post,* 2 June 1881; *Pall Mall Gazette,* 6 Nov. 1896.

150. *London Observer,* 18 Sept. 1898; *London Times,* 19 Sept. 1898.

151. *Reynolds's Newspaper,* 22 Aug. 1880.

152. Frederick Sherlock, *Heroes in the Strife; or The Temperance Testimonies of Some Eminent Men* (London: Hodder and Stoughton, 1881), 62; *Glasgow Herald,* 7 Feb. 1881.

153. *Sheffield Daily Telegraph,* 24 Mar. 1881.

154. *London Morning Post,* 2 June 1881; William H. Russell, *Hesperothen: Notes from the West, a*

Record of a Ramble in the United States and Canada in the Spring and Summer of 1881, 2 vols. (London: Sampson Low, Marston, Searle, and Rivington, 1882), 1:95–96.

155. *London Times*, 12, 16 Apr. 1884.

156. *Bristol Mercury*, 9 July 1881; *Sheffield Daily Telegraph*, 9 July 1881.

157. *London Daily News*, 28 Oct. 1880.

158. *London Standard*, 25 June 1880; *Liverpool Mercury*, 26 June 1880; *Portsmouth Evening News*, 26 June 1880.

159. *Pall Mall Gazette*, 1 Nov. 1879; *London Observer*, 2 Nov. 1879; *Manchester Courier*, 3 Nov. 1879; *Newcastle Courant*, 7 Nov. 1879; *London Standard*, 30 Oct. 1885; *Manchester Guardian*, 30 Oct. 1885, 11 Feb. 1886; *London Times*, 10 Feb. 1886.

160. *John Bull*, 8 Aug. 1885.

161. *Leicester Chronicle*, 18 Aug. 1888.

162. *London Times*, 16 Feb. 1891.

163. *Freeman's Journal*, 23 Feb. 1893.

164. *Bristol Mercury*, 14 Dec. 1878; *Freeman's Journal*, 12 Aug. 1876; *Cheshire Observer*, 22 Nov. 1879.

165. *London Morning Post*, 30 Aug. 1882.

166. *Leeds Mercury*, 9 Jan. 1890; *Huddersfield Chronicle*, 11 Jan. 1890.

167. *Sunderland Daily Echo*, 11 Mar. 1895.

168. *Blackburn Standard*, 15, 22 June 1878; *Manchester Guardian*, 18 June 1878.

169. *Newcastle Courant*, 2 Apr. 1880.

170. Stonewall Jackson Solomon, "a boat boy," enjoyed a brief spell of fame in 1888 after saving the life of a child who had fallen into the sea off the Cornwall coast. A Mr. Stonewall Jackson was living in London Road, Peterborough, in 1903. Thomas Stonewall Jackson, a London cigar importer, was involved in a business dispute that went to court in 1909. A Mr. and Mrs. Stonewall Jackson were residing in Middlesbrough in 1919. *London Times*, 28 Sept. 1888, 2 Sept. 1903, 15 Jan. 1909, 27 Sept. 1919. On racehorses named after Jackson, see *Manchester Courier*, 12 Mar. 1877; *Aberdeen Journal*, 14 Mar. 1877; *North Wales Chronicle*, 17 Mar. 1877; *Worcester Journal*, 17 Mar. 1877; *Manchester Guardian*, 30 Mar. 1876, 30 May 1883; *Times*, 6 Oct. 1877, 22 Jan., 24 Sept. 1878, 30 Aug. 1880, 30 May 1883, 20 Mar. 1906; *York Herald*, 2 June 1883.

171. *York Herald*, 29 Feb. 1876.

172. *Derby Mercury*, 24 July 1878.

173. *Essex Standard*, 3 Aug. 1877.

174. *Portsmouth Evening News*, 27 Mar. 1878.

175. Charles R. Low, *Memoir of Lieutenant-General Sir Garnet J. Wolseley*, 2 vols. (London: Richard Bentley, 1878), 1:269–72; *London Examiner*, 7 Sept. 1878.

176. *Pall Mall Gazette*, 29 Aug. 1888; *Birmingham Daily Post*, 30 Aug. 1888; *Belfast Newsletter*, 30 Aug. 1888; *Manchester Guardian*, 30 Aug. 1888.

177. Lord Wolseley, "Military Genius," *Fortnightly Review* 44, no. 261 (Sept. 1888): 297–312.

178. John D. Imboden, "Stonewall Jackson in the Shenandoah," *Century* 30, no. 2 (June 1885): 280–94; *Northern Echo*, 1 June 1885; *Manchester Guardian*, 1 June 1885; Robertson, *Stonewall Jackson*, 827.

179. *Pictorial Missionary News*, 1 Apr. 1889, 1 Dec. 1890; *Home and Foreign Missionary Record for the Free Church of Scotland*, 2 Apr. 1894; *Juvenile Missionary Magazine*, 1 Mar. 1898.

180. Henry M. Field, "Stonewall Jackson," *Harper's New Monthly Magazine* 83, no. 498 (Nov. 1891): 907–15; *Exeter and Plymouth Gazette*, 3 Nov. 1891.

181. G.F.R. Henderson, *Stonewall Jackson and the American Civil War*, 2 vols. (London: Longmans, 1898), 1:60–61, 386, 410, 2:193, 246, 249, 313, 458. James Robertson recognizes Henderson as one of Jackson's "most loyal defenders" but also points to errors in the book. Wallace Hettle states that while the book's emphasis on maneuverability and speed was attractive to European strategists, "it is sometimes hard to distinguish where Stonewall Jackson's ideas on strategy end and Henderson's begin." Hettle believes that its reliance on information received from southerners made the book pro-Confederate. Robertson, *Stonewall Jackson*, 229, 256, 357, 711, 797, 817, 833, 839–40, 848, 860–61, 869, 883; Hettle, *Inventing Stonewall Jackson*, 104–7.

182. *London Times*, 4 Aug. 1897, 23 Sept., 24 Nov. 1898.

183. *London Standard*, 14 Oct. 1898.

184. *Pall Mall Gazette*, 13 Oct. 1898.

185. *Manchester Guardian*, 21 Dec. 1898.

186. Lt. Gen. Sir Henry Brackenbury, "Stonewall Jackson," *Blackwood's Edinburgh Magazine* 144, no. 998 (Dec. 1898): 721–38. Brackenbury's review was also discussed in the newspapers; see, for example, *Newcastle Courant*, 17 Dec. 1898.

187. Advertisers made this a selling point: *London Times*, 19 Jan. 1899.

188. *Edinburgh Review* 189, no. 337 (Jan. 1899): 48–75.

189. See, for example, *Australasian*, 29 Oct. 1898.

190. See *London Times*, 28 Sept. 1899, 18 Oct. 1900; Wolseley's introduction in G.F.R. Henderson, *Stonewall Jackson and the American Civil War*, 2nd ed., 2 vols. (London: Longmans, 1899), 1:x, xiv; and reviews in *London Morning Post*, 28 Sept. 1899; *London Daily News*, 12 Oct. 1899. On Jackson's resignation, see Robertson, *Stonewall Jackson*, 314–21; Gwynne, *Rebel Yell*, 184–91.

191. See, for example, *London Times*, 9 Mar. 1903.

192. *London Times*, 31 May, 22, 29 Nov., 13 Dec. 1905.

193. *London Times*, 28 July 1904; *Sheffield Daily Telegraph*, 28 July 1904.

194. Wolseley, *Story of a Soldier's Life*, 2:117–18.

195. *Sheffield Evening Telegraph*, 21 Mar. 1900; *Leicester Chronicle*, 25 Aug. 1900.

196. *Dundee Courier*, 10 July 1900; *Freeman's Journal*, 2 Jan. 1900.

197. Hugh Dubrulle, "A Military Legacy of the Civil War: The British Inheritance," *Civil War History* 49, no. 2 (2003): 153–80; Brian Holden Reid, "'A Signpost That Was Missed'? Reconsidering British Lessons from the American Civil War," *Journal of Military History* 70, no. 2 (2006): 385–414; Tal, *American Civil War in British Culture*, 33–66.

198. *London Times*, 3 June, 10 Oct. 1902; *Sheffield Evening Telegraph*, 1 Dec. 1902; *Manchester Courier*, 6 Dec. 1902.

199. Theodore Roosevelt, *Oliver Cromwell* (London: Constable, 1900), 6, 105, 171; *London Morning Post*, 1 Dec. 1900.

200. *Manchester Guardian*, 11 May 1892; *London Times*, 27 Feb., 6 Nov., 5 Dec. 1899, 28 Aug. 1900, 28 Dec. 1901, 22 Aug. 1903; *London Observer*, 2 Apr. 1899.

201. *Friend of India*, 18 Aug. 1898, 22 June, 20 July 1899; *London Times*, 18 July 1899, 22 Sept. 1904, 7 Jan. 1905.

202. *London Times*, 28 Dec. 1901.

203. *Parliamentary Debates*, 4th ser., 19 Feb. 1900, vol. 79, cols. 348–49; 13 May 1901, vol. 93, cols. 1547–48; 14 July 1904, vol. 138, cols. 101–3; 19 Mar. 1908, vol. 186, cols. 867–68; *Parliamentary Debates*, 5th ser., 3 Apr. 1911, vol. 7, cols. 837–38; 12 Mar. 1912, vol. 35, col. 981; 24 Mar. 1913, vol. 50, cols. 1434–36.

204. *London Times*, 26 Mar., 8 July 1913, 24 Mar. 1914, 3 Oct. 1916, 16 Nov. 1917; *Parliamentary Debates*, 5th ser., 7 July 1913, vol. 55, cols. 67–82.

205. *Western Times*, 16 Nov. 1914.

206. *Essex Newsman*, 22 Aug. 1914.

207. *Tamworth Herald*, 13 Nov. 1915.

208. *London Times*, 16, 18 Apr. 1917, 21 Mar., 16 Dec 1918, 15, 22 July 1919.

209. *London Times*, 30 Oct. 1917; David Lloyd George, *The Great Crusade: Extracts of Speeches Delivered during the War* (New York: George H. Doran, 1918), 208–9.

210. *Hull Daily Mail*, 4 Jan. 1918.

10. "PRESENTED BY ENGLISH GENTLEMEN"

1. *London Times*, 24 Sept. 1862; Hope, *Social and Political Bearings*, 6; and Hope, *American Church*, 11–12.

2. *London Times*, 17 Oct. 1863.

3. "Stonewall Jackson," *Saturday Review* 15, no. 396, 30 May 1863, 689–90.

4. *Liverpool Mercury*, 2 June 1863; *London Standard*, 2 June 1863; *Sheffield Independent*, 2 June 1863; *Dundee Courier*, 1 June 1863; *Birmingham Daily Post*, 2 June 1863; *Newcastle Journal*, 3 June 1863; *Chelmsford Chronicle*, 5 June 1863; *Royal Cornwall Gazette*, 5 June 1863; *Preston Chronicle*, 6 June 1863; *York Herald*, 6 June 1863; *Newcastle Courant*, 5 June 1863; *Huddersfield Chronicle*, 6 June 1863; *Leeds Times*, 6 June 1863; *Manchester Courier*, 6 June 1863; *Lloyd's Illustrated Newspaper*, 7 June 1863; *Essex Standard*, 10 June 1863.

5. *Manchester Guardian*, 27 June 1863; *Dundee Courier*, 2 July 1863; *Westmorland Gazette*, 4 July 1863; *Morpeth Herald*, 4 July 1863; *London Morning Post*, 8 July 1863; *Sheffield Independent*, 9 July 1863; *Birmingham Daily Post*, 9 July 1863; *Leicestershire Mercury*, 11 July 1863; *Northampton Mercury*, 11 July 1863; *Southampton Herald*, 11 July 1863; *Bucks Herald*, 11 July 1863; *Bristol Mercury*, 11 July 1863; *Stirling Observer*, 16 July 1863; *Exeter Flying Post*, 22 July 1863.

6. *London Daily News*, 15 July 1863.

7. *Leeds Times*, 18 July 1863.

8. *Freeman's Journal*, 21 July 1863; *Devizes and Wiltshire Gazette*, 23 July 1863; *Worcester Journal*, 1 Aug. 1863; *North Devon Journal*, 6 Aug. 1863.

9. *London Index*, 4 June, 2 July 1863. Hotze, editor of the *Index*, believed that Jackson's death moved the British people more than any other event in the war. Acquaintances in London told him that the death of a "foreigner" had never elicited such a response. Donations for the statue were listed in the *Index*. By the beginning of 1864, well over a hundred named individuals had made contributions, along with several firms and some anonymous donors. See John D. Bennett, "General Jackson's Statue," *Crossfire* 75 (2004): 25–26; and Bennett, *London Confederates*, 114–15, 169; Sebrell, *Persuading John Bull*, 129–30; Doyle, *Cause of All Nations*, 252; Charles P. Cullop, "English Reaction to Stonewall Jackson's Death," *West Virginia History* 29, no. 1 (1967): 3–4.

10. *John Bull*, 18 July 1863. Pro-northern newspapers in Britain made no allegations about Foley, apparently in the belief that he took the commission for art's sake and not as a political statement. Foley also assisted in the design and production of the Great Seal of the Confederacy. Bennett, *London Confederates*, 102.

11. *London Daily News*, 8 Aug. 1863; *Royal Cornwall Gazette*, 14 Aug. 1863.

12. *Norfolk Chronicle*, 8 Aug. 1863.

13. *London Observer*, 9 Aug. 1863.

14. *London Daily News*, 26 Aug. 1863.

15. Blackett, *Divided Hearts*, 49–51, 166, 185, 222–23; Campbell, *English Public Opinion*, 131.

16. *Derby Mercury*, 16 Sept. 1863; *Stirling Observer*, 17 Sept. 1863; *Exeter and Plymouth Gazette*, 18 Sept. 1863; *Aberdeen Journal*, 23 Sept. 1863; *Leeds Times*, 26 Sept. 1863; *John Bull*, 26 Sept. 1863; *Newcastle Journal*, 30 Sept. 1863; *Essex Standard*, 30 Sept., 2 Oct. 1863; *Cork Examiner*, 18 Sept., 2 Oct. 1863; *Belfast Newsletter*, 16 Sept., 2 Oct. 1863; *Leicester Chronicle*, 3 Oct. 1863; *Lancaster Gazette*, 3 Oct. 1863; *Caledonian Mercury*, 14 Sept., 3 Oct. 1863; *Wrexham Weekly Advertiser*, 10 Oct. 1863.

17. *London Morning Post*, 30 May 1864; *Manchester Courier*, 31 May 1864; *Newcastle Journal*, 31 May 1864; *Sheffield Daily Telegraph*, 31 May 1864; *Manchester Guardian*, 1 June 1864; *Belfast Newsletter*, 1 June 1864; *Derby Mercury*, 1 June 1864; *Sheffield Independent*, 1 June 1864; *London Standard*, 1 June 1864; *Liverpool Mercury*, 2 June 1864; *Leeds Times*, 4 June 1864; *Jackson's Oxford Journal*, 11 June 1864; *Westmorland Gazette*, 11 June 1864.

18. *London Times*, 21 July 1864.

19. *London Standard*, 4 Aug. 1864; *Manchester Courier*, 5 Aug. 1864; *Belfast Newsletter*, 9 Aug. 1864. Bennett, *London Confederates*, 169, notes a discrepancy between the available bank records and the published subscription lists of 1864 and 1865. (This probably reflects the outgoings for adverts, printing, and other expenses.) The account at Coutts became inactive in 1877.

20. *Stirling Observer*, 4 Feb. 1864; *Newcastle Guardian*, 6 Feb. 1864.

21. *Devizes and Wiltshire Gazette*, 25 Aug. 1864; *Newcastle Guardian*, 27 Aug. 1864.

22. *London Standard*, 11 Nov. 1875.

23. *Huddersfield Chronicle*, 14, 18 Jan. 1873; *Passing Events at Home and Abroad*, no. 4, 25 Jan. 1873, 54.

24. *London Standard*, 24 Aug. 1870; *London Morning Post*, 25 Aug. 1870.

25. Mark E. Neely Jr., Harold Holzer, and Gabor S. Boritt, *The Confederate Image: Prints of the Lost Cause* (Chapel Hill: University of North Carolina Press, 2000), 44–54, 219; John Esten Cooke, *Stonewall Jackson: A Military Biography* (New York: D. Appleton and Co., 1876), 517–18; Bennett, *London Confederates*, 115, 191; Robertson, *Stonewall Jackson*, 756; Drew Gilpin Faust, *This Republic of Suffering: Death and the American Civil War* (New York: Knopf, 2008), 155.

26. *London Index*, 22, 29 July 1865; *John Bull*, 5 Aug. 1865; *Manchester Guardian*, 8 Aug. 1865; *Essex Standard*, 9, 11 Aug. 1865; *Hull Packet*, 11 Aug. 1865.

27. *North Devon Journal*, 4 Jan. 1866; *London Standard*, 13 Jan. 1866.

28. See, for example, *Boston Daily Advertiser*, 16 Aug. 1865.

29. Long, *In the Shadow of the "Alabama,"* 153.

30. *London Standard*, 12 Aug. 1870; *Pall Mall Gazette*, 12 Aug. 1870; *London Morning Post*, 12 Aug. 1870; *London Times*, 13 Aug. 1870; *Manchester Guardian*, 13 Aug. 1870; *Bury and Norwich Post*, 16 Aug. 1870; *Glasgow Herald*, 16 Aug. 1870; *Nottinghamshire Guardian*, 19 Aug. 1870.

31. *Bury and Norwich Post*, 23 Aug. 1870; *Friend of India*, 22 Sept. 1870.

32. *London Times*, 18 Aug. 1870.

33. *London Times*, 23 Aug. 1870.

34. *London Standard*, 19 Aug. 1870.

35. *Pall Mall Gazette*, 15 Aug. 1870.

36. *Boston Daily Advertiser*, 24 Aug., 6 Sept. 1870; *North American and United States Gazette*, 24 Aug. 1870; *Milwaukee Daily Sentinel*, 2 Sept. 1870; *Frank Leslie's Illustrated Newspaper*, 17 Sept. 1870; *San Francisco Daily Evening Bulletin*, 21 Sept. 1870.

37. *Freeman's Journal*, 8 Sept. 1874; *London Times*, 14 Nov. 1874; *Aberdeen Journal*, 25 Nov. 1874; *Sheffield Daily Telegraph*, 28 Nov. 1874.

38. *London Morning Post*, 4 May 1875; *London Observer*, 9 May 1875; *Ipswich Journal*, 25 May 1875. A picture of the Jackson statue was included in the *Royal Academy Album* of December 1875. *London Times*, 8 Dec. 1875.

39. *Pall Mall Gazette*, 3 June 1875.

40. *Manchester Weekly Times*, 25 Sept. 1875; *Freeman's Journal*, 25 Sept., 4 Oct. 1875; *Dundee Courier*, 25, 28 Sept. 1875; *London Daily News*, 25 Sept. 1875; *Bradford Observer*, 25 Sept. 1875; *Hampshire Telegraph*, 29 Sept. 1875; *York Herald*, 11 Oct. 1875.

41. *London Times*, 29 Oct. 1875. Reports about the passage, reception, and unveiling of the statue had been sent by a correspondent in Philadelphia: *London Times*, 6, 28 Oct. 1875.

42. *London Times*, 30 Oct. 1875.

43. *Manchester Guardian*, 29 Oct. 1875; *Bradford Observer*, 29 Oct. 1875; *Belfast Newsletter*, 29 Oct. 1875; *Freeman's Journal*, 29 Oct. 1875; *John Bull*, 30 Oct. 1875; *Preston Chronicle*, 30 Oct. 1875; *Graphic*, 30 Oct. 1875; *Bury and Norwich Post*, 2 Nov. 1875; *North Devon Journal*, 4 Nov. 1875.

44. *Leeds Mercury*, 29 Oct. 1875; *Bucks Herald*, 30 Oct. 1875; *Belfast Newsletter*, 30 Oct. 1875; *North Wales Chronicle*, 6 Nov. 1875.

45. *Pall Mall Gazette*, 28, 29 Oct. 1875.

46. *London Standard*, 29 Oct. 1875.

47. *London Standard*, 11 Nov. 1875.

48. These details, and the correspondence between Hope and Johnson of July and August 1873, were included in the appendix of Cooke's *Stonewall Jackson*, 515–19. The New York edition of 1876 was an expanded version of what Cooke had first published in 1866. Another biography published in 1876, and containing details about the statue, was written by Sarah N. Randolph, southern apologist and granddaughter of Thomas Jefferson. See Randolph, *The Life of Gen. Thomas J. Jackson* (Philadelphia: Lippincott, 1876), 358–63. Randolph relied heavily on earlier works, especially Dabney's. Hettle, *Inventing Stonewall Jackson*, 41–42, 64–66. A picture of the statue was included at the end of the biography written by Jackson's widow some years later: Mary Anna Jackson, *Life and Letters of General Thomas J. Jackson* (New York: Harper, 1892), 478. A larger version, published in 1895, included two pictures of the statue as well as Hope's correspondence and an account of the statue's presentation and unveiling: *Memoirs of Stonewall Jackson by His Widow Mary Anna Jackson* (Louisville, Ky.: Courier-Journal Printing, 1895), 627–34.

49. Hope's letter to Kemper, the governor's message to the legislature, the official acceptance of the statue, its arrival in Richmond, and a description of the statue and pedestal were all included in Cooke, *Stonewall Jackson*, 520–31. Hope had written a second time to Kemper, on 23

May 1875, regarding completion of the statue and pedestal. See Library of Virginia, Executive Papers of Governor James L. Kemper, 1874–77, box 2, folder 8.

50. *London Standard*, 11 Nov. 1875; *Inauguration of the Jackson Statue: Introductory Address of Governor Kemper and Oration by Rev. Moses D. Hoge, D.D., on Tuesday, October 26, 1875* (Richmond, Va.: R. F. Walker, 1875); Cooke, *Stonewall Jackson*, 545–66. Hoge's speech was also included in Hoge, *Moses Drury Hoge*, 425–47. Of the Virginian commissioners appointed to make arrangements for the statue, Jubal Early appears to have been the most assiduous. See letters dated 21 Mar., 14 May, 25 June, 28 July, 29 Sept., 5, 22 Oct., 10 Nov. 1875, in Library of Virginia, Executive Papers of Governor James L. Kemper, 1874–77, box 2, folders 6 and 8–10, box 3, folders 2–4.

51. *London Standard*, 11 Nov. 1875.

52. *London Standard*, 11 Nov. 1875.

53. *Richmond Dispatch*, 30 Oct. 1875.

54. *Richmond Dispatch*, 26, 27, 30 Oct. 1875; *Alexandria Gazette*, 26 Oct. 1875.

55. *Chicago Inter Ocean*, 30 Oct., 26, 30 Nov. 1875; *Independent Statesman* (Concord, N.H.), 4 Nov., 9 Dec. 1875; *Milwaukee Daily Sentinel*, 18 Nov. 1875; *Daily Whig and Courier*, 1 Dec. 1875.

56. *New York Times*, 24 Sept., 27 Oct. 1875.

57. *Frank Leslie's Illustrated Newspaper*, 27 Nov. 1875.

58. *Galveston Daily News*, 16 May, 9, 29 Sept. 1875; *Georgia Weekly Telegraph*, 18 May, 14, 21 Sept. 1875; *North American and United States Gazette*, 11 Sept. 1875; *Daily Arkansas Gazette*, 11 Sept. 1875; *Chicago Inter Ocean*, 11, 24 Sept. 1875; *St. Louis Globe-Democrat*, 11, 24 Sept. 1875; *San Francisco Daily Evening Bulletin*, 21 Sept. 1875.

59. *Observer*, 2 Jan. 1876; *Pall Mall Gazette*, 3 Jan. 1876.

60. "Statue of General 'Stonewall' Jackson," *Art Journal*, n.s., 3 (1877): 25.

61. *London Observer*, 24, 31 Dec. 1876; *Sheffield Independent*, 4 Jan. 1877; *Southampton Herald*, 6 Jan. 1877; *Northampton Mercury*, 6 Jan. 1877; *Nottinghamshire Guardian*, 12 Jan. 1877; *Worcester Journal*, 13 Jan. 1877; *John Bull*, 13 Jan. 1877.

62. *Hastings and St. Leonards Observer*, 8 Dec. 1877. Descriptions of Richmond by American writers tended also to include the Jackson statue: see, for example, *Galveston Daily News*, 12 May 1882.

63. These pieces were subsequently collected and published together by G. E. Wright as *A Visit to the States: A Reprint of Letters from the Special Correspondent of "The Times"* (London: Times Office, 1887–88).

64. *London Times*, 3, 5, 6 Oct. 1887.

65. *Richmond Dispatch*, 30 June 1896.

66. Hettle, *Inventing Stonewall Jackson*, 69–85; Robertson, *Stonewall Jackson*, 759; Neely, Holzer, and Boritt, *Confederate Image*, 159; Gaines M. Foster, *Ghosts of the Confederacy: Defeat, the Lost Cause, and the Emergence of the New South, 1865–1913* (New York: Oxford University Press, 1988), 89; Charles Reagan Wilson, *Baptized in Blood: The Religion of the Lost Cause, 1865–1920* (Athens: University of Georgia Press, 2009), 156–57; B.A.C. Emerson, *Historic Southern Monuments: Representative Memorials of the Heroic Dead of the Southern Confederacy* (New York: Neale, 1911), 249.

67. David W. Blight, *Race and Reunion: The Civil War in American Memory* (Cambridge: Harvard University Press, 2001), 77; Mark S. Schantz, *Awaiting the Heavenly Country: The Civil War and America's Culture of Death* (Ithaca, N.Y.: Cornell University Press, 2008), 37, 64–65, 121, 218, 221.

68. Foster, *Ghosts of the Confederacy*, 55, 57, 62, 82, 116, 135, 185; William A. Blair, *Cities of the Dead: Contesting the Memory of the Civil War in the South, 1865–1914* (Chapel Hill: University of North Carolina Press, 2004), 54, 58–59, 65–66, 88–93; Wilson, *Baptized in Blood*, ix–xi, xiii, 18–20, 24, 27, 31, 33, 35, 51, 54, 120, 127–28, 133–35, 144–45; Wolfgang Schivelbusch, *The Culture of Defeat: On National Trauma, Mourning, and Recovery*, trans. Jefferson Chase (New York: Picador, 2003), 67–69.

69. Blight, *Race and Reunion*, 64–65, 77, 80; Wilson, *Baptized in Blood*, 18–24.

70. Faust, *Republic of Suffering*, 50, 154–56, 158, 161, 240. The "steady business" in "Stonewall relics" has been noted in Tony Reichhardt, "The Death and Life of Stonewall Jackson," *Historic Traveler* 3, no. 3 (1997): 48, 52–53.

71. Faust, *Republic of Suffering*, 148; Robert C. Cheeks, "Fifty Years after Stonewall Jackson's Death," *America's Civil War* 10, no. 1 (1997): 24–28; Gary W. Gallagher, "Perfect Southern Soldier," *Civil War Times* 51, no. 6 (2012): 18–20; Foster, *Ghosts of the Confederacy*, 59.

72. Neely, Holzer, and Boritt, *Confederate Image*, 20–21, 24, 31, 55, 59, 109–11, 113–15, 117, 122, 126, 133, 135; Bennett, *London Confederates*, 114–16, 123, 127; Blight, *Race and Reunion*, 167, 262–63; Reichhardt, "Death and Life," 46–54. The many memorials to Jackson included some that were not part of the Lost Cause movement: for example, a window in a black church in Roanoke, Virginia. Its pastor had been a pupil in Jackson's Sunday school in Lexington before the war. Wilson, *Baptized in Blood*, 26.

73. K. M. Rowland, "English Friends of the Confederacy," *Confederate Veteran* 25, no. 5 (1917): 198–99. (The magazine was the organ of the United Confederate Veterans and later of the United Daughters of the Confederacy, the Sons of Confederate Veterans, and the Southern Memorial Society. It ceased publication in 1932 but was revived in another form in 1984.) Foster, *Ghosts of the Confederacy*, 59, refers to the Jackson statue as "the gift of a British admirer rather than the product of a popular fund-raising effort," which is not quite correct. There *was* a fund-raising drive but in Britain rather than the South. In his account of the statue, Charles Cullop contends that "Jackson in death contributed significantly to improvement of the Southern image in England" and "an upsurge of English popular sympathy for the Confederacy" (though his evidence is hardly exhaustive). See Cullop, "English Reaction," 2, 5.

74. Samuel J. Graber, "Twice Divided Nation: The Civil War and National Memory in the Transatlantic World" (PhD diss., University of Iowa, 2008), 485, 490, 492, 513–39. See also his "British Tribute to Virginia Valor: Unveiling the Stonewall Jackson Memorial Statue," *American Nineteenth Century History* 9, no. 2 (2008): 141–64.

75. Graber, "Twice Divided Nation," 387–88, 394–95, 399–400, 403–6, 409–11.

76. Blackett, *Divided Hearts*, 1–5, 48–49.

77. David Blight does not go this far—he states that the only reason for the delay was Foley's preoccupation with other projects—but Blight does recognize that delay worked out well for the South. Thanks to good luck and good timing, the unveiling of the Jackson statue could be a "celebratory funeral" for the Confederacy (and quarrels, especially over the involvement of blacks in the day's events, were not allowed get in the way). Blight, *Race and Reunion*, 79–81, 83–84; Blair, *Cities of the Dead*, 106, 118–20. Blight's verdict on the delay is echoed by Charles Reagan Wilson: it was due to Foley's other commissions, and it was "propitious" for the South because "home rule" had been achieved by the time the statue was completed. The statue was "the result more of English than of Southern effort." Wilson, *Baptized in Blood*, 19. According

to Long, *In the Shadow of the "Alabama,"* 144–45, the unveiling was delayed by postwar tension between Britain and the United States and because the statue needed alterations.

78. This is an observation, not a complaint. I wish to thank Dr. Graber for sending me a copy of his work.

79. Graber, "Twice Divided Nation," 488–90, 507–12, 518. Bennett, *London Confederates,* 115, 134, also argues that British commitment to the South was limited—in which case the Jackson statue becomes even more remarkable as one of its enduring expressions. Thomas Sebrell sees the statue as "a joint effort" between the *London Index* and Hope. The *Index* failed to persuade the British government to recognize the Confederacy, but the statue is proof that it did not fail to have a lasting legacy. Sebrell, *Persuading John Bull,* 204–5.

80. Sebrell, *Persuading John Bull,* 205.

81. Grant, *American Civil War and the British Press,* 7, 16–17, 41; Doyle, *Cause of All Nations,* 97; Sebrell, *Persuading John Bull,* 9; Kinser, *American Civil War and the Shaping of British Democracy,* 43.

82. The medals were discussed in correspondence between VMI superintendent Francis Smith and Governor Kemper dated 6, 8 May, 5 July 1876, 14 Feb., 30 May 1877. See Library of Virginia, Executive Papers of Governor James L. Kemper, 1874–77, box 3, folders 10 and 12, box 4, folders 4 and 7. See also James M. Morgan, *The Jackson-Hope and the Society of the Cincinnati Medals of the Virginia Military Institute* (Verona, Va.: McClure Press, 1979), 2–9; Sebrell, *Persuading John Bull,* 206.

83. *New York Independent,* 16 Mar., 18 May 1876; *Boston Daily Advertiser,* 12 May 1876; *Atlanta Constitution,* 16 May 1876; *St. Louis Globe-Democrat,* 21 May 1876; *San Francisco Daily Evening Bulletin,* 25 May 1876.

CONCLUSION

1. Jonathan Leib, "Separate Times, Shared Spaces: Arthur Ashe, Monument Avenue, and the Politics of Richmond's Symbolic Landscape," *Cultural Geographies* 9, no. 3 (2002): 286–312; Josh Sanburn, "A Confederate Monument Solution," *Time,* 3 July 2017; *New York Times,* 9, 18 July 1995. For British comment, see, for example, *Economist,* 15 July 1995, 22 Jan. 2000.

2. *Economist,* 15 Feb. 2003.

3. *London Times,* 17 Aug. 2017.

4. Valerie Parkhouse, *Memorializing the Anglo-Boer War of 1899–1902: Militarization of the Landscape* (Kibworth: Matador, 2015).

5. Tal, *American Civil War in British Culture,* 80–81, 83, 94, 97–98, 113.

6. *Economist,* 20 Nov. 1943, 5 May 1945.

7. *Economist,* 28 May 1938, 30 Mar. 1957.

8. *Economist,* 27 Apr., 9 Nov. 1968, 4 Feb. 1989.

9. *New York Independent,* 6 May 1869.

10. *Little Rock Daily Republican,* 1 Dec. 1873; *San Francisco Daily Evening Bulletin,* 10 Dec. 1873.

11. *Harper's Bazaar,* 17 May 1879.

12. *New York Daily Graphic,* 29 May 1880; *Boston Daily Advertiser,* 30 Mar. 1881; *St. Louis Globe-Democrat,* 5 Apr. 1882.

13. *New York Independent*, 28 July, 24 Nov. 1887, 19 Jan. 1888; *American Architect and Building News*, 5 Nov. 1887; *Church Review* 51, no. 180 (Jan. 1888): 119.

14. *Boston Daily Globe*, 21 Oct. 1887; *Raleigh News and Observer*, 21 Oct. 1887; *Milwaukee Daily Sentinel*, 21 Oct. 1887; *Daily Whig and Courier*, 21 Oct. 1887; *San Francisco Daily Evening Bulletin*, 21 Oct. 1887. A few stories about Hope's absent-mindedness and "very singular" manners made it into the *San Francisco Daily Evening Bulletin*, 11 Nov. 1887, and *New Orleans Daily Picayune*, 27 Nov. 1887.

15. *Chicago Tribune*, 21 Oct. 1887.

16. *Chicago Daily Inter Ocean*, 23 Oct. 1887.

17. *New Orleans Daily Picayune*, 26 Oct. 1887; *Galveston Daily News*, 29 Oct. 1887.

18. Tal, *American Civil War in British Culture*, 8, 125–26, 148, 162.

INDEX